THE DEVON GENTLEMAN

The Life of Sir Peter Carew

THE
UNIVERSITY
OF HULL
PRESS

Cottingham Road
Hull
HU6 7RX

A CIP catalogue record for this book is available from the British
Library.

© John A Wagner

Published 1998

Paperback ISBN 0 85958 669 3

Printed by LSL Ltd, Bedford, England

THE DEVON GENTLEMAN

The Life of Sir Peter Carew

J. A. Wagner

THE UNIVERSITY OF HULL PRESS

For Donna

CONTENTS

ABBREVIATIONS USED IN THE NOTES

APC	*Acts of the Privy Council*, ed. J.R. Dasent, 13 vols. (London, 1890-1949)
BL	British Library, London
Cal. Carew	*Calendar of the Carew Manuscripts*, ed. J.S. Brewer and William Bullen, 6 vols. (Nendeln, Liechtenstein, 1974)
Cal.SP Dom.	*Calender of State Papers, Domestic*
Cal.SP For	*Calendar of State Papers, Foreign*
Cal.SP Ireland	*Calendar of State Papers Relating to Ireland*, ed. H.C. Hamilton, E.G. Atkinson, and R.P. Mahaffy, 11 vols. (London, 1860-1912)
Cal.SP Scotland	*Calendar of State Papers Relating to Scotland*, ed. J. Bain et al. vols. I, IV (Edinburgh, 1898-1952)
Cal.SP Span.	*Calendar of Letters, Despatches, and State Papers Relating to the Negotiations Between England and Spain*, ed. Royall Tyler et al., 13 vols. (London, 1969)
Cal.SP Ven.	*Calendar of State Papers and Manuscripts, Relqating to English Affairs, Existing in the Archives and Collections of Venice*, ed. R. Brown et al., vols. VI, VII (London, 1864-98)
CCR	*Calendar of the Close Rolls*
CFR	*Calendar of the Fine Rolls*
CPR	*Calendar of Patent Rolls*
DNB	*Dictionary of National Biography*
DRO	Devon Record Office, Exeter
HMC	Historical Manuscripts Commission
Hooker, *Description*	John Hooker, *The Description of the Citie of Excester* (Exeter: Devon and Cornwall Record Society, 1919)
Hooker, "Life"	John Hooker, "The Discourse and Discovery of the Life of Sir Peter Carew," MS 605, Carew Manuscripts, Lambeth Palace Library, London. Reprinted in *The Life and Times of Sir Peter Carew, Kt.*, ed. John Maclean (London: Bell and Daldy, 1857)
Lambeth	Lambeth Palace Library, London

LP	*Letters and Papers (Foreign and Domestic) of the Reign of Henry VIII*, ed. James Gairdner et al., 21 vols. (London, 1862-1932)
PCC	Prerogative Court of Canterbury, Will Registers
PRO	Public Record Office, London
StPap	*State Papers of King Henry VIII,* 11 vols. (London:G. Eyre and A. Strahan, 1830-52)
WSL	Westcountry Studies Library, Exeter

ACKNOWLEDGMENTS

I am deeply indebted to Retha M. Warnicke, chairperson of the Department of History at Arizona State University, and to Roger D. Adelson, professor of history at Arizona State, for their encouragement and support of this project. Both are outstanding historians and educators. I must also thank Ron Smith, professor of history at Arizona State, for carefully and patiently reading and criticizing a long manuscript. I also owe thanks to Eugene Bronski for his careful reading of the manuscript and page proofs, and to Michael Bronski for vital computer advice and assistance. I am also deeply grateful to Susan Slesinger and Anne Thompson at the The Oryx Press for graciously allowing me leave time to undertake archival research and to Tom Brennan for his expert preparation of genealogical tables. Siobhán O'Rafferty, acting librarian at the Royal Irish Academy in Dublin, and Dr. Mark Nicholls, Department of Manuscripts and University Archives at the Cambridge University Library, kindly helped me obtain microfilms of relevant materials held by their institutions. The staffs of Hayden Library at Arizona State University; of Lambeth Palace Library, the Public Record Office, and the British Library in London; and of the Devon Record Office and Westcountry Studies Library in Exeter were all exceedingly friendly and helpful. Finally, despite all the advice and assistance of the foregoing, this work would not have been possible without the patience and love of my wife, Donna. Even though Sir Peter Carew took far more of my time and attention than either of us had expected, Donna was never anything to me but patient, supportive, and loving.

PREFACE

In writing this life of Sir Peter Carew, my task was set for me some 400 years ago by a distinguished predecessor. John Hooker of Exeter concluded his narrative of the life and career of Sir Peter Carew, his friend and patron, by humbly conceding that his work was "not so effectually done, nor so exactly performed, as the matter requires." Hooker was too modest, for without his work Sir Peter would today be little remembered and any attempt at his biography would be exceedingly difficult, if not impossible. Having confessed his inadequacies, Hooker continued: "[H]aving done my good will herein, I pray the good acceptation thereof, hoping that which by me is omitted by others shall be supplied and amended."[1] That was my charge—to supply and amend, from other sources and new ideas, the lackings in Hooker's well accepted and widely quoted portrait of Sir Peter Carew.

In the preface to his book *Court and Country: Studies in Tudor Social History*, A.L. Rowse attested to the good "acceptation" of John Hooker's efforts. Rowse called Sir Peter Carew a "familiar character," and so he is. Sir Peter Carew's name appears frequently in studies of Tudor figures and events. Anyone exploring Henry VIII's French wars in the 1540s, the Prayer Book Rebellion during Edward VI's reign, Wyatt's Rebellion against Queen Mary, English activity in Ireland under Queen Elizabeth, or the history of Tudor Devonshire will encounter Sir Peter Carew. But the Sir Peter so encountered is always John Hooker's Sir Peter. The brief background that follows any mention of Carew in numerous Tudor studies comes invariably from the pages of Hooker. Many historians have quoted Hooker's description of the young, willful Peter Carew being tied to his father's hounds as a punishment for truancy. Even Rowse, in a brief chapter that he hoped would "add something new to our knowledge" of Carew, relied heavily on Hooker's work. John Hooker's Sir Peter Carew is indeed familiar.[2]

Hooker's Sir Peter is also a character. Hooker relished telling how Sir Peter sang "fremen" songs with Henry VIII and regaled the king with his adventures at the Turkish court; how he impressed the Scots and French courts with his manners and boldness; how he was ever foremost when there was military service to be done; and how he dealt fairly, honourably, and generously with friends and enemies alike. Hooker recorded with verve and pleasure how Carew fought for Henry VIII, crushed those who rebelled against Henry's son, and outsmarted the murderous agents of Henry's daughter. Finally, Hooker described in great detail what he himself had witnessed, how Sir Peter, in his mid-fifties, sailed for Ireland to restore to his family lands lost almost 200 years earlier.

For a sixteenth-century figure, a contemporary biography is a rare distinction. Hooker's work gives us much precious detail about Carew's life, personality, and youth—detail that we should not otherwise have, and that we lack for a great many more famous or influential figures of the period. Hooker portrayed Sir Peter as a soldier, courtier, and adventurer, and rightly so, for he was all three. But Hooker overemphasised his hero's exotic travels and military adventures, making Carew's career seem not only striking and exceptional, which it was, but also highly atypical of its times, which it was not. Carew's deserved reputation as a swashbuckler and man of action has made unfamiliar many other aspects of his character and career, aspects that mark him as both a representative of his own age and as a harbinger of the age to come.

Sir Peter Carew gave over 40 years service to four Tudor monarchs, and his family's identification with the dynasty went back to Bosworth Field. But the reasons why Sir Peter served, how he served, and when he ceased to serve went beyond mere love of adventure and a military man's notions of honour and loyalty. In his actions and decisions, Sir Peter responded as fully as other members of his class to the contemporary influences of religious belief, political and economic ambition, family history, and national pride and identity. In all the incidental references to Sir Peter Carew in studies of Tudor England, little is said of his Protestant convictions, political motivations, personal ambition, or family tradition of service to the dynasty. This book integrates these and other recoverable parts of Sir Peter's makeup into the image of Hooker's well-known and engaging daredevil, seeking to overlay an affectionate tribute to a friend with an honest and well-rounded portrait of a man, and a recounting of a life with an examination of what that life can tell the twentieth century about how a Tudor gentleman lived in the sixteenth century.

Supplementing Hooker with other sources on the life of Sir Peter can "add something new" to our knowledge of the service given by the Tudor gentry to the Tudor state, as well as to our knowledge of Carew himself. Sir Peter Carew is a pattern for Tudor gentlemen who were political and military servants of a lower level, whose ties to their counties were at least as strong as their ties to the court, who served not at the council board or as army commanders, but as local administrators, ship captains, and conduits of information and instructions.

Carew is also an interesting study in the development of the attitude and spirit that characterised the Elizabethan age. He is the Elizabethan age foreshadowed in Henrician, Edwardian, and Marian times. His youthful wanderings on the continent in the 1520s presaged, in a rather haphazard way, the formal Grand Tour made by the sons of the English nobility and gentry from Elizabethan times through the eighteenth century. His desire to see new sights and new peoples, his restlessness to be active and accomplishing, grew out of the same creative and explorative urges that led Elizabethan sailors and colonisers into the ocean sea, to the New World, and to distant parts of the Old World. His arguments for and efforts toward the colonisation and anglicisation of Ireland described later Elizabethan and Stuart settlement activities in America and elsewhere.

Sir Peter Carew's life is also a window into Tudor Devon and the interaction and interrelation of the active and ambitious gentlemen who ran the counties of the West Country for the monarch, and for themselves. Elizabethan exploration and colonisation efforts drew their energy, resources, and personnel in disproportionate measure from the gentry of the West Country, from families, like the Carews, with long-standing West Country names and connections. Sir Peter Carew was in his personality and outlook a harbinger for the Raleighs, Gilberts, Grenvilles, and Drakes who came later. These bright names in the annals of Elizabethan seafaring and colonisation were western men all. Sir Peter was the one who went before them, the one who made straight the path these others would follow and enlarge.

The life and career of Sir Peter Carew also speaks to the power, or lack thereof, of religious belief as a political motivation. Hooker's biography of Carew says much about Hooker's own Protestantism, but tells us less about the nature of Sir Peter's beliefs and the impact of those beliefs on his career. The life of Sir Peter Carew raises many questions that speak to religious concerns. Was Carew sent to quell the Prayer Book Rebellion in 1549 only because of his military experience and western connections, or did his anti-Catholic opinions also play a part in the choice? Did he oppose Philip's coming in 1554 because it threatened domination by foreigners, or because it promised unwanted religious changes? Did he vigorously pursue his lost Irish lands to uphold his rights, to relieve his boredom, to fill his purse, or to stamp out false and superstitious religion? What role, if any, did religion play in the burst of energetic exploration that animated a host of West Country gentlemen in Elizabethan times?

Because Carew's long service to the Crown was broken by a serious lapse into rebellion under Mary, his career also says something about the limits of loyalty and service. The reasons for Sir Peter's leading role in the 1554 uprisings, largely ignored by Hooker, are explored in this book, as is the possibility that Sir Peter turned informant for the Marian government against other Protestants. Carew's subsequent pardon by Philip and Mary and re-employment by Elizabeth, as well as his brother's re-employment by Henry VIII after the religious upheavals in Calais in 1540, illustrate how valuable were political, military, and administrative experience and ability to the Tudors, no matter what questionable personal or religious beliefs might come attached to those qualities.

This book also examines Carew's ambition, for position and land, and its impact on his standing among his West Country neighbors and the troubles it caused for Elizabeth's government in Ireland. Sir Peter and his family profited much from the misfortune of others, especially the downfall of the marquis of Exeter in 1538; loyalty thrived on reward, as well as on patriotism, honour, and the thrill of adventure. Fear of losing access to reward has its place along side religion in explaining Carew's actions in 1554. Carew's inability to live within his means, despite significant reward and favor from the Crown, caused much and motivated much in his life.

Finally, I have looked at Carew as one member of a family with a long tradition of service to the Tudor dynasty. That service, although profitable, was often hazardous. Sir Peter's grandfather died in the king's army in 1513; his elder brother George went down with the king's ship in 1545; and his cousin Peter fell before the queen's Irish enemies in 1580. Being a Carew was to be a westerner, an Englishman of long and honourable lineage, and a servant of the Tudor dynasty. No study of Sir Peter Carew could ignore his family and its long-standing connection to Devon and the West Country.

This book is intended as a corrective to the valuable, but one-sided portrayal of Sir Peter Carew that heavy reliance on Hooker alone has brought down to us. A.J. Slavin has written that in Tudor history the study "of men not of the first flight is necessary if we are to replace the shadow with the substance of knowledge," if we are to prevent our understanding of institutions, offices, and systems from advancing "more rapidly than our understanding of the men filling the offices and making the systems work."[3] The life of Sir Peter Carew is a valuable instrument for humanising studies of Tudor classes, courts, administrations, and social structures, a way to put an interesting and engaging face on a series of important but often dry undertakings.

[1] John Hooker, "The Discourse and Discovery of the Life of Sir Peter Carew," in *The Life and Times of Sir Peter Carew, Kt.*, ed. John Maclean (London: Bell and Daldy, 1857), p. 119. Hereafter cited as Hooker, "Life."

[2] A.L. Rowse, *Court and Country: Studies in Tudor Social History* (Athens: University of Georgia Press, 1987), p. x.

[3] A.J. Slavin, *Politics and Profit: A Study of Sir Ralph Sadler 1507-1547* (Cambridge: Cambridge University Press, 1966), p. viii.

PROLOGUE

A NOBLE AND WORTHY KNIGHT

Sir Peter Carew was a man of rare distinctions. He traveled the continent extensively as a youth and young man, experiencing the courts of France and Turkey, the culture of Renaissance Italy, and the wars of Hungary. He did all this long before such continental travels became fashionable among the young men of the English nobility and gentry. In the 1560s, Sir Peter strongly advocated and sought himself to undertake the English colonisation of Ireland, and there is some evidence to indicate that he was interested in the previous decade in seeing England compete with Spain in the exploitation of the New World. These interests and ideas spearheaded the Elizabethan movement for English settlement in Ireland and predated by over a decade the initial Elizabethan attempts to establish English colonies in North America.

Sir Peter Carew's most striking distinction is his membership in the small and select company of sixteenth-century English figures who became the subjects of contemporary biographies. Only a few non-royal Englishmen of this century were so honoured, among the best known are Cardinal Thomas Wolsey and Sir Thomas More.[1] The first of these the powerful minister of a powerful king and the second revered by many as a saint and martyr—from these examples it would seem that the century bestowed its attention only on the lives of the truly memorable and the extraordinary. But not every English figure of the time who could be so described found a biographer—for instance, neither Cromwell nor Shakespeare nor Raleigh did so. Such distinction required not only a memorable subject, but a literate biographer who knew and respected his subject. Wolsey's biographer was his gentleman usher George Cavendish; More's was his son-in-law William Roper. Sir Peter Carew found his biographer in his solicitor and friend, John Hooker.

The writings of John Hooker are the most important sources for the life of Sir Peter Carew. Book VI of Hooker's edition of Holinshed's *Chronicles* devotes several pages to Carew's character and to his activities in Ireland.[2] For Sir Peter's involvement in putting down the Prayer Book Rebellion of 1549, Hooker's various separate accounts of the rebellion as a whole are the most important sources. The account of the rebellion preserved in the Bodleian Library is thought to be the earliest, for it mentions some "yet living but being sorry and ashamed of their folly I do suppress their names." Another version is preserved in the Guildhall, and yet another version, containing information not found in the other two versions, was inserted by Hooker in Holinshed. A slightly condensed version was also included by Hooker in his *Description of the Citie of Excester*.[3] For his life of Carew, Hooker seems to have collected from the general narrative of the rebellion the particulars of Carew's activities in the summer of 1549. In his biography of Carew, Hooker refers to a "pamphlet," the availability of which made a repeat in the biography of the details of Sir Peter's role in the rebellion "not pertinent."

The most important source for the life of Sir Peter Carew is Hooker's biography of his late patron. The original manuscript of the Carew biography is preserved in MS 605 of the Carew Manuscripts at the Lambeth Palace Library. A version of the biography was first published by Sir Thomas Phillips in *Archaeologia* in 1840. In 1857, John Maclean published the manuscript again under the title *The Life and Times of Sir Peter Carew, Kt.*, including with the biography an extensive introduction and a selection of State Paper documents relevant to Carew. The entire biography was published a third time in 1867 as part of the frontmatter to the first volume of the *Calendar of the Carew Manuscripts*.

The most detailed portion of the biography concerns Carew's pursuit of his land claims in Ireland between 1568 and 1575, the period of Carew's life with which Hooker was personally acquainted. This portion is in large part a summary of the detailed notes of Carew's legal proceedings before the Irish Council as recorded by Hooker in MS 606 of the Carew Manuscripts. For Carew's life before 1568, Hooker relied on "such instructions as have been delivered to me" and on the recollections of Sir Peter himself.[4] By "instructions," Hooker probably meant research involving Sir Peter's papers, and interviews with those who knew Sir Peter, including, possibly, Sir Gawen Carew, Sir Peter's uncle; Lady Margaret Tailboys, Carew's wife; and various other Carew relatives and friends who would still have been plentiful in Devon and Exeter in the 1570s and 1580s. Sir Gawen lived until the mid-1580s, and could have provided information about Sir Peter's youth, his activities at the court of Henry VIII, his participation in the wars of the 1540s, and his roles in the rebellions of 1549 and 1554. The anecdotes relating, for instance, to Carew's solitary chat with Francis I during the French embassy of 1546, his exile in Venice and Germany in 1554-55, and his terrifying voyage back to England after being kidnapped in 1556 must ultimately have come from Carew himself, whether related directly to Hooker or through a third person.

The biography is largely a collection of anecdotes about Sir Peter linked together by such vague chronological connectors as "not long after this" or "in the next spring." Hooker's chronology is often confused or difficult, especially for the period before about 1545. The dates for Carew's continental sojourn and for some of his activities in the 1530s are particularly confused. (See Chapter 2 for a discussion of the difficulties in dating precisely Carew's birth and the years of his first stay on the continent.) Vague though Hooker's chronology can be for episodes in Carew's life, Hooker is usually correct when he dates major historical events. The anecdotes record events that for some reason stuck in Sir Peter's memory, such as the joust at Edward VI's coronation; showed Sir Peter in a good or honourable light, such his impressing of the Scots during the garter embassy to James V in 1535; recalled some dramatic episode, such as Carew's escape from Vannes's Venetian assassins in 1554; or perhaps impressed Hooker, such as the old Irish gentlewoman who called Carew a dead man arisen as he rode by her door. A common theme of almost all the anecdotes is the honour, courage, or accomplishments of Sir Peter Carew—a theme resulting probably from both the type of information Hooker got from his sources and from his friendship and admiration for his subject.

John Hooker closed his life of Sir Peter Carew by undertaking to "declare and set down his nature, conditions, and disposition."[5] Hooker accomplished this task by writing a frank but affectionate summary of the personality and character of the Sir Peter Carew whom he had known well, a summary that might serve us as an excellent introduction to a man the twentieth century knows not well at all. Although admitting that some readers might judge him "to speak more of affection than of truth," Hooker was willing nonetheless to "boldly. . . affirm" the truth of Sir Peter as he knew it.

> [I]f the planets have any influence in the genesis and course of man's life. . . then, certainly, it should seem that they did consent, and agree, to pour out of every of their influences to the benefit of this gentleman; for he was most plentifully endowed with the gifts which nature yields concerning the body, and adorned plentifully with such virtues of the mind as do appertain and are incident unto a gentleman; without which virtues there can be no nobility, nor any be a gentleman.[6]

Carew, continued Hooker, had not only the nobility of his lineage—his descent from the ancient and august families of Carew and Courtenay, but the nobility of a virtuous mind and character, without which "the substance and ground of nobility fails," despite lengthy pedigrees and broad acres.

Before assessing Carew's inner ornaments, Hooker described his outer appearance.

Concerning his body: he was of mean [middling] stature, but very well compact, and somewhat broad, big boned, and strongly sinewed, his face of a very good countenance, his complexion swarte [swarthy] or cholyryke, his hair black, and his beard thick and great. He was of good strength and agility, being skillful and apt to all exercises as do belong and appertain unto a gentleman.[7]

This description is confirmed by the Gerlach Flicke portrait of Sir Peter Carew now found in the royal collection at Hampton Court. The portrait depicts a stout, broad-shouldered man with a long dark beard extending down to the chest, and a head of thick, dark hair; although painted about 1550 the portrait closely corresponds to Hooker's description of the older Sir Peter, as he appeared in the 1560s or the 1570s, the years when Hooker knew him. The round full face of the portrait seems an older, darker version of the face of Sir George Carew, Sir Peter's oldest brother, as Holbein sketched him in the early 1540s.[8] Hooker described Carew's appetite at table as moderate and ascribed it to an abhorrence of gluttony, but this sparing use of "meat and drink" was perhaps also an attempt to overcome portliness, a tendency suggested by the robust torso depicted in the Hampton Court portrait. The face in the portrait has a broad nose and a high forehead, and, while not handsome, justifies Hooker's description of it as "a very good countenance." The chest and shoulders in the portrait certainly exhibit the compactness and strength described by Hooker, and definitely suggest (at least in a younger day) agility and athleticism. The portrait allows one to accept Hooker's descriptions of the striking figure the young, well-appareled Peter Carew cut at the English, French, and Scottish courts in the 1530s and 1540s.

From the appearance of Carew's body, Hooker moved to the appearance of Sir Peter's soul, which Hooker found to be even more pleasing than Carew's face and gentlemanly bearing. Hooker described his friend as an "earnest promoter of God's true religion, and a patron to all godly preachers," as well as "a great favorer of all Protestants, and most godly affected to all good and godly men." At the end of Henry VIII's reign and the beginning of Edward VI's, "when the Gospel began to have his entry," Sir Peter appointed himself protector of Simon Hayne, the Protestant dean of Exeter and member of the committee appointed in 1547 to devise a new liturgy for the Edwardian Church. Hayne was "sundry times accused and impeached" for his reformist sermons by Exeter conservatives, whose desire to do bodily harm to the dean was firmly thwarted by Carew. Later in Edward's reign, both Sir Peter and his uncle Sir Gawen Carew performed the like service for William Alley, the prebend of St. Paul's in Edward's time and an Elizabethan bishop of Exeter. Alley's enemies so threatened him as to prevent him from mounting the pulpit. The two Carews on a number of occasions bodily escorted Alley to the pulpit and stood guard over him while he delivered his sermon. Although himself unlearned in the Scriptures, Carew's respect for the word of God and the men who preached it was strong; he maintained a preacher at his own expense for the instruction of his household and the benefit of his neighbors and friends in Devon.[9]

Carew's piety was simple and devout. He would not take a meal or lay down to sleep without first saying a prayer. Having once perceived, wrote Hooker in a typical classical allusion, "that Lachesis had given over her spinning," Sir Peter took his death with courage and faithful resignation, giving himself up to prayer, remorse for his sins, and pleas for divine mercy. Carew's religious beliefs were strongly and sincerely held, seemingly grounded not on theological study and personal contemplation but on convictions planted early and deep and never thereafter challenged. Although the exact origins of Carew's Protestantism are unknown, the nature of his beliefs suggests that he came by them earlier rather than later in life. Carew could certainly have encountered Lutheranism among the armies of Charles V in Italy in the 1520s, when he spent six years wondering about the continent largely on his own. He was an impressionable 14 or 15 years old in 1528 when he first came into the service of the prince of Orange, the commander of the imperial armies in Italy. The corruption of the papacy and the Roman Church spurred reformist impulses in the young Thomas Cromwell when he saw them first-hand; they may well have done the same in the young Peter Carew when he also saw them close up a decade or so later.[10]

The reformist current that swept the English court during the height of the Boleyn/Cromwell influence in the 1530s could well have reinforced the beliefs Carew carried back with him from the continent in 1532. The anti-papal rhetoric of the Henrician reformation would have fit well with any anti-papalism Carew had absorbed in Italy. Judging from Carew's later piety, his anti-papalism, unlike the king's, was largely unmixed with politics and so carried him on by the 1540s to full-blown Protestantism, a destination to which Henry VIII never permitted himself to come. This explains how Sir Peter got himself committed to ward at the end of 1545 for possessing forbidden books, and his frequent and open support of Protestant preachers and practices in the friendlier religious environment of Edward's reign. An interesting question is what if any impact Peter's continental reformism may have had on the religious beliefs of his brother George and his uncle Gawen. Both were Protestants by the 1540s, judging from Sir George's experience in Calais after 1539 and from Gawen's run-in with the council in 1543 for eating meat in Lent. The possibility that both George and Gawen had imbibed the religious conservatism of their early patron the marquis of Exeter, and had somehow involved themselves, as had the Exeters, with the Nun of Kent in 1533, suggests a transformation of their religious opinions during the course of the 1530s. Did Peter have anything to do with this transformation, or was it motivated more by attachment to Cromwell?

Hooker commended Sir Peter for endeavoring always to inject his understanding of the Christian message into his relations with others. He took seriously his positions as justice of the peace and of the quorum, and of custos rotulorum of Devon, and sought to perform his duties completely and correctly. He dealt with "every man according to his desert, punishing the evil, succouring the oppressed, and favoring the good." In his official duties, Carew could be neither corrupted nor influenced. This is certainly a description of Sir Peter in the 1560s, when he interested himself both in tracking down a reprehensible wife-beater named John Parker, and in furthering the ecclesiastical career of the godly John Wolton. It is a less fitting description of Sir Peter a decade earlier, when he did not scruple at tampering with a jury to prevent Robert Warren from obtaining remedy at common law in Devon for his suit to recover an old debt from the Carews. Sir Peter does seem to have been a genuinely upright and honest man whose favor and influence were not ordinarily to be bought or induced, but who could be brought to questionable practices by the force of his own needs and interests. The Carew that Hooker knew in Devon and Ireland in the 1560s and 1570s attests to the former qualities; the earlier Carew who acquiesced in Queen Mary's accession and likely betrayed Sir John Cheke and the Dudley conspirators to the Marian government attests to a moral flexibility that arose whenever Carew's own livelihood was at stake.[11]

Hooker believed one of Carew's faults was gullibility. Sir Peter often believed whatever he was told and could be taken in by "smooth speeches" because he "more hastily credited than tried" the information he was brought. John Dudley, Lord Lisle, when he chose Carew to requite an insult given to young Lord Herbert at the French court in 1546, certainly knew how easily and effectively Sir Peter could be worked up to hasty, ill-considered action. Many another man would have thought twice about picking a fight with a French courtier in the presence of the French king and dauphin. The deception practiced upon Carew by a Spaniard from Constantinople in 1541, and repeated by a French prisoner of war in 1543 are examples of Carew's simplicity and lack of skepticism. The possibility that Carew was somehow used by Sir William Paget in the kidnapping of Cheke in 1556 is also strengthened by what Hooker told us of Carew's gullibility. But, conceded Hooker, once he had learned the truth, Sir Peter "could not lightly brook" his deceivers, "nor show them any favor or countenance" thereafter.[12]

Carew's worst fault, in Hooker's opinion, was his excessive and often unwarranted "beneficence and liberality." Hooker believed that Carew took the Christian injunction to give rather than to receive to unacceptable extremes. Carew's "whole disposition was such that a man might say he was born to be friendly to all men, and liberal to every man; for his purse, his apparel, his horses, or whatsoever he had, it was common to his friends, and ready for every man, and rather would lack himself than his friends should want." If one were to describe, wrote Hooker, all the gifts and favors Carew had bestowed in his lifetime, "they should not be so infinite as strange." In other words, Carew was not only imprudent in what he gave away, but indiscriminate in whom he gave things to. What's more, Carew was an overgenerous host, going well beyond his means to ensure the comfort of guests and friends.

> [F]or a fault it was imputed unto him that as he could not guide his purse within the rule of liberality, no more could he, many times, satisfy his eye with sufficiency; for if any personage of countenance were at any time invited at his table, although the same were sufficiently fraughted with store and plenty, yet he thought he had never enough, but all was too little.[13]

Hooker wanted his friend to temper the Christian maxim with the wisdom of Cicero who advocated giving only what one could afford and only to such as deserved it. Because Carew did not follow this advice "there ensued many inconveniences which blemished so noble a virtue."

Carew was not entirely adverse to the wisdom of Cicero; indeed, the Roman was one of his favorite authors, and he followed closely the Ciceronian injunction to use all things in moderation. Carew was given neither to gluttony, nor covetousness, nor drunkenness, nor sexual license, qualities which Hooker could not resist casting in classical terms.

> For, albeit, he had his imperfections, yet he was not known to be wrapped in the dissolute net of Venus, nor embrowed with the cup of Bacchus, he was not carried with the blind covetousness of Plutus, nor yet subject to malice, envy, or any notorious crime; but had a mind free from all such foul vices and incumbrances.[14]

There is no hint, either in Hooker's works or in any other sources of Carew's life, that Sir Peter was ever interested in or involved with any woman other than his wife, Lady Margaret Tailbois. Nor do we find him involved in any drunken brawls or in any other unseemly episodes, unless of course one wishes to call Carew's rebellion against and collusion with the Marian government unseemly. Aside from the questionable nature of Sir Peter's Marian activities, there are no incidents in his life to parallel Sir Gawen Carew's violent encounter with members of the king's guard in 1538. Sir Peter's behavioral excesses seemed always to come "in good causes and for the commonwealth."

Hooker was most insistent on Sir Peter's immunity from sexual vice.

> [H]e neither inordinately sought other men's goods, nor unlawfully desired another man's wife, nor any strange woman: whereof I, the writer hereof, upon my own knowledge, can this affirm, that during the time of my acquaintance with him, I could never perceive nor see any countenance, gesture, behavior, or any signs, at all, of his liking that way. For he never would gladly be in company with any woman of a suspected name, nor whereby he himself might be had, or grow into, any suspicion.[15]

Sir Edmund Butler or Sir Christopher Chivers, the two major Irish land-holders whose lands Carew claimed as his own, might have quibbled with Hooker about Carew's lust for other men's goods, but Lady Margaret seems truly to have had no cause for complaint about her husband's fidelity. The relationship between Sir Peter and Lady Margaret is difficult to characterize because we have so little direct information about it. Judging from the rather ill-received and desultory courtship described by Hooker, the match was probably not based on great passion or overwhelming physical attraction; we have no physical description of Lady Margaret, although some beauty was required to attract the attention of Henry VIII, as Lady Margaret apparently did in 1538. For the free-spending Carew, Lady Margaret's landed wealth was clearly a strong attraction. The revenues from her extensive estates in Lincolnshire and the West Country helped replace the revenues Carew lost under Queen Mary and poured into his Irish venture after 1568. But the marriage was based on more than land; Lady Margaret's continual efforts on her husband's behalf during his long period of exile and imprisonment after 1554 betoken affection and respect, as well as a sharing of interests and values. Lady Margaret seems to have been every bit as bold and direct as her husband, and perhaps more politically astute and a better judge of character than Sir Peter. She took her suits for Carew's pardon and rehabilitation to the most likely sources of success, as her careful wooing of Sir William Petre and King Philip attest. And Carew returned her affection with his own. In his will, Carew called her "my loving wife Lady Margaret Tailbois," who has "used herself most kind and loving to me." He also named her executor, entrusting to her the administration of his beloved Irish barony of Idrone, a sure sign of his respect and love.[16]

Although Carew would not trust his body to vice, he would risk it willingly in the service the state and the grim lottery of war. "Concerning the valientness of his body," Hooker wrote that

> there was not any man lightly who could excel him therein; for, whether there was
> any service to be done at sea or at land, at home or abroad, in time of war or peace,
> he was one and the same man, always most ready and forward therein, for no pains

could discourage him, no perils daunt him, no fear quail him, nor enemy appall him; but with the first he would be foremost, as sundry examples are to be alleged hereof, to his great commendation and praise.[17]

"Forward" and "persistent" are words that describe Carew's approach to state service, as his military and navel exploits of the 1540s demonstrate, and to his personal interests, as the whole course of the Irish venture proves. Sir Peter was always given to leaping before looking, a quality that made him ideal for tasks of honour that required bravery and boldness, such as adorning a garter mission to a foreign court or requiting the mannered insults of a foreign courtier, but much less useful for missions requiring caution or circumspection, such as containing the spread of disorder or disaffection at the start of the Prayer Book Rebellion in 1549. To be fair, Somerset's hope of pacifying the western dissidents was probably vain, and the situation into which Sir Peter and his uncle Sir Gawen were tossed was exceedingly difficult. Although the possibility of maintaining quiet in the West Country in 1549 would have been small in any case, Carew's penchant for acting without thinking eliminated the possibility altogether.

Although not given to contemplation, Carew was not unintelligent. His youthful disdain for book learning was legendary, but he came to feel his lack of learning keenly in later life. His want of formal education led him to Hooker when he sought proofs of his Irish land claims from his family archive in the 1560s; his painful awareness of his lacking is most evident in his November 1568 letter beseeching Cecil not to deprive him of the legal services of William Peryam.[18] Without Peryam, Carew felt himself at a loss to continue his legal proceedings. Yet Sir Peter seems to have done what he could to remedy his educational deficiencies. He had some facility in languages, being "very perfect" in French and also fluent in Italian, and Hooker wrote that he read widely in all three of his languages, especially works on government, mathematics or geometry, and the military arts. In these areas, "sharp was his understanding, pithy were his arguments, and deep was his judgment."[19] Carew was eager to learn and to understand practical things that he could put to immediate and effective use, both for his own benefit and for that of the state.

Carew made himself especially proficient in military affairs, an expertise recognised and appreciated by successive English governments. Carew's military reputation was partially responsible for his appointment by the Edwardian Council to the pacification of the West in 1549, for his pardon by King Philip in 1556, and for his appointment by Elizabeth to the Scottish mission in 1560 and to prepare an expedition against pirates in 1564. Hooker left no doubt as to the scope of Carew's military expertise.

> [S]uch was his skill and experience in martial affairs, that he could pitch a camp, martial [sic] a field, set array, and order the battle, with such wisdom, dexterity, and policy, as should be to the best advantage and safeguard of the army, and the most annoyance to the enemy; besides skill he had in directing the government, and knowledge (of) what appertained to a general, what to a captain, what to a soldier, and finally to all other things incidental and appertaining to the course of wars, either at the seas or at the land.[20]

Carew's expertise also extended to military architecture; he had some knowledge of ship design, fortress layout, and the siting and construction of artillery platforms. The most obvious example of Carew's talents in these areas is his report to the queen of the French fortress at Leith and the reasons for the failure of the May 1560 assault on the fortress by the Anglo-Scottish army.[21]

Carew's interest in architecture and building was not confined to military structures. He largely rebuilt the manor house at Mohun's Ottery, and "bestowed great masses of money" on building houses, mills, barns, and other structures on his properties; he also built ships for himself, including a small bark with which he planned to supply his rebellion in Devon in 1554[22] and the bark *Peter* with which he supplemented his small anti-pirate fleet in 1564-65.[23] He also had several small vessels busily ferrying supplies, household goods, and intelligence from Hooker back and forth across the Irish Sea after 1568. Whether Sir Peter engaged in a little irregular piracy of his own, as did his friends the Killegrews, cannot be known with any certainty. His sly remark to Sir Nicholas Throckmorton about having a small bark "to work his practice by," spoken in the context of plotting a rebellion, could have meant many things. Carew was likely aware of whom among the Devon gentry was involved in or supporting piracy, and the poor result of Carew's 1564-65 expedition against pirates may have been due in part to his reluctance to make strenuous efforts against his western friends and colleagues. Carew cannot be called a pirate but his seamanship, and especially his knowledge of ships and western waters, cannot be doubted.

Although the Irish landholders who suddenly found their estates threatened by Carew's claims in the 1560s may have agreed with A.L. Rowse's characterisation of him as an "old buccaneer,"[24] Hooker, who knew him well during those same years, saw Sir Peter as the pattern of a proper English gentleman. In his life of Carew, the admiring Hooker grouped his friend's many fine qualities into four categories: justice, fortitude, prudence, and temperance.[25] He made a strong case for all, except perhaps prudence, which must be qualified as pertaining to Carew's military and local administrative activities, and not to his impracticality in personal matters and inability to live within his means. The man who emerges from Hooker's biography and from the weight of supplementary sources was honourable, restless, and forceful, and his life mirrored his personality—bold, brave, active, and extravagant. Within his spheres of interest—military affairs and building—Sir Peter's mind was inquisitive and open. But in other areas, Carew tended to be more rigid and opinionated, seeing few shades of gray once his mind was made up. He took the world at face value, neither deceiving nor expecting deceit. All in all, as this book will show, Sir Peter Carew could be a loyal servant, a powerful adversary, and a firm friend.

1   George Cavendish's "The Life and Death of Cardinal Wolsey" and William Roper's "The Life of Sir Thomas More" were published in Richard S. Sylvester and Davis P. Harding, eds., *Two Early Tudor Lives* (New Haven, Conn.: Yale University Press, 1962).

2   Vernon F. Snow, ed., *Holinshed's Chronicles of England, Scotland and Ireland*, vol. VI (London, 1808; reprint, New York: AMS Press, Inc., 1976), pp. 375-78.

3   John Hooker, *The Description of the Citie of Excester* (Exeter: Devon and Cornwall Record Society, 1919), pp. 55-96.

4   Hooker, "Life," p. 109.

5   Ibid.

6   Ibid., pp. 109-10.

7   Ibid., p. 110.

8   The sketch of Sir George Carew is part of a collection of Holbein drawings preserved at Windsor. The collection also includes a drawing of Sir Gawen Carew. Sir Gawen seems to have a longer, narrower face than his nephews, although the basic facial resemblance across the three likenesses is striking. All three men are bearded, with Sir George's being rounded and more closely trimmed than the pointed chest-length beards worn by Sir Peter and Sir Gawen. Both Holbein drawings are thought to date to the early 1540s. For the Holbein portraits, see K.T. Parker, ed., *The Drawings of Hans Holbein in the Collection of Her Majesty the Queen at Windsor Castle* (New York: Harcourt Brace Jovanovich, Publishers, 1983), #76, #77. For a reproduction of the portrait of Sir Peter Carew, see the cover of this book.

9   Hooker, "Life," pp. 111-12.

10 Ibid., p. 112.

11 Ibid., p. 113.

12 Ibid.

13 Ibid., p. 118.

14 Ibid., p. 114.

15 Ibid., p.117.

16 Will of Sir Peter Carew, PRO, PCC 1 Carew, PROB 11/58.

17 Hooker, "Life," pp. 114-15.

18 Sir Peter Carew to Sir William Cecil, 16 November 1568, PRO, SP63/26/84.

19 Hooker, "Life," p. 115.

20 Ibid., pp. 115-16.

21 HMC, *Salisbury Manuscripts*, App. 4, p. 277.

22 T.B. Howells, comp., *A Complete Collection of State Trials*, vol. I (London: Hansard, 1816), p. 882.

23 List of Charges for Sir Peter Carew's Ships, April 1565, PRO, SP12/36/83.

24 A.L. Rowse, *The Expansion of Elizabethan England* (New York: Harper & Row, 1955), p. 139.

25 Hooker, "Life," pp. 110-11.

CHAPTER 1

AN ANCIENT LINEAGE: THE CAREW FAMILY

The eastern Devonshire town of Honiton cascades down a series of small hills toward the River Otter. Northeast of the town rises the rounded height of Dumpdon hill, cut by ancient country lanes and crested with a tuft of tall trees. If one walks east down the hedge-lined lanes along the hill's south face, one drops eventually into a small, green valley and then rises again into the village of Beacon. Across the hilltop from Beacon, high on the long, gentle slope running down into the valley of the Otter, stands a large farmhouse with a thatched roof and a massive and crumbling stone gateway that seems out of tone and proportion with the house. The current house is nineteenth century in origin, replacing the burned down sixteenth-century mansion to which the gateway once led. The gateway, bearing a fading coat of arms and the crudely carved letters "PC," is all that remains of Mohun's Ottery, the Devonshire home of Sir Peter Carew.

In the sixteenth century, the long and close association of the Carew family with the West Country in general and with Devon in particular was well known and frequently used by the government. The appointments by different Tudor regimes of Sir Peter and his relatives to pacify western rebels, capture western pirates, and command western fleets confirmed the strength of this association. Distant governments could sometimes overestimate the degree of regional influence such long-standing association conferred, but in times of invasion or rebellion—as occurred in Devon in 1497 and 1549—the monarch and Council depended on local leaders to restore order or organize defenses. Since the political and social leadership of most counties and regions in Tudor England rested with an interrelated web of local landholding families, it was important for the Crown to have members of the leadership group firmly in its service. This was especially true in a county like Devon, when the Crown itself owned little land and where the percentage of land owned by titled peers was also low. Some 350 knightly and gentry families owned half the land of the county between them in the early sixteenth century, and many of these families, like the Carews, had been in the county for generations, their names commanding recognition and respect from the local population. By the time Sir Peter Carew and his brother became prominent at the court of Henry VIII in the 1530s, members of the Carew family had served the Crown in Devonshire for almost two centuries.[1]

The family's membership in the landholding class of England went back even farther. A charter issued by King John in May 1212 confirmed to a William de Carrio a grant of the manor of Mulesford in Berkshire first made to William's great-grandfather by Henry I.[2] William de Carrio, whose name likely derived from his Pembrokeshire lordship and castle of Karieu or Carrio, was a nephew of Robert FitzStephen, one of the first Anglo-Norman barons to go adventuring in Ireland in the 1160s. Because FitzStephen died childless, the estates he won in Ireland, especially in County Cork, passed eventually to William de Carrio. In the late thirteenth century, William's great-grandson married the heiress to the rich and extensive Irish barony of Idrone, thus greatly extending the family's holdings and influence in Ireland. The recovery of Idrone was to become the consuming passion of the last years of Sir Peter Carew's life after 1568.

In the early fourteenth century, Nicholas Carew, a son of the Idrone heiress, married the sister and heir of Sir John Peverell of Ermynton in Devon.[3] This marriage forged the first connection between the Carew family and the county of Devon. Through the Peverell marriage, the Carews acquired the Devon manors of Weston Peverell, Ashford, and Mamhead.[4] The manor of Mamhead, which was a wedding gift from Sir John Peverell to his sister and new brother-in-law,[5] stayed in the family until the sixteenth century, when Sir Peter sold it, like so many other long-held family lands, to meet his pressing debts.[6] Nicholas, who died about 1312, was the first Carew to live at least part of the time in Devon.[7] He built up the family's holdings in Devon in the same way his ancestors had secured the family's position in Ireland, by marrying his son to the heiress of a wealthy local family. This marriage to the daughter and heir of William de Mohun brought to the Carew family the Devon manors that were to be the foundation of the sixteenth-century Carews' wealth and influence. The Mohun inheritance included the Devon manors of Golmeton, Monckton, Stoke Fleming, and Ottery Mohun (or, as it came to be called, Mohun's Ottery), as well as the lordship of Dartmouth.[8]

Despite their growing influence in Devon, the fourteenth-century Carews were still deeply involved in the affairs of Ireland. John Carew, grandson of Nicholas, received a summons to the Irish Parliament of 1331, and served as lord chief justice of Ireland in 1340 and as a member of the retinue of Lord Justicier Ralph Ufford from 1344 to 1346. He was named one of three "keepers of the peace" for County Carlow, the county in which much of Idrone was located, in 1345-46, and he negotiated for the government during this same year with certain Irish rebels. He was escheator of Ireland in 1349 and is so titled again in the 1350s; he served briefly as lord justicier of Ireland in 1349 or 1350. About 1359, he attended a great council in Waterford, and died in Ireland about 1363.[9] John Carew was part of the king's army at Crecy in 1346 and perhaps also at Calais[10]; his son, who also took part in the siege of Calais in 1347, died fighting the king's "Irish enemies"[11] about 1353.

By the late fourteenth century, an Irish resurgence had stripped the Carews of effective control of most of their Irish estates, and Thomas Carew, John's grandson, ceased to be an Irish landholder. He strengthened the family's position in Devon and the West Country by loyally serving the new Lancastrian dynasty in its wars in Wales and France. He was involved in Henry IV's campaigns against Owen Glendower in 1403,[12] and served with Prince Henry at the siege of Aberystwyth in Wales in 1407.[13] By 1412, Thomas had achieved knighthood.[14] In 1414-15, Henry V directed Thomas to patrol the seas for 50 days,[15] foreshadowing the naval service a future King Henry would demand from Thomas's sixteenth-century descendants for a future invasion of France. Thomas was coleader with the earl of Devon of the Devonshire contingent in the army at Agincourt in 1415,[16] and continued to serve Henry V in various military roles until the king's death in 1422.[17] The capable military service Sir Thomas Carew gave the fifth Henry was to be strongly echoed in the next century by the like service done by Sir Peter Carew for the eighth Henry.

Under Sir Thomas, the family's landed interests centered firmly on Devonshire and the West Country. Over the next several generations, the family increased its landholdings in the region through marriage, particularly through a series of matches with the leading noble family of the West, the Courtenays. Before his death in 1431, Sir Thomas initiated the first Carew-Courtenay union between his son and a granddaughter of the Courtenay earl of Devon, a match that would bring 17 Devonian and Cornish manors into the Carew family. Sir Peter Carew would himself be a product of a later marriage between the two families. Through luck and a series of well-planned marriages with the Courtenays and other important West Country families, the fifteenth-century Carews consolidated the wealth and position the sixteenth-century Carews were able to exploit to achieve favor and recognition at the Tudor court and in Tudor military campaigns.

The seat of the fifteenth-century Carews was Mohun's Ottery, the Devon manor acquired from the Mohuns over a century earlier. Each of the masters of Mohun's Ottery was summoned to Parliament by writ as Baron Carew, a distinction enjoyed by the head of the family since the thirteenth century. By the birth of Sir Peter's grandfather, Edmund Carew, in 1464, the Carews stood in the upper ranks of the Devon gentry in terms of wealth, lineage, and family connections.[18] Edmund Carew, who was only six years old at his father's death,[19] inherited manors worth over £60 per year; these estates, with various other properties outside the county, assured Edmund a comfortable if not spectacular income.[20] When he came of age, Edmund enlarged his landholdings through a marriage to the daughter and coheiress of William Huddesfield, future attorney general of Henry VII.[21] In 1485, Edmund placed his family and his resources at the service of Henry Tudor, choosing to fight for Tudor at Bosworth Field. A grateful and victorious Henry Tudor knighted Edmund two days after the battle.[22] Edmund's decision to support the house of Tudor set a pattern of loyalty and service that his grandson, Sir Peter Carew, followed with diligence throughout most of his life.

Sir Edmund Carew served Henry VII faithfully in various capacities, both military and political. In 1497, Sir Edmund assisted in the defeat of Perkin Warbeck's invasion of the West Country, and his brother John earned a knighthood for his services against Cornish rebels at the battle of Black Heath.[23] After Henry VII's death in 1509, Sir Edmund and his brother took part in the continental wars of young Henry VIII, a service which cost both men their lives. Sir John put to sea in the royal service in 1512, just as his great-nephew Sir Peter Carew was to do for an older Henry VIII some 30 years later. Sir John died on 10 August when his ship, the *Regent,* was set alight and exploded during a duel with the French ship *Cordelier.* Sir Edmund died in a similarly dramatic fashion during Henry VIII's invasion of France in 1513. On 22 June, Sir Edmund was one of several captains attending a council of war in Lord Herbert's tent outside the besieged city of Therouanne. As the captains deliberated, a bullet shot from the town passed through the tent, killing Sir Edmund as he sat at council. This sudden intrusion of death into their midst not unnaturally dismayed the assembly, "but the lord Herbert comforted them with manly words, and so his death was passed over."[24] Sir Edmund's body was brought to Calais on 26 June and buried in the Chapel of the Resurrection in the Church of St. Nicholas just before the king himself arrived in Calais on 30 June.[25]

Sir Edmund's death left his heirs a troubling financial legacy. To furnish himself for the 1513 expedition, Sir Edmund mortgaged some of the most ancient family estates and borrowed heavily from the Crown. His untimely death cost the family several valuable manors, including Mulesford, the manor granted by King John in 1212, and Carew Castle in Wales, the long-held property from which the family derived its name.

The burden of Crown debt contracted by Sir Edmund entangled his son, Sir William Carew, and his grandsons, including, eventually, Sir Peter Carew, with the royal exchequer for decades. Inherited debt, and the inability to stay out of new debt, were to be important factors in the course of Sir Peter Carew's adult life, affecting his actions and decisions on a number of occasions.

Sir Edmund left four sons. The eldest, Sir William Carew, Sir Peter's father, was born about 1483.[26] Sir Thomas, the second son, served with the earl of Surrey at Flodden in 1513. The two younger sons, George and Gawen, born in 1498 and 1503, respectively, were placed by their father's will in the custody of their eldest brother.[27] George Carew became a churchman and a scholar, being presented to the parish church at Lydford in Exeter diocese in September 1533.[28] He later held several important ecclesiastical appointments—archdeacon of Totnes, dean of Exeter, and, under Elizabeth, royal chaplain and dean of Windsor.[29]

The other brother, Gawen Carew, was no more than two or three years older than his eldest nephew, Sir William's first son George, and only about 10 years senior to his nephew Peter. In the 1520s, Sir William attached this youngest brother and his own eldest son George to the household of Henry Courtenay, the marquis of Exeter and a maternal relative of the family.[30] Being of his nephews' generation, Gawen's long career closely paralleled both of their careers, and frequently intersected with Peter's after George died in 1545. Uncle and nephew fought together to put down rebellion, plotted together to raise rebellion, and suffered together the consequences of their mutual treason.

Some time before 1504, Sir William married Joan Courtenay of the Powderham Courtenays, cousins of the comital branch of that family.[31] The couple had three sons—George, Philip, and Peter—and one daughter —Cecily. Joan outlived her two oldest sons, not dying until 1554.[32] Little is known about the middle son Philip, except that he too chose to go adventuring and became a Knight of Malta. He died fighting the Turks some time before his brother George's death in 1545, and he had no children, for neither he nor any heirs stood in the way of youngest brother Peter being found George's heir.[33] Cecily married Thomas Kirkham of Blackadon. Because she was the only one of Sir William's children to have issue, such of the family's West Country holdings as survived Sir Peter's need for money passed to her daughter Thomasine and her son-in-law Thomas Southcote.[34] Mohun's Ottery remained in the Southcote family for several generations after Sir Peter Carew's death in 1575.

After 1513, Sir William Carew struggled with the consequences of his father's indebtedness to the Crown. He appeared before Wolsey and the bishop of Winchester on 25 November 1514 to receive directions for the payment of the debt by yearly installments.[35] His father's name still appeared in a list of Crown debtors made in 1517, and on 1 February 1521 Sir William came before the king's commissioners to make payment on a large debt of £1100.[36] Sir William Carew was still making payment by annual installments on sums owed to the king in 1530.[37] The Devon subsidy rolls for the mid-1520s, a period of unprecedented taxation to finance the king's French wars, provide some indication of the value of Sir William's Devon holdings at this time and the enormity of the debt he faced. For the subsidy of 1525, Mohun's Ottery, Monckton, and the family's core lands in Axminster hundred had an assessed valuation of just over £66. The manor of Stoke Fleming and other Carew lands in Coleridge hundred stood assessed at £40 for 1526-27, the last two years of the four-year subsidy.[38] At this valuation, William Carew's tax bill in Devon for the 1524 subsidy, at the rate of 1s in the £ granted by Parliament, was in excess of £5. Sir William's annual income from his Devon lands was thus a little more than £100. He had additional income from lands outside the county, but this figure was significantly diminished by the loss of Carew Castle and the other properties mortgaged or sold by his father. Sir William's total annual income from land in the 1520s was probably not over £150, well over the average gentry income for the period of about £80 per year, but just at or under the average for knightly families.[39] Sir William's income was sufficient to make him a substantial landholder in the county, but too small to carry easily a burden of Crown debt put at over £1000.

This was the family of Sir Peter Carew—the immediate family, whose members directly affected Sir Peter's own life, and the more distant ancestors, whose lives and decisions determined Sir Peter's social rank, economic position, and political opportunities. The life of Sir Peter Carew echoed with the lives and deeds of his ancestors, familial echoes of a strength and clarity unknown in the lives and careers of such other politically important figures of the sixteenth century as Sir William Paget or Sir Ralph Sadler. Such men rose from obscure families to the highest counsels of king and kingdom. They became the secretaries, councilors, and diplomats the Tudor state needed to function. To explain their new positions and the attendant rewards to a status-conscious society, they often had devised highly fictionalised genealogies and family histories. Sir Peter Carew never cut a great figure in these increasingly important fields, but he had no need to fictionalise his past. The familial echoes he heard rang back over 500 years and called him to Ireland, to the West Country, and to military service for his prince.

---

1   Joyce Youings, *Sixteenth-Century England* (New York: Penguin Books, 1984), pp. 54-55.

2   Maclean, *Life and Times*, Appendix I.

3   Sir William Pole, *Collections Towards a Description of the County of Devon* (London, 1791), pp. 129-30; A.W. Searley, "Haccombe. Part VII. Early Carew Period," *Transactions of the Devonshire Association for the Advancement of Science, Literature, and Art* 56 (1924): 312-13.

4   Pole, *Collections*, pp. 129-30, 333-34.

5   Manor of Mamhead Records, DRO, MS 484M, T8/1. This document is dated
    tentatively to 1275. It confirms Sir John Peverell's gift of Mamhead to "Nicholas of
    Karru" and to his wife, "Alice," Peverell's sister.

6   Pole, *Collections*, p. 259.

7   Searley, "Haccombe," p. 313.

8   Thomas Westcote, *A View of Devonshire in MDCXXX*, (Exeter, 1845), p. 225; Pole,
    Collections, pp. 285-86; Searley, "Haccombe," p. 314.

9   "Sir John Carew." *DNB*, p. 962.

10 R.N. Worth, *A History of Devonshire* (London, 1886), p. 83; John Burke, *A
    Genealogical and Heraldic History of the Commoners of Great Britain and Ireland*, vol. 1
    (London, 1836), p. 266.

11 "Sir John Carew," *DNB*, p. 962.

12 John Lavan Kirby, *Henry IV of England* (London: Constable & Company, 1970),   p.
    153.

13 Christopher Allmand, *Henry V* (Berkeley: University of California Press, 1992),   pp.
    32, 35 n.

14 *Inquisitions and Assessments Related to Feudal Aids, 1284-1431*, vol. VI (Kraus Reprint,
    1973), p. 416. In Burke, *A Genealogical and Heraldic History*, p. 267, Sir Thomas,
    who is mistakenly referred to as Sir John, is said to have been knighted by Richard II.

15 Allmand, *Henry V*, p. 223. Allmand (p. 227) lists Thomas Carew among Henry V's
    best and most experienced naval commanders, and describes him as one who enjoyed
    "high social position" during the reign.

16 William R. Harwood, "The Courtenay Family in the Politics of Region and Nation in
    the Later Fifteenth and Early Sixteenth Centuries." (Ph.D. diss., Cambridge
    University, 1978), p. 32. See also "Sir John Carew," *DNB*, p. 962.

17 In 1416, Thomas commanded 300 men-at-arms at sea as an honour guard to convey
    the Emperor Sigismund to England for his talks with the king. Thomas also served
    for a time as captain of Harfleur, and, in 1418, he was ordered to defend the passage
    over the Seine for the king's army. In 1417, Carew was again keeping the seas for
    the king. A commission of 10 February 1417 orders the muster of a company of 316
    men-at-arms and 632 archers to put to sea under Carew from Dartmouth on 1
    March following. See Pole, *Collections*, p. 85 and *CPR*, Henry V and Henry VI, 10
    February 1417 (London: HMSO, 1897-1911), p. 85.

[18] Youings, *Sixteenth-Century England*, p. 55.

[19] Abstract of Inquisition Post Mortem of Sir Nicholas Carew, 10 October 1471, WSL, File 37 (38).

[20] Ibid.

[21] *Calendar of Inquisitions Post Mortem*, Henry VII, vol. II (Kraus Reprint, 1973), p. 178.

[22] William A. Shaw, *The Knights of England*, vol. II (London, 1906), p. 23. Edmund Carew is included in a listing of knights made at the battle or between the battle and the king's coronation in October. Family tradition has Edmund knighted on the field or within days after the battle.

[23] Ibid., p. 30.

[24] Snow, *Holinshed's Chronicles*, III, p. 576; LP, I(2), 2053 (6ii), 2392; *Chronicle of Calais*, Camden Series #35 (London: Camden Society, 1846), p. 12. Edward Hall, *The Union of the Two Noble and Illustrious Families of Lancaster and Yorke* (London, 1809), p. 538 quotes Lord Herbert as consoling the appalled gathering as follows: "this was a chance of war, if it had hit me you must have been content, a noble heart in war is never afraid of death."

[25] *Chronicle of Calais*, p. 12; LP, I(2), 2391.

[26] J.L. Vivian, ed., *The Visitations of the County of Devon* (Exeter, 1895), p. 135.

[27] Inquisition Post Mortem of Sir Edmund Carew, PRO, C142/30/88.

[28] LP, VI, 480.

[29] Vivian, *Visitations*, p. 135; *CPR*, Elizabeth I, vol. I, 27 April 1560, (Kraus Reprint, 1976), p. 339. George's two sons, Peter and George, made names for themselves in Ireland after being brought to that island by their older cousin Sir Peter Carew in the 1570s. The elder of these two boys, Peter, was Sir Peter Carew's principal heir and inherited the recovered Irish barony of Idrone. Charles I ennobled George, the younger cousin, in the 1620s as the earl of Totnes. The Carew Manuscripts at Lambeth Palace, which contain John Hooker's life of Sir Peter Carew, are the collected papers of George Carew, earl of Totnes.

[30] LP, IV(1), 1792.

[31] Vivian, *Visitations*, p. 135.

[32] Harwood, "Courtenay Family," p. 1; Vivian, *Visitations*, p. 135; Inquisition Post Mortem of Sir George Carew, PRO, C142/73/20.

33 Vivian, *Visitations*, p. 135; Inquisition Post Mortem of Sir George Carew, PRO, C142/73/20.

34 Vivian, *Visitations*, p. 135; *Calendar of Deeds and Documents*, Exeter City Library, DRO, #68402.

35 LP, I(2), 3483.

36 Ibid., II(2), 3087; III(1), 1153.

37 Ibid., IV(3), 6792.

38 T.L. Stoate, ed. *Devon Lay Subsidy Rolls 1524-7* (Bristol, 1979), pp. 33, 236-37.

39 Although the average income for knights and gentlemen varied from county to county, an average income during this period of £150 to £200 for knightly families is a reasonable estimate. See W.G. Hoskins, *The Age of Plunder: The England of Henry VIII 1500-1547* (London: Longman, 1976), pp. 54-55 and Youings, *Sixteenth-Century England*, pp. 54-55.

CHAPTER 2

A BRIEF BUT EVENTFUL CHILDHOOD

"Apart from isolated and fanciful tales," writes a well respected Tudor historian, "we begin to know most politically important sixteenth-century people only when they are already public figures."[1] Sir Peter Carew is a rare exception to this general rule. Something of his childhood and early years has been preserved by his solicitor and friend, John Hooker of Exeter. Because Hooker was, to use Richard Carew's words, a "commendable painful antiquary,"[2] Sir Peter found him to be the ideal agent to undertake advance research among the Dublin Castle archives, a task vital to preparing Carew's suit for recovery of his family's Irish lands and quite beyond Sir Peter's own capacities and temperament. For the better part of five years, Hooker remained in Ireland, either attending Sir Peter when he was present or representing him when he was not. Hooker's duties as Sir Peter's agent in Ireland were diverse, ranging from collecting and analyzing ancient records, to drafting legal documents, renting houses, and borrowing money. During the course of this close association, the two men developed an appreciation for each other's abilities and talents. Carew showed his respect for Hooker by turning to the Exeter native again and again for vital assistance in the conduct of his difficult Irish affairs. Hooker embodied his respect for his friend and patron in a more enduring form. Sometime after Carew's death in 1575 and before his own in 1601, Hooker wrote a lively and engaging biography of Sir Peter based in part on his own experiences in Sir Peter's employ and in part on the reminiscences and memories imparted to him by Sir Peter and others. We are therefore indebted to John Hooker for most of what we know about the first two decades of Sir Peter Carew's life.

For the period between Peter Carew's birth and his rather abrupt arrival at the court of Henry VIII at about age 18, Hooker recorded a series of events in Carew's life that we know from no other sources. These events help us to explain and understand some of the chief characteristics and behavior patterns of the adult Sir Peter Carew. The childhood and youth that Hooker preserved was a short launching pad into an adult life of travel and adventure, military and courtly service, and bold, direct action. At about the age of 12, or perhaps even earlier, Peter Carew left his family to enter the service of a foreign courtier at a foreign court. Within a year or two of that, the boy found himself in the midst of the Franco-imperial wars in Italy. By the time he returned to England to parents who were astonished to see him alive, the experience of war on both the French and imperial sides, and of court life under no less than five different patrons or protectors had transformed a willful, unlettered boy into a well-mannered young gentleman fluent in French and Italian and intimately acquainted with continental armies, courts, and personalities. The need to survive taught young Peter how to function as a courtier and a soldier, roles already congenial to both his nature and his family heritage. Courts and camps became his natural environment, and the traits and characteristics encouraged by those environments—gallantry, bravado, eagerness for military glory—became important elements of his personality.

Sir Peter Carew, wrote Hooker, "was born at Mohun's Ottery, in the year of our Lord, 1514." Peter was the third son of Sir William Carew, and a grandson of Sir Edmund Carew, who had been slain only the year before at Henry VIII's siege of Therouanne. Having other sons, and perceiving Peter to be "very pert and forward," Sir William thought it best the boy acquire some learning and thereby be brought "to some advancement." Therefore, when Peter was about 12 years old, his father took him to Exeter and lodged him with Thomas Hunt, whom Hooker described as a draper and alderman of the city.[3] Hunt was a tenant of the Carews, holding of Sir William a tenement and garden in the Exeter parish of All Hallows upon the Walls.[4] Hunt was apparently a man of means and position in Exeter; he was admitted to the corporation about 1512 and served twice as mayor, in 1515 and again in 1523.[5] For both mayoral periods, the Exeter records call him a baker, but his listing among the aldermen in 1521 agrees with Hooker in calling him a draper. Hunt was still alive in 1540 when he and John Midwinter, a fellow member of the Exeter Common Council, were fined and committed to ward for "using very unseemly speeches the one against the other" in the council chamber.[6]

Hunt was to look after the boy while he attended the grammar school of a Master Freers. John Maclean, the nineteenth-century editor of Hooker's biography of Carew, could find no particulars on Freers, but conjectured that he was one of the four brothers who maintained St. John's Hospital, which, along with its grammar school, was dissolved in the 1530s. Hooker called Freers "a very hard and cruel master," and blamed young Peter's frequent truancy at least in part on this cruelty. But given the boy's subsequent record as a student, Hooker's other stated reason for Peter's poor school attendance seems more convincing—Peter Carew "had no affection to his learning." Young Carew preferred to spend his days roving about the streets of Exeter, a practice of which the school master bitterly complained to the unfortunate Thomas Hunt. Hunt was then forced to rove about the streets himself to find the young truant and return him to his studies. On one occasion, Hunt found the boy playing about the city walls. When the draper tried to lay hands on him, Peter climbed to "the top of one of the highest garrets of a turret of the said wall." Hunt tried to coax Peter off the turret, but received from the boy only the promise to cast himself over the wall should Hunt attempt to reach him. "I shall break my neck," shouted Peter, "and thou shalt be hanged, because thou makest me to leap down." Afraid the boy might actually do as he threatened, Hunt left servants to watch him and hurried home to send for Sir William, requesting him to come as soon as may be and deal with his exasperating son.[7]

At Sir William's next arrival in Exeter, Hunt apprised him of this and other of his son's mischievous episodes. Sir William then applied a novel disciplinary technique. He tied Peter "in a line, and delivered him to one of his servants to be carried about the town, as one of his hounds, and they led him home to Mohun's Ottery, like a dog."[8] This unorthodox method of punishment must have been effective (or perhaps singularly ineffective), for Hooker says the boy remained tied to one of his father's dogs for some time thereafter.

Sir William did not give up on Peter's education. He took the boy to London and "earnestly requested" the school master of Dr. John Colet's foundation at St. Paul's to see what he could do with Peter. The school master did his best to meet the father's request, but like Master Freers, he found the son "more desirous of liberty than of learning." On his next visit to London, Sir William inquired of the master as to his son's progress, hopeful of some good report. His hopes were dashed. Despite his best efforts, the master "in no wise could frame this young Peter to smell to a book, or to like of any schooling"; the boy, Sir William was told, "neither loved the school nor cared for learning." Peter was not and never would be a scholar. It would be better, advised the school master, for Sir William to take back his youngest son and "employ him in some other thing."[9]

While walking in St. Paul's, perhaps pondering what to do with his wayward and obstinate son, Sir William had a stroke of luck—and Peter had the course of his life radically altered. Sir William happened upon an old acquaintance—Hooker did not name the man—who was then serving at the French court. The two men fell to talking; Hooker implies an old familiarity between the two which they now pleasantly renewed. Peter, attending on his father that day, attracted the notice of the other man, who inquired as to whom the boy was. Being told the boy was Sir William's son, the acquaintance proposed that Peter should come with him to France to be trained up as a gentleman at the French court.

The man promised to do as much for Peter "as if he were his own son." Hooker, in probable understatement, said Sir William "was contented, and did accept the offer."[10] Sir William would likely have been something more than "contented" to have his problem so satisfactorily resolved. And Peter, although Hooker said nothing about the boy's feelings, must have been even happier, the prospect of travel and adventure appealing to him far more than any further schooling.

Before Peter's trip could commence, Sir William had to furnish his son with the apparel and other necessaries of a gentleman's page. Once at the French court, Peter's new master, whom Hooker later revealed to be a Frenchman, for a time treated his new page well, training him in the ways of a gentleman and making much of him. But when Peter's clothes wore out and wanted replacing, the master found himself less taken with his page and reduced the boy to the role of a lackey. From this position, Peter tumbled even further, being banished to the stables and the care of his master's mule. Characteristically, the boy was not at all unhappy with these demotions; the stables afforded him some measure of the "liberty" to explore that he so valued, and the work put him in the daily company of men and boys with whom he was comfortable. He was, as he evidently recalled to Hooker, "content with his estate."[11]

This period of contented servitude ended when John Carew of Haccombe in Devon, a distant cousin of Sir William's, came to the French court seeking to indulge his own desire for overseas travel and adventure. John Carew descended from one of the younger brothers of Peter's great-great-grandfather Sir Thomas, who in the 1440s had unintentionally endowed his siblings with generous portions of his maternal inheritance by slapping his mother's face during a quarrel. Hooker called John Carew "a gentleman of great courage and valour, and desirous to serve and see countries"; he had come to the French court bearing letters of recommendation from Henry VIII to the French king, Francis I, who gratified Carew's desire for service and new sights by giving him the charge of a company of horses bound for the wars in Italy.[12]

One day, while present in the French court, John Carew emerged from the court gate and found himself among a large, boisterous crowd of lackeys and horseboys. As he made his way through the boys, he was startled to hear one of them call out to "Carew Anglois!" Curious to know who this "English Carew" was, he asked the boys around him, who pointed out one of their own number. Upon carefully examining this "all too ragged, and very simply appareled" mule boy, Carew was shocked to understand that he was Peter Carew son of his Mohun's Ottery cousin. Carew quickly had the boy's whole story, how his patron had brought him to France as a page but then thoughtlessly and ungraciously relegated him to the stables rather than pay to keep him well appareled and supplied. Taking the boy in charge, the indignant John Carew searched through the court until he found Peter's negligent master and "so talked [to] him and so reproved him" for his mistreatment of Peter that the courtier was soon right willing "to forgo his page, and so seek a new lackey."[13] And so the continental adventures of young Peter Carew entered a new phase.

By Hooker's account, John Carew seems to have remained at the French court for some time; for after reappareling his ragged cousin, he resumed Peter's interrupted training as a gentleman. John took the boy about the court, instructing him "in riding and other such exercises as most meet for one of service." Peter's training was again interrupted when he and his kinsman accompanied Francis I and his army into Italy on the campaign that was to end in disaster for Francis at the siege of Pavia. Hooker claimed John Carew died on the way to Pavia, before the battle was fought. This would place his death some time before 24 February 1525, the day of the battle. No sooner had Peter lost a second patron than he acquired a third. A French nobleman in the royal army whom Hooker called the "Marquis of Salewe" [the Italian marquis of Saluzzo], a friend of

John Carew's and familiar with his young kinsman's story and situation, took the boy into his service. Peter was therefore present in the marquis's retinue at the battle of Pavia, where the French king was taken prisoner and the marquis slain by "a shot of a gun."[14]

Peter, "perceiving fortune to frown upon the French side," boldly took himself into the imperial camp to find a new patron among the winners. The prince of Orange, one of the imperial commanders, soon took a fancy to the boy and "received him into his entertainment." In the prince's service, Peter once again was well contented and continued with Orange for a year and a half, until the prince's death. Peter evidently made a powerful impression on the prince's family and household, for the "Princess" desired him to remain in the family's service and continued for some time to give him "very good and honourable entertainment."[15]

A French manuscript entitled "l'Histoire Généalogique de la Maison de Carew," which John Maclean found in the possession of the Cornish branch of the Carew family in the nineteenth century, gives Peter yet another patron. This document states that Peter Carew served as a page to the constable of Bourbon at the sack of Rome in May 1527.[16] Bourbon, a French subject in rebellion against his king, had fought on the imperial side at Pavia; his death in the attack on Rome two years later only further enraged his already mutinous troops, who plundered the city as mercilessly as the Goths had done a thousand years earlier. If this Cornish tradition is factual, Peter's initial imperial patron after Pavia was Bourbon, whose death at Rome obliged the boy to transfer his service to a second imperial commander, the prince of Orange. Hooker mentioned neither Bourbon nor Carew's presence at the sack of Rome, but this tradition accords well with Hooker's assertions about the time of John Carew's death and Peter's presence at the battle of Pavia.

But how credible are Hooker's assertions? Hooker's account of

Peter Carew's adventures up to and at the battle of Pavia are exciting, but are these adventures likely to have been those of a boy of 10 or at most 11 years of age? If Peter Carew was indeed born in 1514 and was actually present at Pavia as Hooker stated, then he was only about 10 years old when he crossed the Channel, for he had to leave England at least by the middle of 1524 to allow time for his tenure in the stables and his tutelage under John Carew before his trip to Pavia in February 1525. Ten seems too young for the gentlemanly training and martial experiences Hooker described. Indeed, Hooker said the boy was 12 when he left England. Sir Peter Carew's recollection some 40 years later that he was about 12 when he became the Frenchman's page may have been faulty, and he could actually have been a few years younger. Another possibility is that Hooker got Carew's birth year wrong, and that Carew was born before 1514 and was then indeed about 12 years old when he left for France in the year before Pavia. Although the evidence is fragile and will not bear much weight, the case for Peter Carew's birth date being earlier than 1514 can be made.

According to heralds' visitations of Devon from the Elizabethan and early Stuart periods, Peter Carew was about 33 years of age at the time of his brother George's death in 1545.[17] This would place Peter's birth around the year 1512. From the age given for him at the time of his father's inquisition post mortem in 1537, George Carew's year of birth can be estimated at about 1505.[18] The two brothers' youngest uncle, Gawen Carew, was called age 40 "or thereabouts" in January 1543 in city of London records, which suggest a birth year for him of about 1502 or 1503.[19] As a Henrician courtier and soldier, Peter was closely associated with his brother and with his uncle. The two brothers served together in the 1540s—captains of horse in the king's army and captains of ships in his navy. In 1549, Peter and his uncle received a joint commission from Lord Protector Somerset to pacify the Prayer Book rebels of Devon and Cornwall. Nephew and uncle, usually in that order, were both frequently named to commissions for various causes in Devon and neighboring counties. The inference to be drawn from the equal or near equal ranks and levels of military service between the two brothers in the 1540s, and the frequent close association in royal service of nephew and uncle thereafter, is that the differences in ages between Peter and his brother and uncle were not great. If Peter was born in 1514 as Hooker stated, the age gap between him and Gawen would have been 12 years (or more) and between Peter and George at least 9 years. Although 1514 remains possible, moving Peter's birth back to the period 1510-1512 would narrow the age difference between Peter and his brother and uncle and better explain the close association of the three men in their public careers.[20] An earlier date also agrees with the age given for Peter at the time of his brother's death and makes him a more likely 13-15 at the battle of Pavia.

Moving back the year of Peter Carew's birth is one way to untangle Hooker's confused chronology, but there is an even better way to resolve Hooker's contradictions. Hooker's error may not have been in misplacing the year of Carew's birth, but in misplacing Carew himself, specifically, in putting him at the battle of Pavia. If Hooker was correct in placing Carew's birth in 1514 and his departure for France at age 12, then that departure could not have occurred until 1526, a year or more after Pavia. This chronology is supported by a number of other sources. For one thing, we know that John Carew of Haccombe did not die on his way to Pavia in 1525, for in the spring of 1528 he wrote a letter to Henry VIII from the French camp before Naples.[21] Michele-Antonio, the marquis of Saluzzo, whom Hooker claimed was slain at Pavia, was still alive in July 1527 when Wolsey wrote to Henry VIII about the recent accord concluded between the marquis, Francis I, and the Venetians.[22]

We can place John Carew in France in August 1527. In the summer of that year Wolsey crossed to France as the king's lieutenant, empowered to deal in a number of weighty matters, including the consequences arising from the Pope's virtual imprisonment by the imperial army after its sack of Rome. The incapacity of the pope to freely exercise his office had serious consequences both for the administration of the Church and the prospects of obtaining a divorce for Henry VIII. In September, William Knight, a royal envoy on his way to Rome, stopped at Compiégne to report to Wolsey. In a letter to the king on 12 September, Knight wrote that Wolsey had sent Gregory Casale "in company with Sir Robert Jarnegham and Carrew Hacham, towards Monsieur de Loutrek, 14 days past." After recommending the two Englishmen to Lautrec, who commanded the French army bound for Italy, Casale planned to go with all speed to Rome.[23] If Peter Carew was discovered by his kinsman in the summer of 1527, as seems likely, then his initial arrival in France in 1526, when, by Hooker's reckoning, he was about 12, is also probable. In any event, Hooker is clearly wrong about the date of John Carew's death and about Peter's need to find a new patron after Pavia.

Odet de Foix, seigneur de Lautrec, led a French army over the Alps into Italy in August 1527. By November, he had overrun most of Lombardy. From his conference with Wolsey at Compiégne, where he had concluded a new accord with Henry VIII, Francis I ordered Lautrec to march into the Spanish-controlled kingdom of Naples.[24] John Carew and his companion Robert Jernigam accompanied Lautrec's force into Naples, for Jernigam wrote to Henry VIII of the army's arrival in the kingdom on 10 February 1528.[25] On 26 April, Jernigam wrote again, this time from "the Camp, lying within a mile and a half of the town of Naples," to tell the king of recent military events, including a successful ambush laid by the marquis of Saluzzo, who had joined Lautrec's army in early February.[26] Two days later John Carew wrote to the king from the same camp to inform him of Jernigam's death the previous evening of a sickness that had descended upon him eight days before. Jernigam had not wished to tell the king of his illness because he believed he would soon recover. After asking for letters patent granting him "such lands and tenements" as the king had given to Jernigam, Carew concluded with a promise to keep the king informed of events. However, no more letters from Carew are extant because he died shortly thereafter of the same disease that had carried off Jernigam.[27] By late summer, the entire French army was suffering from the illness. In June, reports from Naples said Saluzzo was dead of the disease and Lautrec was ill with it.[28] The reports of Saluzzo's death were premature, but Lautrec died on the night of 15 August. The next day, a trumpeter appeared before the gates of Naples to announce Lautrec's death and the marquis of Saluzzo's succession, by Lautrec's dying appointment, to command of the depleted French forces. The new commander's first act was to request some balsam from his enemies to embalm his predecessor's body.[29]

The epidemic that claimed Lautrec was apparently not confined to the French camp, for within Naples the city's imperial viceroy, the prince of Orange, also fell ill during August.[30] Philibert de Chalon, prince of Orange, to whom Hooker claimed Peter Carew attached himself after Pavia, was only in his mid-twenties in 1528, but already a seasoned and successful commander.[31] In late August, an attack from Naples overran the disintegrating French camp; only Saluzzo and about 1,500 infantry escaped, taking refuge in the nearby town of Aversa. Orange, although not yet fully recovered, hurried to the town with artillery to force its quick surrender.[32] Saluzzo capitulated by 4 September, and Aversa, despite Orange's attempts to prevent it, was sacked by imperial troops. The marquis became a prisoner of war, but was treated honourably and allowed to move about freely.[33] By 8 September, Saluzzo's life was dispaired of, a dangerous fistula having formed in a knee wound caused by a splinter of stone blasted from the walls of Aversa during the siege.[34] He was, however, still alive in early October, when Edward Lee reported his captivity to Henry VIII.[35] Orange too was unwell; his recent exertions at Aversa caused a relapse of his fever and forced him to retire to Castilnovo for a change of air.[36] Saluzzo died on 19 October 1528, four days after a fully recovered Orange returned to his duties.[37] With the marquis dead, as Hooker claimed, of "a shot of a gun," Peter Carew, at some time during this war-weary Italian autumn, took himself into the imperial camp and the service of the prince of Orange.

The siege of Naples fits Hooker's account of Peter Carew's continental adventures in the 1520s much better than the siege of Pavia. All Hooker's key actors were present at Naples and all are confirmed by other sources as playing the general roles Hooker assigned to them. John Carew died some months before the siege came to its conclusion, and some months before the death of the marquis of Saluzzo, giving Peter Carew sufficient time to attach himself to the marquis after his kinsman's death. The conclusion of the siege in late 1528 accords well with Hooker's chronology. Peter Carew probably arrived in France in 1526, when he was about 12 by Hooker's birth date of 1514. He was likely rescued by John Carew in the summer of 1527. Peter's cousin was a squire of the body and was granted an annuity of 50 marks in May 1527.[38] He may have left for France shortly thereafter and could have spent part of the summer with Peter at the French court before the two left for Italy with Lautrec in late August. By the autumn of 1528, John Carew and the marquis of Saluzzo were dead and Peter Carew, then about 14 or 15, entered the service of the prince of Orange. Hooker might have been in error about the year of Peter Carew's birth, although Carew's likely presence at the siege of Naples in 1528 lends greater credibility to 1514 as the year of his birth. Hooker was undoubtedly wrong about Carew's presence at the siege of Pavia in 1525, and the Cornish tradition recalling Peter's service with Bourbon at the sack of Rome in May 1527 is also unlikely. In the spring of 1527, Peter was still at the French court tending his negligent master's mule and waiting to be discovered by his kinsman.

The collapse of French power in Italy after Naples turned the usually indecisive Medici pope, Clement VII, into a convinced imperialist.

Only Charles V could combat Lutheranism in Germany and the Turks in the Mediterranean, and, of perhaps even more importance to Clement, only Charles could help restore the pope's Medici relatives to power in Florence. The treaty of Barcelona of June 1529 called for Medici restoration in Florence and the return to Rome of certain papal territories in exchange for Clement's promise to crown Charles emperor and to absolve of guilt all those responsible for the sack of Rome in 1527.[39] The treaty had both an immediate and a long-range impact on the life of Peter Carew. Its immediate effect was to propel Orange and his army into Tuscany and a prolonged siege of Florence. Its more momentous consequence was the decision by the newly imperialist pope to revoke to Rome the divorce suit of Henry VIII then being tried in England, an action that was to topple Wolsey and lead to England's break with the Roman Church.

Hooker wrote little about what Carew experienced in the service of the prince of Orange during the year after the siege of Naples, and no other source mentions Peter Carew's presence in Italy, but we can follow the prince's movements during the period and from them make an educated guess as to Carew's life in this year. Orange remained in Naples during the last months of 1528, although the wretched condition of the kingdom made a speedy departure of the imperial army imperative.[40] By 3 March 1529, Orange had left Naples with an army of 9,000 "good and well-disciplined" troops for Florence.[41] By August 1529, after months of threatening the city, Orange received his instructions for the reduction of Florence.[42] A siege of the city began before the end of the year,[43] and dragged on through the early months of 1530; Orange spent as much time during these months struggling with a stingy pope and stiff-necked mutineers as with the enemy.[44] Conditions both inside and outside the city grew increasingly difficult as the siege continued. In July, Sir Nicholas Harvey wrote Henry VIII that the imperial camp at Florence, like the French camp at Naples two years before, was suffering from plague. Word from the camp was so grave that the emperor was "in doubt of the Prince of Orange his chief captain, and the residue of his people there."[45] Orange, however, managed to avoid the plague, only to be slain on 3 August 1530 leading a cavalry charge at Gavinana.[46] In four years on the continent, Peter Carew had left or lost four patrons. Since the prince's heir was his young nephew Réné of Nassau, Carew's fifth patron was, as Hooker claimed, a woman, either the late prince's sister, Claudia, or his mother, Philiberta of Luxembourg. Hooker referred to Carew's new patron simply as "the Princess," so it is not absolutely clear whether he meant the mother or the daughter. The former is the more likely, since Philiberta enjoyed the "usufruct" of the principality of Orange after her son's death.[47] Had Hooker meant the younger woman, he would probably have referred to her as countess of Nassau.

Hooker did not say whether or not Peter Carew had any part in the prince of Orange's invasion of Tuscany in 1529 or in his siege of Florence in 1530. He wrote only that the boy, who was at least 15 and 16 in these years, well liked his service with the prince and "continued with this lord in his court about a year and a half,"[48] a time reference that fits well the period elapsed between Saluzzo's death late in 1528 and Orange's death in August 1530. Hooker said plainly that Carew "was at the siege of Pavia," though, as we have seen, his presence at that siege is far less likely than his presence at either of the later sieges of Naples and Florence. Even if he got wrong the exact siege at which Peter Carew was present, Hooker had clearly understood that the boy experienced something of the warfare and military life that was so readily to be had in Italy at this time. Carew's siege experience was probably in the disease-ridden French camp outside Naples. The reference to service in Orange's "court" may mean that Carew's experience of the actual fighting before Florence, in whose spirited defense served the likes of Michaelangelo, was limited. However, Peter Carew's later taste for campaigning, which was so evident during his service in the armies of Henry VIII in the 1540s, makes it probable that he would have found service before the walls of Florence quite congenial. Beyond doubt, these years in Italy gave Peter Carew a taste of the dirt, death, and disease of war as well as the courtly cosmopolitanism of a Renaissance noble's household.

After six years away from home, Peter Carew finally decided to leave the service of the princess, for he was "now grown to ripe years, and somewhat languishing in desire to see his friends and country." Since Peter's departure for France appears to have taken place about 1526, this desire to return home must have come on him about 1531/32 when he was reaching the "ripe" age of 17 or 18. His service with the princess lasted for a year or more after the death of her son, the prince of Orange. Since the first date we can put to Peter Carew's presence in England is October 1532, when he accompanied the king and Anne Boleyn to Calais for a meeting with the French king, his return in late 1531 or early 1532 makes chronological sense. The princess was so fond of young Peter that she at first refused his request to leave her service. The princess, wrote Hooker, could not part with him

> for so honest was his conditions, and so courteous was his behavior, and so forward in all honest exercises, and especially in all prowess and virtue, that he had stolen the hearts, and gained the love of all persons unto him, and especially of the princess.[49]

Nonetheless, she at last relented, perhaps giving way to the dogged persistence that Carew would display to similar good effect on later occasions. Once persuaded, the princess threw herself into the task of providing the young man with all things necessary for a triumphant home-coming—new apparel, letters of recommendation to Henry VIII and Sir William, a gold chain, a full purse, and two deferential attendants. So outfitted, Peter took his leave, with many promises on the princess's part of "a gentleman's entertainment" should he ever decide to return, and many humble thanks on his part.[50]

Immediately upon his arrival in England, Peter took himself to the court, the king then being at Greenwich. After his experiences on the continent, Peter had no doubt that the court was where his future lay in England. The king found himself faced with a richly appareled young Englishman, fresh from the Renaissance courts of France and Italy and fluent in the languages of both countries. Henry read the princess's letters carefully and examined Peter closely, finding him "to be answerable to the princess's report and commendations." Indeed, Henry so well liked the young man that he took Peter into his service immediately. Peter's servants also did well, receiving 500 crowns from the king and royal letters of commendation and thanks for the princess. Peter then asked leave of the king to visit his parents in Devon, for he had not seen either of them in six years. Henry granted the request and Peter rode with his servants to Mohun's Ottery where he dramatically presented himself to his parents as they sat together in the parlor. The astonishment of Sir William and his wife was complete.

> The said Sir William and his lady, at this sudden sight were astonished, much musing what it should mean that a young gentleman so well appareled, and so well accompanied, should thus prostrate himself before them; for they thought nothing less than of their son Peter, who having been away from them about six years, and never heard of, did think verily that he had been dead and forlorn.[51]

Sir William apparently had some difficulty accepting the courtly young man as the same disobedient boy he had dispatched to France years before. It needed the help of the princess's glowing letter to fully convince him. But once persuaded, Sir William was "not a little joyful," and received his prodigal son with gladness and welcome. Sir William and Joan, said Hooker, entertained Peter's impressive attendants "in the best manner they could." After a few days at Mohun's Ottery, Peter begged leave of his father to return to court and to conduct his attendants on the first leg of their journey back to the princess. Bearing rich rewards and

letters of thanks to their mistress, Peter's two travel companions departed
for home shortly thereafter. Peter Carew then returned to the court of his
king, a new phase of his life about to begin, his brief but eventful childhood
at an end.[52]

---

[1] Slavin, *Politics and Profit*, p. 14.

[2] Richard Carew, "The Survey of Cornwall," in *Richard Carew of Antony: The Survey of
    Cornwall etc.*, ed. F.E. Halliday (London: Andrew Melrose, 1953), p. 130.

[3] Hooker, "Life," pp. 3-4.

[4] Hooker, *Description*, p. 696.

[5] Maclean, *Life and Times*, p. 4 n. Hooker, in his *Description*, pp. 869, 871, indicated
    that Hunt was mayor in 1517 as well.

[6] Hooker, *Description*, p. 933.

[7] Hooker, "Life," pp. 4-5.

[8] Ibid., p. 5

[9] Ibid., pp. 5-6.

[10] Ibid., pp. 6-7.

[11] Ibid., p. 7.

[12] Ibid., pp. 7-8.

[13] Ibid., pp. 8-9.

[14] Ibid., pp. 9-10.

[15] Ibid., p. 10.

[16] John Maclean, *The Life and Times of Sir Peter Carew, Kt.* (London: Bell and Daldy, 1857), p. xiii.

[17] Vivian, *Visitations*, p. 135.

[18] Inqusition Post Mortem of Sir William Carew, PRO, C142/59/106.

[19] S.T. Bindoff, ed., *The House of Commons 1509-1558*, vol. I (London: History of Parliament Trust, 1982), pp. 572-73.

[20] Indeed, the profile of Sir Peter Carew in Bindoff, *House of Commons*, I, p. 578 gives 1510 as the year of his birth, a date based on the estimated year of birth of his brother, Sir George Carew.

[21] John Carew to Henry VIII, 28 April 1528, *StPap*, VII, pp. 67-68. See also LP, IV(2), 4215.

[22] Thomas Wolsey to Henry VIII, 16 July 1527, *StPap*, VII, p. 217.

[23] William Knight to Henry VIII, 12 September 1527, *StPap*, VII, p. 1.

[24] R.J. Knecht, *Francis I* (Cambridge: Cambridge University Press, 1982), p. 215.

[25] Robert Jernigam to Henry VIII, 10 February 1528, *StPap*, VII, p. 49.

[26] Robert Jernigam to Henry VIII, 26 April 1528, *StPap*, VII, p. 66; for Saluzzo's arrival in the French camp, see *Cal.SP Span.* III(2), 315. References to *Cal.SP Span.* are document numbers, not page numbers, unless otherwise noted.

[27] John Carew to Henry VIII, 28 April 1528, *StPap*, VII, pp. 67-68.

[28] *Cal.SP Span.*, III(2), 457.

[29] Ibid., 533.

[30] Ibid.

[31] Karl Brandi, *The Emperor Charles V* (London: Jonathan Cape, 1970), pp. 270-71.

[32] *Cal.SP Span.*, III(2), 536.

[33] Ibid., 539.

[34] Ibid., 540.

[35] Edward Lee to Henry VIII, 6 October 1528, *StPap*, VII, p. 102.

[36] *Cal.SP Span.*, III(2), 539.

[37] Ibid., 576.

[38] LP, IV(2), 3142 (11).

[39] Knecht, *Francis I*, p. 218.

[40] *Cal.SP Span.*, III(2), 585, 597.

[41] Ibid., 639.

[42] Ibid., IV(1), 106.

[43] Orange wrote to the emperor from "the camp close to Florence" in mid December. See *Cal.SP Span.*, IV(1), 233.

[44] The pope was eager for the Medici restoration in Florence, but much less eager to contribute to the cost of the venture. In April, Clement complained to the emperor of a letter from Orange asking for immediate funds to prevent a mutiny among the Swiss troops, see *Cal.SP Span.*, IV(1), 287. In May, the emperor was told of Orange's resolution to invest the city more closely, and of another mutiny among Spanish troops, see *Cal.SP Span.*, IV(1), 306. On 27 June, the emperor informed the pope of Orange's further need for 16,000 ducats to pay his troops, see *Cal.SP Span.*, IV(1), 362.

[45] Nicholas Harvey to Henry VIII, 11 July 1530, *StPap*, VII, p 246.

[46] *Cal.SP Span.*, IV(1), 402.

[47] Maclean, *Life and Times*, p. 10 n.

[48] Hooker, "Life," p. 10.

[49] Ibid., p. 11.

[50] Ibid.

[51] Ibid., pp. 12-13.

[52] Ibid., p. 13.

CHAPTER 3

THE COURT OF HENRY VIII

As a henchman, or royal page, Peter Carew was an official member of the royal chamber staff and as such had limited access to the king. His sudden and dramatic appearance at the English court created something of a stir, and piqued Henry's interest enough to buy Carew, at least temporarily, more royal attention than his position would otherwise have warranted. The king took "great delight and pleasure" in Peter, and found him to be "very witty, full of life, and altogether given to all such honest exercises as do appertain to a gentleman, and especially in riding, for therein he had a special love and desire." Peter was exactly the type of vigorous young man Henry VIII liked. What's more, the young man could speak from first-hand knowledge of personalities and fashions at the French court and of military practice in Italy. The king appreciated Peter's excellent French, "which was as ripe in him as his own natural English tongue," and the two would talk together often about the French court. Carew "could name every nobleman in France, in what credit and countenance he was in the court." In this regard, Peter's arrival at the English court was especially timely, for the king was "minded. . . to go to Calais, and there to meet with the French king." From young Carew, Henry VIII hoped to glean useful intelligence that would help him prepare for this meeting. The more the king talked with Peter Carew, "the more he delighted in him."[1]

Having rid himself of Wolsey, the king after 1530 lacked a reliable minister capable of influencing or manipulating the papal Curia in his behalf. In terms of clout at the papal court, idle threats were no effective substitute for an English cardinal. Henry's divorce suit continued to languish. The king then hit upon the idea of enlisting the aid of the

French king and his more abundant supply of cardinals. In 1531, Henry began suggesting through his envoys that the two kings meet again, as they had once before at the Field of Cloth of Gold in 1520. Initially, Francis was unwilling, but by the summer of 1532 the meeting was agreed upon. To please Henry, Francis also invited Anne Boleyn, the newly created marquis of Pembroke.[2] The pope viewed the upcoming meeting with concern, sure that "it will be to his prejudice" and hopeful for "the usual effect . . .that the princes will be more at variance after the interview than before."[3] The French ambassador in England put it about that the meeting was being held only "for the purpose of resisting the Turk, and driving him out of Christendom." But Eustache Chapuys, the imperial ambassador, would have none of that. "The King," he wrote Charles V, "is taking with him a legion of doctors and monks who are in his favor about the divorce." Some "conference about the divorce" would surely take place, and Henry would no doubt seek to have the matter discussed and decided by the French Council and cardinals.[4]

On 11 October, Henry, trailing Anne Boleyn and a large and noble retinue, landed at Calais for the third time in his life. He had first been in the town 29 years before, just days too late for the burial there of Sir Edmund Carew. Now Sir Edmund's 18-year-old grandson came to Calais at the king's side. Indeed, bragged Hooker, Peter Carew was "one of the chiefest about the king."[5] The royal party stayed at Calais for over a week, until the French king's arrival in Boulogne on 19 October. Two days later the two monarchs met on English territory midway between Calais and Boulogne, and then rode together to Boulogne for several days of meetings and festivities. Neither queen was present; Queen Catherine of England, an aunt of Charles V, could not attend for obvious reasons, and Henry was not anxious for the French Queen, a niece of Charles V, to be present either. The problem was solved by eliminating all women from the Boulogne meetings; Anne Boleyn remained behind in Calais. On 24 October, the two kings rode together to the English town, where Henry played the consummate host and Francis danced and talked with Anne. On 28 October, Henry held a chapter of the Garter at which Philippe de Chabot, the lord admiral of France, and Anne de Montmorency, the great master, were installed into the order.[6] The king appointed Peter Carew as one of the admiral's attendants at this ceremony, where Peter's bearing and behavior drew the attention and the "great commendation and praise" of the French king.[7] The next day the kings rode to the frontier, embraced, and parted amicably, Francis having agreed to make Henry's great matrimonial cause his own.[8]

Despite his high profile about the king in Calais, Peter Carew did not advance beyond the position of henchman for another two years. Around 1534, when he was "above the age of a gentleman of that service," 20 year-old Peter Carew was appointed to be a gentleman of the privy chamber.[9] With this new appointment, the young man made a great advance in terms of position at court and opportunity of access to the king. Moving from henchman to gentleman of the privy chamber, Carew went from service in the king's outer or public chamber to service in the privy chamber, the king's suite of private apartments to which access was tightly controlled.

In early 1535, Henry dispatched Peter Carew to another Garter presentation; Carew accompanied Lord William Howard to Scotland to offer the honour to James V. The Garter Chapter that elected James was held on 20 January, and Howard left for Scotland immediately afterward.[10] Carew's courtliness and "behavior after the French manner," and especially his fluency in the French language, convinced the Scots that he was some great French lord.[11] Chapuys reported to Charles V that the English embassy was well received in Scotland, although he could not refrain from noting that the Scottish king's reception of the Garter "was very poor in comparison with what was done at the reception of that of your Majesty."[12] Chapuys also claimed that James had dismissed the English ambassador as quickly as good manners allowed, for he had feared the English party would contaminate his court with heretical doctrines.[13] Hooker claimed that the Scottish court was much taken with Carew, more than with any other member of Lord Howard's retinue. By late March, Peter was back at the English court, where he was "well commended and rewarded" by the king for the fine figure he had cut among the Scots.[14]

In the late 1530s, the fortunes of the Carew family at court experienced a series of ups and downs. George Carew, Peter's elder brother, was implicated in the Nun of Kent affair in 1533, as were George's former patrons, the marquis and marchioness of Exeter.[15] The Nun's confession named many people, including the Princess Mary and Sir Thomas More, as having heard and listened to her revelations concerning the bleak prospects for the king's reign and afterlife. "Sir George Carew and his brother" and "Mrs. Katharine Champer, his brother's wife"[16] were among those mentioned by the Nun as being part of a sympathetic circle of western adherents clustering around the marquis of Exeter and his wife. Because George is unlikely to have been knighted by 1533, his identification with this circle is not absolute; but George's past association with the Exeter household makes the identification likely. If Katharine Champer is Katherine Champernon, as also seems likely, then the reference is to George's aunt, not his sister-in-law. Katherine was sister to George's uncle Gawen, whom the Nun may have called George's brother, a misidentification that was to befall Gawen several times in his associations with his nephews. Gawen's former connection with the Exeter household makes him a stronger candidate than Peter for the person the Nun identified as George Carew's "brother." Other than this probably incorrect reference, there is no evidence that Peter Carew was involved in the matter of the Nun of Kent. Certainly Hooker made no mention of it. The Carews were accused of nothing more than having had the Nun's revelations shown to them, and George Carew's subsequent advancement in the royal service suggests that any involvement he might have had in the matter did not have lasting consequences. Because George, his brother, and uncle later proved themselves loyal to the king and unfriendly to the old religion, any Carew involvement in the Nun of Kent affair was probably more a matter of association with the marquis of Exeter and his circle than, as Mattingly suggested, of active plotting with Eustace Chapuys, the imperial ambassador, to support Catherine of Aragon and the conservative religious interest.[17]

In 1536, over a year after Peter was favored with appointment to the Scottish embassy, George secured election to Parliament as a knight of the shire for Devon in the place of his recently deceased uncle Sir William Courtenay. George was knighted some time between the Devon by-election in January 1536, when he was given no title, and October of that year when "Sir George Carew" was one of those appointed "to attend upon the king's own person" during the continuance of rebellion in the north. Certain members of Parliament had been knighted on 9 July when Cromwell was raised to the peerage; Carew may have been among that group.[18] At the end of the year, Sir George was chosen sheriff of Devon for 1537.[19]

Sir William Carew died in his mid-fifties some time during 1536, or perhaps even late in 1535, leaving Sir George as the master of Mohun's Ottery and new head of the family. Sir William's undated will was proved in 1537, the same year inquisitions post mortem were held into his estates in Devon, Cornwall, and Dorset.[20] Joan Carew was named her husband's executrix and George Carew was found to be his father's heir to the manors of Mohun's Ottery, Monckton, Stoke Fleming, and Southton in Dartmouth. George also inherited Manerlegh in Devon and a number of other manors pledged to the king under the terms of certain indentures made with the Crown in 1515 for repayment of debts incurred by the testator's father, Sir Edmund Carew. Luffingcote manor in Devon was enfeoffed to the use of Joan until she had received sufficient revenues from it to settle her husband's debts, then the manor was to pass to George. All

Sir William's goods and chattels went to his wife, who, with George, was enjoined to select a burial site for Sir William's body in the parish church of Luppitt and to care for his still living mother. Sir William left each of his household servants "not having a dwelling place or land wherein to live" one year's wages.

The path of Gawen Carew's advancement at Court was somewhat bumpier than his nephews'. In early 1531, he married Anne, the daughter of Sir William Brandon and sister of Henry VIII's friend and favorite, the duke of Suffolk. Anne had been a widow since about 1529; her first husband, Sir John Shilston, had been a member of another prominent Devon family. When Anne died, some time before 1540, Shilston's manor of Wood in Devon came into the possession of Gawen Carew. Anne was probably at least 10 years older than Gawen, her marriage to Shilston having taken place in 1513 when Gawen was about 10 years old.[21] Gawen's marriage set a pattern of marriages to older widows to which his nephew Peter also adhered. This marital pattern brought the sixteenth-century Carews wealth and social connections, but deprived them of a next generation of heirs. Neither Sir George nor Peter nor Gawen, despite six marriages between them, had any children. For Gawen, the prestigious connection to Suffolk did not bring many rewards. In October 1532, Suffolk asked Cromwell to favor his new brother-in-law "at the next election of sheriffs for Devonshire," but Gawen did not become sheriff until 1548, over two years after Suffolk's death.[22] Gawen received a license to import 500 tuns of Gascon wine and a quantity of Toulouse wood in December 1536, and to export with three other gentlemen 14,000 pounds weight of bell-metal in July 1540, but few other favors came his way at this time.[23]

Perhaps Gawen's talent for getting into trouble slowed his advancement somewhat. In the spring of 1538, the court erupted with a series of violent altercations. In one of these incidents, Gawen and his servant fought with a sergeant of the guard and one of his yeoman; the battle left the sergeant "sore hurt," the yeoman dead, the servant in Newgate, and Gawen in the Compter.[24] By the following year, Gawen had recovered sufficient favor to be appointed with Peter to the king's new bodyguard, the Gentlemen Pensioners,[25] and in January 1540 Gawen and Peter were among the 50 "gentlemen called pensioners" who lined Henry VIII's way as he went to receive Anne of Cleves into London.[26] But Gawen was in trouble again in the spring of 1543. The Council examined Carew and several others for "eating of flesh and keeping an open board thereof during Lent." Some of those examined said they had a license from the king to do as they did; others admitted their fault and submitted. We do not know which course Gawen Carew took, but all were dismissed "after a good exhortation."[27] If Gawen had been involved in plots with Chapuys in Queen Catherine's behalf in 1533, his religious convictions had apparently undergone some change by the start of the 1540s.

The arrival of Anne of Cleves was only the first of many times that Peter and his uncle Gawen were joined in the same service. In 1539, Henry, probably following the fashion of the French court, expanded his personal bodyguard by forming a band of 50 gentlemen, with their own officers and standard, called the Gentlemen Pensioners. Because members of the guard served by turns in the king's outer chamber, a place among the Pensioners was eagerly sought after.[28] The appointment of the Carews, nephew and uncle, to the Pensioners illustrates their high standing at court and explains their involvement in the ceremonies surrounding the arrival of Anne.[29] Hooker implied that Peter was not only part of welcoming the lady into London but also present at Anne's reception into Calais as one of sundry "lusty gentlemen meet for this service" who accompanied the earl of Southampton to the continent for the official greeting of the new queen on English territory and "the wafting of her from thence into England." As usual with Hooker, we are told that Peter so well acquitted himself as to reap richly deserved "praise and commendation."[30]

If Peter did travel to Calais, he likely met his brother George, who had been in the town since March 1539 as captain of Rysbank, one of the main fortifications of the Calais enclave. George Carew took part in the festivities surrounding the arrival of Anne of Cleves in the town in December. On 5 December, George and Mr. Knolles ran together at the tilt —Knolles breaking three staves and Carew one.[31] Sir George Carew was present on 11 December when Lord Lisle and most of the Calais Council met Anne and conducted her to Henry's representative, the earl of Southampton.[32] On the night of 18 December 1539, while Anne and her party waited in Calais for storms to abate, Sir George Carew's wife died, and was buried the following day.[33] Thomasine Carew was the daughter of Sir Lewis Pollard.[34] The Pollards were another important and long-standing western family.

After the excitement of Anne's arrival in England had died down, the attention of the "young lusty gentlemen" of the English court turned toward eastern Europe and the victories there of the Ottoman sultan, Sulieman the Magnificent. Rumors of wars and tales "of the great Turk, and the royalty of his court, and what a mighty prince he was" aroused intense speculation as to what the mysterious and exotic Turkish court was really like. Many young men of the English court proclaimed their desire to travel to the Ottoman Empire and see for themselves if Sulieman deserved his grand appellation. In some cases, the loud expression of such a desire was perhaps nothing more than the fulfillment of court expectations —young gentlemen were supposed to crave adventure, danger, and glory. Peter Carew was absolutely serious about making such a trip. Unlike most other young courtiers at the time, he had already experienced adventure, danger, and glory. He knew better than other young English gentlemen his age what to expect of continental travel. He had already seen distant peoples and places and he had found that seeking after new sights and new adventures was to his liking. Of all those expressing a desire to see Sulieman the Magnificent, none was more ardent than Peter Carew, "whose chief desire was to travel countries, and to see strange fashions."[35]

Peter's enthusiasm for the venture infected his cousin John Champernon, son of Peter's aunt Katherine and her husband Sir Philip Champernon. The two young men were eager to begin their trip at once, "thinking every one day ten before the journey could be taken in hand." The king, when the plan was made known to him, commended their courage and spirit of adventure, but had no wish to risk them "in so perilous a journey, wherein more fear was to be thought of loss to their persons than profit of their travels." The king's refusal left the two cousins with nothing but enthusiastic persistence and "sundry mediations" to wear the king down and overcome his opposition. At length they were successful, and Henry granted his license. Like the princess of Orange before him, Henry VIII found Peter Carew was not easily dissuaded from a course of action once he had made up his mind.[36]

Having given his consent to the venture, Henry assisted in preparations for it by liberally furnishing the two young men with money and letters of commendation to various important nobles in France and Italy. In "the spring next following," the two cousins and a friend named Henry Knolles took leave of the king and of their friends at court and sailed to France. The three travelers spent the summer and autumn sightseeing in France and Italy, and then passed the winter in Venice, where Carew and Champernon secured a safe conduct to travel to Constantinople from the Ottoman ambassador. In the spring, the two cousins parted from Knolles, who remained in Venice, and took ship to Ragusa on the Dalmatian side of the Adriatic. The city was at this time nominally independent, although it paid tribute to the Porte. It was a Christian outpost on the edge of the Ottoman Empire and an important node on the main trade and travel route to Constantinople. From here, Carew and Champernon followed the overland road taken by all diplomats and merchants bound for Sulieman's court.[37]

Upon their arrival in Constantinople, the two young Englishmen were closely questioned as to who they were and what business they had in the Ottoman capital. Despite their safe conduct from the Ottoman ambassador in Venice, they were nervous about revealing their true identities and purposes—that they were gentlemen of the English court come solely to see the Ottoman court. Such reasons from such persons could be easily misconstrued and so put the young travelers in considerable peril. To avoid this, they claimed to be alum merchants, a plausible story, since the sultan controlled the main source of alum for Europe in Egypt and the Levant. In their guise as merchants, Carew and Champernon stayed in Constantinople about two months, visiting the sultan's court whenever possible and several times seeing the sultan himself. The two young gentlemen had difficulty maintaining for so long a period the unaccustomed role of a merchant, and this inability "to dissemble their own estates" soon brought them under suspicion and in great danger of arrest. Fortunately, Carew's fluency in French stood him in good stead once again, for his command of the language and his "behavior tasting after the French manner," which could have done little for his believability as a merchant, won him the attention and friendship of the French ambassador to the Porte. The ambassador warned the two of the danger they were in, and arranged to spirit them out of the city on a timely merchant ship bound for Venice. Having benefited from another's assistance, the two cousins did their own good turn for someone else by ransoming and taking with them a Spanish gentleman who had been held captive for six years.[38]

Once they were safe in Venice, Carew and Champernon spent a large sum of money to resupply the Spaniard, who faithfully promised to repay them for their assistance. But once "having liberty and all things at will," the ungrateful Spaniard slipped away, leaving the two young Englishmen without either their money or his thanks. The two travelers quickly forgot this unpleasant episode when they learned in Venice that Ferdinand, archduke of Austria and brother of Charles V, was then laying siege to the Hungarian city of Buda on the Danube. The two, apparently finding their brush with danger in Constantinople to be insufficient adventure for the trip, resolved to journey to Buda "to see the manner of these wars." First, however, they made good use of the king's letters of commendation. They returned to the duke of Seravia, to whom Henry had directed one of his letters and with whom they had stayed for a time upon their first arrival in Italy in the previous year. The duke treated them honourably, welcoming and entertaining them, and "using them as his companions." Carew's command of languages and courtly behavior may have impressed the duke as they had so many others, but a more compelling reason for the duke's hospitality was probably his "yearly pension of the King of England." From Seravia's household, the Englishmen traveled to Milan and the like hospitality of the marquis de Gashayes, another of Henry VIII's pensioners. From Milan, the cousins made their way over the mountains to Hungary and the siege of Buda.[39]

In the fall of 1540, Ferdinand dispatched an army to seize Buda, in which lay the infant son of his recently deceased rival for the Hungarian throne. Defended by 2,500 Hungarians loyal to the child and his family, Buda stood siege all through the winter and into the summer of 1541, when a large Ottoman force was reported to be entering the country to relieve the city.[40] Anxious to see the Turkish military in action, Carew and Champernon determined, apparently in the early summer of 1541, to go to Buda and observe the siege. Throughout the summer, Ferdinand's position at Buda deteriorated; in July, Henry VIII learned from the French that the Ottoman army would soon relieve the city. The desperate siege was now hopeless.[41] By the end of September it was all over. Lord William Howard, the ambassador Peter had accompanied to Scotland in 1535, wrote from Lyon to tell Henry VIII the Turks had arrived at Buda, "overthrown the king of the Romans' [Ferdinand's] men, burnt the bridges, and compelled those who took refuge at Pesta, on the other side of the Danube, to surrender."[42]

Carew and Champernon came to Buda while the siege was still in progress, but apparently not long before its ending in September, for Hooker mentioned the "sundry assails upon the host of Ferdinand" by Buda's defenders that were reported to the western courts all through the summer of 1541.[43]   Since the arrival of the two young Englishmen in Hungary was in the second year of their sojourn, they must have left England in the spring of 1540.   The pair's stay in Constantinople then likely occurred in the late spring of 1541, which would have given them a few weeks in the early summer to enjoy the hospitality of Henry VIII's Italian pensioners before journeying to Buda in about July or August for the climax of the siege.

With the collapse of Ferdinand's army, there was "no further service to be done" in Hungary, so the cousins went to Vienna, where they encountered another English traveler, an old friend named Wingfield. Within a few days, this happy meeting turned to grief; all three fell ill with a "bloody flux" that killed both Champernon and Wingfield. "Immediately whereupon," Peter Carew, "having the disease upon him," took horse back to Venice, where, after some time, he recovered his health. As soon as he was strong enough to make the journey, Carew returned from Venice to England.[44]   Hooker is vague about the length of Carew's second stay in Venice, but we know that he was back in England by 1 June 1542, for on that day Peter Carew, one of the Gentlemen Pensioners, received a license from the king to buy and export 600 unwrought cloths.[45] Carew probably spent the winter in Venice and traveled back to England in the spring of 1542.

As he had done upon his return to England 10 years before, Carew made straight for the court.   Having been gone for two years, and full of tales of strange courts and distant wars, Peter again caused a sensation. The king first demanded to know the whereabouts of John Champernon, and was deeply sorry to hear of his death.   But he was overjoyed at Peter's return and eager to hear in detail the whole story of his journey. "Whereupon," wrote Hooker, Peter recounted the tale—"the orders of France, the manners of Italy, his entertainment there, the government and state of Venice, the majesty of the Turk's Court, the wars of the Hungarians, the description of Vienna, with many other things." Everyone wanted to hear particularly about the sultan and his court and wars, "which the more rare, the more delectable and pleasant they were both to the king and the nobility." Even after the full tale had been told, numerous members of the court, and the king himself, would for some time thereafter engage Peter in further conversation about his experiences.

For the next year or so, until the king's new wars in France engaged everyone's attention, Peter spent his time at court, telling of his journey and partaking of "all such honest exercise as do appertain to a gentleman." Hooker mentioned particularly singing, vaulting, and riding, and said that Carew was almost always a participant in any matches organised at court in any of these exercises. Carew especially excelled in riding; Hooker claimed that in this exercise he was "not inferior to any in the court."[46] Thus, the 1530s were years of advancement at court for Peter Carew, as well as for his brother George and his uncle Gawen. Despite brief brushes with the law and the king's touchy religious sensibilities, all three Carews ended the decade in high favor.

---

1   Hooker, "Life," pp. 13-14.

2   J.J. Scarisbrick, *Henry VIII* (Berkeley: University of California Press, 1968), pp. 305-06; Jasper Ridley, *Henry VIII: The Politics of Tyranny* (New York: Viking, 1985), p. 209.

3   LP, V, 1405.

4   Ibid., 1429.

5   Hooker, "Life," p. 14.

6   LP, V, 1484, 1485.

7   Hooker, "Life," p. 14.

8   Scarisbrick, *Henry VIII*, pp. 307-08.

9   Hooker's chronology for the first years of Carew's service at the English court is
    confused and difficult. Hooker preceded his description of the royal trip to Calais by
    noting that Carew was appointed a gentleman of the privy chamber after two years
    as a henchman ("Life," p. 13). By putting the two events in this order, Hooker
    implied that Henry's meeting with Francis did not occur until two years after Peter
    Carew's sudden arrival at court. Since we know the meeting of the two kings took
    place in the autumn of 1532, Hooker is thereby dating Carew's return to England to
    1530, which fits with his earlier insistence that Carew left England before the battle
    of Pavia in February 1525 and was out of the country for six years. As described in
    Chapter 2, Carew's presence at Pavia was extremely unlikely, and his continental
    sojourn is best dated 1526-32, rather than 1524-30 as implied by Hooker. The
    actual sequence of events in Carew's early career at court is uncertain in Hooker. He
    mentioned the promotion first, but did not establish a firm connection between that
    event and the trip to Calais. He wrote only that the king was "minded on a time to
    go to Calais"; just where this vague "time" stood in relation to the promotion to the
    privy chamber is unclear. It seems best, then, despite Hooker's indications to the
    contrary, to place Carew's appointment to the privy chamber in 1534, two years after
    his journey to Calais with the king.

10 LP, VIII, 69.

11 Hooker, "Life," p. 14.

12 LP, VIII, 429.

13 *Cal.SP Span.*, V(1), 142.

14 Hooker, "Life," p. 15.

15 *Cal.SP Span.*, IV(2), 1149.

16 LP, VI, 1468.

17 Garrett Mattingly, *Catherine of Aragon* (Boston: Little, Brown and Company, 1941), p.
    402.

18   Bindoff, *House of Commons*, I, pp. 573-74.

19   LP, XI, 1217 (23).

20   Inquisitions Post Mortem of Sir William Carew, PRO, C142/59/106 (Devon), C142/58/93 (Cornwall), and C142/59/84 (Dorset); Will of Sir William Carew, "Copies of Transcripts and Extracts from Wills and Other Records Collected by Mrs. Olive Mager," vol. III, WSL, p. 891.

21   Bindoff, *House of Commons*, I, p. 572; III, pp. 314-15.

22   LP, V, 1403.

23   Ibid., XI, 1417 (17); XV, 942 (98).

24   Ibid., XIII(1), 696.

25   Ibid, XIV(2), 783.

26   Ibid., XV, 14.

27   APC, I, pp. 114-15.

28   David Loades, *The Tudor Court* (Totowa, N.J.: Barnes and Noble Books, 1987), p. 52.

29   LP, XXIV(2), 572; XV, 14.

30   Hooker, "Life," p. 15.

31   LP, XIV(2), 638.

32   *Lisle Letters*, V, p. 724.

33   LP, XIV(2), 707.

34   Vivian, *Visitations*, p. 135.

35   Hooker, "Life," pp. 15-16.

36   Ibid., p. 16.

37   Ibid., p. 17.

38   Ibid., pp. 17-19.

39   Ibid, pp. 19-20.

40   LP, XVI, 858; Dennis Sinor, *History of Hungary* (New York: Frederick A. Praeger, 1959), pp. 151-58.

[41] LP, XVI, 1005.

[42] Ibid., 1199.

[43] Hooker, "Life," p. 20.

[44] Ibid., p. 21.

[45] LP, XVII, 443 (8).

[46] Hooker, "Life," pp. 21-22.

CHAPTER 4

THE WARS OF HENRY VIII

In 1536, Sir George Carew began a period of advancement in the royal service that was eventually to entangle him in the dangerous mix of religion and high politics that toppled both Thomas Cromwell, the king's chief minister, and Arthur Plantagenet, Lord Lisle, a bastard son of Edward IV and therefore an uncle of the king. In the late 1530s, Lisle was the king's deputy in Calais. Sir George Carew and Lord Lisle first fell afoul of one another in 1536 when the two became unwitting rivals in a seemingly simple land grant from the king to Lisle that turned into an extremely complicated affair. The episode left Lisle with no great opinion of Carew, an important consequence since Sir George was soon associated with Lisle in the government of Calais.

Early in 1539, the king appointed Sir George to be captain of Rysbank, one of the fortifications at Calais. Carew was also to sit upon a commission charged with looking into how to best fortify Calais, the king being anxious about how the newfound friendship between France and the Empire might threaten the security of the town. Sir George and his wife began their journey to Calais in March 1539. Within weeks of his arrival, Carew wrote to Cromwell with an assessment of the fortifications at Rysbank, which he called "as raw and bare a house of war as ever was seen."

Sir George also quickly immersed himself in the religious differences dividing the Calais Council. By his own account, Sir George identified himself with the council minority that favored the prospering of the word of God, a position that Carew clearly believed was shared by Cromwell.[1]

Carew's membership in this pro-reform minority was confirmed by Henry Lacy, who concluded an October 1539 letter to Cromwell by enthusiastically noting "how my Lord Gray, the High Marshal [Sir Richard Grenville] and Sir George Carowe favour all such as love the word of God well enough and bear them neither grudge nor malice at all, thanked be God thereof."[2]

Although Carew's advocacy of the reform position and his secret letters of information may have found favor with Cromwell, they soon put him at odds with Lord Deputy Lisle and with the king's increasingly conservative religious views. In April 1540, about the time Peter Carew departed on his adventure to Constantinople, a royal commission came to Calais charged with ascertaining the disposition of the Council, officers, and townspeople toward religion and the king's laws. The commission found much diversity on religion in the town, contrary to statute.[3] On 5 April, the commissioners reported to the king that Sir George Carew was a great favorer of certain heretics. Carew also confessed to eating meat in Lent and was found to have comforted certain sacramentaries being sent to London for examination.[4]

Because Carew was a councilor and royal officer, the commission did not proceed against him, as they did against the other suspects, until the king's pleasure was known. Carew himself expressed again a desire to come to England, citing as his reasons poor health and a desire to do the king service.[5] Henry VIII responded to the commissioners on 8 April. The king reserved determination of Carew's case to himself and required the commissioners to give Sir George license to come to England to be examined.[6] In mid-May, Lisle went to the Tower, and the French ambassador reported on 1 June that two others in authority in Calais were also brought to the Tower.[7] One of these was likely Sir George Carew, for on 11 June, one day after Cromwell's arrest, the ambassador wrote the French constable to clarify his earlier report on Carew's confinement in the

Tower. People had assumed, wrote the ambassador, that Carew was imprisoned in the Tower because he was taken there and did not come out again. However, it now appeared that he was taken there only to be examined and to confront Lisle. The experience had so unnerved him that he fell ill with a fear-induced fever and had been unable to leave the Tower until he had sufficiently recovered himself.[8]

Sir George Carew was fortunate. Cromwell went to the block in July; Carew's support of Calais reformers in his behalf was one of the things used by Cromwell's enemies to prove that the minister had been working in Calais against the king's religious purposes. Lisle languished in the Tower until his death in March 1542. Sir George was probably saved by the same fact that later rehabilitated his brother after a major rebellion—good lower level servants, if not implacably hostile, were too valuable to lose.

Sir George's rehabilitation, and the general favor in which all the Carews were held was signalled by the benefits that flowed to the family from the destruction, in late 1538, of their kinsman, the marquis of Exeter. Exeter's young son Edward was thrown into the Tower, where he lay neglected until 1553 when Queen Mary released him to become a thorn in the side of both the state and Peter Carew. Sir George and Peter were born of a Courtenay mother, Sir George and Gawen had served in Exeter's household in the 1520s, and the Carews had been associated with the Courtenays for over a century in the West Country; nonetheless, few families reaped more material benefits from the wreck of the Courtenays than the Carews.

Gawen Carew obtained the keepership of Exeter's park at Chittlehamholt in Devon on 24 October 1539, less than a year after the marquis's execution.[9] The manor of Chittlehampton, except for Gawen's park, went to Sir George and his new wife in July 1544. In December

1542, Sir George was appointed at £30 a year as chief steward of all the late marquis's possessions in the West Country and throughout England.[10] Peter obtained a share in the Courtenay bonanza in 1544, when he received a 21-year lease at £42 rent of all the lands within Okehampton park in Devon, which became an outright grant in perpetuity in 1545.[11]

The strength of Sir George's position in the king's favor was further displayed by the rapidity with which he climbed back into active royal service after he left the Tower. By mid-July 1540, Sir George was named to the commission of the peace and a commission of oyer and terminer for Devon.[12] By early 1541, Sir George had remarried, taking to wife Mary, daughter of Henry Norris of Bray in Berkshire.[13] Carew spent the rest of 1541 at his post in Calais; he was still at Rysbank in the spring of 1542, about the time his brother returned from Venice.[14] In November 1542, the king named Sir George sheriff of Devon for the second time; two years later he was drawing 20s a day as a lieutenant of the Gentlemen Pensioners, the body of gentlemen guards that still included both Peter and Gawen Carew.[15]

In 1543, the outbreak of war with France united the three Carews in the same royal service for the first time since Anne of Cleves's arrival three years earlier. Before the year was out, the orthodox Catholic emperor found himself allied with the schismatic king of England against His Most Christian Majesty, the Catholic king of France, who, for good measure, was allied with the Ottoman sultan. By mid-summer, an English army of about 5,000 men crossed to Calais under Sir John Wallop to assist the emperor in defending the Low Countries.[16] The army rolls for this Flanders campaign listed Sir George Carew as supplying six horsemen and ten foot soldiers and Gawen Carew four of each. An appended list, headed "To Go with Mr. Treasurer," included the names of Sir George, Gawen, and Peter Carew.[17]

Sir John Wallop, commander of the army, had served as lieutenant of Calais, ambassador to France, and captain of Gusines at Calais; he had been one of those named by Sir George Carew in a May 1539 letter to Cromwell as most forward in blocking the advance of reform in Calais.[18] Now Wallop and Sir George, the two former Calais councilors, found themselves serving together again on the army council. Whatever their differences in Calais might have been, Wallop did not seem to hold a grudge; in a postscript to his 27 July letter to the Council in London, Wallop stated his belief that Sir George "will prove a very good man of war, and as mete to serve His Highness, as any other that is come at this time."[19] Sir George held appointment as lieutenant-general of horse. Peter, however, was not to be outdone; he came to France as captain of the romantically named Black Band, a troop of 100 footmen clothed all in black at his own charge.[20]

On 31 July, Wallop reported the army's first skirmishes with the French, and both Carew brothers figured prominently. Ironically, the action took place outside the city of Therouanne, the site of Sir Edmund Carew's death 30 years before. Sir Edmund's grandsons more than made up for his lost opportunities. Wallop laid several ambushes outside the town to draw out the French. The second of these was a concealed group of horse under Sir Richard Cromwell and Sir George Carew. The French refused to be drawn, however, and did not come out until Wallop launched a direct attack on the town. In the ensuing skirmish, Cromwell and Carew left their ensign and their troop outside the range of the guns, "and gallantly gave a hot skirmish unto those that issued out, and drove them back to the town gates and bulwarks." The skirmish lasted a long while and was accompanied by much gun fire, which, despite its great sound, hurt no one. No sooner did this skirmish die down than 24 light horse issued from the town in pursuit of the retiring English. Peter Carew and four other captains of the rearward immediately engaged the French horse in a fierce skirmish, the outcome of which was several dead French horses and one English arrow in one French leg. Even so, the skirmish must for a time have been close, for Cromwell and Sir George, "perceiving them [Peter Carew and his fellow captains] to be somewhat in danger," sent their men back to chase the French into the town. This they did with such good effect that "a good sort" of the Frenchmen almost "had come short home."[21]

Wallop next related to the Council an account of one of the chivalric rituals that from time to time punctuated the real war. Wallop sent the captain of Therouanne, an old acquaintance of his, a letter suggesting that the captain send out any French gentlemen who were willing "to break any staves for their lady's sake" with a like number of English gentlemen. The captain agreed to send out six gentlemen the next morning. Although Wallop indicated that the original offer for the skirmish was his, Hooker said the offer came from the Frenchman and described a heated debate over the advisability of accepting it. Some argued that it was "not good to put in peril the loss of any captain or gentleman, in and for a vain bravery, when a further service of necessity was to be done." But it was just such "vain braveries" that appealed to the Carews and both brothers strongly urged accepting the challenge.[22] The Carews' eagerness for the skirmish accorded with Wallop's own, and six gentlemen, including Peter Carew, were appointed to meet the Frenchmen, 40 courses a man. The first courses went well for the English; Peter "broke his staff very well, and had another broken on him." Hooker added that Peter ran his first course so well as to "almost overthrow both horse and man." The pleasant gallantry of the event evaporated, however, when Wallop's man Calveley, "by the evil running of a Frenchman's horse," was run through the body and severely injured. Having survived the guns of real war the previous day, Calveley's life was now threatened by the splintered staff of chivalry. The wounded man was carried into Therouanne from which Wallop received word the next day that his servant had some chance to live.[23] Hooker, in his typical mirroring of Peter Carew's exuberance, said nothing of Calveley's dreadful mischance.

For the next three months, the English army took part in the siege of Landrecy. During this period, Sir George signed, as a member of the army council, a series of letters to the king and London Council describing military operations and the course of the siege.[24] Wallop wrote on 28 August of a battle between the English troops and some of the emperor's men. Sir George Carew was among those officers who helped to persuade the English troops to break off their assault on the imperial camp. When an imperial colonel swaggered into the English camp later offering to shoot Wallop, Sir George had to be prevented from putting honour before allied relations and running the man through with his sword.[25] On 10 October, Sir George almost suffered the fate of his grandfather, when his companion on an inspection of a trench before Landrecy was shot by a bullet fired from the city walls.[26] By early November, the allied force had lifted the siege of Landrecy and removed to Cambray, where the French king was then located. Hopes of bringing Francis to battle were dashed when he raised his camp secretly in the night and withdrew with speed into France.[27]

Discovery in the morning of the French flight led to a furious allied pursuit in which the emperor himself took part. In this chase, Sir George Carew, being, in the apt phrase of Hooker, "more forward than circumspect," was taken prisoner with several other English gentlemen.[28] Carew and his companions were so zealous in their pursuit that they outstripped their men and found themselves without support when the French rear guard suddenly turned on them. Wallop reported to the king on 6 November that the fates of Sir George Carew, Sir Thomas Palmer, and Edward Bellingham were unclear, although rumor declared that Carew and Bellingham were slain.[29] The next day Wallop was still unsure whether the missing men were alive or dead.[30] By 10 November, Wallop had received a letter from Oudart du Bies in the French camp saying that du Bies had seen an unwounded Carew in the custody of a band of Italians under Count de Sansegand. Du Bies believed Carew would be well treated, for the Italians were more interested in ransoming than killing prisoners. Indeed, du Bies advised Wallop not to inquire too frequently after Carew, or the Italians would raise their ransom demand.[31]

Peter Carew undertook to win his brother's release by capturing a French gentleman whom he could trade for Sir George. Peter carried the Frenchman back to Calais, new appareled him, and concluded an agreement with him whereby the Frenchman agreed either to have Sir George sent home or to send Peter sufficient money for his brother's ransom. Then, like the Spaniard Peter Carew and John Champernon had rescued from the Turks, the Frenchman departed and neither returned Sir George nor paid any ransom.[32] Once again Peter had proved too trusting. Sir George remained in French hands for some months until the king intervened and won his release.[33]

In 1544, the grand Anglo-imperial invasion of France began; Henry VIII crossed the channel himself to lead his army in person. The army rolls for this year list all three Carews under the Pensioners. Sir George was to bring 20 horsemen, Peter five, and Gawen seven. Sir George was also to provide 80 archers and 120 pikemen, while Peter and Gawen were to find two and four archers, respectively.[34] Sir George, as a lieutenant of the Pensioners, received 20s a day in wages for the three months from July to September 1544.[35] Part of the English force was commanded by the duke of Suffolk, Gawen Carew's former brother-in-law. Peter was attached to this part of the army, being again captain of a band of horse.[36] Both Peter and Sir George were present at the siege of Boulogne, Sir George having for a time in July the oversight of the gunners and archers holding a trench outside the great gate toward Montreuil.[37] According to Hooker, Peter was one of the first to enter Boulogne at the surrender of the town on 14 September 1544, and was soon thereafter charged with taking the castle of Hardelow, which was about five miles outside Boulogne. The French commander holding the castle fled upon hearing that Carew was coming to besiege the place. Fifty soldiers and 100 peasants surrendered along with the castle. Carew then entered the undefended fortress and held the place with a garrison of 50 men until the king returned to England on 30 September. Hooker, who disapproved of Peter's natural generosity, remarked that while at Hardelow Carew "kept as liberal a house and as great a port as never more bountifully in all his life."[38]

While master of Hardelow, Peter Carew had the famous encounter with Henry VIII that was recorded by Hooker. Upon Suffolk's summons, Carew left Hardelow in the charge of his lieutenant, Richard Reynolds, a Devon man who married into the Southcote family that eventually came into possession of Mohun's Ottery. Suffolk sent Carew to the king with a message. After Peter delivered the message, the king asked him why and by what warrant he had left his post at Hardelow. Carew answered that he had come by order of Suffolk, the general in command in the field. The king said this was no sufficient warrant, and then told the young man why.

> Learn this for a rule: so long as we ourselves are present there is no other general but ourselves, neither can any man depart from his charge without our special warrant. And therefore you being thus come hither without our commandment, you are not able to answer for the same if we should minister that which by law we may do.[39]

Carew immediately humbled himself and begged the king's pardon. The king himself had taught Peter the supreme lesson that all who served Henry VIII had to learn—the will of the king was paramount.

An anonymous diary of the 1544 invasion of France gives a somewhat different chronology for Peter's tenure at Hardelow Castle. The diarist stated that a small castle just six miles from Boulogne surrendered on 28 July, a month and a half before the surrender of the town. This diary confirms that the castle, which was thought to house great riches, was entrusted to the keeping of Peter Carew.[40] This dating puts the castle in Carew's charge for two months, a more likely period of time than the bare two weeks allowed by Hooker. Even Hooker's own complaint about Carew's generosity implied a longer stay at the castle than two weeks. Carew's encounter with the king could have occurred any time during the last six or seven weeks of the Boulogne siege, rather than being confined only to the king's harried last weeks on the continent.

On 18 September 1544, the day Henry VIII entered his newly won town of Boulogne in triumph, Charles V abandoned his English ally and made peace with the French. The English were now left to face the French army alone, and in the last two weeks of September Henry had some tense moments wondering if the dukes of Norfolk and Suffolk could safely bring their armies into Boulogne. If Hooker is right that Carew's misstep occurred during these weeks, Henry's imperious response can probably be at least partially ascribed to his anxious state of mind at this time. However, the dukes brought their forces to safety and Henry left for England on 30 September.[41] The year ended with Boulogne firmly in English possession.

Peter Carew left his charge at Hardelow Castle at the end of September and attended the king on his return journey.[42] Soon after his return to England, Peter Carew shifted his service from the land to the sea. On 20 October, he advised the Council to begin shipping much needed supplies to Calais and Boulogne; he had observed only two French vessels during his passage to England and believed that a storm had scattered the French fleet and now provided an opportunity to resupply the English towns.[43] Shortly thereafter, Peter Carew put to sea with the fleet commanded by Sir John Dudley, with whom Sir George Carew had commanded a naval campaign against pirates in 1537. Dudley had been created Viscount Lisle in 1542 and was named lord admiral the following year. A navy list of 29

October 1544 shows Peter Carew as captain of the 230-ton *Primrose*, which carried a crew of 160.[44] On 13 November, the *Primrose* was involved in a battle with several French men-of-war just off the French coast. These vessels tried to protect themselves from the English by running in close to the shore behind some herring boats, several of which foundered in their haste to get away from the warships. Peter saved some of the herring men by pulling them from the water and bringing them aboard the *Primrose*.[45] The admiral's fleet kept the seas during that whole winter, which was "for the most part foul, and full of storms and tempests," until the French returned to their harbors and no further service was to be done in the Channel.[46]

Without his imperial ally, Henry could not encounter with the French king on land, and after the loss of Boulogne, the French king was eager to strike back at Henry. Thus, the land war of the previous year became a war at sea in 1545, providing bountiful opportunities for naval service for all three Carews. Peter and Gawen still held appointment as Gentlemen Pensioners,[47] but the new year found both of them, as well as Sir George, commanding the king's ships.[48] By early summer, Francis I had sent his galleys into the channel to harass the sea connections between England and her continental towns. Henry VIII responded by ordering the admiral to sea with a fleet of 45 vessels, of which one was a ship Hooker called the *Francisco Hardado*, a former Venetian ship. This 700 ton vessel, which was otherwise called the *Great Venetian*, was commanded by Peter Carew.[49] Hooker reported an encounter with the enemy off Newhaven, where Carew was among the first in the fleet to catch sight of a flotilla of 20 French galleys. Carew was so eager to engage the enemy he almost attacked without waiting for the rest of the fleet. Fortunately, the English fleet attacked as a unit, for the battle lasted two days and "became very hot and sharp." When the wind blew, the English ships had the advantage; when the wind fell, the French galleys prevailed. At length, the seas grew rough and the galleys were forced to retire, leaving the seas and the victory to the English. The admiral wanted to pursue the French, but his larger ships drew too much water to follow the galleys into the shallows off the French shore.[50] The optimistic cast of Hooker's account of the naval actions of the early summer of 1545 is misleading. In early June, the English fleet had encountered not only galleys, but also some 200 other French vessels massing for a descent on England. Lisle fought an indecisive action and was driven by the weather into Portsmouth, where the king then lay "languishing and listening to hear news of his navy."[51] By 24 June, all ship captains, including Sir George and Peter Carew, had been ordered to Portsmouth,[52] where the king himself would coordinate defenses against French raids and the threatened French invasion.

With the English fleet in Portsmouth to refit, the French galleys used this English inactivity and a favorable sea to raid along the south coast of England and land on the Isle of Wight, where they caused much damage. They even rowed arrogantly back and forth in Portsmouth harbor before the eyes of the king himself. At the sight of his enemies' boldness, Henry VIII "fretted, and his teeth stood on edge, to see the bravery of his enemies to come so near his nose, and he not able to encounter with them."[53] Henry set up his headquarters at Southsea Castle on the Portsmouth headland, within sight of the Isle of Wight. An army under the ailing duke of Suffolk collected around the castle and feverish efforts were made to concentrate the fleet at Portsmouth and prepare it for sea. There was need of haste, for a French fleet of 150 large ships, 50 smaller vessels, and 25 galleys set sail under Admiral Annebault from various French ports for Portsmouth and the Isle of Wight on 6 July. Annebault arrived off the Isle of Wight on Saturday 18 July, and promptly sent a number of galleys toward Portsmouth to view the disposition of the English ships.[54]

As the French fleet gathered unbeknownst to the English behind Wight, Henry VIII met with Lord Admiral Lisle and his chief captains aboard the *Great Harry* to take a meal and map strategy. Peter, Sir George, and Gawen Carew were all present at this meeting. At some point during the meeting, the king appointed Sir George Carew vice-admiral of the fleet, the office Sir George's Uncle Thomas had achieved some 30 years earlier. For his flagship, Sir George had the *Mary Rose*, one of the finest vessels in the fleet. The *Mary Rose*'s captain was another westerner, Roger Grenville, whose three-year-old son would grow up to one day fight a naval battle of his own aboard the *Revenge*. As he took his meal, the king ordered that someone climb to the top of the *Great Harry*'s mast and scan the seas for enemy ships. "The word was no sooner spoken but that Peter Carew was as forward, and forthwith climbed up to the top of the ship." The king called up for news and Peter reported three or four sails that he took to be merchantmen. But within a short time the southern horizon sprouted dozens of sails and Peter shouted to the king that a large fleet of warships was massing off Portsmouth. This could only be the French fleet. The king sent his ship captains, including Peter and Gawen Carew, scurrying back to their vessels. Henry VIII then called for a long boat to take him ashore, but tarried long enough to hold hurried private conversations with the lord admiral and the new vice admiral. The king's last act before leaving the *Great Harry* was to place around Sir George Carew's neck the traditional insignia of his new office, a gold whistle on a chain.[55] The king then left the ship, and the fleet hummed with preparations for battle.

Sieur Martin du Bellay was an officer in a cavalry force embarked on the French fleet in the summer of 1545. In 1580, du Bellay published an account of the naval actions fought between the English and French fleets during that summer. Du Bellay described in detail the inconclusive action of 18 July.

> The enemy's force consisted of sixty picked ships well arrayed for war, fourteen of which, helped by a strong land breeze, came out of Portsmouth with such alacrity and in such fine order, that one had the impression that they were going to engage

our whole fleet on their own. But when our Admiral sent the rest of the galleys forward, the remainder of their force also came out of the harbour to meet them. . . . After a long fight with gun-shot, the enemy began to slip to the left to the shelter of the land. This was a place where their ships were defended by a few forts that stood on the cliff behind them and on the other side by hidden shoals and rocks, with only a narrow and oblique entrance for a few ships at a time. This withdrawal, and the approaching night, put an end to the first day's fighting, without our having suffered notable loss from their cannon shot.[56]

Sunday 19 July was a fine summer day. In the morning, the sea was calm with no breath of wind. These were ideal conditions for the French galleys, which rowed into the harbor firing at close range on the becalmed English ships. The English could not stir in the face of the French fire, while the galleys could row about dodging the English guns. Being higher and bulkier than the galleys, the English ships were hit by most every shot sent their way. Finally, the wind arose, beginning to blow out of the harbor from the north, and the ebb tide began to run, also from north to south, from the English toward the French. The big English ships began to move. The French galleys hurried to the protection of their fleet as the *Great Harry* and the *Mary Rose*, flying the red-crossed flag of St. George and trailing green Tudor streamers, came around before the wind. From Southsea Castle, where he was surrounded by the tents and pavilions of Suffolk's army, the king had a broad, unobstructed view of the entire battle area to seaward. No one could remember seeing as many great ships in one place as covered the water of Portsmouth harbor on that day.

As the wind caught her sails, the *Mary Rose* began to heel. The ship was soon leaning so much that Gawen Carew, on the deck of his own ship, the 600-ton *Matthew Gonson*,[57] asked his ship's master what this strange maneuver meant. The master replied that if she continued to heel as she was "she was liked to be cast away." Gawen brought his vessel in close to the *Mary Rose* and called out to his nephew, "asking him how he did, who answered that he had a sort of knaves he could not rule." From Southsea Castle, just over a mile away, the king and Mary Carew, the vice admiral's wife, watched the *Mary Rose* heel over and slip under the waves until only two tilted masts protruded from the water.[58]   The horrified watchers are said to have heard a long wail issue from the doomed ship as it carried most of its 700 crewmen below the water with remarkable speed.[59]   Du Bellay estimated that only about 35 of the lighter armed sailors were able to swim to safety; anyone in armor had no chance.[60] Mary Carew fainted at the sight, the king himself helping to comfort her. The king, said Hooker, was "oppressed with sorrow of every side," but as he tended to Mary Carew, he prayed "that of a hard beginning, there would follow a better ending."[61]   No one knows what Peter Carew thought as the stunned fleet moved forward carrying him past his brother's watery tomb and into battle.[62]

Valient efforts were made in the months following the disaster to raise the *Mary Rose*, but all were unsuccessful.   Lord Admiral Lisle complained of the loss from active service to the recovery operations of "three of the greatest hulks of the fleet," including the *Great Venetian*, the ship recently commanded by Peter Carew.   It is unlikely that Peter was seriously involved in the salvage attempt, since we know that within a few days of Lisle's letter he was again on active naval service in the *Great Venetian*.[63]

"Many a man," noted John Hooker, having witnessed the death of a brother and come thereby into a large inheritance, "would have given over the service, and have gone home to enter into the possession of those great livelihoods, as which were then left unto him."   But, as Hooker continued with pride, Peter Carew "never made account of any such thing"; he preferred "the service of his prince" and "the doing of his duty."[64]   On 7 August, less than three weeks after the *Mary Rose* disaster, Admiral Lisle related to Paget an example of Peter Carew's martial zeal.

The king had acceded to Carew's request and placed him in command of that wing of the fleet made up of the galleys and other oared vessels; Carew's flagship was to be the *Great Mystres*, a fine new ship out of Portsmouth. But, wrote Lisle, Carew "with piteous moan besought me that he might not be shifted out of his ship." When he realised that further action against the French fleet was imminent, Carew remembered "that he was in a ship able to board one of the greatest of the enemies, and what might be thought in him to forsake such a ship of himself." Lisle consented to Carew's request and suggested to the king that William Tyrrell command the galleys, "since Mr. Carewe is so loth to leave the great ship."[65] Three days later, when Lisle drew up his list of ships and captains in the fleet, Peter Carew was still in command of a crew of 450 in the 700-ton *Great Venetian*, the second ship listed in the main battle of the fleet, right after the *Henry Grace a Dieu*, Lisle's flagship.[66]

Carew did not have to wait long for the action he sought. On 2 September, Lisle, seeking to pay back the French for their raids earlier in the summer on the Isle of Wight and the south coast of England, followed the advice of an informer, whom Hooker called Roybodo, that "there was good service to be done to recompense the Frenchmen" in the bay of Treport on the Norman coast. As word spread through the fleet that a landing would be attempted near Treport, a competition arose over who would be the first to reach the top of the heights overlooking the beach. Such a challenge was irresistible to Carew, and he was one of the first to set foot on French soil. He was not, however, the first to the top of the hill; another Devon man, William Courtenay, whom Hooker misnamed John Courtenay, rushed up the narrow path ahead of Carew and planted his ensign on the height before all others.[67] Courtenay appeared in Lisle's 10 August list of ships and captains as commander of the *Mary James*. Carew's disappointment with his unaccustomed second place finish was assuaged by the sweet retribution meted out by the English army at Treport. Hooker, in his optimistic way, described an English rout of French forces too frightened to stand and fight.

The French who before stood on the cliffs and saw the fleet, seemed to make a great show of some great matters; but the Englishmen were not so soon on the land to go, as they were in haste to run away. Not far from their landing was the town of Treport, which, forthwith, was spoiled, the country preyed, and all French ships in the harbor burned. . . . [68]

In the letter that he "scribbled in the Harry Grace a Dieu, the 3rd of September, athwart of Arundell, at 8th in the morning," Lisle described somewhat stiffer resistance. The French fell back, but continued to assemble "more and more in great troops, and now and then, with some horsemen, skirmished with us as they durst." Lisle used the bulk of the army and several small field pieces to keep back the French and shield one wing of the army as it entered and burned Treport. Two or three nearby villages, several gentlemen's houses, and the abbey were also put to the torch before the entire English force retired in good order to the ships. Peter Carew so distinguished himself in this action that Lisle made to dub him a knight as the fleet was preparing to weigh anchor for Portsmouth. Peter humbly resisted the honour, saying that he had an uncle in the fleet who deserved it more. Gawen Carew was still in command of the *Matthew Gonson*, another of the large ships in the main battle of the fleet. Lisle was angry with himself for trying to knight the nephew without the uncle, and forthwith commended and knighted both Carews for their gallant service. As a further mark of honour, Lisle chose the newly knighted Peter to carry his letter to the king and to describe the action at Treport for the monarch in more detail. In his letter, Lisle praised "this bearer, Sir Peter Carew. . . who did your Majesty, for his own part, such service, that I can do no less of my duty, but commend the same to Your Highness." The king was eager for news of his navy and questioned Carew closely before reading the admiral's letter. Henry so well liked what he heard that he called for his sword to knight the bearer of such welcome tidings. Before the sword could be brought, the king read Lisle's letter and, noting the reference to "Sir Peter Carew," saw that he was too late in his intention. Nonetheless, the king highly commended Sir Peter "and promised him that he should not be forgotten."[69] Shortly thereafter, Henry VIII brought his French wars to a close; three years of war had won Sir Peter Carew a knighthood and a military reputation, but had cost him a brother.

From the autumn of 1545, Sir Peter spent most of his time at court and was often in the company of the king. Henry VIII loved to sing and he found in Sir Peter, who, according to Hooker, had "a pleasant voice," an excellent partner for singing such "fremen" songs as "By the Bank as I Lay" and "As I Walked in the Wood so Wild."[70] Fremen songs were simple rounds or catches for three or more unaccompanied voices, with each singer taking up a part in turn. A songbook containing the particular songs mentioned by Hooker is found among the Royal Manuscripts in the British Library. John Maclean and Sir Henry Ellis, a nineteenth-century keeper of the British Museum Manuscript Department, believed this book to have been the possession of Henry VIII himself, so it may be the book used by the king and Sir Peter when they sang together.[71]

Yet for Peter Carew, the months after Treport were not all singing and courtly exercises as Hooker would have us believe. The Public Record Office preserves a fragmentary letter that was written by Sir William Petre to Sir William Paget on 17 December 1545. This letter describes " a great hurley burley" over certain prohibited books on religion that were being covertly distributed in London. A priest named Octavian was found to be the "great setter forth" of these books and was at the time of writing in the Tower. One of these volumes turned up in the possession of Sir Peter Carew. For his unorthodoxy, Carew was committed to the keeping of John Russell, the lord privy seal, who, as the premier peer in the West since the destruction of the marquis of Exeter in 1538, had recently helped Sir Peter become MP for Tavistock. His spell of confinement with Russell, and later with Lord Chancellor Wriothesley, must have kept Sir

Peter away from the Parliament house for at least part of the November 1545 session. He was released on 13 December, and the letter writer seemed hopeful that the matter was now at an end.[72] Carew's escape without further or heavier punishment may have been due to good timing. On Christmas Eve, Petre wrote again to Paget to say that the king was not displeased with the failure in the just concluded session of Parliament with "the bill of books." Henry was apparently in a conciliatory mood. The king came personally to close Parliament, and his moving speech, during which he wept for the growing dissension over religion, asked all men to unite behind the religious authority of king and Council and not to dispute religion in every alehouse and tavern.[73] Leniency toward Sir Peter's religious faux pas may have partly resulted from this mood of moderation and partly from a reluctance to proceed too far against such an otherwise useful servant.

Of Sir Peter's religious opinions, we have no hint until this sudden confinement for the possession of seditious books at the end of 1545. Sir Peter, who was listed in the grant as "of the household," did receive St. German's rectory in Cornwall in November 1543, but this was probably a reward for his military service of the previous summer.[74] Foreign travel and military service had occupied much of the 1540s for Sir Peter Carew. The calm period of courtly service at the end of 1545 may have been his first extended opportunity to think of something besides foreign courts and ships and sieges. That he should so quickly involve himself in religious difficulties after having the rare leisure to do so, argues for a substantial level of commitment to the "seditious" ideas contained in the books that confined him. Unlike his brother and uncle, who were implicated, if ever so slightly, in the Nun of Kent affair, no evidence exits to connect Sir Peter in any way to the religious conservatives. Carew may have imbibed Lutheranism while a boy in Italy, where reform was rife among the imperial armies. He may have returned to England just in time to blend comfortably into the Henrician reformation. We have no hard evidence for how Sir Peter Carew came by his later Protestantism, but come by it he did. The Protestant environment of the next reign was to suit Sir Peter Carew well, and the Catholic environment of Mary's reign was to suit him ill.

As the reign of Henry VIII closed, Sir Peter found one more opportunity to spend time at the French court. In 1546, "there was a peace concluded between the King of England and the French king, and for establishing thereof, and to receive the French king's oath, the Viscount Lisle, Lord Admiral, was appointed to be ambassador, and among others to accompany and attend him, Sir Peter Carew was one."[75] Lisle was joined in this embassy by Bishop Tunstall of Durham; Dr. Wootton, the dean of Canterbury and York; and Sir Henry Knevet, a privy councilor. Passports and instructions were issued to the ambassadors on 2 July 1546.[76] An 8 July list of "rewards" paid to the ambassadors and their gentlemen attendants "towards their furnitures in their journey into France" confirms Carew's presence on the embassy. He received £40 for his expenses on 1 July.[77] The party's progress toward Paris was slowed by the aged and ailing Tunstall, who could journey neither far nor fast.[78] From Paris, the embassy traveled to Fontainebleau, where the king and the court were then residing. Lisle reported that the embassy arrived on 30 July, and that evening some of the gentlemen in the party desired "to see the dancing and pastime in the King's presence."[79] Lisle does not name these gentlemen, but Sir Peter was probably among the would-be revelers, for Carew certainly wasted little time making his presence known to the French court.

Soon after the English party's arrival in Fontainebleau, one of its youngest members, the 18-year-old Lord Herbert, future third earl of Worcester, was "very coarsely handled and ill treated" by a French courtier. Herbert was with the embassy to gain knowledge of the workings and fashions of the French court. Being so young and inexperienced, he had not the spirit to resent and requite his ill treatment. Lisle, when informed of the incident, was furious, and determined that the offending Frenchmen should have suitable answer for his insult. And the admiral knew the ideal man for such a task.

> But the Lord Ambassador. . .did so storm, and was so grieved therewith, that, calling such gentlemen unto him as he well liked, so opened the matter unto them, that they perceived his mind was that such an injury should not be closed up without some acquittal. Sir Peter Carew was then present, and one unto whom, as they thought, the speeches were especially directed unto, and indeed, he being somewhat warm therein, deviseth how to compass the matter.[80]

Carew compassed the matter shortly thereafter when Lisle and all his attendants came into the presence of the king and the dauphin. As the Englishmen passed through the presence chamber between two rows of the king's pensioners and yeoman, Carew spied the courtier who had abused Herbert. He immediately marched up to the man and "picked such a quarrel with him, that he gave him a box, or blow, under the ear." Although they said nothing, the king and the dauphin were highly offended by the loud and impudent Englishman who started brawls in their presence. But, as with most such incidents recounted by Hooker, even the most outrageous acts eventually redounded to Sir Peter's credit. After being advertised of the reasons for Carew's actions, the king and dauphin likewise blamed their own courtier for his "evil behavior" and commended Sir Peter for his "stout courage."[81]

Carew was able to present himself to the king in a better light on 2 August, probably the day after the incident in the presence chamber. The king, as Lisle wrote Henry VIII, would not let the Englishmen depart until they had joined him in a hunt.[82] The king pursued his game so avidly that he outstripped the rest of his party and found himself alone, except for Sir Peter Carew, whose excellent horsemanship had allowed him to keep pace. Hot and sweaty from his ride, the king fumbled unsuccessfully for a handkerchief to wipe his brow. Carew seized the opportunity to gallantly and graciously offer the king his own handkerchief, which was gratefully accepted. For a few moments, until the rest of the party caught up, Francis I and Sir Peter Carew chatted in a friendly and familiar way. Perhaps they recalled the events surrounding Henry VIII's 1532 meeting with Francis in Calais, when Carew had first attracted the French king's attention. The king took "so good a liking of him as he did afterwards use his company both in hunting and other exercises."[83]

Having won the favor of the king, Carew capped his eventful four-day visit (the English party took their leave on the evening of 2 August) to the French court by challenging to personal combat the Frenchman whom he had captured and sought to trade for his brother back in 1543. As a condition of his release, the young French courtier had agreed either to secure the release of Sir George Carew or to send money to pay his ransom. The Frenchman did neither, and now Sir Peter required satisfaction. Once again, when the facts were known, court opinion sided with Carew and condemned the courtier. Realizing his position, the young man admitted his fault and asked Carew's forgiveness, which he readily obtained.[84]

Before the embassy left, the king showered its members with gifts, but Carew's generosity, which was even more extreme than the king's, sent him home a poorer man than when he came. Not for the last time, Hooker disapprovingly described his future patron's foolish and impractical liberality.

At his being in the court, the French king and the dauphin, having a good affection unto him, did deal very liberally with him, and gave unto him many good and rich gifts; but he was not so apt to receive as he was more liberal to give, for such was his liberality, that he gave not only away that which he received there, but whatsoever he brought of his own with him, insomuch that he left scarce either jewel, horse, or apparel, being worthy the gift, but he gave it.[85]

This generosity purchased him attention and favorable comment at the French court and thanks and commendation at the English court, but Hooker left the clear impression that he believed Carew had made a bad bargain. On 3 August, Lisle, who gave away none of the rich gifts he had received, complained to Paget of the great expenses he had incurred: "I pray God I may have enough to bring myself home. I assure you this journey hath been extremely chargeable, after such sort as I think I shall be fain to hide me in a corner for vii year after."[86] If Lisle felt so terribly out of pocket about his trip, what must have been the monetary cost to the less well-supplied Carew of his French gallantries?

Perhaps Carew had sources of revenue unknown to the precise and proper Hooker. On 3 June 1546, the Council dealt with the complaint of one Baldwin Barbier, a merchant of Antwerp who had lost a ship load of wax and woad "to certain adventurers." These "adventurers" turned out to be John Lasshe, master of one of Sir Peter Carew's ships, and Robert Wayemouth, master of "Mr. Carow Hacene's bark."[87] Thomas Carew of Haccombe was Sir Peter's cousin and son of the man who had rescued the young Peter from the French stables in 1527. The ships appear to have operated out of Dartmouth, the small Devon port under Carew influence; Sir Thomas Dennys and the mayor of Dartmouth were told to order the two ship masters to come up to London and answer for their actions, or to restore the goods they had taken. It was not unknown for West Country gentlemen to supplement their incomes with a little piracy, and past generations of Carews may not have been averse to this practice. For instance, Sir Peter's ancestor Sir Thomas Carew appears to have been involved in some way in the piracy of a West Country compatriot named John Hawley in 1412.[88] Sir Peter may thus have been carrying on an old family tradition, although there is not enough evidence to say this for sure.

Sir Peter associated freely in his treason against Queen Mary with the piratical Killegrew family, whose exploits in western waters were well known. However, at various periods in their lives, both Sir Peter and Sir George spent much time, money, and effort chasing pirates, although in Sir George's case the pirates usually seemed to be non-English. In this episode, Lasshe may have been acting on his own account, although the suspicion remains that Sir Peter's ships may from time to time have reaped their profits in somewhat irregular ways.

With his brother's death, Sir Peter had inherited Mohun's Ottery and all the other Carew properties within and without Devon. Sir George Carew died intestate, but the inquisition post mortem held on 3 April 1546 found Sir Peter to be his heir, the middle brother, Sir Philip, also being dead without issue.[89] On 10 July, Sir Peter was granted livery of all his brother's lands.[90] Sir Peter also fell heir to the family's position and influence in Devon. He was appointed sheriff of Devon in 1546, the year after his brother's death; Sir George had received the same appointment in 1537, the year after his father's death.[91] Given the expense of life at court, and the dimensions of Sir Peter's generous, free-spending ways, the inheritance, if not its circumstances, was welcome. We can gauge the size of Sir Peter's new income from the revenue payments collected by his brother during the previous decade. In October 1539, Edmond Lenthall, a Carew family servant, received for Sir George the following rents from various family estates in Devon and the West: £21 16s 7.5d for the rents of Tamerton, Luffinycott, West Draynes, Faryndon, Trevenyell, and Treweneck; £30 10s 11.5d from Stoke Fleming; £113 3.5d from Mohun's Ottery and Monckton; £6 from Colwaye in Lyme; and £70 8d from Polsloe, the former priory site Sir George was leasing.[92] Total receipts exceeded £240, a sizable sum, especially since not all the Carew lands were listed in this payment. The document is also unclear as to what portion of the year's rent for each manor these amounts represented. Sir George received these monies in Calais, where he was much in need of funds, and probably anxious to get his hands on whatever was available. His surviving receiver's accounts for the early 1540s show that Sir George drew similar sums each year for Mohun's Ottery, Monckton, Stoke Fleming, Polsloe, and several other properties.[93] A month before his death, Sir George acknowledged receipt of over £23 in land revenue, part of which came from the recent monastic acquisition at Newnham and the former Courtenay holding of Chittlehampton.[94] These numbers represent a considerable increase in income over what we know of Sir Edmund's revenues at the start of the sixteenth century. Some of this increase probably came from the rising prices landlords in the century received for sale of their agricultural surpluses, a circumstance of the rising population and increasing scarcity of land due to enclosure and engrossment. Part of the increase in Carew income was probably due to an increase in rents, as Sir George and his father demanded more from their customary tenants as those tenants earned more from the sale of their produce.[95] But a good deal of the Carew gains must have come from the losses of others, i.e., the Courtenay and monastic windfalls. Through new properties gained from these sources, Sir George made good the £30 in family lands that he sold in his lifetime and enlarged the estate from which Sir Peter could draw revenues in the future.[96]

Sir Peter had picked up little himself from the destruction of the Courtenays or the dissolution of the monasteries, the Okehampton lease being the major exception. However, within a year of his brother's death, Sir Peter was selling off some of Sir George's acquisitions from these sources. In July 1546, the month of his glorious extravagance in France, Sir Peter obtained a license to alienate parts of the Chittlehampton and Newnham properties, as well as several other small properties in Devon.[97] Three months later, Sir Peter received another license to alienate further portions of Newnham to Griffin Ameredyth, with whom Carew was to have other land dealings in the future.[98] Extravagance and an inability or disinclination to carefully and closely manage money were to cause serious consequences both for Sir Peter Carew and for the family estates throughout his lifetime.

As the reign of Henry VIII ended, Sir Peter Carew and his uncle Sir Gawen were coming into their own both at court and in the West Country. In Edward VI's reign, Sir Gawen was appointed his nephew's successor as sheriff of Devon. Both uncle and nephew sat in the Parliament of 1545, Sir Gawen as a knight of the shire for Devon. Sir Gawen may even have served in the same capacity for the Parliament of 1542; the damaged parliamentary return for that year leaves some doubt whether the chosen MP was Gawen or Sir George Carew, since all that remains is "G . . . . . r [?]we." If this item refers to a Carew at all, the absence of the knightly designation "miles" makes the as yet unknighted Gawen more likely.[99] The Parliament of November 1545 vested in the king the wealth of the chantries, and in February 1546 commissions were issued under the Chantries Act for the surveying of these institutions throughout the kingdom. Sir Gawen was appointed with the bishop of Exeter and several other gentlemen to survey the chantries in Devon, Cornwall, and Exeter.[100] The power to seize chantries lapsed with the king's death in January 1547, and Sir Gawen was not named to the Edwardian commission. For his work on the 1546 commission, Sir Gawen received £20 in December.[101] As part of this commission, Sir Gawen reported on the free chapel of Ottermoyne in the Carew family's home parish of Luppitt. Ottermoyne had been founded by one of Peter and Gawen's ancestors for the purpose of endowing a priest to say Mass continuously for the family. The chapel was on the manor of Mohun's Ottery, a mile or more distant from the parish church of Luppitt. The bailiff of Mohun's Ottery paid the priest a yearly sum of 66s 8d. It is significant that the 1546 commission found Ottermoyne, which was for some months before the act in Sir Peter's charge, without an incumbent and devoid of any jewels, plate, or other ornamentation.[102] Perhaps Sir Peter's or Sir George's religious interests had preceded the king's economic interests.

The death of Henry VIII on 28 January 1547 brought the first phase of Sir Peter Carew's public career to an end. The advent of a new reign, that of a boy king governed and advised by men of Protestant leanings with whom Carew had served at court and in camp, was to offer Sir Peter new opportunities for the things he craved most—honourable service, influence at court, and adventure.

1 Sir George Carew to Thomas Cromwell, 21 May 1539, PRO, SP1/151/226; LP XIV(1), 1009.

2 Henry Lacy to Thomas Cromwell, 26 October 1539, *Lisle Letters*, V, p. 694.

3 Calais Commissioners to Henry VIII, 5 April 1540, *StPap*, VIII, pp. 299-301

4 Ibid., pp. 302-03.

5 Ibid., pp. 299-303.

6 Henry VIII to the Calais Commissioners, 8 April 1540, PRO, SP1/158/171.

7 J. Kaulek, ed., *Correspondance Politique de MM. de Castillon et de Marillac* (Geneva: Slatkine Reprints, 1971), #224.

8 Ibid., #227.

9 LP, XIV(2), 435 (41).

10 Ibid., XVII, 1251 (11).

11 Ibid., XIX(1), 610 (44); XX(1), 620 (50).

12 Ibid., XV, 942 (75).

13 Ibid., XVI, 1500 (30b); Vivian, *Visitations*, p. 135.

14 LP, XVI, 580 (41), 703, 1174, 1311; XVII, 127, 210, 829.

15 Ibid., XVII, 1154 (75); XIX(2), App. 10.

16 Scarisbrick, *Henry VIII*, pp. 439-40.

17 LP, XVIII, 832.

18 Sir George Carew to Thomas Cromwell, 21 May 1539, PRO, SP1/151/226; LP XIV(1), 1009.

19 Sir John Wallop to the Council, 27 July 1543, *StPap*, IX, p. 455; also LP, XVIII(1), 960. Wallop did not hold a grudge, unless one wants to read something into the fact that Carew's mention in the postscript was made necessary by Wallop's failure to include his name in an earlier list of those in the army who were eager to do the king's service.

20 Hooker, "Life," pp. 22-23.

21 Sir John Wallop to the Council, 31 July 1543, *StPap*, IX, pp. 457-60; also LP, XVIII(1), 979.

22 Hooker, "Life," pp. 23-24.

23 Hooker, "Life," p. 24; Sir John Wallop to the Council, 31 July 1543, *StPap*, IX, pp. 457-60; also LP, XVIII(1), 979.

24 LP, XVIII(2), 13, 43, 65, 129, 187, 267, 325.

25 Ibid., 92.

26 Ibid., 266.

27 Hooker, "Life," pp. 24-25.

28 Ibid., p. 25.

29 LP, XVIII(2), 345.

30 Ibid., 352.

31 Ibid., 347, 365.

32 Hooker, "Life," p. 25.

33 Bindoff, *House of Commons*, I, p. 574. Sir George was apparently held for a time in Montreuil, for in the following summer he and Sir Thomas Palmer were able to give the king valuable intelligence about the town, having been the only Englishmen recently inside the walls (LP, XIX(1), 903).

34 LP, XIX(1), 275.

35 Ibid., XIX(2), 524 (18).

36 Hooker, "Life," p. 26.

37 LP, XIX(2), App. 10, pp 485-86.

38 Ibid., XIX(2), 424; Hooker, "Life," p. 26.

39 Hooker, "Life," pp. 26-27.

40 LP, XIX(2), App. 10, pp 485-86.

41 Scarisbrick, *Henry VIII*, pp. 448-49.

42 Hooker, "Life," p. 27. Sir George's service lasted into October, for he was one of those placed in charge of transportation between England and the continent. His main role was to transport the sick and wounded to England and prevent the desertion of able-bodied men from their posts in Calais and Boulogne (LP, XIX(2), 414, 415).

43 LP, XIX(2), 465.

44 Ibid., 502.

45 Ibid., 601.

46 Hooker, "Life," p. 28.

47 LP, XX(2), App. 2 (vi).

48 Ibid., XXI(2), Add. 2, 1697.

49 Hooker, "Life," p. 28; Order of Sailing and Engagement for the Fleet, 10 August 1545, *StPap*, I, p. 811.

50 Hooker, "Life," pp. 29-30.

51 Ibid., p. 30.

52 LP, XX(1), 1022.

53 Hooker, "Life," p. 31.

54 John Entick, *A New Naval History: or, the Compleat View of the British Marine* (London, 1757), p. 158

55 Hooker, "Life," pp. 31-33.

[56] Du Bellay's original manuscript is in the Carisbrook Castle Museum on the Isle of Wight, but an English translation of part of the manuscript was reprinted in 1757 in Entick's *New Naval History*. See pages 158-60 for an account of the naval actions fought on 18 and 19 July 1545.

[57] Order of Sailing and Engagement for the Fleet, 10 August 1545, *StPap*, I, p. 811.

[58] Hooker, "Life," p. 33.

[59] Alexander McKee, *King Henry VIII's Mary Rose* (New York: Stein and Day, 1974), p. 66. For a detailed account of the sinking of the *Mary Rose*, see pages 51-67. McKee led the expedition that discovered the remains of the *Mary Rose* in the 1970s.

[60] Entick, *New Naval History*, p. 160.

[61] Hooker, "Life," p.34.

[62] No one was sure what had happened to the *Mary Rose*. Hooker drew his explanation from Sir George Carew's last words.

> It chanced unto this gentleman [Sir George Carew], as the common proverb is—the more cooks the worse pottage, he had in his ship a hundred marines, the worst of them being able to be a master in the best ship within the realm; and these so maligned and disdained one the other, that refusing to do that which they should do, were careless to do that which was most needful and necessary, and so contending in envy, perished in frowardness. (Hooker, "Life," pp. 33-34)

The negligence Hooker suspected may have been in leaving open the gunports as the ship got underway and in failing to secure the ship's big guns. The calm seas and stationary combat of the morning would likely have made such precautions seem unnecessary. A Fleming among the survivors confirmed this for the imperial ambassador—when the *Mary Rose* heeled over with the wind the water rushed in by the lowest row of gunports, which had been left open after the morning's action (LP, XX(1) 1263; *Cal.SP Span.*, VIII, 101). Hooker said the *Mary Rose* was carrying some 700 men, and du Bellay said 500 or 600; either estimate was far more than the ship's normal complement of 415 (Hooker, "Life," p. 33; Entick, *New Naval History*, p. 159; McKee, *Mary Rose*, p. 66). Perhaps she had taken on extra infantry for a battle to be fought just off the English coast. The extra weight of 300 additional men would have brought the open gunports dangerously low in the water and the movement of the unsecured guns would have made the ship unstable. As water poured in the lower decks, the ship would heel more and more to one side until she toppled over completely and sank. This is what Sir Walter Raleigh thought happened; in his "Essay on the Invention of Shipping" he wrote: "Her loss was occasioned by a little sway in casting her about, her ports (she had but one gun deck) being only 16 inches from the water" (Maclean, *Life and Times*, p. 128). Du Bellay believed that the *Mary Rose* "was sunk by our cannon"; he thought the French galleys had heavily damaged both the *Mary Rose* and the *Great Harry*, which he claimed would have suffered the same fate as the *Mary Rose* had not other English ships come to its aid (Entick, *New Naval History*, p. 160). The *Mary Rose* remained on the bottom of Portsmouth harbor until 1982, when its remains were carefully lifted from the ocean and placed in a specially constructed drydock in Portsmouth.

63 Lord Lisle to Sir William Paget, 2 August 1545, *StPap*, I, p. 801; LP, XX(2), 62.

64 Hooker, "Life," p. 37.

65 LP, XX(2), 62.

66 Order of Sailing and Engagement for the Fleet, 10 August 1545, *StPap*, I, p. 810. Carew's choice was a wise one, for if he had transferred to the *Mystres* he might not have taken part in the upcoming action against the French. On 20 August, Lisle chronicled for Lord St. John the many problems of the *Mystres*. After encountering foul weather, the ship had suffered such damage that she was no longer seaworthy. "Her main mast is loose in the Pawtners, and the cross trestles both of her foremast, and also of her main mast, are broken." Lisle had no choice but to send her back to Portsmouth and summon the king's shipwrights to devise some way to repair her. See Lord Lisle to Lord St. John, 20 August 1545, *StPap*, I, p. 820.

67 Hooker, "Life," pp. 34-35.

68 Ibid., pp. 35-36.

69 Lord Lisle to Henry VIII, 3 September 1545, *StPap*, I, p. 829; Hooker, "Life", pp. 36-38.

70 Hooker, "Life," pp. 38-40.

71 Maclean, *Life and Times*, p. 40 n.

72 Sir William Petre to Sir William Paget, 17 December 1545, PRO, SP1/212/47.

73 Sir William Petre to Sir William Paget, 24 December, 1545, PRO, SP1/212/110.

74 LP, XVIII(1), 982 (47).

75 Hooker, "Life," p. 40.

76 LP, XXI(1), 1177.

77 Ibid., 1235.

78 Ibid., 1327.

79 Ibid., 1405.

80 Hooker, "Life," p. 42.

81 Ibid., pp. 42-43.

82 LP, XXI(1), 1405.

83 Hooker, "Life," p. 43.

84 Ibid., pp. 43-44.

85 Ibid., p. 44.

86 LP, XXI(1), 1406.

87 APC, I, p. 444.

88 Allmand, *Henry V*, p. 320. Hawley is said to have seized a French vessel with the help of "a hundred men or more armed and arrayed in manner of war." Devon was even further from the center of power in London in the early fifteenth century than it was in Sir Peter's time.

89 Inquisition Post Mortem of Sir George Carew, PRO, C142/73/20.

90 LP, XXI(1), 1383 (34).

91 Ibid., 472, 773 ii(3).

92 Rent Receipts of Sir George Carew, 2 October 1539, PRO, SP1/153/163.

93 LP, XVIII(2), 226.

94 Ibid., XX(1), 923.

95 Hoskins, *Age of Plunder*, pp. 64-65.

96 Bindoff, *House of Commons*, I, p. 574.

97 LP, XXI(1), 1383 (110).

98 Ibid., XXI(2), 332 (91).

99 Bindoff, *House of Commons*, I, p. 572.

100 LP, XXI(1), 302 (30).

101 Ibid., XXI(2), 775 (109).

102 Lawrence S. Snell, ed., *The Chantry Certificates for Devon and the City of Exeter* (Exeter: James Townsend and Sons, Ltd., 1963), p. 31.

CHAPTER 5

THE PRAYER BOOK REBELLION OF 1549

The death of Henry VIII altered the political and religious landscape of England, replacing the old king's unquestioned authority and cautious reforms with the shaky leadership and moderate but sincere Protestantism of the new king's uncle, the duke of Somerset. The new reign also brought changes to the lives of Sir Peter Carew and his uncle. Sir Peter and Sir Gawen had both fallen from the old king's favor for brief spells, mainly for deviating too widely from the narrow channel of Henry's twisting orthodoxy. The personalities of Sir Peter and Sir Gawen lacked the devious, calculating subtlety of the king, preferring more direct approaches to desired ends. The king knew that the Carews were loyal and useful, if occasionally willful, servants. Henry knew how to use loyalty and talent, and how to curb willfulness. The duke of Somerset lacked the old king's abilities in directing and controlling royal servants. As a result, the Carews found their service for Protector Somerset less valued and less successful than had been their service for Henry VIII, and the West Country found the Carews' exercise of local authority and influence less business-like and less effective and more arrogant and quarrelsome than in the past.

The greatest change to come to Sir Peter Carew's life with the new reign had its origins in the last months of the previous reign. During the last year of King Henry's life, Sir Peter was "wrapped in Venus bands, and stricken with Cupid's darts," to use Hooker's phrase. The object of Carew's affections was a lady of the court, Margaret, Lady Tailboys, widow of George, Lord Tailboys, and daughter of the Lincolnshire knight Sir William Skipwith. The lady apparently did not share Sir Peter's feelings, for his suit had "many ague days" and, despite Carew's undoubtedly strenuous efforts, prospered not at all. But Carew was not one to moon about the court over his unrequited love. As in the past, when persuasion failed him, Sir Peter employed persistence and high level mediation.[1] This technique had won him permission to depart the princess of Orange's court in 1532 and leave to embark on his adventure to Constantinople in 1540; it now won him his love and a wife and her not inconsiderable estates.

After returning from the French court in August 1546, Sir Peter took his failing marriage suit to the king, "humbly beseech[ing] his highness to stand his good lord" with the reluctant lady. The king, however, "seemed to strain courtesy at the matter" and had no "good liking thereof." Whether the king objected to being employed as a matchmaker or to the match itself or to both is unclear. Whatever the case, Henry VIII had a change of heart, which Hooker predictably put down to the king's reconsideration of Sir Peter's "worthiness and nobility," but which is probably better ascribed to Carew's talent for doggedly pursuing his purposes until they were attained and perhaps to Henry's poor health. Henry now entered into the role of matchmaker, writing "most earnest letters" to Lady Tailboys on Carew's behalf and promising to give the newlyweds and their heirs £100 in land. This promise may have turned the tide–it likely increased Sir Peter's desire for the match–for "howsoever her liking of him was before," she now yielded to the king's persuasion "and was contented." But before the wedding could be celebrated, King Henry died.[2]

Henry VIII's initial objections to Carew's suit may have sprung from Lady Margaret's past connections to the royal family and to the king himself. In January 1538, Henry VIII had been a widower for only three months, but interest in his future marriage plans was already beginning to generate speculation and rumor. On 3 January, John Husee wrote to his master, Lord Lisle, to proudly describe his merry reception by the king and

Cromwell as he delivered Lisle's gift to the king on New Year's day. Then, in lines that almost whisper of themselves, Husee wrote cryptically that

> [m]y Lord of Wiltshire is again now in the Court and very well entertained. The election lieth betwixt Mrs. Mary Shelton and Mrs. Mary Skipwith. I pray Jesu send such one as may be for his Highness' comfort and the wealth of the realm. Herein I doubt not but your lordship will keep silence till the matter be surely known.[3]

The earl of Wiltshire's re-emergence at court meant that the king had apparently forgiven him for being Anne Boleyn's father, and, quite possibly, that the king had a serious interest in his niece, Mary Shelton. By Mary Skipwith, Husee meant Margaret Skipwith, whose father, Sir William Skipwith, had about 1533 been one of Cromwell's choices to fill the Lincolnshire seat in Parliament left vacant by the ennoblement of Sir Gilbert Tailboys, Margaret's future father-in-law. Husee's apparently unique reference to the king's amorous interests at this time is too vague to say exactly what the king's relationship to the two women was. But Husee's extreme discretion in the matter and his warning to Lisle to keep silence suggest that Mistress Shelton and Mistress Skipwith were being considered for something more than mere dalliance. Husee's prayer that the selection between the two might lead to the king's contentment and the benefit of the kingdom implied, as Muriel St. Clare Byrne pointed out, that the contest was between potential queens and not just potential mistresses.[4]

The next mention of Margaret Skipwith occurred in a letter of 17 April 1539 from Sir Thomas Heneage to Cromwell. Heneage wrote that he and the lord admiral, the earl of Southampton, had told the king of their proceedings in the matter of Lord Tailboys and "my niece Skipwit," and that the king believed it best that the two be married as quickly as possible.[5] The king's interest in the match was perfectly proper, for George, second Lord Tailboys, was a fatherless minor and therefore a ward of the Crown. But the young man had another connection to the Crown. His mother was Elizabeth Blount, the king's former mistress and the mother of the king's son Henry FitzRoy, duke of Richmond. In 1522, three year's after giving birth to the king's son, Elizabeth married Sir Gilbert Tailboys. The couple were granted lands in Warwickshire and in 1523 acquired extensive lands in Yorkshire by act of Parliament. Sir Gilbert served as a gentleman of the king's chamber and was elected to Parliament for Lincolnshire in 1529. His service in the Commons was brief, for at the end of the year the king created him Baron Tailboys of Kyme. He died in April 1530.[6] The first Lord Tailboys had risen in the world by accommodatingly taking the king's discarded mistress to wife. Evidence suggests that the second Lord Tailboys may have followed in his father's footsteps.

On 26 April, John Husee wrote separate letters to Lord and Lady Lisle. In each letter, his bare mention of the forthcoming marriage between Margaret Skipwith and Lord Tailboys is followed by a warning to keep knowledge of the Tailboys marriage "to yourself till you hear more."[7] Then, on 15 May, in the midst of all manner of unrelated news, Husee wrote a simple, unelaborated statement to Lady Lisle: "The Lord Tailboys is married."[8] Cap. 16 of the acts for private persons passed in the parliamentary session held that spring confirms Husee's hushed secret. The statute for "lady Tailboys' jointure" explained that the king had granted "the custody and marriage of the said Lord [Tailboys] now being of the age of sixteen year and more" to the earl of Southampton, who had recently agreed that Tailboys' should marry the earl's cousin, Margaret Skipwith. The act then rehearsed Tailboys' inability to draw profit from his inheritance during his minority, which prevented him from supporting himself "conveniently and reasonably" and from making any jointure "to the said Margaret, now his wife, towards her necessary living." Tailboys' reward for agreeing to marry a royal mistress may have been an early release from wardship, which would normally have lasted until his 21st birthday. The Tailboys estates were settled on husband and wife for the longest survivor of the couple, and to their heirs.[9] When the brief marriage ended with Tailboys's death in September 1540,[10] the young Lady Tailboys was left a well-landed widow.

In 1546, when Sir Peter Carew sought royal assistance in winning the lady's hand, he was probably asking the king to persuade a former lover to become another man's wife. Margaret Skipwith may well have won Husee's "election," as had her new mother-in-law 20 years before. The king neither arranged nor endowed such a marriage for Mary Shelton.[11] His past relationship with Margaret Tailboys may explain the king's initial reluctance to help Carew. Sir Peter was present in the court in 1539 and could have been aware of the circumstances of Lady Tailboys's first marriage. He may even have counted on lingering affections to help his cause when he chose to take his suit to the king, although such subtlety would be out of character for Carew. It is more likely that Husee's whispered secret never came to the 25-year-old courtier who was soon to be off to Constantinople, and in 1546 Sir Peter came innocently to the king, for it was to the king that he naturally took all great matters. However, Carew was not ignorant of Lady Tailboys's landed wealth. In the last months of 1546, Sir Peter was granted licenses to alienate pieces of property, including some of the monastic holdings granted to his brother. Although contemporary belief expected love to blossom after marriage and not before, there is no reason to discount Hooker's talk of "Venus bands" as merely the romantic convention of the time, or to ascribe Carew's pursuit of the lady solely to land hunger or a need for money. The marriage would withstand the long years of Sir Peter's exile during Mary's reign, when Lady Tailboys worked constantly and effectively for her husband's rehabilitation and return. The affection and respect that husband and wife displayed for one another during this difficult time suggests that Sir Peter really found himself smitten in 1546, although his need for money argues that Sir Peter was looking for just such a landed lady to smite him.

Peter Carew could have met Lady Tailboys and likely did meet Lord Tailboys during the ceremonies and celebrations surrounding the arrival of Anne of Cleves in December 1539 and January 1540. Lord Tailboys, like Peter and Gawen Carew, was a member of the greeting party led by the earl of Southampton to Calais.[12] Tailboys was one of the lords Southampton took with him to dinner on 13 December to comply with Anne's request for some noble folks to come and share her meal with her as she was accustomed to do in her country.[13] Lady Tailboys was part of the group of women scheduled to greet the new queen in England with the princesses Mary and Elizabeth.[14] She stayed on in the court after her husband's death, holding some position in the household of one of the royal princesses. Her name appears in the royal household expenses in both 1540 and 1541,[15] the years of Sir Peter's absence from court to travel on the continent. In 1542, Lady Tailboys was one of those receiving letters of credence concerning her contribution to a loan demanded by the king.[16] Having given to the king, Lady Tailboys in the next year received from him, being granted by letters patent the wardship and marriage of the son of the late Lincolnshire gentleman Anthony Tottoft.[17] In 1546, Lady Tailboys was still "a lady in the court" when she yielded to Carew's persistence and the king's letters.[18]

Dispensation for the marriage of Sir Peter Carew and Lady Margaret Tailboys to be held without banns was granted on 14 February 1547.[19] The couple agreed between them to be married on 20 February, which was also Edward VI's coronation day, a coincidence that Hooker implied was accidental rather than intentional. The new husband honoured his wife by wearing her glove in his headpiece while taking part in a coronation day tournament. Sir Peter and five other knights took on all comers and Carew "acquitted himself very honourably."[20] In his diary, Edward VI said the jousts took place on 21 February, the day after the coronation. According to the king, the five other challengers with Carew were Lord Seymour of Sudeley, the lord admiral and the king's uncle; Sir

Richard Devereaux; Sir Anthony Kingston; Francis Knowles; and Mr. Shelley. The challengers ran six courses against every one of 24 defenders, with an additional two courses against any defender who was willing to run them for the honour of his lady. The king, the lord protector, and many nobles were present at one o'clock when the jousts began. All the courses were nobly run, and neither man nor horse was injured. The day ended with the royal party and the tournament participants returning to the admiral's house for "a goodly supper."[21]

Hooker related an incident that occurred to Carew during the tournament. Among the defenders were certain strangers to the court with whom Sir Peter greatly desired to run a course. He was pleased when he understood that one of the strangers had challenged him, but his pleasure turned to disappointment when he learned that his challenger was instead Mr. Cooke, a gentleman of the court. Carew asked Cooke to withdraw and give place to one of the strangers, but Cooke refused repeated requests to do so. "Well, if he will not," said Carew, "then let it fall out as it may." Hooker wrote with evident satisfaction that Sir Peter overthrew both the stubborn Mr. Cooke and his horse. The outcome of this incident must have particularly pleased Carew, for the recollection of it was vivid enough to him years later to recount it in detail to Hooker.[22]

After the coronation, Carew was "of the mind to sequester himself from the court," and he and Lady Tailboys withdrew to her extensive Lincolnshire estates, "where they remained almost three years."[23] However, Carew was not exclusively resident in Lincolnshire during this period. For one thing, he was sheriff of Devon for 1547, having been chosen by Henry VIII in November 1546.[24] The duties of this office drew him frequently during the king's first year into the West Country, where Sir Gawen was serving on the commission of the peace for Devon, having been appointed in May 1547.[25] Sir Gawen was to be the first Edwardian appointee as sheriff of Devon, succeeding his nephew in the post for

1548.[26] Both men also spent part of 1547 in London, where they sat in the first Parliament of the reign in the autumn, Sir Gawen as senior knight for Devon and Sir Peter as member for Dartmouth. Sir Peter's first appearance in the Commons had been in 1545 as member for Tavistock. An indication of the family's rising standing at court and in the West was the return of all three Carews to the 1545 Parliament; Sir George and Sir Gawen were both elected to represent Devon, although Sir George's death prevented him from actually sitting. Sir Peter likely owed his seat at Tavistock to the influence of Lord Russell, who was lord of the manor and borough. Because he was lord of the borough of Dartmouth, Carew probably had less need of Russell's help in 1547. The Carew family had long held the lordship of Southton in Dartmouth, but the lordship of the borough itself had belonged to the Percy earls of Northumberland until 1537 when it reverted to the Crown. Henry VIII then granted the lordship to Sir George, a further indication that the Carews were, with Russell and others, among the new party of king's men being built up in the West by Henry after his destruction of the marquis of Exeter and the old Courtenay influence.[27]

The only reference to Sir Peter's activities in the first Edwardian Parliament comes from its third session, in late 1549, and concerns a bill exhibited by several Devon clothiers for remitting of the Act of Relief for the making of cloths. On 16 November, the Commons committed the measure to "Mr. Carowe" until the knights of the shire for Devon should return to the House and give answer to the bill. Since Sir Gawen was one of the absent knights, the Carew to whom the bill was delivered was Sir Peter.[28] The second session of this Parliament, which ran from November 1548 to March 1549, saw the passage of much important legislation on religion. "An Act for Abstinence from Flesh" continued "due and godly" abstinence from meat, but for such secular reasons as maintaining the livelihoods of fishermen and preserving supplies of meat. "An Act to take away all positive Laws against Marriage of Priests" affirmed the ideal of clerical celibacy, but repealed all ecclesiastical laws and canons against clerical marriage as a way to end the "uncleanness of living and other great inconvenience" caused by enforced celibacy. The centerpiece of the religious legislation in this session was the Act of Uniformity, which enjoined upon the clergy the exclusive use of Archbishop Cranmer's *Book of Common Prayer* for divine service.[29] In terms of doctrine, conservatives had some reason to be satisfied with Cranmer's work, since his steps toward continental Protestantism were few and cautious. But while bishops argued the doctrinal subtleties of the new prayer book, the simple parishioners of the West Country focused on practical realities as a simpler, more scripture-centered service replaced the familiar ritual and saint veneration of the past, and mundane English replaced sacred Latin as the language of the English Church. In the spring of 1549, Sir Peter Carew was in London participating in the Parliament that approved these changes; by the summer of that year, Sir Peter was in the West Country struggling with the severe and bloody consequences of those same changes.

Sir Peter had been in the West Country in the late summer of the previous year, when he served as vice-admiral for Devon. On 9 August 1548, Lord Admiral Seymour, the lord protector's brother, wrote to Carew and to John Grenville, vice-admiral for Cornwall, with secret Council instructions for the licensing of privateers from the two shires against the French. Although France and England were at peace, the French had recently seized several English fishing vessels, confiscating the cargoes and either ransoming the crews or sending them to the galleys. To retaliate, the protector and Council ordered the admiral and vice-admirals to recruit West Country captains willing to sail at their own risk against the French fishing fleet from Newfoundland as it returned home. Officially, the English ships put to sea to combat the Scots, pirates, and the king's other enemies, but the vice-admirals were secretly to authorize all ship owners and captains to seize the Newfoundland fleet and any other French vessels they encountered. To excuse their actions, the English privateers were to claim that they had been previously spoiled by the French, had received no compensation for their losses, and were now retaliating in kind; or they were to pretend that any victuals or munitions found in the French ship were bound for the Scots, with whom the king was presently at war. All prizes were to be brought to English ports. The vice-admirals were to take bonds of all owners and captains for their good behavior toward the king's subjects and friends and to keep careful records of the burdens, ports, owners, captains, and masters of all ships. They were also to ensure that careful inventories were made of all captured vessels, for if peace continued and the French agreed to redress their acts of piracy, all French prizes or the value thereof were to be restored. The Council promised to compensate the takers if such restoration occurred. If war came, all prizes went to their takers. Because of the seriousness of the service and the secrecy required, four local gentlemen were empowered to act with the vice-admirals—two for Devon and two for Cornwall. Carew's colleagues were his father's old friend Sir Thomas Dennys and another member of the ubiquitous Grenville family, Sir Richard.[30] Despite Sir Peter's absence from court, the first two years of the reign saw him actively employed and highly favored by the new regime.

The third year of the reign, 1549, was to be a difficult and eventful year for Sir Peter Carew. It began with both Sir Peter and Sir Gawen, as well as the latter's brother, Archdeacon George Carew, appearing mysteriously in one of the depositions taken from Princess Elizabeth's servant Katherine Ashley during the investigations into the treasonous behavior of Lord Admiral Seymour. Mistress Ashley, who was a Champernon and the aunt of Carew's cousin Katherine Champernon, mentioned meeting the three Carews and George Eliot in a house in London in late November or early December 1548.[31] The circumstances of the meeting and the Carews' purpose in being there are not clear, but the reference is incidental to the main thrust of the investigation and the

Carews do not again figure in the matter. As vice-admiral of Devon, Sir Peter had been in contact with the lord admiral in the summer as the two coordinated the Council-mandated efforts of western privateers against the French, but there is no hint that Carew had any part in Seymour's many treasons of western provenience. These included fortifying his estate at Sudeley, conspiring with Sir William Sharington to divert funds from the royal mint at Bristol to his private purposes, and neglecting his duties as lord admiral to control, if not actually protect, western pirates who attached themselves to his interest.[32] For all these misdeeds, as well as for his attempts to influence the young king and convince the Princess Elizabeth to undertake an unauthorised marriage with him, the lord admiral, in the cold phrase of his royal nephew, "was condemned to death and died the March ensuing."[33]

The revelations of his brother's treasons and his own acquiescence in his brother's execution damaged the reputation of the lord protector just as a series of dangerous rebellions began to challenge his authority. Within a month of the lord admiral's death, various riots and disorders among the commons came to the attention of the Council. Many of the disruptions reported in the spring of 1549 concerned enclosures. According to Holinshed, the cause of some of the first disorders was the government's proclamation on 11 April ordering all offenders against the enclosure statutes uncovered by commission in the previous year to throw down their enclosures or suffer the penalties prescribed by the statutes. The commons in numerous counties, perceiving the enclosers to be in no haste to comply with the proclamation, took it upon themselves to enforce the order by tearing down hedges, killing sheep and deer, and generally causing havoc.[34] Many of these risings were quickly put down by energetic local gentlemen, but as soon as one fire was stamped out two more flared up. In late May, another proclamation promised speedy remedy of illegal enclosures but also complained of "disobedient and seditious persons, assembling themselves together unlawfully" to usurp royal authority by their riotous self-enforcement of the enclosure laws. All persons engaging in such activity were ordered to cease, while all royal justices and officers were directed to proceed swiftly and sternly against those assembling unlawfully or breaking down enclosures.[35]

These enclosure disorders eventually reached their climax later in the summer in a large-scale rising in Norfolk that could only be crushed by troops and the ruthless leadership of John Dudley, earl of Warwick, who as Henry VIII's lord admiral had knighted Sir Peter Carew in 1545. In 1549, Carew did not partake of his old captain's service in Norfolk; he had his own service to perform against rebels in his own part of the country. Almost simultaneously with the Norfolk rising, an equally large and dangerous rebellion exploded across Cornwall and Devon. The causes of this rising differed somewhat from those of the Norfolk rebellion and most of the earlier disorders. According to John Hooker, the cause of the western rising that year "was only concerning religion which then by act of Parliament was reformed."[36] Because several of the earlier risings had been successfully pacified by gentlemen of local influence, the Council, currently preoccupied with the lord protector's war in Scotland, turned in this western emergency to trustworthy men with military experience who were familiar with the area and its people. Sir Peter and Sir Gawen Carew fit this description perfectly. Sir Peter was on his wife's estates in Lincolnshire when the Council's summons came; Sir Gawen was already in attendance at court.[37] Sir Peter came with all speed to London, where he and his uncle were ordered by the king and Council into the troubled West Country.

Hoping to avoid a full-scale rebellion that might require diversion of extremely expensive and painfully collected mercenaries from his Scottish venture, the protector sent the Carews on a peace mission. A draft memorial to the western sheriffs, dated 20 June 1549, embodies the general instructions outlined in the commission under the king's hand and signet that the Council issued to the Carews.[38] In the memorial, the king accepted that the reported disorders against the prayer book in the West had arisen "rather of ignorance than of malice." Therefore, with the advice of the protector and Council, and at the "humble suit" of "diverse gentlemen," the king offered pardon to the rebels for "all the said contempts and offences heretofor past. So that the said offenders shall never hereafter be troubled or vexed for any such offence hereafter past and done, upon condition that hereafter they do behave themselves towards us as the duty is of loving and obedient subjects."[39] The specific instructions given the Carews echoed these conciliatory sentiments. Sir Peter and his uncle were to consult with the local justices and devise "the best means and ways that they might for the appeasing of this rebellion, quieting of the people, and pacifying of the country." The Carews were to induce the rebels to return quietly to their homes by promising to refer all their complaints and grievances to the king and Council. Only if the rebels stubbornly refused to disperse were the Carews authorised "to use such other good means and ways as might be for the suppressing of them."[40]

Certain members of the Council did not share the protector's taste for gentle persuasion to calm rebellion. These councilors, among whom the ambitious Warwick was prominent, preferred the sterner measures of the late king for dealing with unruly subjects. Warwick had served with Sir George Carew and had commanded Sir Peter Carew in various land and sea campaigns of the 1530s and 1540s. He was well aware what kind of man Sir Peter was, and the tasks he was best suited to perform; Warwick's selection of Sir Peter as the best man to requite the insult to young Lord Herbert during the French embassy of 1546 proved this. While the protector counted upon Sir Peter's familiarity with and influence in the West Country to pacify the rebels, Warwick and his like-minded colleagues counted upon Sir Peter's aggressive nature and military experience to crush the rebels. All the Council factions, although for different reasons, looked upon Sir Peter and his uncle as well suited for dealing with the western disturbances. Henry VIII had found Sir Peter Carew useful for waging foreign wars and impressing foreign courts; Protector Somerset now sent Sir Peter to avoid conflict and maintain internal peace. Bearing peaceful instructions and warlike expectations, Sir Peter would soon prove whether the dead king or the living duke had the better measure of his man.

In his biography of Sir Peter Carew, John Hooker cut short his description of the Prayer Book Rebellion of 1549 for the following reason: "But concerning this rebellion, and the good service this gentleman did therein, the same already at large, being set forth in a pamphlet thereof, it is not pertinent to this matter to treat thereof."[41] Hooker wrote several versions of the events of 1549; the "pamphlet" he referred to was most likely the manuscript now preserved in the Bodleian Library, which from internal evidence appears to be the earliest of Hooker's accounts of the rebellion. The Bodleian account, with some additions and variations, was later incorporated by Hooker into his monumental *Description of the Citie of Excester*, a comprehensive history and description of the city that was published by the Devon and Cornwall Record Society in 1919. Hooker also embodied his description of the 1549 rebellion in his 1587 revision and extension of Holinshed's *Chronicles*.[42] Hooker was in Exeter in the summer of 1549 when the rebels besieged the city, and was therefore, in his words, "*testis oculatus* of the things there done."[43] The *Description*, which has become the standard narrative source for the Prayer Book Rebellion, is also the best description of Sir Peter Carew's role in putting down the uprising.

The rebellion began, wrote Hooker, "at a place in Devon named Sampford Courtenay which lieth westward from the Citie [of Exeter] about sixteen miles." The Act of Uniformity required all priests to begin using the *Book of Common Prayer* on Whitsunday, 9 June. On the appointed day, the priest at Sampford Courtenay complied with the law and used the new service. Some of his parishioners did not find it to their liking, for on Monday 10 June they confronted the priest as he prepared again to say the reformed service and demanded that he "keep the old and ancient religion as their forefathers before them had done." The priest objected, saying that by law he could use nothing but the new prayer book. The protesters stood firm, parroting to the priest the argument that the recently imprisoned Bishop Gardiner and other religious conservatives had put unsuccessfully to the Lord Protector—"king Henry the eighth by his last will and testament had take[n] order that no alteration of religion should be made until king Edward his son were come to his full age." Since Edward was still a minor "and could do nothing," the parishioners of Sampford Courtenay would have no changes in the way divine service was conducted. Whether through fear of his insistent parishioners or out of secret agreement with them, the priest dressed "himself in his old popish attire and sayeth mass and all such services as in times past accustomed."[44]

Word of Sampford Courtenay's defiance of the Statute of Uniformity spread rapidly throughout Devon and gave heart to like-minded persons in all the villages and countryside round about. The common people, wrote a disgusted Hooker, "so well allowed and liked thereof that they clapped their hands for joy and agreed in one mind to have the same in every of their several parishes." The reasons for such misguided joy were clear to Hooker: the Church in Devon suffered from a lack of learned preachers to instruct the people in proper religion, and a scarcity of "well persuaded magistrates" to keep them in due obedience to the king. "Lacking the one and not stored with the other," the commons of Devon fell victim to their own ignorance and "rebellious disposition." Sir Hugh Pollard and a group of the gentlemen living nearest to Sampford Courtenay now tried tardily to supply Hooker's want of "well persuaded" magistrates. They rode to the village and sought to confer with the leaders of the disaffected parishioners. The villagers, having been warned of their coming, refused to talk with the gentlemen until they agreed to leave behind their servants and retainers and meet with village spokesmen in a specially prepared enclosure. Hooker, ever suspicious of anyone willing to accommodate papists, conceded that a desire to avoid violence might have caused the gentlemen to agree to this demand, but thought it more likely, as "was greatly suspected," that some of the gentlemen were sympathetic to the villagers' cause. After all, noted Hooker, the gentlemen with their retainers had the greater number and could have "repressed the small number of the commoners there assembled."[45]

The conference lasted "a pretty while" but accomplished nothing, at least from the government's point of view. The gentlemen withdrew, convincing the villagers "that the game was theirs," and Hooker that the gentlemen "were so white livered as they would not or durst not to repress the rages of the people." The gentlemen's weak response to their strong stand had an electric effect on the commons of Devon. All over the shire, people dissatisfied with the recent alterations in religion gathered together "in great troops and companies" to maintain their quarrel with the king's reforms. The government's worst fears began to come true when mobs of religious protesters from Cornwall crossed into the neighboring county to join their strength with their Devon compatriots. By the middle of June, the situation in the West Country was quickly slipping beyond the capacity of the local justices to deal with it. At this point, the government, still hoping to contain the spreading disaffection, dispatched Sir Peter and Sir Gawen Carew to their native shire.[46]

When the Carews reached Exeter on 21 June, they met immediately with Sir Piers Courtenay, the sheriff of Devon, and showed him the proclamation with which Somerset had armed them on their departure from the court. The document granted pardon to all rioters who immediately ceased such disorders and threatened death to all who persisted in them.[47] Sir Peter quickly took command, summoning all the county justices to a meeting in Exeter. At the meeting, the Carews learned that a large company of the commons, including the original rioters from Sampford Courtenay, had assembled in the village of Crediton, about seven miles from Exeter. After much discussion, the gentlemen decided that Sir Peter should lead a company of gentlemen to Crediton and try to accomplish what Sir Hugh Pollard and his party had failed to do—persuade the unruly commons to return quietly to their homes. Despite Pollard's experience, the general consensus at the meeting was that with "good speeches and gentle conferences" this purpose could be achieved.[48]

The Carews and their companions were quickly disabused of this fond notion when they arrived at Crediton. The rebels—for such they now were—had somehow learned of the Carews' intentions and had prepared for conference not with arguments, but with arms. Sir Peter's party found the entrance into the town barricaded and guarded by men armed with weapons of all types, including guns and bows. Great plow chains had been hung across the road, and several barns and other structures adjoining the barricade were filled with rebels, their weapons protruding ominously from holes knocked in the walls. Seeing that they could not ride into the town, the gentlemen resolved to enter on foot, but were astonished to find themselves still denied entry. Indeed, the rebels refused even to speak with them. The gentlemen, unaccustomed to being "so irreverently and discourteously intreated," took it "in evil part." In their outrage, the Carews forgot for a moment the protector's charge to pacify, not enflame, rebellion. Sir Peter and his uncle, seizing upon what was for them a natural course of action, led their willing companions in a charge of the barricade. However, the fire from the barricade defenders, and especially from the men concealed in the barns, was so galling that the attackers were forced to retreat "with the loss of some and the hurt of many."[49] The Carews' impetuous leadership had led not to pacification, but to the first shedding of blood.

In the confusion of the fight and the retreat of the gentlemen, a servant of Sir Hugh Pollard named Fox managed to creep up to one of the fortified barns and set it on fire. The flames spread rapidly to each of the occupied structures, driving the terrified rebels before it. In no time, both town and barricade were deserted. Sir Peter walked into Crediton unimpeded, but found no one to hold conference with except a few of the aged who could not take to their heels. The reaction following Sir Hugh Pollard's retreat from Sampford Courtenay was mild compared to the explosion that followed the burning of the barns at Crediton. As the Carews led their party back to Exeter, the story of what had happened at Crediton swept over the shire like a strong wind. The tale grew with the telling, until the commons were convinced that the Carews and the other gentlemen "were altogether bent to overrun, spoil, and destroy them." In their anger, the people gathered, in Hooker's colorful phrase, as "a swarm of wasps . . . in great troops and multitudes," ready to repel the enemy who seemed so eager to assail them.[50]

Walter Raleigh, the father of the Elizabethan courtier, chose this tense moment for a foolish display of religious zeal. Raleigh, an outspoken Protestant, had taken as his third wife Katherine Champernon, daughter of Sir Peter's Aunt Katherine and sister of John Champernon, the cousin who had accompanied Sir Peter to Constantinople before dying in Vienna in 1541. Katherine Champernon had already given birth to three sons by her first husband, Otho Gilbert, and was to have two more by Walter Raleigh. All five of these Carew cousins—Sir John, Sir Humphrey, and Adrian Gilbert, and Sir Walter and Sir Carew Raleigh—were to take active parts in English overseas exploration during the Elizabethan period, but Sir Humphrey Gilbert and Sir Walter Raleigh especially distinguished themselves in that field.[51] In June 1549, the senior Raleigh was riding to Exeter through a country lane when he overtook an old woman praying on her rosary. Raleigh asked the woman what she was doing and then proceeded to lecture her on religion. The reformed religion, said Raleigh, had been established by law, and such superstitions as praying on beads had been rightly abolished. As a good and obedient Christian woman she should conform herself to the law or risk suffering the punishment the law "appointed against her and all such as would not obey and follow the same."[52] Whether Raleigh meant this last remark as a threat or as a friendly warning is unclear; it was in any case untrue, for the Act of Uniformity prescribed no penalties against laypersons.

There is no doubt how the woman took Raleigh's comment. "Not liking nor well digesting this matter," the woman ran straight to the parish church in the village of Clyst St. Mary, which was at that moment filled with people attending divine service, and, in another example of Hooker's vivid phrasing, began "to upbray in the open Church very hard and unseemly speeches concerning religion." The excited woman claimed that a gentleman had offered to burn all the commons out of their houses and utterly spoil them unless she gave up her beads and holy bread and water. Hooker denounced the woman's tirade as "very false and untrue," and having no resemblance to her conversation with Raleigh. But since the woman's words only confirmed what they already believed, the parishioners accepted her story without question.[53]

Hooker again employed his wasp image to describe the parishioners flying out of the church and into the village, where they immediately set about constructing Crediton-style fortifications. They laid great trees athwart the bridge that led out of the village toward Exeter, fearful that Sir Peter Carew would at any minute lead his band of gentlemen against them from the city. This possibility caused great apprehension among the villagers, for popular rumor was charging the burning barns at Crediton solely to Sir Peter's ruthlessness. Convinced that Carew meant nothing less than their destruction, the Clyst St. Mary rebels brought several large pieces of ordnance from the nearby town of Topsham and planted them atop the fortifications to make a direct assault on the bridge more risky. Raleigh, meanwhile, had the ill luck to be overtaken by the party of villagers sent out to fetch the ordnance. They were so enraged by the way he had talked to the woman that he was "like to have been murdered" if he had not reached the safety of the chapel in Topsham, from which a group of friendly mariners helped him escape. Raleigh's freedom was short-lived, however; he was captured shortly thereafter by another group of rebels and kept imprisoned under threat of death, like so many other unfortunate gentlemen during this summer, in the church of St. Sidwell's until the end of the rebellion, almost two months later.[54]

Raleigh's adventures probably occurred on Saturday 22 June, the day after the fiasco at Crediton. Carew spent the day in Exeter meeting with Devon justices and city magistrates to discuss preparations for the town's defense should the protector's program of pacification fail, which must by this time have seemed likely. Mayor John Blackaller and his brethren had wisely begun to take precautions a week earlier, canceling the annual Midsummer Watch held on St. John's Eve on 23 June. The event involved a procession through the streets and around the city walls by the mayor, city officials, and representatives of the trade guilds, all clad in armor and livery. After inspection of the city defenses, all participants usually sat down to a meal. Given the growing tension outside the city and the suspected presence of rebel sympathizers inside the city, the magistrates thought it best not to provoke trouble by parading armed men about the town. On 22 June, with Carew's advice, the city magistrates took further measures for Exeter's security. The tailors', shoemakers', bakers', and brewers' guilds were ordered to provide 10 men "in harness, householders or honest and discreet inhabitants," to keep watch on the walls and in every quarter of the town.[55] As these orders were being put into effect, news of the disturbances at Clyst St. Mary reached Exeter.

Sir Peter immediately assembled the remaining justices and gentlemen and conferred with them on the best course of action. Although the Carews had so far been less than successful at pacification, the protector's program was given one more try. The assembly decided to send Sir Peter, Sir Gawen, Sir Thomas Dennys, Sir Hugh Pollard, and several other gentlemen to Clyst St. Mary to try again to talk the rebels into dispersing quietly. On Sunday morning, 23 June, Sir Peter's party issued out of Exeter bound for Clyst St. Mary. As they approached the village, they saw the fortified bridge and realised that they were once again barred from riding into their destination. Having apparently learned nothing about the rebels' determination from his hostile reception at Crediton, and perhaps unaware of the terrible reputation the burning of the Crediton barns had won for him, Sir Peter alighted from his horse and began to walk heedlessly toward the bridge, thinking that he would be allowed to enter the village on foot. By now, Clyst St. Mary was full of rebels from numerous nearby villages. When one of these neighboring rebels, a smith from Woodbury named John Hammon, recognised Sir Peter Carew walking toward his position on the bridge, he, at the urging of some of his fellows, charged his gun and aimed it at Carew. Hammon would have fired, had he not been prevented from doing so by Hugh Osborne, a servant of a local sergeant-at-law named Prideaux. This near miss awoke Sir Peter to his danger, and he retreated to his companions to discuss how best to proceed, since it was clear the rebels would not admit them to the village.[56]

Both Carews had evil names among the commons of Devon and Cornwall even before the episode at Crediton. Hooker wrote that the great "rancor and malice" being directed at Sir Peter by the conservative commons was due in large part to his religion.[57] The Carews were both associated with the protector's Protestant regime, had both profited from the suppression of western monasteries, and had identifed themselves with preachers of reform in the West. Early in Edward's reign, Sir Peter had defended Dean Simon Hayne of Exeter from conservative adversaries who much "maligned and envied" him "for his sincere and true preaching of the Gospel." Later in the reign, both Carews stood guard when William Alley, a future bishop of Exeter, took the pulpit to preach reform in Exeter; Alley's conservative enemies had so threatened him for his preaching that he "durst not to adventure to come again into the pulpit" without the Carews' protection.[58] Sir Gawen's reputation among religious conservatives was no better than his nephew's. He was the holder of much former Church property in Cornwall, including Launceston Priory and the rectory and chapel at Tresmere. In the 1540s, Sir Gawen angered the parishioners at Tresmere by refusing to pay the £5 stipend to maintain a curate. The parishioners sent a deputation to London to complain that Sir Gawen cared more for his profit than their souls.[59] In 1549, then, the Carews' hostility to the old religion was well known among the western commons, and made Sir Peter's seeming willingness to brutally roast adherents of that faith all the more believable. Indeed, it was probably the Carews' reliable Protestantism, as well as their local position and military experience, that made them the protector's first choice for subduing the rising in the West.

Despite their hostile reception and the fruitless example of the earlier talks at Sampford Courtenay, the gentlemen decided to try again to talk to the insurgents. Accordingly, a messenger was sent into the village bearing an offer from the gentlemen to discuss with the rebels any grievances or complaints they had about anything or against anyone. This message caused much doubt and discussion among the rebels, who finally sent word that they would allow only Sir Thomas Dennys, Sir Hugh Pollard, and Thomas Yarde to come into the village to talk. The rebels wanted nothing to do with either of the Carews. Dennys was probably chosen because he was well-known to the people of Clyst St. Mary, being their neighbor at Bicton, and Pollard had apparently shown some sympathy for the conservative cause in his earlier talks with the Sampford Courtenay rioters. Yarde too may have been viewed as a sympathizer. Nonetheless, the three gentlemen had to come alone, bringing no servants or retainers, and had to promise that their waiting companions would attempt nothing against the village while the conference lasted. These promises being given, the three men entered the village at about 10 o'clock in the morning. Denied access, Sir Peter and Sir Gawen waited with the rest of their party by the roadway beyond the barricaded bridge. They waited all through the day and into the evening without any word from their companions in the village. As darkness began to fall, the increasingly restless gentlemen grew alarmed and a short but sharp quarrel arose between those who "in plain speech said they would ride over the water and issue into the town" and the friends and servants of the three men in the village who feared that such a breach of promise might slay their friends and masters.[60]

The argument burned itself out with no action taken, and the waiting continued until one or two of the more militant members of the party rode down to the riverside and used their staffs to gauge the depth of the water as the tide rolled in. This action put the three gentlemen in the village in great peril. Watchers on the bridge raised the alarm, and some of the rebels angrily charged Dennys, Pollard, and Yarde with bad faith. Whether the men who approached the river did this on their own account or on Carew's order is not known for certain. Other accounts of the incident, perhaps reflecting the anger against the Carews preserved in local folk memory, assign responsibility, either directly or indirectly, to Sir Peter. Without giving her source, Frances Rose-Troup, in her 1913 study of the western rising, identified Richard Carwithen, a servant of Sir Peter's, as the man who probed the water.[61] Froude told an imaginatively embellished account of the incident, claiming that Sir Peter and Sir Gawen were themselves responsible for this alarm, riding forward to probe the mud with their lances in search of a way to take their horses across the water and around the bridge. Only the refusal of his men to accompany him prevented Sir Peter from attacking the village "at all hazards."[62] Such impatience for action on the part of Carew is certainly believable; it calls to mind his dangerous willingness in 1545 to engage a flotilla of French galleys without waiting for the rest of the English fleet. It is impossible now to determine whether or not Sir Peter was himself responsible for the incident. In any event, the alarm forced the three gentlemen in the village to scurry over the bridge and back to their restless companions. Sir Peter immediately demanded to know what had been concluded and how their negotiations had fared. The three men gave the laconic answer "well enough," and would say nothing more about their day's work during the two-mile ride back into Exeter.

Once within the walls of the city, the party took a late supper at the Mermaid Inn.[63] When the servants had retired from the chamber, Sir Peter again demanded to know what had transpired in Clyst St. Mary. The envoys reported that the commons agreed to end their disorders if the king and Council would leave the Church as it had stood at the death of Henry VIII, making no further alterations in religion until the king came of full age. This was merely a restatement of the original Sampford Courtenay demands and represented no change at all in the rebels' position. Instead of doing their duty and persuading the rebels to disarm and disperse, the three gentlemen had apparently spent the day negotiating the Crown's religious policy, a matter quite beyond the scope or authority of anyone in the room. The envoys' shocking report momentarily threw Sir Peter into "a great dump," but he quickly recovered and with Sir Piers Courtenay, the sheriff of Devon, "openly, sharply, and in plain terms inveighed against them for their slender or rather sinister dealings in so weighty a cause." Froude portrayed an enraged Carew branding the timid citizens of Exeter "traitors and poltroons" and threatening to call out every gentleman in the county to "slash the rebel dogs into their senses."[64] Froude was perhaps overly dramatic in his descriptions, but the account captures the anger and frustration that must have attended Carew's realisation of his utter failure to accomplish the task he was sent out to do. Rather then suppress the rebels, the gentlemen had actually given the rebels heart. The protector and Council would not be pleased. Foreshadowing the treatment the Council would mete out to him, Carew charged Pollard with allowing the rising to get out of hand in the first place through his equally ineffective actions at Sampford Courtney. Some suspicion of where Pollard and Dennys' true sympathies actually lay was also voiced. Pollard and Dennys sought to excuse themselves as best they could, and then tried to shift blame for intensification of the rising onto Carew and his mishandling of the meeting at Crediton.[65]

Amid discord and rancor, the meeting broke up, and "every man shifted for himself, some one way and some another way." Word of the disarray among the gentlemen in the Mermaid was somehow smuggled out of the city to the rebels that very night. This news and the outcome of the Clyst St. Mary conference emboldened the rebels to blockade all the roads out of Exeter and to entrench themselves at various points around the city. Many of the gentlemen from the Mermaid who tried to leave the city over the next few days were captured and, like Walter Raleigh, held prisoners in various chapels and churches for the duration of the rebellion. Other gentlemen avoided capture only by taking to the woods or otherwise hiding themselves until the commotion was past. Only a few gentlemen stayed in Exeter, for the mayor had made it known that the city's food supply was insufficient to accommodate a large company of gentlemen and their retinues.[66]

In the early morning of Monday 24 June, Sir Peter Carew left the Mermaid and rode east. Finding a road that had not yet been blocked, Sir Peter galloped for Hinton St. George, the Somerset seat of the Paulet family. Here Carew met Lord John Russell, the lord privy seal, who was newly arrived from London with a lord lieutenant's commission and the protector's typically vague instructions for ending the rebellion. Carew had apparently kept the government informed of his progress, or rather lack thereof, for Russell's appointment was clearly occasioned by the government's knowledge of the course of events in the West since Sir Peter's arrival there. Others had also been keeping the government informed of events, for on 26 June the Council responded to letters of 24 June from Sir Thomas Dennys and several other Devon justices who had witnessed the acrimony at the Mermaid on the previous night. Before 29 June, a messenger named

Stowell brought the Council a series of letters from the West that detailed "the whole state and proceedings of the busy people of Devonshire."[67] Carew's ride to Hinton St. George, rather than straight to London, also indicates a foreknowledge on his part of Russell's appointment and mission.

Russell's instructions, dated 24 June, reiterated Somerset's hope that the use of persuasion could prevent the need for force; if Russell found the people "out of frame and not in such order of obedience as were convenient," he was to try to "bring the people with gentleness to such conformity as appertaineth by travail and gentle persuasions." This was simply a restatement of the policy Carew had failed so completely to implement. Tales of Carew's actions and rumors of his intentions had only fed the flame he was trying to put out. In response, Russell's instructions urged him to make special efforts to track down the starters and spreaders of rumors and to charge parents with ensuring that their children and servants were kept quiet and occupied.[68] Rumor and fear were turning many an anxious parishioner into an ardent rebel.

At Hinton, Carew reported the latest developments to Russell, including the frustratingly ineffective conference at Clyst St. Mary and the growing rebel threat to Exeter. The two men agreed that Russell should move westward with his force to Honiton, from which an attempt, if practicable, could be made to reach Exeter. Honiton as a base of operations was probably suggested by Carew, whose home at Mohun's Ottery was only a few miles to the northeast up the valley of the Otter. Carew likely convinced Russell of the futility of Somerset's hope that the use of persuasion could eliminate the need for force. Certainly they discussed the lack of available resources to quell the spreading rebellion, for Carew carried to the Council Russell's request for more men and money.[69] Having planned his next steps, Russell dispatched Carew to London to report to the king and Council.[70]

Once in London, Carew came first before the king, to whom he described the events in Devon of the previous week. The king was greatly grieved by the disloyalty of his subjects and the apparent necessity of giving up for the time being the attempt to subdue Scotland. Edward then commanded Carew to make a full report to the Council. The ensuing scene in the Council chamber was, if anything, more tense and acrimonious than the angry meeting in the Mermaid Inn. Somerset, when he had heard Carew's account, was more aggrieved than the king with the disruption to the Scottish plans. Perceiving "that great troubles were like to ensue" from the rebellion,[71] he angrily charged Carew with causing the commotion through his mishandling of the attempted conference at Crediton. Significantly, Carew stoutly defended himself not by blaming the burning of the barns on Sir Hugh Pollard's servant—upon whom Hooker laid responsibility—but by arguing the necessity of the action under the circumstances. In other words, the military situation demanded it. What's more, Carew now produced the commission given to him at his departure from court. Because this document was written in the king's own hand and given under the king's privy seal, Carew claimed good warrant from the king himself for everything he had done. Lord Riche, the lord chancellor, dismissed the commission "as no sufficient warrant" because it had not passed the great seal and declared that Carew by right should "be hanged for his doings." Never one to back away from a challenge, Sir Peter

answered so stoutly and charged the Duke so deeply that in the end he was willed to return into the country being promised sufficient help both of men and money should be with speed sent down into the country. And to this effect he had both the king's and the Council's letters unto the Lord Privy seal [Russell].[72]

Having already been threatened with the rope for acting without proper authority, Carew determined to take no further chances in this regard when he returned to the troubled West Country.

In his biography of Sir Peter, Hooker somewhat softened his description of Carew's reply to Somerset and Riche. Finding the words directed at him to be "very sharp, and touching the quick," Carew asked pardon to give answer to the charges, and was granted leave to do so. Carew then proceeded

in such pithy manner, and not without a reasonable stoutness, to answer the duke and Lord Chancellor, and also both satisfy the king and council, that he was well allowed and commended for the same; and, in the end, according to his petition, order was taken that both men and money should be sent with speed to the Lord Privy Seal, and he willed to return with speed into the country, and there to follow the service for the repression of the rebellion.[73]

This account is consistent with Hooker's usual portrayal of Sir Peter in the "Life": a strong but courtly gentleman able always to turn initial ill will into commendation. The mention here of Carew's petition for reinforcements to Russell's army confirms that Carew and the lord privy seal had discussed the need for greater military strength to crush the rising at their brief Hinton St. George meeting. However, Hooker made no mention here of Carew's demand for letters from king and Council to document both his own reappointment and the government's promise to reinforce Russell. The angrier exchange described in the *Description*, followed as it is by the pointed demand for sufficient warrant for future actions and promises, seems to better capture Sir Peter's personality and the tension of the times and is probably the more accurate account. Both accounts indicate the reluctant abandonment of the pacification policy for the "repression of the rebellion." The failure of Somerset's desired policy, and the detrimental impact of that failure on his Scottish plans, lay at the root of the protector's anger with Carew, who made both a convenient and likely scapegoat for the collapse of Somerset's plans. The high standing Sir Peter had enjoyed at court almost continuously since 1532 was, despite his reappointment by the Council, seriously jeopardised.

Upon returning to Devon, probably about 29 or 30 June, Carew found Russell still in Honiton, barred from proceeding any further toward Exeter by blocked roads and alarming rumors of growing rebel numbers. The welcome letters and promises of speedy resupply that Carew brought only strengthened Russell's determination to go no further without reinforcement. For the next few weeks, Russell divided his time between Honiton and Mohun's Ottery, awaiting in vain the fulfillment of the government's pledges. On 2 July, the rebels completed their encirclement of Exeter and laid the city under siege. For the next month, they sought by every device, including the clandestine activities of sympathesizers within the walls, to persuade or force the city to capitulate. Hooker, who was himself trapped within the besieged town, described in detail the various rebel stratagems.[74]

While Exeter suffered the rough attention of the rebels, Russell waited forlornly at Honiton, seemingly ignored by both the rebels and the government. His position grew more precarious every day.

> But having long looked for the same [the promised reinforcement] in vain he was daily more and more forsaken of such of the common people as who at the first served and offered their service unto him; and having but a very small guard about him he lived in more fear than he was feared; for the Rebels daily increased and his company decreased and shrank away and he not altogether assured of them which remained.[75]

Given this tense situation, it was not surprising that rumors of the fall of Exeter and a new rising behind him in Salisbury convinced Russell to take the panicky advice of several Dorset gentlemen to retreat eastward to a safer position in Dorsetshire. When word of Russell's withdrawal from Honiton reached him at Mohun's Ottery, Carew at once took horse and furiously pursued the retreating lord lieutenant. He caught up with Russell on the Black Down, where ensued a long and animated conference between the two men. Carew vigorously rejected the arguments of Russell's Dorset advisors, and declared to Russell

> what inconveniences were like to ensue to the encouraging of the enemy, the undoing of the whole country, and the great dishonour unto himself, if he should now leave the country, and give the enemy scope and liberty to go forward.[76]

At last, persuaded that Carew was correct, Russell changed his mind and returned with Sir Peter to Honiton. Here, the lord privy seal remained, except for one night in nearby Ottery St. Mary, spending his days "in more fear than peril."[77]

A long July passed with Russell continually demanding more troops and supplies from the government before he could act, while Somerset constantly demanded more action from the lord privy seal with the troops and supplies at hand. An indication of the government's attitude toward Sir Peter appears in a 12 July letter from Somerset to Russell. The protector responded to an earlier letter from Russell in which the lord privy seal had asked that Sir Peter and Sir Gawen Carew be named his councilors to assist and advise him in crushing the rebellion. Somerset, without either care or enthusiasm, left the matter in Russell's hands, telling him that "we refer it to yourself to choose whom you think mete to be called unto you for advice and for understanding of the state of the country."[78] Since Somerset considered the Carews responsible for "the state of the country," who better for Russell to turn to for an understanding of it. Clearly, however, the Protector was in no mood to grant anything to the Carews.

In the last week of the month, on about 27 or 28 July, the rebels at last took notice of Russell; "understanding of his distressed state," they moved a force toward Honiton to try his strength and perhaps also his will. By this time, Russell had received reinforcements in both men and money, including a troop of Italian mercenaries—the first time in centuries that an

English government had deployed foreign troops against Englishmen. When the rebels were come to the Otter bridges at Feniton, about three miles west of Honiton, Russell consulted with Sir Peter and Sir Gawen as to the best course of action. The Carews typically advised an immediate attack, and, after much discussion, the decision was made to march toward the rebels "and give the onset upon them." Accordingly, "without further delay or much talk it was done out of hand," and the next morning Russell and the Carews came upon what must have been by now a familiar sight for Sir Peter and Sir Gawen—a barricaded and defended bridge. Russell was forced to secure the bridge by "bold adventuring," which translated into seizing it by sheer weight of numbers while artillery swept the other bank to hold back the rebels massed in the meadow just beyond. Several of the company were wounded in the "adventuring" on the bridge, including Sir Gawen, who, for his undoubted boldness, took an arrow in the arm.[79] Sir Gawen's last appearance in Hooker's account had been during the long wait outside Clyst St. Mary while the three gentlemen conferred so ineffectually inside. He did not apparently accompany his nephew on the stormy trip to London, but his presence at Feniton indicates that he escaped Exeter before the siege cut the city off from the outside. It is likely that he escaped the city with Sir Peter on the morning of 24 June and stayed with Russell at Hinton St. George and Honiton through the long summer.

Once the bridge was secured, Russell's men poured across to attack the rebels on the opposite bank. Locals can still today point out to curious travelers the site of the bloody meadow beside the Otter near Feniton. The battle in this meadow was fought with "good store of blows and bloodshed." The rebels were at last driven off and Russell's soldiers had just given themselves over to spoil when some 200 Cornish rebels suddenly set upon them again. Caught unawares, many of the spoilers "paid dearly for their wares." Russell and Carew quickly marshaled their troops, but the fight was for a time "very sharp and cruel, for the Cornish men were very lusty and fully bent to fight out the matter." The rebels were at last put again to flight, leaving behind, by Hooker's probably inflated estimate, about 300 dead in the meadow for the two engagements. Russell's men pursued for about three miles, and the normally cautious lord privy seal exhibited a Carew-like determination to boldly follow the rebels all the way to Exeter. This boldness proved short-lived, however, for Russell's fool, Joll, rode up from Honiton in a panic with a report that all the church bells to the east were ringing the alarm and calling together the men of the countryside to congregate and assail the government forces from behind. The sharp fights in the meadow and the surprise attack of the Cornish men gave this report credibility, and Russell withdrew to Honiton.[80]

In Honiton, Russell was again reinforced. Being now "of a very good comfort and courage," Russell wrote to the mayor of Exeter to tell him the city's deliverance was at hand. On Saturday 3 August, Russell, Carew, and a force now in excess of 1,000 men left Honiton and marched toward Exeter. Russell's army camped that night beside a mill near Clyst St. Mary, the site of Carew's failed conference. Rebels from the village attacked the camp next morning, but were driven off. Russell and Carew then attacked the village itself, where, according to Hooker, the startling number of 6,000 rebels had gathered. Carew was determined to enter the village that had so far denied him all access. An assault of the village began, but broke up in panic when Sir Thomas Pomeroy, one of the rebel captains, having hidden "himself in a furse close" until the attackers passed by, suddenly popped up and ordered his trumpeter and drummer to sound out. Russell's men once again retreated in the fear of being suddenly attacked from behind. This precipitous retreat allowed the defenders to rush out of the village and haul off some of Russell's supply wagons. Realizing they had been deceived, Russell and Carew prepared another assault. Russell was informed that every building in the village was packed with armed men, and that the only safe way to proceed was by the example of Credition, that is, setting the entire village on fire. This plan was carried out, but instead of fleeing, as they had done at Crediton, the rebels gathered in the center of the village and continued to resist. Many on both sides were slain in the fighting before the rebels were at last defeated. Hooker wrote that about 1,000 rebels were dead, with a large number burned to death in the fire, and several of Russell's gentlemen, including Sir William Francis, were slain in the assault.[81]

Passing through the village, Carew now found himself at the other end of the bridge that had defied him earlier. The tide was once again flowing and a way had again to be found over the rushing waters that Sir Peter's party had probed so earnestly a month and a half earlier. John Yarde, a local gentleman, led Russell and a party of horse that likely included Sir Peter across the river, but the bulk of the army could not cross until the bridge had been cleared of rebels and obstructions. Russell promised 400 crowns to anyone who could knock out the rebel cannon that commanded the approaches to the bridge. This drew an immediate response from one of his men who dashed forward "more respecting the gain than forecasting the peril." The gunner on the bridge killed his rash attacker with one shot, but the resulting need to reload allowed one of Russell's party on the opposite bank to ride up to the gunner and shoot him. The bridge was now quickly cleared of obstructions and Russell's men passed over to the other side. As night descended, death came once more when Lord Grey, another of Russell's captains, reported seeing a great company of rebels marching through the twilight from the direction of Woodbury. To best meet this new threat, it was decided to kill the large number of rebel prisoners taken in the day's fighting. Hundreds of men died to enhance the chances of meeting an attack that never came. Whatever Grey had seen, it was not an attacking force of rebels. Finally, 4 August came to an end; it had been a bloody Sunday.[82]

Fighting resumed on Monday 5 August, as the rebels about Exeter rushed forward to halt Russell's advance. So "great was the slaughter and cruel. . . the fight" that Grey reportedly said he "never in all the wars that he had been did know the like." The rebels were defeated again, and Russell's army spent the night in Topsham, the village in which Walter Raleigh had experienced his narrow escape from enraged rebels back in June. Word of their defeat robbed the remaining rebels of their courage, and the siege of Exeter melted away during the night. Local gentlemen, including many of those who had weeks earlier slipped so fearfully away from the Mermaid, suddenly found themselves freed from imprisonment and made their way to the walls of Exeter to give the town the first word of its deliverance.

Early on the morning of Tuesday 6 August, Russell, accompanied by the Carews, came with his army to Exeter. Russell stayed in the town about 10 days, "rewarding the good and punishing the evil." Among those receiving rewards were Sir Peter and Sir Gawen Carew.[83] To Sir Peter, Russell gave the lands in Devon and Cornwall of John Wynslade, a Cornish gentleman who had thrown in his lot with the rebels. Wynslade's lands had a yearly value of £73 14s 10d. The king confirmed the grant in May 1550.[84] Sir Gawen did even better, receiving the lands of Humphrey Arundell of Cornwall, one of the most active rebel leaders. Manors and lordships in Devon and Cornwall worth £108 18s 8d per year came into Sir Gawen's possession as a reward for his service against the rebels. The king confirmed Sir Gawen's grant in March 1550.[85]

Had Somerset remained in power, the king's confirmation of Russell's generous grants to the Carews might never have occurred. Although Sir Peter and his uncle had secured the favor and gratitude of Russell, they had fallen out of favor with the lord protector, who continued to blame their heavy-handedness for aggravating the western rising. But Somerset's hostility was not as devastating to Sir Peter as it might appear at first glance. The unsuccessful rebellions in the West and in Norfolk caused a successful rising in the Council. Blamed for a misguided leniency that fostered the summer rebellions, Somerset was deposed and imprisoned in the Tower in October by the men who had taken the field to rectify his mistakes. The earl of Warwick became the new power in the Council and behind the young king, and Warwick was well acquainted with the Carews and the ways they could be best employed to serve the state. Thus, by the spring of 1550, a change in leadership of the Council had restored Sir Peter and his uncle to favor at court.

The evil name Sir Peter had won among the western commons was likewise balanced by the good will he won from the city of Exeter. During his days in Exeter after 6 August, Russell appointed Carew to an informal council of trusted gentlemen charged with providing advice and assistance to the city magistrates as they wrestled with the aftermath of the siege. In his letter to the mayor, Russell identified lack of such good advice from the local gentry as the main reason the city had suffered a siege in the first place.[86] Carew was already familiar to the city fathers, having borrowed £40 from them earlier in the year. Alderman Griffin Ameredyth, whose name appeared frequently during this period in financial and land transactions involving Sir Peter, was part of the arrangements made for repaying the loan. The city now granted its new advisor a pension of £2 per year for life and a hogshead of wine at the delivery of the patent, "for his travail and good will to the city and for his counsel hereafter."[87] From 1549 until the end of the reign, Sir Peter continued to advise the Exeter magistrates and to exert a growing influence on the city administration. For instance, in June 1550, he wrote to the mayor from Mohun's Ottery recommending one Mr. Sture "as a continual councilor," and asking rather high-handedly what remuneration the city would give Sture.[88] Sir Peter and his uncle, now connected securely to Russell, who was himself securely connected to the new Council leadership, were about to become important and influential figures in Exeter.

But first the lingering embers of the rebellion had to be stamped out. During his stay in Exeter, Russell shook off the timid lethargy of the summer and set to work with a will restoring order to the city and the region. He was "very sharp and severe" with captains and ringleaders of the rebellion, but "pitiful and merciful" to those who merely followed, and "did daily pardon infinite numbers" of them. Sir Peter and Sir Gawen apparently remained with Russell in Exeter during this period, for both set out for Sampford Courtenay with the lord privy seal on about 16 August. Word had arrived in Exeter that the remaining rebels were gathered in the village under the leadership of Humphrey Arundell, who was perhaps not yet aware that his lands had just been handed over to Sir Gawen. These obstinate rebels, fumed Hooker, were "fully bent to maintain their quarrel and to abide the battle."[89] Russell marched forth boldly now with his full power. On Saturday 17 August, Russell found the rebels "strongly encamped" before the village. He sent Herbert and Lord Grey with part of the army, including a troop of Italian mercenaries and a number of cannon, to assail the camp, which they did so effectively that the rebels soon fled toward the village. But Arundell had one trick left. As the pursuit of the retreating rebels began, and while Russell was himself still in the rear conducting forward the supply carriages, Arundell led the bulk of his force in a surprise assault on the rear of Grey and Herbert's men. This sudden turn of events, wrote Russell, "wrought such fear in the hearts of our men as we wished our power a great deal more." Leaving Herbert to pursue alone, Grey had to turn part of their joint force and meet Arundell's onslaught. This rapid redeployment apparently unnerved the rebels, for the fight with Arundell degenerated into a mere artillery duel, which, nonetheless, allowed Herbert time to drive the rebels he was pursuing into "plain flight." With this wing of the rebel force eliminated, Russell could concentrate his forces against Arundell, whose men "fled without one blow" when they saw the entire royal army coming against them. 700 rebels were cut down in the pursuit and many more were captured; Russell believed even greater execution would have occurred "had not the night come on so fast." The back of the rebellion was at last broken.[90]

Russell, Sir Peter, and the rest of the royal captains spent the night on horseback. In the morning, word came that Arundell had fled to Launceston in Cornwall, where, in his desperation, he tried to incite the townspeople to murder the gentlemen they held prisoner. But cooler heads among the townspeople, understanding that Arundell's destruction could purchase their salvation, freed the gentlemen and then assisted them in seizing and confining Arundell and five or six other rebel leaders who were with him. Upon this news, wrote Russell, "I. . .incontinently sent both Mr. Carews with a good band to keep the town in stay."[91] Within a few days, Russell followed the Carews to Launceston, taking Arundell off their hands and sending Sir Peter in pursuit of a remaining band of rebels said to be in flight to the east. Carew and Sir Hugh Paulet, "with a great company attending upon them" caught this band in Somerset near the village of King's Weston. Carew and Paulet quickly subdued the rebels, taking their leader, a gentleman with the ominously prophetic named of Coffin, back to Exeter as a prisoner.[92]

The rebellion in the West now faded into horrid memory, as men like Sir Anthony Kingston, whom Russell appointed provost marshall for Cornwall, fanned out from Exeter seizing and executing hundreds of rebels in both counties. Priests and village leaders suffered particularly. This aftermath, which offered the surviving rebels such sights as the popular vicar of St. Thomas in Exeter hanging from his church tower attired in his popish vestments,[93] cemented among the western commons a hatred and sullen distrust of the region's pro-government gentlemen, and especially of the Carews. While seemingly enhanced with the government by the outcome of the rebellion, Sir Peter's influence in the West Country was greatly weakened among the commons by their perception of his role in putting down the rebellion. That role was to earn Sir Peter some immediate rewards and cause him many future troubles.

1   Hooker, "Life," pp. 44-45.

2   Ibid., pp. 45-46.

3   John Husee to Lord Lisle, 3 January 1538, *Lisle Letters*, V, #1086.

4   *Lisle Letters*, V, p. 11.

5   Sir Thomas Heneage to Thomas Cromwell, 17 April 1539, PRO, SP1/131/161; also LP, XIV(1), 790.

6   "Sir Gilbert Tailboys," *DNB*, p. 342.

7   John Husee to Lord Lisle and to Lady Lisle, 26 April 1539, *Lisle Letters*, V, #1394, #1395.

8   John Husee to Lady Lisle, 15 May 1539, *Lisle Letters*, V, #1414.

9   *Lisle Letters*, V, pp. 12-13.

10 LP, XVI, 19.

11 *Lisle Letters*, V, p. 13.

12 LP, XIV(2), 572 (3ii).

13 Ibid., 677.

14 Ibid., 572 (3v).

15 Ibid., XVI, 380, 1489.

16 Ibid., XVII, 312.

17 Ibid., XVIII(1), 802 (52).

18 Hooker, "Life," p. 44.

19 D.S. Chambers, ed. *Faculty Office Registers 1534-1549* (Oxford: Clarendon Press, 1966), p. 289.

20 Hooker, "Life," p. 46.

21 J.G. Nichols, ed., *Literary Remains of King Edward the Sixth*, vol. I (London, 1857), p. ccc.

22 Hooker, "Life," pp. 46-47.

23 Ibid., p. 47.

24 LP, XXI(2), 472, 773 ii(3).

25 CPR, Edward VI, vol. I, 26 May 1547, p. 82.

26 Ibid., vol. V, 27 November 1547, p. 317.

27 Bindoff, House of Commons, I, p. 68.

28 Journal of the House of Commons, 1547-1628, (London, 1803), p. 11.

29 See T.E. Tomlins, ed., The Statutes of the Realm, vol. IV (London: The Record Commission, 1810-1822), pp. 65-66 for the act concerning the eating of flesh, p. 67 for the act concerning clerical celebacy, and pp. 37-38 for the Act of Uniformity.

30 Council Instructions to West Country Vice Admirals, PRO, SP10/4/39; Lord Admiral Seymour to Sir Peter Carew, 9 August 1548, PRO, SP10/4/40.

31 Deposition of Katherine Ashley, 4 February 1549, Cal.SP Dom., Edward VI (London: HMSO, 1992), #196.

32 W.K. Jordan, Edward VI: The Young King: The Protectorship of the Duke of Somerset (Cambridge, Mass.: Harvard University Press, 1968), pp. 368-82.

33 W.K. Jordan, ed., The Chronicle and Political Papers of King Edward VI (Ithaca, N.Y.: Cornell University Press, 1966), pp. 10-11.

34 For the 11 April proclamation, see Paul Hughes and James Larkin, eds., Tudor Royal Proclamations, vol. I (New Haven: Yale University Press, 1964), pp. 451-53. See also Snow, Holinshed's Chronicles, III, pp. 916-17.

35 Hughes and Larkin, Proclamations, I, pp. 461-62.

36 Hooker, Description, p. 56.

37 Hooker, Description, p. 59; see also Snow, Holinshed's Chronicles, III, p. 940.

38 Hooker, "Life," p. 47.

39 Nicholas Pocock, ed., Troubles Connected with the Prayer Book of 1549 (London: Camden Society, 1884), p. 5.

40 Hooker, Description, p. 59.

41 Hooker, "Life," p. 53.

42 Frances Rose-Troup, *The Western Rebellion of 1549* (London: Smith, Elder, & Co., 1913), p. 426.

43 Hooker, *Description*, p. 55.

44 Ibid., p. 55, 57.

45 Ibid., pp. 56-58.

46 Ibid., pp. 58-59.

47 Hughes and Larkin, *Proclamations*, I, pp. 462-64.

48 Hooker, *Description*, p. 60.

49 Ibid., pp. 60-61.

50 Ibid., p. 61.

51 Robert Lacey, *Sir Walter Ralegh* (New York: Atheneum, 1973), p. 5.

52 Hooker, *Description*, p. 62.

53 Ibid., pp. 62-63. Hooker probably heard about the conversation in the country lane from Raleigh, with whom he was well acquainted. How he learned about what the woman said in the church at Clyst St. Mary is another question.

54 Ibid., p. 63.

55 Rose Troup, *Western Rebellion*, p. 152.

56 Hooker, *Description*, pp. 63-64.

57 Ibid., p. 63.

58 Hooker, "Life," pp. 111-12.

59 A.L. Rowse, *Tudor Cornwall: Portrait of a Society*, 2nd ed. (New York: Charles Scribner's Sons, 1969), p. 213.

60 Hooker, *Description*, p. 64.

61 Rose-Troup, *Western Rebellion*, p. 149.

62 J.A. Froude, *History of England from the Fall of Wolsey to the Death of Elizabeth* (New York: Charles Scribner's Sons, 1881), p. 169.

63 Rose-Troup, *Western Rebellion*, p. 150.

64 Froude, *History of England*, p. 169.

65 Hooker, *Description*, p. 65.

66 Ibid., pp. 65-66.

67 Pocock, *Troubles*, pp. 12, 15.

68 Ibid., pp. 9-10.

69 Hooker, "Life," p. 52.

70 Hooker, *Description*, p. 81.

71 Hooker, "Life," p. 51.

72 Hooker, *Description*, p. 81.

73 Hooker, "Life," pp. 51-52.

74 Hooker, *Description*, p. 82. For Hooker's account of life in Exeter during the siege, see *Description*, pp. 66-81.

75 Ibid., p. 82.

76 Hooker, "Life," p. 52.

77 Hooker, *Description*, p. 82.

78 Pocock, *Troubles*, p. 26.

79 Hooker, *Description*, pp. 83-84.

80 Ibid., p. 84.

81 Ibid., pp. 85-87.

82 Ibid., pp. 87-89.

83 Ibid., pp. 90-91.

84 *CPR*, Edward VI, vol. III, 21 May 1550, pp. 406-07.

85 Ibid., 5 March 1550, p. 340.

86 HMC, *Report on the Records of the City of Exeter* (London, 1916), Letter 20, p. 21.

87 Wallace T. MacCaffrey, *Exeter, 1540-1640: The Growth of an English County Town* (Cambridge, Mass.: Harvard University Press, 1958), p. 212.

88 *Calendar of the Archives of the City of Exeter*, DRO, #25.

89 Hooker, *Description*, p. 94.

90 John, Lord Russell to Duke of Somerset, 23 August 1549, BL, Harleian MS 523, f. 51.

91 Ibid.

92 Hooker, *Description*, p. 950

93 Ibid., p. 94.

CHAPTER 6

THE NORTHUMBERLAND REGIME

In the years following the Prayer Book Rebellion, Sir Peter Carew weakened his standing among his fellow western gentry by displaying an arrogance and high-handedness that signaled clearly the position and influence he believed himself to hold with the government of Warwick, who in October 1551 was created duke of Northumberland. This loss of influence with the western gentry was to prove an altogether more serious matter for Carew than his low standing with the western commons. When the accession of Mary deprived him of the support of a friendly government, Carew found himself isolated and utterly unsupported when he became the rebel and tried to lead his western colleagues against the new regime. But in 1550, as Carew began to flaunt his growing power and position, these events lay in the future.

Several examples of Sir Peter's standing in the county in the second half of Edward's reign and his abrupt and overbearing use of that standing can be cited. The borough of Dartmouth archives for the reign of Edward VI speak of a bitter dispute at this time between the borough and Carew. The mayor, bailiffs, and burgesses of Dartmouth complained to the Council of their expulsion from Dartmouth Castle by Carew, who immediately had new locks and keys made to prevent their re-entry.[1] The Carew family had long held the manor of Southton in Dartmouth and the lordship of Dartmouth Castle, but Sir Peter seemed to be carrying the exercise of his lordship beyond its traditional bounds. A second petition to the Council from the Dartmouth magistrates complained of Carew's seizure of the town bulwark and chain, and explained the difficulties the town faced in regaining possession.

[F]orasmuch as the said Sir Peter Carewe is a man of worship within the said county and greatly friended and allied there and that therefore it may chance if your said orators should attempt to put him out of possession of the said fort that in doing thereof they might happen not only to break your grace's peace but also some manslaughter or worse inconvenience might ensue thereby.[2]

The town prayed the Council to send letters of injunction under the privy seal to Carew directing him to give up the fort. Although the outcome of the dispute is unknown, the Council evidently made some investigation of the matter, for a series of interrogatories concerning the bulwark were prepared by the town to be put to Carew.[3] The magistrates' belief that "manslaughter or worse" would be required to foil Sir Peter's purposes is a jarring testimony to the reputation Sir Peter's manner and behavior were winning for him in the West Country at this time.

Dartmouth was not the only town with which Carew became embroiled. In 1552, a dispute between Sir Peter and the city of Exeter grew so intense that the Council had to step in and impose a settlement. The trouble actually started when servants of Sir Peter's uncle, George Carew, the dean of Exeter, got into a fight with several city officers. Sir Peter seems to had injected himself into the fray on behalf of his uncle's men. Carew's typically angry intervention only retarded reconciliation and escalated tensions. The Council commanded both Sir Peter and his uncle and the city to make peace and ordered Dean George's servants to apologize for their behavior.[4] On 23 July 1552, the Council sent a letter to Sir Peter requiring him to remain in friendship with the townspeople of Exeter despite the recent jar that had occurred between him and them. This letter may refer to the dispute arising from the actions of Dean George's servants, although its reference to the citizens of Exeter having been tried and found at fault in the matter seems to indicate a new dispute or the original disagreement taken to a new phase. A letter was also sent to the mayor and people of Exeter willing them to continue in friendship with Sir Peter. The Council marveled that the city should make such "grievous complaints" of Carew, since they seemed to have so small an occasion to do so.[5] Whether these letters represented a new complaint, or merely an extension of the old, they illustrate Carew's penchant for abrupt action and the use of force to handle disputes and achieve desired ends.

The best example of Carew's arrogance and sharp dealing during this period appears in the records of a suit brought before Star Chamber by Robert Warren, administrator of the estate of the late John Lane. The records of the case are undated, but the approximate time of the suit can be determined by reference to the sheriff of Devon who served the accompanying writs, Sir Thomas Dennys. Dennys served eight times as sheriff of Devon, starting back in 1508, six years before Sir Peter's father first held the post. However, only Dennys' last two tenures, 1550 and 1554, could be possible years for Warren's suit. Since Sir Peter was to spend almost the whole of 1554 in exile on the continent, 1550 is the logical date for this incident. In his petition to the king and Council in Star Chamber, Warren rehearsed the failure of his attempts to recover £100 borrowed by Sir William Carew, Sir Peter's father, from John Lane in 1521. After Sir William's death, Warren demanded payment first from Sir William's wife and then from Sir Peter when he became his father's heir in 1545. When Carew utterly refused to pay, Warren obtained a writ of *extendo facias* against Sir Peter's lands, goods, and chattels. The sheriff of Devon, Sir Thomas Dennys, to whom the writ was directed, begged Warren to go no further with the suit until he or his attorneys had more fully discussed the matter with Carew. Respecting the good will Dennys bore for his friend's son, Warren agreed. Carew, however, proved "obstinate against all reason and conscience and would not fall into any reasonable agreement." Warren's writ in the meantime expired, forcing him to obtain another. A jury was finally impaneled in the case in Exeter Castle during the Easter sessions.[6]

The extent of Sir Peter's influence in the county became clear when the matter came before the jury. The 17 freeholders on the panel, being "more afeared of the displeasure of the said Sir Peter than regarding justice or their duty and obedience," then and there "before the face and body of the whole shire by the sinister means of the said Sir Peter utterly refused to pass upon the said charge." When Undersheriff Gaverocke threatened "to set fines upon any of their heads" if the jurors failed to observe their oaths and do their duty, the panel astonished him by still refusing to deal in the case, no matter what fines he tried to impose. The jurors absolutely refused to proceed until they had spoken to Carew and understood his pleasure in the case, whether he wished them to pass on the matter or not. Whereupon, recited the horrified Warren, the entire jury marched out of the castle to begin a diligent search of Exeter for Sir Peter, "to the great admiration of all who beheld them and to the evil example" of all the king's subjects in Devon. After conferring privately with Carew, the panel returned and asked to see the recognizance Sir William Carew had entered into before the mayor of Exeter in 1521 and a true copy of the inquisition taken on Sir William's death. According to Warren, the inquisition proved that Sir William's manors of Mohun's Ottery, Stoke Fleming, Churchill, Monckton, Ashwater, Mamhead, Weston Perverell, and Golmeton, among others, were extendible for the debt. These estates, which the inquisition of 1537 valued at almost £160 per year, were the heart of the ancient Carew lands; it is no wonder Sir Peter did not want possession of them transferred to Warren by the operation of the writ.[7]

Warren claimed that he presented the inquest with sufficient evidence to prove that Sir William was possessed of the aforementioned lands at the time the recognizance was made; what's more, the jury knew of their own special knowledge that this was true. Carew did not and, indeed, could not show anything to the contrary. Nonetheless, the jury delivered themselves of an astounding verdict; they found that Sir William Carew was not seised of any property in Devon at the time the recognizance was made, or at any time in his life. The Carew family had been land-holders in Devon for over 250 years, and every person in Exeter Castle on that day knew it. The jurymen absolutely refused to reconsider their verdict, and then added insult to injury by refusing to return to Warren the copy of the inquisition shown to them as evidence.[8]

Because no jury in Devon would find for Warren against Carew by reason of Carew's "power and friendship," nor for the same reasons punish the jurymen for their untrue verdict, Warren found himself without remedy at common law. He therefore requested the king and Council to summon Carew to appear before them in Star Chamber and to compel Carew to pay the original £100 debt as well as Warren's costs and damages. Fearing that even in London Carew's "power and friendship" might be too strong, Warren sweetened his suit by reminding Northumberland's impecunious government that Sir Peter probably still owed a large sum to the Crown as well. In November 1514, Sir William Carew had appeared before Wolsey to pledge the manors of Mohun's Ottery, Stoke Fleming, Churchill, and Monckton, which were valued at Sir William's death at £71 per year, against payment of the sum of £1040 owed by Sir William to the king. None other than Sir Thomas Dennys had recorded the agreement of February 1515 whereby Henry VIII was to have 100 marks per year from these manors until the full £1040 had been paid. In his complaint, Warren assumed that this debt to the Crown must have been satisfied and that the estates were now extendible for the debt to Lane. He nonetheless requested that the Council look into matter, and call in any of Carew's Crown debt that might still be outstanding, thereby freeing the manors to be extended under the writ for satisfaction of his claim.[9]

Warren's complaint most likely caused the reordering of the Carew family's Crown debts that was finalised by patent on 16 December 1552. The patent rehearses the complicated history of these debts since the time of Sir Edmund Carew, Sir Peter's grandfather. The late Sir

Edmund owed Henry VIII £1400. Three obligations found among the records of the treasurer of the chamber indicated that Sir Edmund, his second son Thomas of Bickleigh, and his son-in-law Philip Champernon had bound themselves for the debt on 20 July 1510. After Sir Edmund's death, his son Sir William, in the February 1515 indenture mentioned by Warren in his Star Chamber complaint, pledged to a royal commission headed by Wolsey to repay the debt by half yearly installments of 50 marks. For security, the commission recovered against Sir William "by writ of entree in the past" the manors of Mohun's Ottery, Stoke Fleming, Churchill, Monckton, and various other lands and rents in Devon.[10]

According to the patent, an examination made in 1552 revealed that £760 of the original £1400 was still unpaid. By 1552, Sir William, his brother Thomas, and his brother-in law Champernon were all dead, and Sir Peter, as last living heir to Sir Edmund and Sir William, was inheritor of any remaining family debts to the Crown. The investigation also discovered that Sir Peter not only owed the unpaid portion of his grandfather's original debt, but two unpaid debts incurred by his late brother Sir George: a 1538 obligation to the Crown for £40 and a further £100 assessed upon Sir George as a benevolence granted to Henry VIII. The total family indebtedness to the Crown inherited by Sir Peter Carew in 1552 was therefore £900. For these long-lingering obligations, the king now granted Sir Peter full pardon and release.[11]

The king's forgiveness of debts incurred by his grandfather, father, and brother did not, however, extend to debts incurred by Sir Peter himself, which turned out to be significant. Carew and his brother-in-law, Sir William Skipwith of Grimesby in Lincolnshire, had bound themselves on 1 December 1547 to the executors of Henry VIII's will to pay a debt of £920 owed to the Crown in Augmentations for 230 fodder of lead. The brothers-in-law gave bonds for £1100 to pay in full by Christmas 1551. A year after that due date, the £920 had not been paid. Carew was also in arrears to Augmentations for rent on the late marquis of Exeter's estate at Okehampton Park in Devon, on which Henry VIII had granted a lease to Sir Peter in 1544. The total amount owed by Carew for both the lead and the arrearage in rent was £986 13s 4d. Under the patent of 1552, the king allowed for payment of this sum in yearly installments of £47, and ordered Augmentations to take surety from Sir Peter in lands for that yearly value.[12]

Sir Peter also acknowledged his share of a large debt owed to the Crown by a group of Devon gentlemen and Exeter citizens, including John Chichester and Griffin Ameredyth. How the debt was contracted is not explained, but the group bound themselves for £2500 on 15 December 1547 to pay by Ascension 1556. As their part of the debt, Carew and Chichester each owed £1080 8s 8d. To this amount, the Exchequer added £33 6s 8d owed by Carew for a "contribution" assessed on his wife, Lady Tailboys, by Henry VIII. Carew's total debt in Exchequer was therefor £1113 15s 4d. For settlement of this debt, the king was content to receive yearly installments of £53 8s beginning on All Saints day 1552. Carew had to give further surety in lands to the Exchequer for this annual sum.[13] Sir Peter's total outstanding debt to the Crown in 1552, in both the Court of Augmentations and the Exchequer, was over £2100, a huge sum for which the bulk of the family estates now stood pledged.

This burden of debt probably accounts for many of the business and land transactions Carew entered into during this period. In December 1550, for instance, Sir Peter joined with Sir Gawen, the earl of Bedford [Russell], Richard Duke, and Michael Wynston in a mining venture in Devon. Wyston had discovered deposits of iron ore and of the earth called "moor coal" which was needed to extract iron from the ore, in the king's forests of Exmoor and Dartmoor. The king allowed the partners to mine the ore without payment, but required them to build all necessary mills and furnaces and to pay the Crown 6s 8d for every ton of iron produced.

The grant was extended also to the heirs of the partners, so the work might "have continuance forever."[14]

Such a project promised much for the future, but the initial capital outlay needed to start production could have done little to alleviate Carew's immediate financial needs. To raise ready cash, Carew turned, during Edward's reign, but especially after 1550, to the granting of future interests in parcels of the family estates for an immediate cash payment. For instance, in February 1551, Sir Gawen and his second wife Mary Wotton and Sir Peter and Lady Margaret purchased from the king for £4 a license to grant certain lands to Walter and John Yong and their heirs. Sir Peter and Lady Margaret granted several messuages and farms in the Devon parish of Axmouth for an unspecified consideration, and the Yongs regranted the lands to the Carews in survivorship for their lives.[15] The Carews therefore retained use of the lands until the death of the longest lived spouse, when the properties came to the possession of the Yongs or their heirs. In 1552, just prior to the issuance of the royal patent restructuring Sir Peter's debt to the Crown, Carew concluded several such arrangements for various pieces of the Devon manor of Mamhead, which had come into the Carew family by marriage in the late thirteenth century. Sir Peter, for example, concluded a bargain and sale with Gilles Balle for certain lands in Mamhead, Wood, and Golyford.[16] One Walter Baker purchased other lands, messuages, and gardens in Mamhead and Golyford from Sir Peter and Lady Margaret; Carew had to give Baker a bond of £40 for performance of all the covenants included in the agreement.[17] A third bargain and sale concluded by Carew during the year gave Nicholas Parre an interest in two messuages, two gardens, 60 acres of land, and 20 acres of pasture in Mamhead and two smaller manors.[18] In July 1552, John Parre obtained an interest in certain other gardens, wastes, and pastures held by Carew for a consideration of £27 14s.[19] Three months later, Carew obtained a license for £8 16s 9d to grant his Devon manors of Chittlehampton and Newenham to Sir Hugh Pollard and his heirs.[20] Both of these former monastic parcels had been picked up by Sir George Carew in the early 1540s. The parcels of land involved in the transactions of 1552 do not seem to have been large; Sir Peter was at this time in his late thirties and probably still had hopes of an heir, whose future estate he did not wish to diminish in any significant way. Later, in Elizabeth's reign, as hope of an heir faded away, Carew would continue similar transactions, but for larger amounts of both land and cash.

The ascendancy of Northumberland in London and Russell in the West Country after 1549 brought Sir Peter and the rest of his family solid rewards, both in terms of property and influence. Northumberland bound important aristocrats and gentry to himself through liberal distribution of lands, titles, and offices. Confirmation of Russell's land grants of August 1549 were the Carews' immediate rewards. Russell himself did particularly well. In January 1550, the king raised him to the earldom of Bedford and gave him a free gift of lands worth £300 a year.[21] From the spring of 1547 to the summer of 1549, Sir Peter's activity in the West had been somewhat limited by his decision to spend much of his time on his new wife's extensive estates in Lincolnshire. But by the end of 1550, Carew was again active and prominent in western affairs. On 16 December, Sir Peter and Sir Gawen were named with their kinsman Arthur Champernon, Sir Thomas Dennys, and Sir Hugh Pollard to two commissions charged with collecting in Devon and in Bristol the third installment of a relief granted to the king by the Parliament of November 1547.[22] A year later, on 4 December 1551, Sir Peter and his uncle were named to a commission with the bishop of Exeter, Dennys, Pollard, and others to inquire into the rise in corn and food prices in Devon. The commissioners were to determine if greedy and covetous persons were responsible for the price rises and to apprehend all such offenders.[23] In between these two commissions, in May 1551, Sir Peter was sent on a familiar mission—conveying the garter to a foreign monarch. Carew was one of the knights dispatched to France with the marquis of Northampton to bestow the garter on the new French king,

Henri II, and to solicit the friendship of the French government for Northumberland's regime. For this service, Sir Peter received £50. Among Carew's companions on this trip were Sir Henry Sidney and Sir John Perrot, with whom Carew would be associated in Ireland in the late 1560s, and Sir Nicholas Throckmorton and Sir William Pickering, with whom Carew would plot rebellion in the next reign.[24] Hooker, unfortunately, wrote nothing of this episode, so we have no way of knowing if this trip to the French court was as eventful as Carew's last visit there in 1546.[25]

An indication of the status the Carews were according themselves at this time appears in the licenses that both Sir Peter and Sir Gawen were granted in June 1551 to retain more servants and household officers than those specified in the Act of Retainers. The licenses, which were granted for life, allowed both Carews 40 retainers for their households in the offices of steward, understeward, bailiff, and game keeper. They could give any retainer a badge or livery, but they could not retain any servant of the king. For any offense committed against the Act of Retainers since 25 January 1551, the two men received pardons.[26] The reign also brought ecclesiastical status to George Carew, Sir Peter's uncle. In March 1547, George Carew, then archdeacon of Totnes, received a license to be nonresident from all benefices for five years, while using the emoluments and titles of the offices to support study overseas.[27] The archdeacon did not apparently stay abroad for the whole five years, for in June 1551 George received another license for nonresidence, this one for all benefices, with or without cure, currently held or to be held. The second license refers to him as king's chaplain and prebendary of Exeter and Wells Cathedrals.[28] We know that George was in Exeter long enough in the following year to embroil his nephew in the nasty spat with city officials over the behavior of his servants. The dispute, as we have seen, grew serious enough to attract the attention of the Council.

Both Sir Peter and Sir Gawen were especially active on the government's behalf in the West Country in the last years of Edward's reign. In September 1551, for instance, the Council called upon Sir Peter, Sir Thomas Dennys, Sir Hugh Pollard, Sir Arthur Champernon, and the bishop of Exeter to investigate the spreading of rumors about the unsoundness of the coinage in Exeter and the West. Two men held in Exeter for spreading such rumors were to be released on bond by the city magistrates to appear before the commission for examination. If these two or any others were found guilty of rumor mongering, which by a recent proclamation was prohibited, the commission was to punish them and then report their proceedings to Bedford.[29] Sir Peter acted alone in August 1552 in the matter of one George Browne and the captain of Brest's son, both of whom were in trouble with the Council for "misusing" the king's subjects in some unspecified fashion.[30] In the following spring, Sir Peter cooperated once again with Dennys and with Anthony Harvey in attempting to apprehend Thomas Browne, master of the *John of Apsam*, who was expected to return soon from Flanders.[31] Two days later, the Council ordered Sir Peter and Dennys to examine one Bodenham in a case involving seditious speech.[32] Two weeks later, in early May 1553, Sir Peter and Dennys joined Sir Gawen, Champernon, William Strowde, and the bishop of Exeter on a commission to apprehend Walter Hele and examine him as to his preaching. If the accusations against Hele proved true, the commission was to inform the Council so that punishment could be administered. If the accusations proved groundless and were made only in malice, the commission was to dismiss Hele "with some good lesson."[33]

The last months of Edward's reign found Sir Peter much involved in the Devon phase of the government's nation-wide expropriation of church goods. Northumberland had continued and even accelerated the protestantizing of the English Church begun by Somerset. A second Act of Uniformity, passed in April 1552, authorised a new prayer book that drastically reformed and simplified the English worship service. Use of the plate, vestments, altar cloths, and lavish ornamentation associated with the sacrifice of the Mass was now by law forbidden. These valuable items were to be confiscated to the use of the Crown, which during Northumberland's time was more than usually strapped for cash. Several inventories of church plate and goods had already taken place during the reign: one was carried out by the bishops in December 1547 and a second was conducted by the sheriffs and justices of the counties in February 1549. Concealment and illegal sales of church goods were rampant, as pious or opportunistic church wardens acted to forestall the rumored expropriation. When the Act of Uniformity took effect in November 1552, and the expropriation order was issued early in 1553, local commissions fanned out quickly to the churches in their county or area of responsibility to prevent too much of the government's newly acquired property from slipping through its fingers.[34] Sir Peter Carew and his uncle both found themselves on the commission for Devon.

The Carews were natural choices for this work, given their well-known reformist views. The ferreting out of church goods once used for the superstition of the Mass was likely a congenial task for both Sir Peter and his uncle. The earl of Bedford and Sir Hugh Pollard were among those serving with Sir Peter and Sir Gawen on the 1553 Devon commission for church goods. The commissioners were to inventory the plate, jewels, vestments, bells, and other ornaments of the churches, chapels, brotherhoods, guilds, and fraternities in every parish in the county. They were to pay particular attention to comparing their list of goods with the previous inventories, and to make diligent search for all missing items. Anyone caught concealing or otherwise appropriating church goods was to be imprisoned and reported to the Council.[35] Sir Peter was also named to the church goods commission for the city of Exeter; his colleagues on this commission included the bishop and mayor of Exeter and Sir Thomas Dennys.[36]

The animosity generated between Carew and Dennys and Pollard by the events of June 1549 does not seem to have interfered with the close and frequent association of the three men on various commissions and for various causes during the years of Northumberland's regime. The bitter accusations and denunciations uttered during the stormy meeting at the Mermaid Inn apparently did not prevent the men from working together. The memory of the high words at the Mermaid did not seem to affect the normal gentry administration of Devon, but in 1554, in decidedly abnormal times, Sir Peter's call for his fellow gentlemen to take Devon into rebellion against the Crown fell on deaf ears, some of which may have been too full of the harsh echoes of the Mermaid to hear him.

Whatever their private thoughts about one another, the Devon and Exeter commissioners set diligently to work on the lengthy and difficult task of inventorying the goods in the county and city churches. In Exeter, which was still much in favor in London for its stout loyalty in 1549, Carew and Dennys and their colleagues had to allow certain parishes to sell over £200 of church goods to raise funds for the construction of a canal much desired by the city administration. The commissioners bound the city to repay this sum on demand, but Exeter was able eventually to have even the bond canceled.[37] Such details took a great deal of time to complete. The commissions had been issued in early March, but the Devon commissioners did not submit their report until 16 June. They warned that certain inaccuracies between their inventory and the work of earlier commissioners were likely due to the incorrect evaluation of certain items in the previous lists; pieces described in the earlier inventories as made of gold or cloth of gold appeared on the examination of the current commissioners to be made of baser materials. To soften this disagreeable news, the commission hastened to inform the Council that they found the people quiet and conformable to the government's proceedings, and glad of the increase in the king's treasure.[38] It would have been surprising had the commissioners found the people of Devon to be anything else so soon after the bloodshed for religion of 1549.

While Sir Peter made careful search through the churches of Devon for royal property, the young king of England lay dying. When Edward departed this life on 6 July 1553, he took with him the political hopes of the duke of Northumberland, the ecclesiastical hopes of Archbishop Cranmer, and the bright future in both spheres that had lain before Sir Peter Carew. The political and religious landscape of England, which was so congenial to Sir Peter during most of Edward's reign, turned decidedly unfriendly to the Devon gentleman after July 1553. So unfriendly was the climate, that the loyal courtier, soldier, and servant of two Tudor monarchs became an open and notorious rebel against a third.

---

1   Calendar of the Archives of the Borough of Dartmouth, DRO, #703.

2   Ibid., #742.

3   Ibid., #3308.

4   MacCaffrey, *Exeter*, pp. 229-30.

5   APC, IV, pp. 101-02.

6   Court of Star Chamber Records, Edward VI, PRO, STAC 3 4/23.

7   Ibid.

8   Ibid.

9   Ibid.

10 CPR, Edward VI, vol. IV, 16 December 1552, pp. 398-400.

11 Ibid.

12 Ibid.

13 Ibid.

[14] Ibid., vol. III, 21 December 1550, pp. 344-45.

[15] Ibid., vol. IV, 4 February 1551, p. 44.

[16] Manor of Mamhead Records, DRO, MS 484M, T1/7-9.

[17] Ibid., T6/1-2.

[18] Ibid., T15/1.

[19] Ibid., T15/2.

[20] CPR, Edward VI, vol. IV, 18 October 1552, p. 248.

[21] Diane Willen, *John Russell, First Earl of Bedford: One of the King's Men* (London: Royal Historical Society, 1981), p. 84.

[22] CPR, Edward VI, vol. V, 16 December 1550, pp. 352, 361.

[23] Ibid., vol. IV, 4 December 1551, p. 141.

[24] Nichols, *Literary Remains*, pp. 316-17; APC, III, p. 271.

[25] Indeed, Hooker's account of the 1546 visit is so crammed with adventure that it is possible he consolidated events from the two separate trips to the French court into one episode. See Chapter 4 for a discussion of Carew's activities at the French court in 1546.

[26] CPR, Edward VI, vol. III, 11 June 1551 (Gawen), 29 June 1551 (Peter), p. 312.

[27] Ibid., vol. I, 27 March 1547, p. 102.

[28] Ibid., vol. IV, 6 June 1551, p. 168.

[29] APC, III, p. 356.

[30] Ibid., IV, p. 118.

[31] Ibid., IV, pp. 258-59.

[32] Ibid., IV, p. 261.

[33] Ibid., IV, p. 268.

[34] W.K. Jordan, *Edward VI: The Threshold of Power: The Dominance of the Duke of Northumberland* (Cambridge, Mass.: Harvard University Press, 1970), pp. 386-94.

[35] CPR, Edward VI, vol. IV, Undated, p. 394; 3 March 1553, p. 414.

36 Ibid., Undated, p. 396; 3 March 1553, p. 416.

37 Jordan, *Threshold*, p. 394.

38 Devon Commissioners to the Council, 16 June 1553, BL, Stowe MS 141, f. 54.

CHAPTER 7

THE REBELLION AGAINST THE MARRIAGE

For the years of Queen Mary, John Hooker's biography of Sir Peter Carew becomes much less helpful a source than for earlier years. Of Sir Peter's reasons for involving himself in the conspiracy against the queen's marriage that led to Wyatt's rebellion, Hooker said nothing. Of Sir Peter's treasonous role in the unfolding of that conspiracy, Hooker wrote little. Of Carew's activities against the queen's government while in exile in France, Hooker took no notice. Of the possibility that Sir Peter arranged the betrayal of a Protestant friend and fellow exile into the hands of a regime then engaged in burning heretics, Hooker gave no hint. Only when the lonely and penurious Sir Peter, wandering forlornly about Europe, ingeniously escaped several traps laid for his capture by the queen's agents in Italy does Hooker again provide colorful, anecdotal detail. Opportunities to relate the display of Sir Peter's wit, the triumph of his honour, and the advancement of his fortunes were few for the reign of Mary, leaving Hooker with little to say about his patron during these troubling years.

Hooker's silence, especially concerning the origins of the conspiracy against the queen, leads one to wonder whether he is not telling what he knows or simply knows nothing to tell. Hooker's biography makes no attempt to deny Carew's involvement in the plot, no attempt to defend his actions, and no attempt to vilify the queen for so misusing a loyal servant. It simply relates, in a sort of literary monotone, the bare outline of events, rising to rich detail only when narrating Sir Peter's successful escapes, both from England initially and from the queen's men later while in exile. The details of the secret flight to the Dorset coast and of back alley bravado in Italy could only have come to Hooker from Sir Peter's lips. The details of plots and treason and possible betrayal were likely kept from Hooker's ears by Sir Peter's understandable reticence, for Hooker would have happily championed with his pen his patron's protestations and explanations had they been forthcoming. The silence of Hooker's pen betokens Sir Peter's silence. And just what that silence betokens, the next two chapters will endeavor to uncover.

The death of Edward VI and the accession to the throne of his Catholic sister Mary signified a total reversal of fortune for many powerful men in England, including Sir Peter Carew. In Edward's last years, while the national government in London and local administration in the West Country were in the hands of his old comrades John Dudley, duke of Northumberland, and John Russell, earl of Bedford, Sir Peter Carew was "one of the chiefest in most credit" both in London and the West Country.[1] Northumberland, Bedford, and Carew were all long-time servants of Henry VIII, agents, either directly or indirectly, of the late king's dismantling of a Church the new queen cherished above all things and for which she had grievously suffered. For these men, the accession of Mary changed much and threatened much. Both King Edward and Northumberland understood what was at stake—the one for his country, the other for himself—when they made their audacious and desperate attempt to circumvent the normal working of hereditary succession and the statutory working of Henry VIII's will and keep Mary from the throne. Mary's accession promised not only to alter religion beyond Sir Peter's liking, but to cut Sir Peter off from access to the power, influence, and wealth that flowed from the Crown, access that he had enjoyed almost without let since his return from the continent in 1532. New men, who had suffered in the political wilderness for years, either for their loyalty to the new queen or to her old religion, could look forward to the future. Men like Sir Peter Carew, who had prospered with the policies and leadership of the two previous reigns, could but look back at what was gone and seek to make the best of what was to come.

This indeed seemed to be Sir Peter's intention when in mid-July 1553 he confounded expectation by ignoring the Council's proclamation of Queen Jane. He caused Queen Mary to be proclaimed in his lordship at Dartmouth and in the nearby town of Newton Bushel. Carew did this knowing full well "that there was like to ensue a great alteration in religion if the Lady Mary should be proclaimed queen," and that the religion to which he "was well affected" she "utterly did abhor."[2] Loyalty to the Crown was deeply ingrained in Carew and strong enough to override, in this instance, any personal misgivings about the new monarch. In late July, after Northumberland had been taken into custody but before Mary had left Colchester for London, the new queen dispatched a letter of thanks to Carew and the gentry of Devon for their support. The queen thanked the Devon men for their "faithfulness and true hearts ready to serve and to have defended us against our traitors and rebels."[3] Among those receiving thanks with Carew were Sir Gawen Carew, Sir Arthur Champernon, and John Chichester, all of whom would be implicated with Sir Peter in a major rebellion within six months, and Sir Thomas Dennys, John Ridgeway, and John Prideaux, all of whom would in six months be engaged in thwarting Carew's rebellion. Unlike her father and brother, Mary would prove unable to transform Carew's loyalty to the English Crown into personal loyalty to her.

Carew had no part in the attempt to foist Queen Jane upon the realm. Since 1550, he had spent most of his time in Devon, and in the spring of 1553, he was heavily involved in the Northumberland regime's expropriation of church goods, serving on the Devon and Exeter commissions for inventorying such goods. The work of these commissions went on well into June; the Devon commission submitted its report only days before the scheme to exclude Mary from the succession was finalised in London.[4] Carew was in London in March 1553 for the meeting of Edward VI's last Parliament; Sir Peter sat for the first time as member for Devon, having sat earlier for Tavistock and Dartmouth in the Parliaments of 1545 and 1547, respectively. The purpose of this, the shortest of all Tudor Parliaments, was to pass the government's much needed subsidy bill and then adjourn without keeping the increasingly ill monarch too long in the public eye.[5] The session ended on 31 March, and Sir Peter was back in Devon before the outcome of the king's illness became apparent and made necessary the *Devise* for altering the succession.

Although Sir Peter was not part of the king's scheme to replace Mary with Jane Grey, Northumberland and the other councilors who had tied their futures to the dying king's will clearly expected Sir Peter to support them when their plot became known. Hooker wrote cryptically that no one outright condemned Carew for his proclamation of Queen Mary—which would have been unwise in any case given Mary's success in taking the throne—but several "of great countenance, and in high authority, were offended with him, because he did not advertise unto them his own bent, and the disposition of the people" of the West.[6] Of whom Hooker was speaking here, one can only speculate. Certainly there were those on Queen Jane's short-lived Council who might have had cause to be disappointed in Sir Peter, and it may be some of these men to whom Hooker referred. But Northumberland himself had the most cause to be offended with Carew's seemingly quick and easy decision to back Mary. Besides having had a long naval association with Sir Peter and his late brother, Northumberland had knighted Sir Peter after the action at Treport in 1545, had given Sir Peter opportunity to bring himself to the French king's attention during the peace mission of 1546, and had created through his favor Sir Peter's high position and influence in the West Country since 1550. That Sir Peter Carew would align the West with Mary likely never occurred to Northumberland as he formulated his plot. If he thought about Carew at all as he lay in the Tower, he probably did so with resentment.

Carew's action was unexpected enough to draw the attention of other observers, even in a month filled with attention-grabbing events. The four imperial ambassadors then in London wrote Charles V on 27 July that an important lord of the West had declared for Mary and that the 700 or 800 horsemen the lord had sent to Mary from Cornwall passed through London the previous day.[7] Northumberland came a prisoner to the Tower on 25 July, passing through streets filled with people "calling him traitor without measure."[8] The duke's son, Lord Robert Dudley, arrived at the Tower the following day, along with the bishop of London and the marquis of Northampton, in whose party Sir Peter had gone to bestow the garter on Henri II in 1551. Queen Jane, now once again plain Lady Jane Grey, and her new husband, Northumberland's son Guildford Dudley, never left the Tower; they merely exchanged the royal apartments for less sumptuous quarters. Jane's father, the duke of Suffolk, found himself in the Tower by 28 July, the same day the fortress greeted Sir John Cheke, tutor to the late king. Cheke would survive this stay in the Tower, but would return again a prisoner in three years' time, accompanied by a fellow prisoner—Sir Peter Carew. The future shared fate of Cheke and Carew could not be foreseen in the summer of 1553. While Cheke languished, Carew, if not warmly embraced by the new queen, was at least free and safely positioned, untainted by any involvement in Northumberland's plot and credited with securing the West Country for Mary.

On 3 August 1553, while new prisoners were yet passing into the Tower, three old prisoners came out. On this summer evening the queen passed triumphantly through London to the Tower where she found kneeling before her on Tower hill three men long held close prisoner within the fortress.[9] The queen bid them rise, kissed each, and saluted them as "my prisoners."[10] The three were the aged duke of Norfolk, whom Henry VIII had sent to the Tower for treason and released now as a good Catholic; Stephen Gardiner, whom Somerset had imprisoned for opposing his religious innovations and released now to serve as Mary's chancellor; and, the longest held of the three, Edward Courtenay, the son of George and Gawen Carew's old patron, the marquis of Exeter. Imprisoned for most of his life, young Courtenay was released now to his mother, a long-time and loyal friend and partisan of both Queen Catherine and Princess Mary. It was for Mary and her mother that the marchioness had so dangerously entangled herself, and her husband, in the Nun of Kent affair in 1533. Both Exeters had survived that episode, in which many people were marginally implicated, including, as we have seen, George Carew, his aunt Katherine, and his uncle Gawen. But the marquis was a descendent of Edward IV, the most prominent and influential surviving member of the legitimate Yorkist line, which Henry VIII had once expressed himself desirous of ending.[11] Henry acted on that desire in 1538 when he sent the marquis, and his Yorkist cousins in the Pole and Neville families, to the block for treason. At his father's death, Edward Courtenay, then about 12, disappeared into the Tower, not to come out again until he was 27.

During Edward's imprisonment, the Courtenay interest, which had been so powerful in the West Country in the fourteenth and fifteenth centuries, was broken up. George, Gawen, and Peter Carew all acquired portions of the former Courtenay estates in the West in the 1540s. When, soon after his release, the queen raised Courtenay to his family's ancient peerage, the earldom of Devonshire, steps were taken to at least partially reconstitute the Courtenay lands and position in the West. On 28 September, a huge grant of reversions was made to the new earl to support his dignity and rank. The grant included the manors of Raskere in Cornwall and South Alyngton and Skyrydon in Devon, which had been given for life to Gawen Carew and his wife in 1541; the Devon manors of Chittlehampton and Newenham, which had been given to Sir George Carew and his heirs in 1544; and certain lands with the park of Okehampton in Devon, which had been granted to Sir Peter Carew in 1544.[12] This grant was a first sign of the possible limitations to be placed in the future on the influential position Sir Peter had enjoyed in Devon under Northumberland. Still, the Carews had risen in western society in the fifteenth century in part through their close association, by marriage and otherwise, with the Courtenays. The Courtenay interest was rising again, on a national as well as on a western basis, and the position in the West Country Sir Peter and his brother had built on the Courtenay fall in the 1530s might be maintained by reattaching to the Courtenay rise in the 1550s.

This may well be one reason Sir Peter quickly involved himself with the movement to marry Courtenay to the queen. The young earl was now about all that remained of the Yorkist line, and as such, appeared to many to be the ideal solution to the thorny political problem raised by the unaccustomed accession of a woman to the throne. Mary needed a husband. A party, led by Lord Chancellor Gardiner, who had befriended Courtenay while the two were in the Tower, formed rapidly around the young earl as the best candidate for Mary's hand. The party's formation was helped by fear of the competition. As soon as Mary was securely seated on the throne, Charles V began cautiously exploring the possibility of marrying her to his son Philip. Throughout September and October 1553, the emperor's ambassador in England, Simon Renard, moved skillfully and in secret to persuade the queen to accept Philip. On 29 October, the queen made her decision; she would follow her natural inclinations and marry the emperor's son. Having won over the queen, Renard now faced a far more formidable task—making the Spanish match palatable to a hostile country.

Any foreign match was unpopular, for no one knew just how far a non-English husband could persuade the queen to involve England in fighting the wars and pursuing the interests of his country. Courtenay was an Englishman, of royal Plantagenet blood; his long years in the Tower kept him from being well known and from making enemies. Those years also kept him inexperienced and immature, and hid a weak, foolish, and unstable nature. All these traits would become evident soon enough; but for the moment, Courtenay had the support of Gardiner, much of the Council, and many in the country. He also won by default the backing of the French king, who stood ready to oppose anything that favored the imperial interest but who lacked a strong candidate of his own for Mary's hand. Antoine de Noailles, the French ambassador in England, was soon deep in plots to prevent the Spanish marriage and promote the match with Courtenay. In the weeks before Mary's first Parliament opened on 5 October 1553, rumors of the supposedly secret Spanish proposal swirled about London. So too did a series of pamphlets, such as the "Discourse of an English Gentleman," that argued stenuously against the Spanish connection. Both the rumors and the pamphlets were the work of Noailles acting in secret with the Courtenay party as it prepared to work through Parliament to compel Mary to take an English husband.

Throughout the autumn of 1553, a parade of opponents to the Spanish marriage passed secretly though a secluded garden gate at the back of Noailles' house. An unnamed associate of Courtenay's came at the ambassador's invitation on the night of 7 September. Noailles, who had just been assured from another source that the Spanish proposal was real, told his visitor to urge Courtenay and his friends to begin constructing a party of supporters to work in his behalf in the upcoming Parliament.[13] Who Noailles' visitor was on this night is unclear, but it seems likely that Sir Peter Carew was among the pro-Courtenay MPs who passed through the ambassador's gate later while Parliament was in session.[14]

Sir Peter sat for Devon in Mary's first Parliament, as he had in Edward's last Parliament seven months earlier. We know nothing about his positions or activities in this Parliament except what we can glean from the appearance of a mark next to his name on a Crown Office List of the knights and burgesses in this Parliament. As Jennifer Loach notes in her study of the Marian Parliaments, the true meaning of this list is difficult to discern. The list is headed "they which stood for the true religion are signed thus +," and 60 names, including Carew's, bear the mark. The meaning of "true religion," of course, depends upon the point of view of the unknown maker of the list. But it is unlikely Carew's name would appear on a list of those zealous for the Catholic faith, and, as Loach has shown, many of the other men listed showed themselves to be clearly of the reformed religion in the 1560s and 1570s, whatever their opinions might have been in the 1550s.[15] Three men who were soon to be involved with Sir Peter and others in plotting against the queen's Spanish marriage—Sir Edward Rogers, Sir Nicholas Throckmorton, and Sir Edward Warner—also were marked for "true religion." It seems likely then, that the men denoted on this list had in some way shown themselves in this Parliament to favor reformed religion and, by implication, to oppose at least part of the queen's conservative religious program.

The names on the list cannot be associated with support for or opposition to any particular bill debated in this Parliament. Loach has tried without success to identify the marked names as those who opposed a measure repealing various Edwardian religious statutes, such as the 1549 and 1552 Acts of Uniformity. The list might also refer to those members who expressed reluctance during debate to support a bill "for avoiding treasons and praemunire," which was strongly supported by the queen. This measure repealed all definitions of treason not contained in Edward III's act of 1352 and all new felonies and definitions of praemunire enacted since 1 Henry VIII. Since one of the treasons to be repealed was denying the royal supremacy, the measure raised the possibility of reintroducing papal authority into England, which, as Mary related to Cardinal Pole, occasioned much debate and opposition.[16] Whatever the list's exact origins, Sir Peter's inclusion on it indicates his choice to identify himself during the session with those who did not enthusiastically endorse the queen's whole religious program.

Before Parliament dissolved on 6 December, the Commons presented the queen with a petition asking her to take a husband from within the realm. Courtenay and his friends, including Sir Peter, had apparently acted upon Noailles's advice to build a parliamentary party in favor of his marriage to the queen. The petition was prepared in late October, but the queen stalled its presentation until 16 November. The delay allowed the queen to formally accept the Spanish marriage proposal at a secret audience with Renard on 8 November, thereby reducing the petition to irrelevance before it could even be presented.[17] The queen unwisely allowed the unsuspecting Commons deputation to go forward with the presentation of their already doomed petition. Believing their request would be seriously heard and considered, the deputies were astonished when the queen cut off the speaker in the middle of his speech and denounced the Commons for meddling in her affairs. Forcing her to take a husband she did not want would, she scolded the MPs, "cause her death, for if she were married against her will she would not live three months, and would have no children."[18] The speaker and his colleagues did not quite know what to make of this outburst, but before November was out everyone knew that the queen had accepted the Spanish proposal and rejected Courtenay.

The secret quashing of the Commons petition as it lay unpresented made absolutely clear the lack of influence the anti-Spanish, pro-Courtenay party had at court. Mary had chosen to follow her personal inclinations, and then given her word to act upon the choice. Her reaction to the Commons petition and her unfortunate treatment of its presenters displayed for all the queen's utter refusal to be guided by a popular will that ran contrary to her own. Gardiner continued to talk, and Noailles continued to plot, but neither calm, reasoned argument nor angry public reaction moved the queen.[19] Negotiations for the marriage treaty went forward. There were many in and out of Parliament like Sir Peter Carew, pro-Courtenay men who had been in sympathy and in favor with the previous regime, and who had exercised significant local authority and influence thereby. In the queen's response to the Commons petition, these men saw their former influence reduced to ineffectual begging of a monarch who ignored them, and they now began to fear that their future position would be at the mercy of Philip and his Spaniards. What's more, they began to realize that their range of choices for action to preserve their local positions and their access to royal favor was narrow. To simply acquiesce in the queen's marriage and allow Philip and the Spaniards to enter the kingdom and monopolize the queen's favor and the royal administration was utterly unpalatable. To resist the queen's decision by force, in hopes of changing her mind, or, failing that, replacing her with a more like-minded monarch, was scarcely more appealing.

The inaction of acquiescence never appealed to Sir Peter, but disobeying, indeed threatening, the Tudor throne, which he had served loyally and vigorously for over 20 years, and his family had similarly served since Bosworth, could have been no easy choice for Carew. Yet, on 26 November, only 10 days after the queen's rejection of the Commons petition, Sir Peter was one of a small group of gentlemen who met secretly in London to plan a rising against the Tudor queen. Besides Carew, those later indicted for conspiring against the government at this meeting included Sir Nicholas Arnold, Sir James Croft, Sir George Harper, Sir William Pickering, Sir Edward Rogers, William Thomas, William Winter, and Sir Thomas Wyatt.[20] Another version of the indictment lists Sir Edward Warner and Sir Nicholas Throckmorton among the plotters.[21] Most of the conspirators were gentlemen of standing and influence in their counties, and most had connections at court. Carew, Croft, Pickering, Warner, Thomas, and Throckmorton had achieved influence in their counties through service at court; Carew and Winter gained favor and position through their naval service. Harper, Wyatt, Rogers, and Arnold made names for themselves in London through diligent service in their county administrations. Harper and Wyatt had been sheriffs of Kent, and all four had served on their county commissions of peace. Whether primarily courtiers, soldiers, or JPs, the conspirators were bound by their shared parliamentary experience; of the 11, only Winter had never served in the Commons. Carew, Rogers, Throckmorton, and Warner were members of the current Parliament. Carew, Arnold, Rogers, Thomas, Throckmorton, and Warner had sat in Edward VI's last Parliament in March 1553. All 11 conspirators were conspicuous for their service to either or both of the Edwardian regimes. Although none of the indicted had openly supported Queen Jane, all had acquired wealth, exercised influence, or enjoyed office during the last reign.

Determining the religious opinions of the 11 conspirators is a difficult matter. Carew was clearly a strong Protestant by the time Hooker came to know him in the next decade. His spell of confinement for possessing forbidden books in 1545 and his activities on behalf of Protestant preachers in Devon during Edward's reign show that he was already a Protestant in the mid-1550s. However, he was not so zealous in his faith that he could not adapt himself to Mary's religious conservatism. Carew proclaimed Mary in Devon in July even though he had little liking for her religion. As the plot began to unfold, Sir Peter outlined his reasons for joining it to the duke of Suffolk.

If the queen would forbear this marriage with the Spaniard and use a moderation in the matter of religion I would die at her foot but otherwise I will do the best to place the lady Elizabeth in her stead.[22]

Many of Carew's fellow plotters had the same outlook—they were practical Protestants, happy to be rid of the pope, anxious to retain the church properties they had acquired over the last 15 years, but willing to conform to the queen's religion so far as necessary to retain the queen's favor and their positions. There was probably little liking for the queen's Catholicism to be found around the table at which the conspirators gathered on 26 November. But each of them had known four months earlier what Mary's accession would mean in terms of religion. They had each chosen at that time not to risk themselves or their estates in an attempt to prevent what they foresaw. In those four months, the queen's plans for the English Church had not changed; what had changed, or rather, what had been revealed, was the queen's plans for her marriage. The likelihood of a Catholic restoration had not driven these men into rebellion, but the possibility of a Spanish monopoly of favor and office at court was to them a far more frightening proposition. The plot hatched against the queen by Sir Peter Carew and his colleagues at the end of 1553 was not motivated by religion, but by fear of what a foreign consort would mean to the plotters' influence and position, both in their home counties and at court.

The conspirators received no support or assistance from like-minded members of the nobility. The marquis of Northampton and the earls of Pembroke and Arundel, for instance, had backed Northumberland in July and were much too relieved at having escaped the duke's fate to contemplate any new insurrections. The only nobleman to eventually join the conspiracy was the duke of Suffolk, Jane Grey's feckless father.[23] If action was to be taken against the marriage, it would have to be led by men like Carew—gentlemen of lower rank who had the experience, both political and military, and the connections to organize a broad-based rising and bring it to a successful conclusion. Carew's connections with members of Parliament, important figures in the Henrician and Edwardian military establishments, and the leading gentlemen of the West were considerable. In addition, Carew, ever the francophile, was probably in touch with Noailles, the French ambassador, and was known to Princess Elizabeth's servant Katherine Ashley,[24] and possibly to Elizabeth herself. If the risk was worth taking, the wherewithal for a rising was at hand; and Carew and his fellows stood to suffer enough by the Spanish marriage and to gain enough from a successful rising to make the risk of unsuccessful rebellion worth taking.

Carew's position in Devon made him a key figure in the plot. Devon was of great importance, not only because it stood athwart the Channel sea lanes, but because the Devonian port of Plymouth was reputed to be Philip's most likely landing site. Carew assured his colleagues that Philip could expect a proper English welcome in Devon, for "he trusted his countrymen would be true Englishmen, and would not agree to let the Spaniards to govern them."[25] If Devon, which had so recently shown itself friendly to religious conservatism, could be persuaded by Carew to oppose the marriage and Philip's landfall, the Spaniards could be stopped before ever establishing a foothold in the country. What's more, Devon was the seat of Courtenay's lands and power, and the conspirators were relying upon Courtenay to put himself and his resources at their disposal. As a fellow westerner, Carew was the conspirators' chief contact between Courtenay and the West Country, where the young man's name carried more weight than his seldom seen person. Coordinating with the earl of Devon proved a difficult task, for the nervous and unstable young man posed a constant threat of detection. Several times before the end of the year Noailles had to talk the earl out of abandoning his colleagues and fleeing the country.[26] But the Devons, earl and county, were central to the conspirators' plans, and Sir Peter had chief responsibility for usefully involving the one and successfully raising the other.

The conspirators' plan of action unfolded gradually during November and December. All agreed that the likelihood of forcing Mary to change her mind was remote. The queen's overwrought reaction to the Commons marriage petition displayed clearly the depth of her commitment to the Spanish marriage and the strength of her emotional connection to Charles V and her mother's family. To keep out the Spaniards, Mary must go. But how was she to be replaced and by whom? Just before Christmas, William Thomas suggested that the most effective plan was to assassinate the queen. Thomas, to judge from his writings, was a radical Protestant, and may have been motivated to join the plot as much by hatred of the queen's Catholic faith as by hatred of the Spanish match. Arnold, Croft, and Wyatt were horrified by the idea, or so they claimed later.[27] Certainly no attempt was made to act upon Thomas's suggestion, and the conspirators moved forward under the leadership of Sir James Croft with the idea of replacing Mary with her sister. Although no direct connection between the Princess Elizabeth and the rebellion was ever proven, several of the plotters had access to her. Both Croft and Throckmorton were personally acquainted with Elizabeth, and Carew had at least some connection with members of her household.[28] The next question was how to involve Courtenay. Securing the earl's marriage to the queen had been the original aim of several of the plotters, so transforming Courtenay from Mary's prospective husband to Elizabeth's was a natural step. A second chance at sharing the crown would hopefully keep the nervous earl and his important western influence firmly in the enterprise. As to Mary's fate once her throne was lost, Carew told Suffolk that he would himself lead the ex-queen to the Tower.[29]

With their goals established, the conspirators turned to means. Anything that disrupted imperial plans was obviously of interest to the French, but too deeply involving the French in an enterprise ostensibly aimed at preventing the intrusion of foreign influence into England was clearly unwise. The French ambassador had been working throughout the autumn to foster the marriage with Courtenay and then to stir up disaffection against the Spanish match. Noailles knew something of the activities of Carew and his colleagues, but just how much is unclear. No formal link was established between the conspirators and the French government, even though Carew, predictably, suggested one. In a discussion about how and where to collect the armor and ammunition needed to hinder Philip's landing in Devon, Carew told Throckmorton that he thought it best to approach the French king for armor, ammunition, and money. Throckmorton cautioned Sir Peter to be wary of bringing Frenchmen into the realm "in as much as he could as evil abide the

Frenchmen after that sort as the Spaniards." Throckmorton doubted if the French could give much aid in any case, for most of their military supplies were being consumed in their own wars. Sir Peter backed off at once. Never, explained Carew, had he intended to bring the French into the kingdom, "for he loved neither party" and sought only "to serve his own country, and to help his country from bondage."[30] Carew's affection for things French went back to his boyhood, to his time at the French court in the 1520s.

It has been suggested that Carew developed a particular hatred for Spaniards during this same period.[31]   This is not impossible, for he encountered Spaniards while in Italy in the service of the prince of Orange. The prince is known to have had his troubles with mutinous Spanish troops during the siege of Florence.[32] Also, in 1541, Carew had been victimised by the ungrateful Spaniard he and John Champernon had brought safely out of Turkish captivity to Venice. Once the young Englishmen had paid to reapparel him, the Spaniard forgot his promises of repayment and disappeared.[33] Carew's experiences at Florence and Venice may had left him with a special dislike for Spaniards, but we have no solid evidence for this. Perhaps as a native of the seafaring West, Carew developed a hatred of Spaniards not shared by his co-conspirators from other parts of the country. Certainly the seamen of the West Country displayed little love for Spain during Elizabeth's reign, although to project Elizabethan attitudes back into Mary's reign is probably unwise. If Carew already had an Elizabethan hatred for Spain in 1554, he was well ahead of most of his fellow West Countrymen. Although Sir Peter clearly had an unusual affection for France because of his childhood experiences, it can not be said with any certainty that either those experiences or anything else bred in him an exceptional hatred of Spain. Carew probably joined the conspirators because he shared their main goal as stated by Throckmorton—to prevent control of the English government from falling into the hands of any foreign power.

To achieve this goal, the conspirators finally agreed on a definite plan of action on 22 December. Carew, working with Courtenay, would organize and lead a rising in Devon, while Croft, Wyatt, and the duke of Suffolk would do the same in Herefordshire, Kent, and Leicestershire, respectively. All four risings would begin on Palm Sunday, 18 March 1554, and converge on London to sweep the queen from her throne.[34] In the matter of supplies for the Devon rising, Carew told Throckmorton that he had a small bark of his own "to work his practice by."[35] This comment was perhaps a sly hint as to Sir Peter's own piratical capabilities or, at least, to his connections with those in the West Country who had such capabilities. At about this same time, the French constable informed Noailles of the appearance at the French court of an Englishman who claimed to represent "8 or 10 English gentlemen" and who offered to the French "8 or 9 good warships" that his group expected soon to have under their control.[36] This mysterious Englishman was likely Henry Killigrew, a member of a Cornish family that was "notorious" for aiding and practicing piracy. Killigrew was a friend of both Carew and Rogers, was in France in January before the rebellions started, and was one of Carew's companions in exile in France later in the year.[37] Carew, of anyone, would be alive to the need of seapower to prevent the Spanish landing, and he had already betrayed to Throckmorton his willingness to involve the French in the rebellion. It is therefore likely that Sir Peter had sent Killigrew into France to enlist support, perhaps without informing his less Francophile colleagues. It is also likely the Sir Peter was already practicing with Protestant, seafaring gentlemen of the West Country, like the Killigrews, to give the rebel cause some measure of naval strength. If so, Sir Peter must have begun these activities before he left London, just before Christmas, to begin preparing the West Country to rise against the Spaniards.

Upon his arrival in Devon, Sir Peter set about organizing his part of the rebellion with more zeal than discretion. On about 18 December, a servant of Sir Thomas Dennys brought his master "secret intelligence" as

Dennys met in Exeter Castle with his colleagues on a commission of gaol delivery. Thomas Hawse of Exeter had been sent by person or persons unknown to inquire of Sir Thomas Pomeroy, a local gentleman, whether or not he intended to allow the king of Spain to land in Devon. By his manner of asking, Hawse left no doubt that the people he represented expected a negative reply. Pomeroy wisely answered that he did not intend to meddle in the matter.[38] Pomeroy had been one of the leaders of the 1549 Prayer Book rising. By popping out of hiding behind the royal lines and ordering his drummer and trumpeter to strike up, he had caused a brief panic among Russell and Carew's men during their assault on Clyst St. Mary a few days before the final relief of Exeter. His unexpected retention of his head—but not his lands—after the rebellion is usually put down to his decision to surrender voluntarily to the royal forces and to the possibility that he helped apprehend his fellow rebels.[39] That Carew should approach one of the Prayer Book rebels is hard to explain, unless Pomeroy owed some unknown favor from 1549 or Carew thought he could in some way intimidate Pomeroy into helping spread anti-Spanish rumor and disaffection throughout the county. Rumor had been the volatile fuel that set the Prayer Book rising alight across Devon; perhaps Pomeroy had some special expertise in this area.

The questioning of Pomeroy, whatever the reasons behind it, served only to alert Dennys and John Prideaux, a fellow commissioner, to the possibility of a plot to forcibly resist Philip's landing. Dennys, who was serving his eighth term as sheriff of Devon in 1554, and Prideaux decided to approach John Chichester and ask point-blank if he was part of or knew of any plan being formulated by anyone to prevent Philip from landing. Prideaux hinted in his later deposition that he and Dennys had some information indicating Chichester's possible involvement in such a plan, and stated outright that they went to him because he had great trust and great possessions in the county, "which by common prudence should refrain any man to do any wicked deed."[40] What Prideaux did not say was that Chichester had well-known connections with Sir Peter and Sir Gawen Carew. He had served with Sir Gawen as knight for Devon in the Parliament of 1547 and he had been associated with the Carews during the 1549 rising.[41] However, if either of the Carews were in any way suspected at this time, Prideaux made no mention of it. Chichester denied any knowledge of or involvement in any plot, and there the matter rested for the moment.

Over Christmas, suspicion that a rising against the marriage was somehow being plotted in the West Country continued to grow. On 23 December, Noailles reported a rumor in London that Plymouth was openly preparing to resist the Spaniards.[42] By 2 January the Council knew or suspected enough against Sir Peter to summon him by letter to London for questioning.[43] Five days later, Renard, the imperial ambassador, reported that "heretics" were plotting against the marriage and seeking to induce either Courtenay or Princess Elizabeth to lead them. "[O]ne Carew," who lived somewhere in the West, was the only rebel Renard could definitely name. The Council, wrote Renard, had summoned Carew, intending to throw him into the Tower, a fate he richly deserved, for he was "the greatest heretic and rebel in England and in Parliament plotted for Courtenay and opposed the restoration of religion."[44] Carew, with his zealous, forthright manner and lack of circumspection, was clearly proving to be miserably inept at intrigue.

In Devon, meanwhile, Sir Peter's ill-fitting cloak of secrecy began to slip off entirely. In the weeks between Christmas day and Epiphany, the county was awash with rumors that the prince of Spain was about to descend on the West Country "with a great navy and a great puissance." On 8 January, Sheriff Dennys came to Exeter for the Devon Christmas sessions, which were to start the next day. That evening Dennys dined with Prideaux and several cathedral officials, including Dr. John Moreman, the newly installed Catholic dean of Exeter and one of young John Hooker's teachers. During the course of the meal, a local vicar entered and reported that Sir Gawen Carew had, for purposes unknown, ordered harness to be secretly prepared in the dean's house in Exeter during the days of Christmas. This was, to say the least, highly suspicious. Sir Peter Carew also came under suspicion when the diners heard that he too had spent Christmas in Exeter, rather than on his estates. Before breaking up, the company around Dr. Moreman's table agreed among themselves to try to discover by secret means the truth about the Carews' sinister holiday activities.[45]

But with the Carews, there was little need for secrecy. During the sessions next day, Sir Peter, Sir Gawen, Chichester, and Sir Arthur Champernon approached Dennys to tell him of their concern over a growing belief among the people of the county that the rumored landing of the king of Spain in Devon would be "a great distraction to the country." If such a landing by the prince of Spain was the queen's pleasure, answered Dennys, "it were no subject's part to let it. . .but to be therewith contented." Anything but content with this answer, Sir Peter suggested that it was nonetheless the duty of the queen's justices in the county to make her aware of the situation. Dennys and Prideaux thereupon wrote a letter to this effect to the queen, but Carew so disliked what the two gentlemen had written that he drafted his own letter and presented it to the gentlemen on 10 January.[46] This letter, which Paget described with alarm to Renard a week later, was a blatant attempt to enlist the gentry leadership of Devon into the rebel cause. Renard misinterpreted Paget's description of the regular Devon sessions as an extraordinary meeting of local gentlemen summoned by Carew and eight or ten supporters. According to Paget, Carew attempted to persuade the assembled gentlemen to sign a letter declaring their intention to resist Philip's landing in the West Country. With his typical extravagance, Carew described for the gentlemen the horrible consequences of submitting to foreigners who would do as they pleased in England, even to the point of violating men's daughters. This,

declared Carew, no Englishman could suffer; even death would be preferable
to such degradation.[47] Both Paget, in his account of Carew's letter, and
Prideaux, in his account of the Devon sessions, agreed that Carew failed to
arouse any support. Dennys and Prideaux attempted to deflect Carew
from his purpose by asking John Ridgeway to write a compromise letter
for all the justices to consider the next day. Ridgeway's letter was
apparently never sent, for that same night news reached Exeter that Philip
was to land at Portsmouth, not Plymouth. Ridgeway's letter to the queen
was replaced by a letter from all the justices which advised the Privy
Council of the many anti-Spanish rumors then floating about the county.[48]
Because Carew ultimately sent his letter, or a later draft of it, to London,
he apparently still had hopes of persuading the Devon gentry to rise
against the marriage, even though to this point his attempts at frightening
the justices into opposition with warnings of Spanish evil doing had made
little progress.

In the following week, a new set of rumors swept Exeter. Certain
gentlemen of Devon were said to be ready to seize control of the city,
having for the attempt secret stores of harness and supplies hidden all
about Exeter. The rumors gained substance on 17 January 1554, when a
servant of Sir Peter Carew led through the city's west gate six horses close
packed with harness and handguns drawn from Carew's armory at
Dartmouth Castle.[49] This dangerous parade was a sign of Sir Peter's
growing desperation. He had tried to avoid complying with the Council
summons of 2 January by pleading lack of horses as his excuse for not
appearing.[50] By this ploy, Carew hoped to buy himself the time he needed
to rally the Devon gentry to his cause at the Christmas sessions. But this
effort had clearly failed. Instead of rising in fear of the Spaniards, the county
was nervously awaiting Sir Peter's rising. The lack of enthusiasm for
Carew's cause no doubt stemmed in large part from the natural reluctance
to undertake the risks of rebellion. However, Carew's inability to attract
the support of his many relatives and long-time colleagues suggests other

more personal reasons for his failure. Of relatives, only Sir Gawen and Sir Arthur Champernon gave Sir Peter any support. Champernon was Sir Gawen's nephew and Sir Peter's cousin, brother to the John Champernon who had died in Vienna in 1541 while traveling the continent with Sir Peter. The only other local gentlemen to follow Carew seem to have been advanced Protestants, interested mainly in preventing the restoration of Catholicism. Dennys, who was returned with Carew for Devon to Mary's first Parliament, stood solidly against his former colleague, as did most of the other principal gentlemen of the county. Here, perhaps, was the repayment of some old debts, both those incurred in the summer of 1549 and during the rule of Northumberland. The charges of treachery Carew leveled at Dennys and others during the Prayer Book rebellion, and his arrogant exercise of influence in Devon while enjoying the favor of Northumberland and Russell may have caught up with Sir Peter in January 1554. Carew's assurance to his fellow conspirators of Devon's support for their enterprise proved hollow. The Council would not wait much longer for Carew to appear voluntarily; his situation was grave. Carew's clumsy efforts at building support had jeopardised not only himself, but the entire anti-Spanish conspiracy. His failure, so unexpected to himself, now caused Carew to panic.

On 16 January, Prideaux dined again in Exeter with Dr. Moreman and several of the previous week's company; the group discussed the strange rumors and doings currently abroad in Devon and each diner renewed his pledge to inform the others of any news that came his way. Upon returning that evening to Honiton, which is only about three miles from Carew's home at Mohun's Ottery, Prideaux learned from a servant that the earl of Devon had been seen within the past week in Sir Peter's company. Prideaux immediately summoned the eyewitness who said the earl arrived at Mohun's Ottery with one servant about dinner time on 10 January. Prideaux was not fully convinced the story was true, but thought enough of it to send at once to Dennys, telling him to come with all speed to Exeter.[51] Between his flamboyant performance at the Christmas sessions and the six horses loaded with harness, Carew had thoroughly alarmed Dennys and thrown Exeter and Devon into an uproar.

In London, meanwhile, Renard wrote the emperor that the Council had summoned Carew a second time (although the Privy Council register records only the 2 January summons) and received for answer not another excuse, but the virtual declaration of rebellion Carew had presented to the justices at the Devon sessions the week before.[52] On 16 January, the Council dispatched a letter to Dennys ordering him to send Carew to London for examination.[53] The queen showed Renard several letters to the Council signed by Carew and seven other western gentlemen. These letters appear to have been composed after the letter of defiance presented to the Devon sessions, for their content and tone were very different. According to Renard, Carew and his colleagues asked to be excused for their earlier belligerence because they had not known then of the queen's intentions concerning the Spanish marriage. They had believed that the Spaniards were coming armed to oppress the English people. Such excuses were fantastic, at least on Carew's part; as a member of the October Parliament, residing in London the entire autumn, he could not have been so misinformed about the queen's intentions. Carew's excuses were therefore dismissed as merely a device for hiding his true intent—preventing restoration of the Roman Church. The queen then informed Renard of the order to seize Carew and her intention to take all necessary measures to crush the intended rebellion.[54]

Dennys received the Council's order about 18 or 19 January, and news of the sheriff's intention to arrest Sir Peter reached Mohun's Ottery about the same time. Sir Gawen may have brought the news to his nephew on the morning of the 19th[55] when he reached Mohun's Ottery after a breathless night escape from Exeter. The magistrates conducted that night a search of the town; Sir Gawen, fearing himself to be the object of the search, sent one of his servants to the south gate at about 10 o'clock to create a distraction. The servant did this by offering the porter two shillings to let him out of the gate to catch a ship that was supposedly waiting for him to embark. Sir Gawen then scaled the walls of the city and went on foot three miles through the winter darkness to John Christopher's house. Hindered in his progress by his boots, Sir Gawen cut them and had to borrow a new pair and a horse from Christopher. Sir Gawen next rode to the house of William Gibbes and from there to Mohun's Ottery, where he and Sir Peter armed themselves and began gathering men to defend the manorhouse against assault by Dennys. Sir Gawen later deposed that he and his nephew eventually gathered around themselves some 70 armed adherents.[56]

In an effort to gain time, the Carews wrote to Dennys on the 19th, assuming in their letter an air of aggrieved innocence. Having heard that Dennys was preparing to apprehend them, "for what matter we know not," the Carews thought it good to tell the sheriff that

> . . .we are as true and as faithful subjects unto the queen's highness as any whatsoever they be within the realm, and intend to observe and follow her religion as faithfully as they that are most affected unto it. Wherefore, knowing ourselves without offence towards her majesty, we can not but wonder for what cause you should prepare, with force, to take us. And if it be so that you have any such commission from her highness, or her most honourable council, we heartily pray you so advertise us, and we shall, without rumor or stirring, immediately repair unto you wheresoever you shall appoint us. Whereas if you do the contrary, you shall drive us to stand to the best of our powers for our liberty until such time as we shall better understand your authority.[57]

Having backed themselves into a corner, Sir Peter and his uncle sought desperately for means to extricate themselves, trying both fair words and threats on the sheriff. Dennys, meanwhile, was having his own problems.

At about the same time the Carews were composing their letter, word reached London that "sir Peter Carowe, sir Gawen Carowe, sir Thomas Dey[nis]. . .with diverse others, were up in Devonshire resisting of the king of Spain's coming, and. . . had taken the city of Exeter and the castle there into their custody."[58] This rumor may have been the work of Carew's colleagues in London, attempting either to misrepresent what had occurred at the Devon Christmas sessions or to circulate as encouragement to other potential rebels what they had expected to occur there. In either case, the rumor served to make the government suspicious of Dennys just when Dennys was most in need of its trust. To deal with disaffection in Devon before it got out of hand, the queen's council, about 22 or 23 January, dispatched Sir John St. Leger there, much as the late king's council had sent Sir Peter Carew to the West Country almost five years before. But by the time of St. Leger's appointment, events both in London and in Devon were moving rapidly toward a crisis.

On 21 January, Gardiner summoned the earl of Devon to his presence and drew from the frightened young man the full story the Council had sought to extract from Carew, had he obeyed their summons. It is not clear whether the chancellor had heard the rumor picked up by Prideaux of the earl's mysterious night visit to Mohun's Ottery on 10 January. The growing certainty that Carew and some segment of the western gentry were involved in a plot against the marriage may have been sufficient to make Gardiner suspicious of the young western earl he had come to know so well in the Tower. In any event, the government now knew that Carew was just one part of a much larger enterprise. The conspirators in London, who seemed to come by much better intelligence much more quickly than the government, knew that they were discovered within twenty-four hours of Countenay's disclosures. The rising could not wait for March, but would have to take place at once. By 22 January, Wyatt was rousing his followers in Kent and Croft was preparing to leave the capital to warn Elizabeth.[59] On the same day, the queen wrote to Sir

Hugh Pollard—whom Carew had accused of treachery in 1549—and other Devon gentlemen ordering them to suppress false and malicious rumors in the county about the prince of Spain's coming. To aid them in this, the queen sent to Devon an explanation of the articles contained in the treaty with Spain, which the gentlemen were to declare openly to the people to ease their minds.[60]

As these events unfolded in London, Dennys attempted to carry out his original instructions to arrest Sir Peter Carew and send him to the Council for questioning. Unlike the way Sir Peter had himself proceeded in the similarly explosive situation of 1549, Dennys moved with caution, hoping to avoid violence if at all possible. This hope was difficult of achievement, for Mohun's Ottery was strongly fortified and the local gentlemen not well prepared with weapons and harness to launch an assault. Dennys thought about bringing up artillery, but none was readily available and the earth was so soft and wet that the guns could probably not be transported even if they could be found. Carew's letter of the 19th, if its sentiments were genuine, gave the sheriff a way out of this quandary. Taking Sir Peter at his word that "he would come to me at all times," Dennys "signified unto him the queen's pleasure and commandment, commanding him, in her grace's name, to be with me at Exeter the day following at ten of the clock before noon."[61] This message was taken back to Mohun's Ottery by the Carew servant who had brought Sir Peter's letter to the sheriff. Passing out of the walls of Exeter about midnight on the 20th, this man confided to the porter that the earl of Devonshire had within the week made a midnight visit to Mohun's Ottery accompanied by only two servants. This information was of course brought to the attention of the city magistrates, and confirmed the same basic story that Prideaux had heard and conveyed to Dennys four days earlier.[62]

The Carews seem to have been afflicted with singularly loose-lipped servants, for it was one of Sir Gawen's men who one day later revealed to a traveling companion the details of his master's flight over the walls of Exeter. It was "like to be a busy world," continued the gossiping servant, who then disclosed his current mission to be delivery to his mistress of a letter from Sir Gawen directing his wife to smuggle his harness out of Exeter by concealing it in several hand baskets. For good measure, this most unreliable of messengers also revealed all the precautions Sir Gawen had taken to prevent discovery of the letter, including concealing it in the sole of the servant's shoe.[63] All this information made its way quickly to Dennys and the city authorities, who promptly sealed off Exeter and thereby prevented any Carew sympathizers within the walls from reaching Sir Peter.

At Mohun's Ottery, confusion reigned. No one in the manor-house knew how much the government knew about the anti-Spanish plot or what action to take. Should the conspirators stay together and maintain themselves at the Carew manor until the rising began and they could issue forth to support it, or should they disperse and each man try to save himself as best he could? By Sunday morning, 21 January, Sir Arthur Champernon had come to the latter conclusion. On that morning, Champernon sent to his neighbor John Ridgeway asking Ridgeway to come with all speed and speak with him. Knowing that Champernon had just come from Mohun's Ottery, Ridgeway declined, wanting to be in no way associated with whatever was taking place at the Carew manor. Champernon sent again the next day to both Ridgeway and the mayor of Totnes, acquainting both with the urgency of his need to see them, but neither Ridgeway nor the mayor would stir until their own messenger had returned from Champernon's house at Modbury with confirmation of all that Sir Arthur had said in his letter. Whereupon, on Tuesday morning, 23 January, Ridgeway, the mayor, and several other merchants of Totnes finally rode out to Modbury. According to Champernon, Carew had summoned him to Mohun's Ottery to enlist his aid in a plan to resist the landing of the prince of Spain. The two cousins quarreled when

Champernon refused to participate; Sir Arthur declared that "forasmuch as now he knew the queen's pleasure was to have the prince of Spain into England, that he would embrace the same, and show himself obedient to his power unto the queen's pleasure therein." Champernon begged his listeners to "not mistrust him therein," and, in so doing, made the impression he no doubt intended, for next day Ridgeway wrote to Dennys that he and the men of Totnes "think verily he spoke as he meant, and will earnestly do the same."[64]

In closing, Ridgeway informed the sheriff that the people living around Totnes were quiet and well contented with the prince of Spain's coming, "and do much malign against such gentlemen as would the contrary." What's more, the men of Totnes were well armed and prepared, at the sheriff's bidding, to resist any gentlemen who went about "to levy any power otherwise then appartaineth to the duty of their allegiance." Here was further confirmation of the utter disinterest most of Devon had in Sir Peter Carew's rising against the Spaniards. The gentry of Devon had, despite London's uninformed anxiety, already turned their backs on Sir Peter. From Ridgeway's report, and from the careful measures taken by the Exeter authorities to guard the city,[65] it appeared that the townsfolk and common people of Devon did the same. Sir Peter directed his energetic if ineffective efforts at his own class, perhaps expecting little from the conservative commons he had fought five years earlier. Sympathy with the queen's religion and reluctance to incur again the consequences of rebellion were probably enough to keep most men quiet. But condemnation of rebel gentlemen and a willingness to take up arms against them betokened outright hostility, not mere indifference. Just as the ill will Carew had earned in 1549 among the gentry of Devon had helped disorder his confident plans to raise the county, so had the ill will he earned that same year from the commons of Devon helped to cause confusion within the walls of Mohun's Ottery and drive his nervous cousin to abandon him.

About the time Champernon left Mohun's Ottery, Sir Peter, according to Hooker, received "some secret intelligence from one who was then both of countenance, and in authority (and who, if Sir Peter should have been apprehended, did doubt of his own case)."[66] Since information about this secret message could only have come from Carew himself, it is not surprising that only Hooker knew of it. Hooker's ostentatious non-identification identifies the sender as the earl of Devon, who, despite his confession to Gardiner on 21 January, was at liberty until taken to the Tower on 12 February. Carew had taken extraordinary measures to maintain contact with the earl, and Courtenay may have used one of these channels to get a message to Carew. St. Leger, for instance, investigated a system of post horses that Carew had set up between London and Devon for swiftly conveying the earl to the West Country.[67] The earl was also later alleged to have carved upon his guitar a special cipher for use in communicating with Carew.[68]

The message that came to Mohun's Ottery about 22 January may have been a simple warning to Carew that the government knew all; Courtenay had seen to that himself. But the message may also have told Carew, immured as he was in Mohun's Ottery, what was happening elsewhere in Devon. Any hope of a rising in the county had utterly collapsed and everyone was rushing to pin blame on Carew. That knowledge was available at court by 23 January, when Renard related it to the emperor. All those who had signed Carew's letter at the Christmas sessions now claimed they did so only because Carew told them Philip was landing among them with an armed multitude and that the queen needed to be made aware of it. When they understood that Philip's landing in England was the queen's pleasure—the same excuse pled by Champernon to his neighbors—they realised that the entire incident had been stirred up by Carew and rallied at once to the queen's cause. Renard claimed that two of these former associates had already come up to London to acquit themselves of their unfortunate association with Sir Peter.[69]

On the same day Renard wrote to the emperor, Carew wrote to Dennys to explain why he could not keep his promise to come to the sheriff in Exeter. Several messages may have passed between Dennys and Carew between Saturday the 20th and Tuesday the 23rd, for Carew mentioned making his promise to the sheriff's messenger, but the sheriff's original order to meet him in Exeter had come back to Mohun's Ottery via Carew's servant. In any event, Carew now declared his intention to depart immediately for London. Sir Peter expected to answer fully all charges against him, "whatsoever mine enemies shall allege against me."[70] Even Hooker implied that this was no more than a ruse to further delay Dennys, for he wrote that Carew was barely started on his journey to London when he met with a servant sent some time earlier "to two of his dearest friends, the one in Wiltshire and the other in Dorsetshire." This is once again an apparently unique piece of information from Sir Peter himself. The sending of messengers into neighboring shires indicates that Carew suspected his growing isolation in Devon; Hooker implied that Countenay's "secret intelligence" precipitated the planned ride to London, but Champernon's abandonment was probably also a factor. The servant confirmed Carew's suspicions, whatever their origins, by telling him that "no friendship was to be had" in either Wiltshire or Dorset.[71]

Despite this setback, Carew's resources were not exhausted. He still had sufficient connections in Exeter to send a secret messenger there to borrow a sum of money for himself.[72] Another messenger was dispatched to Walter Raleigh, whose bark stood ready at Weymouth to convey Sir Peter to safety overseas.[73] Carew also found safe and secret lodgings with another friend near Weymouth for three or four days before sailing from the port on the evening of Sunday 28 January. According to Hooker, Carew rode to Weymouth "appareled like unto a serving man, and attending upon one of his company, as his servant."[74] The number and composition of this company varies with the different accounts of the embarkation. John Graynfyld, who investigated Carew's escape for St. Leger and

Dennys, had three unnamed gentlemen passengers described to him—
"one being a little man, the other of a mean stature, the third a more
longer young man." One of these gentlemen wore a gold chain about his
neck and another remarked at departing that the "King of Spain would
come shortly, he shall be as well barked at as ever man was."[75] It is hard
to determine which of these three was Carew and impossible to know who
the other two might have been. What's more, Hooker's assertion that
Carew came disguised as a servant does not jibe with Graynfyld's information,
unless Carew discarded his disguise before embarking. It is possible the
vague account gathered by Graynfyld and forwarded to the Council by St.
Leger does not describe the departure of Sir Peter Carew but of three other
gentlemen.

A second report of the escape said Carew embarked at Weymouth
on Thursday 25 January with Andrew Tremayne, John Courtenay, and
James Kirkham, and indicated that a Killigrew was already aboard the
vessel to receive Sir Peter.[76] Having only left Mohun's Ottery on the 23rd,
Sir Peter's completion of all departure arrangements in two days is hard to
credit. The presence of a Killigrew is possible; several members of that
family were in exile in France with Sir Peter and Henry was already active
there on Sir Peter's behalf in early January. Courtenay, Tremayne, and
Kirkham were all young Devon gentlemen and likely enough companions;
Courtenay and Tremayne were both known to have been active among the
exiles.[77] Hooker adds his usual touch of drama by relating a dream that
came to Lady Tailboys on the very night her husband was to board
Raleigh's bark. In the dream, Sir Peter slipped as he was boarding the
vessel, fell into the sea, and, like his brother, was drowned. The dream so
unnerved Lady Margaret that she immediately dispatched a messenger to
Weymouth to see if her husband was alive. Upon arriving in the port, the
messenger was told that Sir Peter had indeed slipped and fallen into the sea
and would have drowned had not a bystander quickly pulled him out.[78] It
is hard to see where Hooker could have gotten this story, if not from Sir

Peter or Lady Margaret, but Graynfyld's informant, who "stood by the boat when they shipped themselves,"[79] made no mention of the incident. This lacking throws further doubt on Graynfyld's information, although the second account of Carew's departure does not mention Sir Peter's near drowning either.

Once safely aboard the bark, Sir Peter ordered the vessel to sea. They had not gone far, however, before a terrible storm arose and so tossed the small bark about as to threaten the whole company with drowning. The vessel rode out the storm but was driven by the wind almost back to Weymouth, and some members of the company suggested landing to await better weather. Carew absolutely refused to land, fearing that they would all be caught if they did so. He made the whole company stay aboard as the bark bobbed in the water just off shore awaiting a turn in the wind. Sir Peter probably avoided capture by his refusal to land.

On 26 January, the queen's letters proclaiming both Carews; Wyatt, who had risen in Kent; the duke of Suffolk, who had risen in Leicestershire; and others traitors circulated among the lord lieutenants of the counties.[80] The whole West Country was seeking Carew and his associates. St. Leger focused his attention on Carew's castle at Dartmouth. During the last reign, relations between Sir Peter and the town of Dartmouth were bad. Carew had seized the fort that guarded the haven and the town authorities complained to the Council that only violence could dispossess him. Now, with Sir Peter believed to be a fugitive somewhere on the waters off Devon, St. Leger received many a "credible report" about Carew's intimate familiarity with the coasts near the town and castle of Dartmouth. As St. Leger explained to the Council, Sir Peter had often boasted that "if he were the king's enemy he could get the fort that the town had there, and burn the town with fewer than a hundred persons, and let into the haven such as pleased him." The key to accomplishing Carew's boasts, so St. Leger was told, was to land a force in surprise behind the town at a place called Blackpool. If Carew could make such a landing, he would have the town, haven, and castle at his mercy. The town's opinion of Carew was such that the magistrates convinced themselves and St. Leger that a landing was likely, and St. Leger explained to the Council the steps being taken to keep both Dartmouth and Blackpool under constant watch.[81] The watchers never saw what they were seeking, for well to the east a small bark off Weymouth caught a change in the wind and made for the open sea on a journey that would take it to Normandy.

When Sir Peter, upon receipt of his "secret intelligence," slipped away from Mohun's Ottery on 23 January, the other gentlemen gathered there with him did likewise. It is hard to say what plans, if any, were made by the conspirators before their separate departures. Because of the speed and success of his arrangements, Carew, it seems likely, already had in mind to take himself overseas when he left the manor. The government knew him for the ringleader of rebellion in the West and lesser men implicated in the rising were falling all over themselves to cast blame on him. Rather than be the Northumberland of this rising, the designated one to suffer for the sins of the many, Carew may have seen escape as his only chance for survival. What's more, the chance to return to France, to the continent, even under the present unfortunate circumstances, may have appealed to Carew more than to most other men.

Carew's chief confederates seem to have departed Mohun's Ottery with no such plan of action. From Mohun's Ottery, Sir Gawen rode to his house at Tiverton, from where he addressed a letter to Dennys on 24 January. The letter is an even more extreme expression of the injured innocence displayed in the Carews' joint composition to Dennys of 19 January.

[I]t is bruted that the gentlemen should gather themselves together, and levy a power to stand in the field. I marvel not a little to hear of these imagined lies. I do assure you, by the faith I bear to the living God, there was no such matter of gathering together of any gentlemen, nor no repair of any other, but only as heretofore it hath been accustomably used. And for mine own part, I had no more with me than I do accustomably use to ride withal, which was but viii persons, and Sir Peter Carew, his household servants. But the very occasion of my repair to Sir Peter was that you had gathered a power (as it was showed us) to apprehend us both, and what commission or authority you had so to do we knew not, and upon that consideration wrote unto you our former letter, for if you had sent, declaring that you had such a commission from the queen's highness, we would have come to you as humble and obedient subjects, according to our bounden duties.[82]

From Tiverton, Sir Gawen rode to the house of another nephew, John Carew of Bicklegh, son of his deceased brother Thomas. News of Sir Gawen's presence at Bicklegh soon reached St. Leger, who asked Sir Roger Bluet to write to John Carew "concerning other secret affairs between the said John Carew and him." By this means, Carew was induced to come to Bluet's house without alarming his uncle. St. Leger demanded to know why John gave shelter to the queen's enemies, for so Sir Gawen was. John answered that his uncle "came unto him unlooked for, and as a man, unto his knowledge, which had not offended." To prove his own innocence, John Carew then offered to deliver his uncle into St. Leger's hands.[83]

Instead of accepting this offer, St. Leger gathered a force of some 30 gentlemen and retainers, including John Carew, and rode to the house of Sir John More, where recent intelligence put another one of the fugitives from Mohun's Ottery, William Gibbes. Gibbes's house had been one of Sir Gawen's stops on his midnight flight the week before to Mohun's Ottery. At the Christmas sessions in Exeter, Gibbes had declared his opinion that any man unwilling to defend the county from the Spaniards, who would "ravish. . . wives and daughters, and rob and spoil the commons," should have his throat cut. He singled out Dennys and Prideaux as particularly fit for such treatment. Thereafter, until he withdrew with Carew to Mohun's Ottery, Gibbes seems to have stalked about Exeter with half a dozen armed servants talking wildly about how his own throat was in danger of being cut by the murderous Dennys.[84] For all his previous bluster, Gibbes surrendered himself "very gently and peaceably, without resistance." With Gibbes safely in tow, St. Leger pressed on to Bicklegh, where Sir Gawen, forewarned of the party's arrival, waited "with all humility" outside the gate to greet his captors. Sir Gawen "submitted himself, with like submission as the said William Gibbes." St. Leger then brought both his prisoners to Exeter, where, he informed the Council on 29 January, "I have them in safe keeping."[85]

By early February, St. Leger had added another bird to his collection. Sir Arthur Champernon saved St. Leger the trouble of tracking him down by coming to Exeter and offering his services, "to the uttermost of his power," to the queen. This ostentatious offer, which had apparently also been made to Dennys, did not impress St. Leger, who immediately threw Champernon into "sure keeping" with his uncle. William Thomas, who had followed Sir Peter west from London, was not so accommodating. After much careful searching and "espial for him many secret ways," the most St. Leger could discover was that Thomas had left Mohun's Ottery for Wales around 21 January. Sir Peter Carew, wrote St. Leger to the Council on 4 February, was rumored to have taken ship at Weymouth some days earlier. He enclosed a copy of Graynfyld's information and described the precautions being taken to prevent Sir Peter from making a surprise landing along the Devon coast.[86]

The separate departures from Mohun's Ottery of uncle and nephew raise many questions. Why did Sir Gawen not accompany his nephew? Did Sir Gawen know when he left Mohun's Ottery that his nephew planned to flee the country? Why did Sir Gawen take so few apparent pains to hide his whereabouts? For Sir Peter Carew and William Thomas, the two men at Mohun's Ottery who had been involved in the plot against the marriage from the beginning, from the first secret meeting in London, the consequences of capture were far more severe than the consequences awaiting those who had thrown in their lot with Sir Peter only after his return to Devon. The latter could and did go some way toward excusing themselves, as Champernon's actions and Sir Gawen's letter attest. Sir Peter Carew and William Thomas wasted no time on excuses, kept themselves secret, and bent all their energies towards escape. It is possible that Sir Gawen, and perhaps also Gibbes, led St. Leger just enough of a chase to the west to distract his attention from Sir Peter's eastward flight to the Dorset port of Weymouth. Sir Gawen may have thought a spell of imprisonment and royal displeasure worth his nephew's life.

Dennys and St. Leger may also have been something less than assiduous in their efforts to find Sir Peter. Preventing Sir Peter from launching a rebellion against the queen was one thing; handing over a long-time friend and colleague to the queen's tender mercies once that rebellion was safely suppressed was quite another. One of the most interesting aspects of the life of Sir Peter Carew is the light it sheds on the complex web of relationships that linked the gentry of a particular county. The families of Dennys and Carew had long worked side by side in the administration of Devon. Sir Thomas Dennys and Sir William Carew were close friends. Dennys could quarrel with Sir William's son during the tense situation of 1549, but still speak for that son's interests a year later when Robert Warren brought suit against Sir Peter, and could still work effectively with Sir Peter on numerous royal commissions. In 1554, Dennys struggled to prevent Sir Peter from leading Devon into rebellion, but he seems to have been happy enough to see his old friend's son escape the ax, whatever his transgressions. The body of gentlemen who administered Devon for the Crown, like similar groups of gentlemen in the other counties, were a family, whose members could quarrel violently among themselves, but who showed an amazing capacity to close ranks when destruction threatened any one member.

If Sir Gawen had indeed sacrificed his freedom for his nephew, he might have been amused, in his new lodgings in Exeter Castle, to have read in the imperial ambassadors' dispatch of 29 January that Sir Peter Carew "and his brother" had fled into France. Although Wyatt's phase of the premature rebellion was about to consume the government's attention, the whereabouts of the dangerous Sir Peter Carew was still very much a topic of interest in London. According to the ambassadors, Carew had been so bold as to write before his departure to a member of the Council to boast that he knew "a king who would treat him better than the queen had done."[87] Such an impetuous taunt would not have been out of character for Carew, who would shortly in France make a number of provocative statements to his fellow exiles, but there is no other evidence of this letter beyond its mention by the not always trustworthy ambassadors. On 31 January, Gardiner assured the ambassadors that Carew and his supporters were hiding somewhere in the West and would soon be caught.[88] But Gardiner's assurances were hollow. Carew and his little band of shipmates were no longer in English waters. Carew's phase of the rebellion was over, even as Wyatt's phase was about to begin. For Sir Peter Carew, two long years of exile lay ahead.

---

[1] Hooker, "Life," p. 53.

[2] Ibid., p. 54.

[3] HMC, *Exeter Records*, pp. 366-67.

[4] Sir Peter and the other commissioners reported from Devon on their activities on 16 June. See Devon Commissioners to the Council, BL, Stowe MS 141, f. 54. Five days

later, on 21 June, the great officers of state, the peers, the chief royal officials, and the judges were summoned to sign the king's letters patent excluding Mary and Elizabeth from the succession and settling the Crown on Jane Grey. See Barrett L. Beer, *Northumberland: The Political Career of John Dudley, Earl of Warwick and Duke of Northumberland* (Kent, Ohio: Kent State University Press, 1973), p. 154.

5   Bindoff, *House of Commons*, I, p. 578; Jordan, *Threshold*, pp. 504-10.

6   Hooker, "Life," p. 54.

7   *Cal.SP Span.*, XI, p. 120.

8   The arrival at the Tower of Northumberland and his chief co-conspirators is carefully recorded in *A Chronicle of England During the Reigns of the Tudors* by Charles Wriothesley, edited by William Douglas Hamilton, vol. II, new series, no. 20 (London: The Camden Society, 1877), pp. 90-91.

9   Wriothesley, *Chronicle of England*, II, pp. 94-95.

10 John Gough Nichols, ed., *The Chronicle of Queen Jane, and of the Two Years of Queen Mary* (London: Camden Society, 1850), p. 14.

11 LP, XIII(2), 753.

12 *CPR*, Mary and Philip and Mary, vol. I, 28 September 1553, (London: HMSO, 1936-39), pp. 253-54.

13 René Aubert de Vertot, *Ambassades de Messieurs de Noailles en Angleterre*, vol. II (Leyden, 1763), pp. 174-75.

14 For more on the French ambassador's visitors that autumn, see E. Harris Harbison, "French Intrigue at the Court of Queen Mary, *American Historical Review* 45 (April 1940): pp. 547-49.

15 Jennifer Loach, *Parliament and the Crown in the Reign of Mary Tudor* (Oxford: Clarendon Press, 1986), pp. 83-84.

16 Loach, *Parliament and the Crown*, pp. 83-86; the full Crown Office list is printed in Bindoff, *House of Commons*, I, Appendix XI, p. 16.

17 *Cal.SP Span.*, XI, p. 349.

18 Ibid., p. 364.

19 In late November, Noailles still believed that rising opposition to the proposed treaty would force the queen to change her mind. See Vertot, *Ambassades*, II, p. 271.

20 Indictment of 1553 Conspirators, 7 April 1554, PRO, KB27/1174 Rex V.

21 Indictment of 1553 Conspirators, 7 April 1554, PRO, KB8/29, r2

22 Exeter Indictment of Sir Peter Carew and Others, 13 September 1554, PRO, KB27/1176, Rex III.

23 While his daughter languished in the Tower, Suffolk narrowly escaped the ax and regained his freedom. As a convinced Protestant tainted indeliably by Northumberland's coup attempt, Suffolk was, in a sense, living on borrowed time. His involvement with the November plotters was simply a matter of paying the debt he had avoided in July.

24 Deposition of Katherine Ashley, 4 February 1549, *Cal.SP Dom.*, Edward VI, #196.

25 T.B. Howells, comp., *A Complete Collection of State Trials*, vol. I (London: Hansard, 1816), p. 882.

26 Vertot, *Ambassades*, II, pp. 253-54, 255-56,

27 Howells, *State Trials*, I, p. 863; *Chronicle of Queen Jane*, p. 69.

28 E. Harris Harbison, *Rival Ambassadors at the Court of Queen Mary* (Princeton, N.J.: Princeton University Press, 1940), p. 112.

29 Exeter Indictment of Sir Peter Carew and Others, 13 September 1554, PRO, KB27/1176, Rex III.

30 Howells, *State Trials*, I, p. 882.

31 Loach, *Parliament and the Crown*, pp. 225-26.

32 *Cal.SP Span.*, IV(1), 306.

33 Hooker, "Life," pp. 19-20.

34 Howells, *State Trials*, I, p. 883.

35 Ibid., p. 882.

36 Harbison, *Rival Ambassadors*, p. 117.

37 Amos C. Miller, *Sir Henry Killigrew: Elizabethan Soldier and Diplomat* (Leicester: Leicester University Press, 1963), pp. 3-17.

38 Declaration of John Prideaux, 24 January 1554, PRO, SP11/2/27.

39 Philip Caraman, *The Western Rising 1549: The Prayer Book Rebellion* (Exeter: Westcountry Books, 1994), pp. 88-89, 104, 115.

40 Declaration of John Prideaux, 24 January 1554, PRO, SP11/2/27.

41 Bindoff, *House of Commons*, I, pp. 638-39.

42 Vertot, *Ambassades*, II, p. 342.

43 APC, IV, p. 382.

44 *Cal.SP Span.*, XII, p. 16.

45 Declaration of John Prideaux, 24 January 1554, PRO, SP11/2/27.

46 Ibid.

47 *Cal.SP Span.*, XII, p. 34.

48 Declaration of John Prideaux, 24 January 1554, PRO, SP11/2/27.

49 Articles for Watch and Ward in Exeter, 24 January 1554, PRO, SP11/2/25.

50 *Cal.SP Span.*, XII, p. 31.

51 Declaration of John Prideaux, 24 January 1554, PRO, SP11/2/27.

52 *Cal.SP Span.*, XII, p. 31.

53 APC, IV, p. 385.

54 *Cal.SP Span.*, XII, p. 34.

55 Sir Gawen's servant stated that his master went over the city wall on the night of Friday 19 January, and Sir Gawen himself later deposed that he went over the wall on the night of 25 January. Since Sir Gawen was at Mohun's Ottery on 19 January when he and Sir Peter sent their letter to Dennys, his escape from the city was probably the previous night. Unless there were two escapes from Exeter, Sir Gawen was probably incorrect about the date being 25 January. See Articles for Watch and Ward in Exeter, 24 January 1554, PRO, SP11/2/25 and the Deposition of Sir Gawen Carew, 28 January 1554, PRO, SP11/3/34-35.

56 Articles for Watch and Ward in Exeter, 24 January 1554, PRO, SP11/2/25; Deposition of Sir Gawen Carew, 28 January 1554, PRO, SP11/3/34-35.

57 Sir Peter Carew and Sir Gawen Carew to Sir Thomas Dennys, 19 January 1554, PRO, SP11/2/4.

[58] *Chronicle of Queen Jane*, p. 35.

[59] Harbison, *Rival Ambassadors*, pp. 126-27.

[60] Queen Mary to Sir Hugh Pollard, 22 January 1554, *Cal.SP Dom.*, 1547-1580 (London: HMSO, 1856), p. 56.

[61] Sir Thomas Dennys to the Council, 25 January 1554, PRO, SP11/2/31.

[62] Articles for Watch and Ward in Exeter, 24 January 1554, PRO, SP11/2/25.

[63] Ibid.

[64] John Ridgeway to Sir Thomas Dennys, 24 January 1554, PRO, SP11/2/23.

[65] Articles for Watch and Ward in Exeter, 24 January 1554, PRO, SP11/2/25.

[66] Hooker, "Life," pp. 56-57.

[67] Sir John St. Leger to the Earl of Arundel, 26 January 1554, PRO, SP11/2/35.

[68] *Cal.SP Span.*, XII, p. 139.

[69] Ibid., p. 41.

[70] Sir Peter Carew to Sir Thomas Dennys, 23 January 1554, PRO, SP11/2/19.

[71] Hooker, "Life," p. 57.

[72] Ibid.

[73] Deposition of Sir Gawen Carew, 28 January 1554, PRO, SP11/3/34-35.

[74] Hooker, "Life," p. 57.

[75] John Graynfeld to Sir John St. Leger, Sir Thomas Dennys, and Sir Roger Bluet, 3 February 1554, PRO, SP11/3/17.

[76] Deposition of Sir Gawen Carew, 28 January 1554, PRO, SP11/3/34-35.

[77] Christina Hallowell Garrett, *The Marian Exiles: A Study in the Origins of Elizabethan Puritanism* (Cambridge: Cambridge University Press, 1938), pp. 131, 209, 309.

[78] Hooker, "Life," p. 58.

[79] John Graynfeld to Sir John St. Leger, Sir Thomas Dennys, and Sir Roger Bluet, 3 February 1554, PRO, SP11/3/17.

80 Queen Mary to Lord Lieutenants, 26 January 1554, *Cal.SP Dom.*, 1547-1580, p. 57.

81 Sir John St. Leger to the Council, 4 February 1554, PRO, SP11/3/15.

82 Sir Gawen Carew to Sir Thomas Dennys, 24 January 1554, PRO, SP11/2/21.

83 Sir John St. Leger to the Council, 29 January 1554, PRO, SP11/2/56-57.

84 Deposition of Sir Gawen Carew, 28 January 1554, PRO, SP11/3/34-35.

85 Sir John St. Leger to the Council, 29 January 1554, PRO, SP11/2/56-57.

86 Sir John St. Leger to the Council, 4 February 1554, PRO, SP11/3/15; John Graynfeld to Sir John St. Leger, Sir Thomas Dennys, and Sir Roger Bluet, 3 February 1554, PRO, SP11/3/17.

87 *Cal.SP.Span.*, XII, p.55.

88 Ibid., p.64.

CHAPTER 8

THE EXILE

By the first week of February 1554, Dr. Nicholas Wotton, Mary's ambassador in France, knew that Carew was in Paris. A rumor in the French court said a great "milord" had come to seek King Henri's aid against the English queen. On 10 February, Wotton demanded an audience with the king to whom he denounced Carew as a rebel and a traitor. If the king wanted friendly relations with England, he should deny Carew refuge in France and send him back to England a prisoner. To do any less, declared Wotton, would be to abet a rebel. Henri replied that he had never heard of Carew and denied that he would ever support anyone against the queen. But despite the king's smooth denials, Wotton learned that Carew had seen the king before leaving Paris for Rouen on 9 February.[1] Carew's move to Rouen caused fears for the safety of Calais,[2] which were heightened when the deputy of Calais shortly thereafter reported that the king had given Carew three ships and placed him in command of 1,000 dissident Englishmen currently being assembled in France for service against the queen. The crushing of Wyatt's rebellion somewhat calmed fears of what Carew might do, and on 16 February the queen felt confident enough to scold Noailles for the way his master was allowing Carew to threaten her from French soil.[3]

The scolding only seemed to convince Noailles that the queen feared Carew, for next day he urged the constable to send Carew back to England at once to help in "stirring up a rising."[4] On 22 February, the queen again warned Wotton to watch the proceedings of Carew and the other English exiles closely. The queen, convinced that Carew and King Henri were conspiring secretly against her, had received intelligence that

Carew was in Rouen seeking to hire English ships and seamen for some suspicious enterprise.[5] In an audience with the king on the same day, Wotton announced the defeat of Wyatt and again demanded the arrest of Carew. The king, who had seen Carew during his visits to the French court in 1546 and 1551, again denied knowing him. However, now that he understood this Carew to be a traitor, the king agreed to seize him, if possible, and return him to England along with every other English refugee guilty of crimes.[6]

Wotton's demands, Henri's denials, and Noailles' urgings all indicated the paramount position among the English exiles accorded to Carew by both the English and French governments. The number of English political exiles in France grew rapidly after Wyatt's rebellion flared out. By mid-March the band included Sir William Pickering, Carew's fellow conspirator, and a sizable contingent of Courtenays, Killigrews, and others from the West Country.[7] Carew and his West Country friends had naval and seafaring experience, and no one knew what damage they could cause if Henri gave them ships and safe harbors to roam the channel at will. The anxiety these exiles, and particularly Carew, caused the English government was amply demonstrated by Noailles' tense interview before the Council on 15 March. Gardiner told the ambassador that the queen did not fear Carew and his band of renegades, was determined to have Carew extradited, and marveled that the French king would give aid and comfort to such traitors. When Noailles flatly denied that Henri was supporting Carew, Lord Howard angrily contradicted him. Noailles suggested that if Howard cared to go to France the king would give him warrant to arrest Carew. The ambassador then launched into a long discourse on the greater difficulty of capturing a criminal in France than in England, concluding with mention of the greater natural compassion of French people and more bountiful mercy of French princes. However, the English outrage over Carew worried Noailles enough for him to recommend to the constable two days later that Carew be warned to "restrain himself a bit more, both in his presence and in his language." Noailles also suggested that Carew keep himself better concealed and change his residence more frequently so as to limit English opportunities to track his activities. For his own ease, Noailles suggested that Wotton be given every means to arrest Carew, both for the ambassador's and the queen's amusement.[8]

Noailles' recommendations proved timely. On 9 March, Renard told the emperor that he had learned through spies of a French fleet, supposedly in preparation for Scotland, but actually meant for an attack on England. The fleet was being readied on Carew's advice, the rebel having told Henri that the English were more willing to have the French than the Spanish and would not resist.[9] On 24 March, English agents reported Carew, Pickering, and other exiles in Caen, where Carew and Pickering were about to be placed in command of 200 sail to intercept Philip on his way from Spain. Three ships full of Englishmen were already at sea under Killigrew watching for Philip.[10] Four days later another English agent reported an increase in Carew's retinue, whose members were so well treated that their collusion with the French king could no longer be doubted. Carew showed none of the restraint recommended by Noailles when he urged his comrades to stand with France against the hated Spaniards.

> Are we not allianced with Normandy? In what ancient house is either there or in France, but we claim by them, and they by us? Why then should we not rather embrace their love, than submit ourselves to the servitude of Spain?[11]

The agent did, however, detect a willingness among at least some of the exiles to leave off their French allegiance. He believed that if they were assured of their lives, they would gladly return to England.

Carew, meanwhile, seemed indefatigable in his attempts to harm the queen. In mid-March, Wotton complained to the French of the *Sacre*, a ship of Dieppe given to Carew with money to outfit her by the captain of Dieppe Castle on Henri's orders. To a new demand for Carew's extradition, the French king responded with complaints about the way his ambassador was being treated. He denied the *Sacre* was in Carew's hands; that vessel had been given to other Englishmen whose intent was to fight the king's enemies, not Queen Mary.[12] A week later, word had Carew with a French fleet in Brittany, and the queen's officers in Cornwall reported the capture of a ship bearing 20 Englishmen sent by Carew to reconnoiter western coasts.[13] Other rumors said Carew was preparing to fall on the Isle of Wight, to seize the Scellies and rouse the West to rebellion, or simply to roam the channel preying on English ships.[14] A report on 27 March had Carew returning from Brittany, where he left his ships in the charge of John Courtenay, his fellow passenger on Raleigh's bark, to Abbeville, where the French king was allegedly gathering a great force.[15] Even the emperor picked up word of Carew's activities, warning Renard on 2 April that Carew was helping plan French attacks on Wight and the West Country.[16]

The queen continued to angrily demand Carew's extradition, and Noailles continued to recommend that some show be made of arresting him.[17] The French king made some move in this direction, promising Wotton that Carew, Pickering, and others would be apprehended, but at the end of March, to Wotton's knowledge, no attempt had been made to arrest any of the rebels.[18] The queen even enlisted Cardinal Pole, on his way to England, to take up Carew's extradition with Henri.[19] Carew, apparently weary of the constant watch being kept on his movements, finally broke the official wall of denial that surrounded him by sending a letter to the French constable. This letter was shown to Wotton on 14 April. In the letter, Carew said he left England for his personal safety, not for conspiring against the queen; he suffered because he would not allow his country to be oppressed by strangers. Carew wondered why Wotton pursued him, sending men everywhere to seek him out. He expressed a desire to meet with Wotton and demanded that he be sent immediately to the queen for punishment if any wrongdoing could be proved against him. On the heels of this communication from Carew, Wotton was contacted by Pickering's servant, who claimed his master wanted to talk to the ambassador about certain matters. Wotton refused to see either man without the queen's consent.[20]

By late April, the first open cracks appeared in the unity of the English exiles. On 25 April, Pickering and one or two others stole away to Lyon while Carew was on a visit to the French court. Pickering felt mistreated by his comrades, and intended to take himself into Italy or Germany. The exiles had clearly come to mistrust one another, for Wotton heard that upon finding Pickering and his fellows gone, the remaining exiles immediately assumed that Wotton had sent them to the queen to confess what they knew. Wotton reported unsuccessful exile attempts to overtake and kill the fugitives, and believed their lives were still in danger from the French king, who had expected Pickering to accompany Carew to court and would be angry at the break in exile ranks. Before departing, Pickering had told Wotton through a servant that the French would land, at Carew's urging, in late summer in Essex and Wight. To assist with these plans, Carew had an unknown Englishman spying for him in England. Renard's spies also discovered connections between Carew and several leading men in England, learning from Carew's secretary of his master's habit of smuggling letters into England hidden in slippers.[21] Wotton recommended that the queen grant Pickering mercy, for he seemed a man both able and willing to do the queen good service.[22]

The queen, meanwhile, dismissed Carew's letter to the constable as an impudent attempt to excuse his treason. Claiming his enterprise was aimed only at preventing foreign domination was but a pretense to hide his hatred of the queen's religion. Carew was a manifest danger to the queen's person and the whole realm.[23] In May, Carew wrote directly to Wotton requesting him to sue the queen for pardon and expressing a willingness to submit to the queen if she showed a willingness to grant mercy. Carew and his fellow exiles complained of their poverty and of the French king's distrust and unwillingness to employ them.[24] On 29 May, the queen responded, declaring Carew's offense to be great but desiring to show mercy if Carew was indeed sincere in repenting his fault and earnest in his desire to serve. There could be no pardon, however, until Carew confessed his fault in full and declared to Wotton the complete circumstances surrounding his misdeeds.[25]

Carew was apparently unwilling to confess, for no more was heard from him until mid-July, when Wotton picked up rumors that Carew was determined to leave France for Italy.[26] Within a few days, Wotton learned that Carew, having promised on his arrival not to leave France without the king's consent, had sent Henry Killigrew to the French court to declare to the king his intention to leave the country and to request the king's permission to do so. The constable kept Killigrew waiting four days, before taxing him with all the king had done for Carew and complaining bitterly of the inconstancy of Englishmen. However, on 10 July, Killigrew was told that Carew could leave if he wished. Sir Peter left after midnight the next day for Venice, a natural and familiar destination for him. Wotton's informant said Carew had great difficulty raising money for the trip and was likely to live miserably in Venice.[27] Before leaving Paris on 11 July, Carew wrote again to Wotton, who forwarded the letter to the queen on 29 July. In this letter, Carew expressed his deep regret for the past and denied that he ever meant to harm the queen's person. He simply could not bear a foreign yoke and had rashly despised to live as a subject of the prince of Spain, and so had sought by various means both in England and France to hinder the queen's purpose. Carew then confessed his error in planning and undertaking such evil deeds and professed unfeigned repentance. To prove to the queen his absolute submission to her, he was voluntarily leaving France, where he had lived as a gentleman in the king's favor, to dwell in poverty in another country unless the queen extended her own favor to him. Carew closed by begging Wotton to stand his good friend.[28]

Standing friend to Carews in trouble was virtually a full-time job for Wotton in the spring of 1554. In February, Wotton learned that his brother-in-law, Sir Gawen Carew, was being brought to London with William Gibbes and Sir Edward Rogers "to abide the order of the law."[29] Sir Gawen was imprisoned in the Tower on 2 March.[30] Wotton lamented to Secretary Petre the miserable state of his sister Mary, who now watched the good match she had made swallowed up in the consequences of her husband's treason.[31] Those consequences came quickly. Already on 30 January Sheriff Dennys was in possession of Mohun's Ottery and Sir Gawen's house at Tiverton; he forwarded inventories of the goods and chattels at each house to the chancellor a week later.

The inventory of Mohun's Ottery allows us to glimpse something of the size and appearance of that now-vanished manor house, as well as something of the Devon lifestyle of Sir Peter Carew. The colorful bed chambers bore names. The steward's chamber contained a great joined bedstead with coverlets of tapestry and hangings of yellow and black, the Carew family colors. Indeed, yellow and black were the dominant colors in most of the bed chambers. The grandly named king's chamber was hung with those colors and contained as well "a joined bedstead, a chair covered with green cloth embroidered," and two small chests. The maiden's chamber boasted "a feather bed" and "a window cloth of red and green say." The yellow chamber, which also contained two featherbeds and much fine bedding, returned to Carew colors for its hangings. The galley held "a Spyres chest wherein is a canapy of thread" and six pair of Dowles sheets (from Brittany), as well as napkins, towels, and table linen. Most of the rooms were described in the inventory by their placement in the house: "the corner chamber next to the barn," "the chamber under the wardrobe," "the chamber over the gate house." The gate house, part of which can still be seen, must have been the most distinctive feature of the house. The chamber over it was hung in red and green say and included a tester of the same colors and material and a "close stool covered with green cloth." The "chamber next over the gate house" contained more bedding, a tester of white and red silk, and a chair "covered with crimson satin embroidered with gold lace." The wardrobe contained "a pair of harness, whereof ii for demilances," and the kitchen yielded "a grater, a mortar, a pestle of brass," and various other utensils of pewter and brass.

Of plate, Mohun's Ottery had little, merely "ii salts of silver whereof one is gilt and the other ungilt, iiii spoons of silver, a stone cup covered with silver, a cover silver for a like cup." Perhaps Sir Peter had conveyed his plate elsewhere as a precaution, or perhaps it was normally housed elsewhere, in London or on the Tailboys estates in Lincolnshire. Outbuildings included the day house, brewhouse, bakehouse, barn, and buttery, and the barton round about the manor house was planted with 30 acres of wheat. Eight horses were listed, several of which had been given to servants in recompense for wages and three that were reserved for use by Lady Margaret. A list of cattle found on the estate was also appended.[32] The inventory of Sir Gawen's house, done on 2 February, listed similar quantities of bedding, tapestries, and hangings of yellow and black, and listed something not found in Mohun's Ottery—books.[33] Both houses were of modest size and scale and not lavishly furnished, probably because the Carews, like Henry VIII himself, took many of their furnishings with them when they traveled. Because the Carews moved about a good deal and spent much time in London, neither house probably displayed the full extent of their means. But both houses fairly represented the comfortable lifestyle the two men had lost.

On 7 April, Sir Peter was indicted in the Guildhall in London with Throckmorton, Croft, Arnold, Pickering, Rogers, Winter, and Warner for conspiring with Wyatt and Harper in London on 26 November 1553 to seize the Tower and make war on the queen with the intention of depriving her of the royal title.[34] Wyatt and Harper had already been separately indicted with Suffolk and others for rebellion. Only Carew and Pickering had escaped the kingdom; all the other conspirators were in custody. Of these, only Croft and Throckmorton were brought to trial, and Throckmorton so ably defended himself as to win an extremely rare acquittal, for which the jury itself spent some months in prison.[35] Croft's jury took the hint and convicted him of treason, but neither he nor most of the other men indicted for conspiracy paid with their lives.[36] Death was the price only for Wyatt, Suffolk, and William Thomas, whose plotting with Carew was compounded by his proposal to assassinate the queen, evidence for which came out at Wyatt's trial. After departing Mohun's Ottery, Thomas was captured and brought to the Tower, where, on the night of 26 February 1554, he tried to commit suicide by "thrusting himself under the pappes with a knife."[37] The attempt failed, and in May a fully recovered Thomas was indicted for plotting the queen's death and for conspiring with Carew at Mohun's Ottery in December 1553.[38] He was executed on 18 May. All the other conspirators indicted with Carew spent varying amounts of time in prison and had their pardons at some point during 1555 or 1556.[39]

Sir Gawen and Gibbes languished in the Tower, unable to be seen by anyone,[40] throughout the summer. On 29 March 1554, Lady Guildford, Sir Gawen's wife, was licensed to receive the revenues of her lands for use only to support herself and her husband. The Council demanded that she stand ready to account to them any expenses incurred by either her husband or herself.[41] On 15 June, she was licensed to receive the revenues of her husband's lands under the same conditions.[42] Although both prisoners remained in the Tower, Sir Gawen and Gibbes were indicted with Sir Peter on 13 September in Exeter.[43] The indictment claimed that Sir Gawen and Gibbes became party to Sir Peter's treasons on 17 January 1554 when he summoned them both to Mohun's Ottery to assist him in waging war on the queen. Both then remained at the manor until Sir Peter's flight, part of an armed force of 40 rebels.[44] Neither man was ever brought to trial. On 18 January 1555, both men were released from the Tower along with Croft, Harper, Throckmorton, Warner, Rogers, and others, leaving the fortress to "a great shooting of guns."[45] The Council bound Sir Gawen for £500 for his "good abearing, order and fine at pleasure."[46] Ten days later, Sir Gawen's brother-in-law, Ambassador Wotton, wrote the Council from Poissy requesting that Sir Gawen be freed.[47] In May, Sir Gawen had to obtain a letter from the Council to halt proceedings of outlawry against him in King's Bench. His promised pardon having not yet passed the great seal, the proceedings of outlawry had continued unabated.[48] On 4 June, the Council allowed him to leave London to put his affairs in order in Devon, provided he returned to London by Ascension day.[49] Sir Gawen finally received his pardon on 2 July 1555; it covered treasons and offenses committed before 1 March 1554 and released to him "all forfeitures" related to his indictment.[50] By mid-1555, Sir Gawen had recovered his freedom and, apparently without further payment, all his lands and chattels as well. If he had indeed ventured himself for his nephew, his gamble had paid off.

Another Carew relative who fell afoul of the queen also came out right eventually. Sir Arthur Champernon was apparently released after a brief imprisonment in Exeter, for there is no record that he was either brought to prison in London or to trial in Devon. By 9 April, he was probably a free man, for on that day the Council ordered all tenants of Sir Peter Carew's manors of Chittlehampton and Newenham in Devon to allow Sir Arthur to collect the rents from these manors owed by Carew to Champernon's wife, the former wife of Carew's late brother George. Champernon was to have payment of the rent due from Carew as if Carew

"had not offended and stayed quiet in the realm."[51]   By noisily letting
everyone know he had left Mohun's Ottery on bad terms with his traitorous
cousin, Champernon had been able to distance himself sufficiently from Sir
Peter to avoid any serious consequences.

Although indicted in April with the other London conspirators,
Sir Peter Carew was singled out by the government from the beginning
as one of the most dangerous rebels. The vehemence of some of the
comments attributed to Carew, especially his expressed willingness to be
"one of the hundred gentlemen that should take the queen and put her
in the Tower," and his continuing treasonous practice with the French
probably accounted for much of the government's attitude. The most
complete list of the government's charges against Carew is found in the
September indictment lodged against both Carews and Gibbes in Exeter.
The Exeter indictment describes Sir Peter as "impie inverse et erronie
religionis [long of impious and erroneous religion]" and quotes his
blustering pledge to Suffolk to remove the queen and "do the best to
place the Lady Elizabeth in her stead" should the queen refuse to give
up the Spanish marriage and moderate her religious doings. Carew is
further charged with levying war on the queen by gathering armed men
about himself at Mohun's Ottery in January 1554, with inducing the earl
of Devon to lead a revolt against the queen, and with departing the
realm without royal license. [52]

Since Carew's body was beyond the government's reach, the
Council moved quickly against the traitor's lands. On 13 June 1554, a
lease of the rectory and parish church of Luppitt, "late in the tenure of
Sir Peter Carew," was made to one John Gammage and one John
Malacke.[53] Luppitt was the ancient parish church of the Carew family
in Devon and burial site of Carew's father, Sir William. On 26 October,
George Jernigan, sewer to Philip and Mary, received a lease of the
former Courtenay properties held by Carew at Okehampton in Devon.

This grant stated flatly that Carew was "attainted of high treason," although the bill of attainder confiscating the estates, goods, and chattels of Carew, Suffolk, Wyatt and 51 others did not pass until 14 January 1555, almost three months after the Jernigan grant and a year after Carew's flight to France.[54] This rush to parcel out Carew's properties before Parliament had officially attainted him supports D.M. Loades's assertion that the government considered Carew an attainted traitor from the presentation of the London indictments in April 1554.[55] Indeed, a bill of attainder against Carew and the others was lost in the April 1554 Parliament through a mysterious dispute over the seizability of entailed lands.[56] It appears as if the government ignored its failure to obtain Carew's attainder in the spring of 1554 and proceeded against his lands as if the bill had passed; the actual passage of the attainder in 1555 then gave a sort of retroactive sanction to actions already taken against the Carew lands. The bulk of the Carew estates, however, remained in the queen's hands until March 1555, when they were granted to James Bassett, a gentleman of the queen's privy chamber. Bassett came of two old western families, the Bassetts and the Grenvilles; his mother, Honour Grenville, married as her second husband Lord Lisle, Sir George Carew's nemesis at Calais in 1539-40. Bassett was an enthusiastic Catholic who sat for Devon in three of Mary's Parliaments; from the queen's point of view, he was a logical choice to succeed to the wealth and influence in Devon once enjoyed by the Protestant traitor Sir Peter Carew. The heart of the ancient Carew lands, including Mohun's Ottery, Monckton, Ashwater, Weston Peverell, and Georgeham passed into Bassett's possession on a 30-year lease. The combined yearly rent of just the five aforementioned manors was almost £150. The Crown agreed to maintain the manor house at Mohun's Ottery, including repairs to the lead roof and all tiles, slates, and timbers. Bassett was held responsible for all other repairs. Since Bassett did not intend to live at Mohun's Ottery, keepers were appointed for the park, house, and garden at wages of 2d per day.[57]

Basset did not receive Carew's movable property. The items inventoried by Dennys at Mohun's Ottery were sold back at their appraised value to Lady Margaret by the Council's instructions in June 1554.[58] On 22 September 1554, Lady Margaret received answer to her petition of Philip and Mary for permission to write to her husband overseas and to send him some "material relief." The king and queen, wishing to show mercy and believing Lady Margaret to be "a good and loving wife," agreed to the request. Lady Tailboys was called before the Council and told she could write to her husband and could for this one time only send him relief out of her own goods.[59] Lady Tailboys insisted that the Council give her a copy of the royal answer to her petition. She was indeed a clever and effective suitor. The household records of Sir William Petre, a member of the Council, record the delivery of "an ambling grey gelding" worth 10s to Petre's steward by Lady Tailboys's servant just five days before the Council answered the petition.[60] Hooker called Sir Peter's wife "a continual suitor and travailler to King Philip, and to the Queen, for her husband." The slight thaw in the government's attitude toward Carew in the autumn of 1554 is probably due in equal parts to Lady Tailboys's strenuous and unremitting efforts on his behalf and to Philip's desire to rehabilitate all disaffected Englishmen whose talents and experience might make them useful to him. The queen certainly displayed little inclination to pardon Carew before Philip's arrival in England in July 1554. Thus, despite the queen's hostility and the loss of his estates, Carew had some cause for hope of improvement in his condition at the end of 1554.

There was certainly need for improvement. The months in France, begun so bravely, had passed in frustration and ended in dejection. The French king had promised much, but delivered little, and Carew, a direct man of bold and rapid action, had found himself mired only in inaction and intrigue. By the summer of 1554, the indecision of the French king, the harassment of English spies, the discord among the exiles, and his own straitened circumstances led him to seek pardon from Mary through Wotton and to leave France as a sign to the queen of his genuine repentance.

Carew's choice of Venice as his next place of refuge is not surprising. Carew had visited the city several times during his sojourn on the continent in 1540-42; after the death of his cousin in Vienna, he had retreated to Venice to recover, staying the whole winter of 1541-42. Carew may also have spent some time in Venice during his residence in Italy in the late 1520s. Peter Vannes, Mary's ambassador in Venice, notified his government of Carew's presence in the city in mid-August 1554. Carew asked to meet with Vannes, but like Wotton in France, Vannes refused to speak with a known traitor without the queen's permission. The Venetian ambassador in Brussels told his English counterpart, Sir John Mason, that the queen should leave Carew in Venice, where he could do less mischief than anywhere else. Everyone had feared what Carew might do in France, where he could at any time have turned to piracy and preyed upon the queen's subjects in the channel. Perhaps, ventured the ambassador, the quiet in distant Venice might help Carew learn obedience and cause him to repent.[61] The Venetian ambassador's remarks indicate the depth of English fears about Carew and his ability to cause trouble. On 2 September, Mason informed the queen of his Venetian colleague's opinion, and told Vannes that he could speak to Carew on his own account whenever he pleased. In what could have been an echo of Philip's sentiments as currently circulated in Brussels, Mason also suggested that Carew was not evil by nature, and that it might be useful to carefully cultivate his loyalty.[62]

Hooker, who passed over the French phase of Carew's exile by recording merely Sir Peter's refusal to serve a foreign prince against his own country, had several heroic tales to tell of Carew's stay in Venice. Peter Vannes, far from talking with Carew about a possible pardon, "sought all the ways he could how he might have him to be taken and apprehended." First, Vannes tried legal means, telling the Venetian government that Carew was not a distressed refugee, to whom the city would naturally give sanctuary, but a notorious rebel and traitor to his queen and his country, whom the authorities would normally arrest and expel. But Vannes did not reckon with Carew's connections within the Venetian government. Hearing of Vannes' charge against him, Carew appealed to his friend Francisco Foscarini, the Venetian attorney-general. Carew and Foscarini had become friends during the latter's term of service with the Venetian embassy at the court of Edward VI. Foscarini visited Carew, heard his story, and assured him that all would be well: "I will. . . repair to the court and see whether any matter be put in against you, which if it be so, I will answer it for you." The Venetian also advised Carew to look carefully to himself and "go not abroad, unless you have good company with you, and that you be also well armed and appointed." Foscarini then went straightaway to the Venetian court and gave "such an effectual and pithy answer" to the bill of information lodged there by Vannes for Carew's arrest that the "bill was rejected."[63]

Frustrated in his first attempt to seize Carew, Vannes now tried "another way." He hired "certain ruffians" to keep watch on Carew's movements, looking for an opportunity to secretly "dispatch and murder him." Carew, taking Focarini's warning to heart, left his lodgings rarely and then only well accompanied. Whether these companions were more Venetian friends of Carew's, an escort supplied by Foscarini, or Carew's servants, Hooker did not say. Whoever they were, they served well their purpose some time later when Vannes laid his "ruffians" in ambush at a street corner "called *ruga causa*," which the ambassador knew Carew must pass to return to his lodgings. Perceiving Vannes's trap, Carew lined his company up by twos, placing himself with a partner in the middle of the group, and so passed quickly by the dangerous corner. The assassins, not knowing which of the company was Carew and hampered in their identification by the dim evening light, allowed Carew's party to pass without challenge, all the while asking each other "'la quelle,' 'which is he?'" Vannes's ruffians apparently had some scruples, for they refused to depart from Vannes's instructions to shoot only Carew and to harm no one else. Hooker depicted the assassins as milling about the corner in confusion until the last members of Carew's company turned around with their own pistols at the ready and asked them what they wanted. Carew returned safely to his lodgings giving thanks to God for his narrow escape.[64]

The close call at the *ruga causa* convinced Carew that he should "no longer tarry there in such dangers and perils." Resolving therefore to leave Venice, Carew turned again to the faithful Foscarini, who helped Sir Peter borrow some money and slip safely out of the city.[65] Foscarini was likely not acting out of friendship alone in helping Carew to escape; Carew's success in eluding Vannes and in obtaining funds probably owed something to the covert support of the Venetian Signory, in whose behalf Foscarini was acting.[66] The length of Carew's stay in Venice is unclear, although it seems to have lasted about nine or ten months, from July or August 1554 to the late spring of 1555. Hooker indicated that Carew went directly from Venice to Strasburg in Germany,[67] but we know that in April 1555 Carew returned secretly to England. On 29 April, the Council ordered the sheriff of Lincolnshire to examine Sir William Skipwith, Carew's brother-in-law, and a Mr. Piersall concerning information laid before the Council by deposition that Sir Peter Carew had come to Lincolnshire, lodged at Skipwith's house, and sent letters to Piersall.[68] In 1556, an action for slander brought by William Lord Willoughby against one Arthur Thimbleby provided further details of Carew's surreptitious visit to Lincolnshire the previous year. Thimbleby alleged that Carew

did land at Hull, and from thence came to William Skipwith's house at Ormsby, and there did lie one night and so went to a place called Frampton near Boston, and there the lord Willoughby and Sir William Skipwith did appoint to meet him, and Raffe Piersall, gentleman, received letters from the said Sir Peter Carew to aid the said Sir Peter Carew with money.[69]

What success Carew had in raising funds from his brother-in-law and the other gentlemen of Lincolnshire, we do not know. This desperate descent into England was both a typical piece of Carew bravado and an indication of the seriousness of Carew's need for money. From Lincolnshire, Carew probably made his way to Strasburg, where Hooker said Carew stayed until he "had news from his lady and wife." Strasburg in these years was the home of a growing group of English Protestant exiles who had left their homes to escape the queen's Catholic church and its increasing use of fire to purge the realm of heresy. Carew perhaps believed that he could find both moral and material support more easily in Strasburg than elsewhere. Because they had fled specifically for religion, most of the Strasburg exiles differed from the political exiles Carew had nominally led in France. Carew's Protestant and Edwardian credentials were powerful enough to gain him full entree to the highest levels of the Strasburg exile community. This entree is attested by Carew's close association in Strasburg with John Ponet, the Edwardian bishop of Winchester, and John Cheke, tutor and friend of Edward VI. While in Strasburg, Carew dashed into Ponet's burning house to save the bishop's "money and treasure" when he heard Ponet "make some moan for his money." Carew ran through the flames "with all his force and might" and then smashed with his foot the cupboard containing the bishop's treasure. As soon as Sir Peter emerged from the burning building, it collapsed into a mass of flame; Sir Peter had once again been miraculously "preserved and saved."[70]

One contemporary historian has argued that Carew, while in Strasburg, discussed with Ponet and perhaps others the possibility of harming the despised Spaniards by striking at their American colonies. As a seafaring westerner in whom exile had bred a hatred of Spaniards, Carew could quite naturally have come to such a notion. If true, Carew, in this idea, as well as in his love of continental travel and his future ventures in Ireland, foreshadowed in Henrician and Marian times an Elizabethan world view. Christina Garrett in her *The Marian Exiles* suggested that a copy of Peter Martyr's *Decades of the New World*, which is now found in the Bodleian Library, once belonged to Carew in Strasburg, where he lent it to Ponet, who in 1555 was engaged in writing his *Short Treatise of Politike Power* (1556).[71] The name "Peter Carewe" appears twice in the Bodleian volume, and the initials "P.C." appear on the title page. The handwriting does not appear to be Carew's, although with Carew's difficult hand it is hard to be certain. Garrett believed the hand to be that of Carew's secretary, who may have followed Carew from France and been among the company of companions in Venice. Marginal notes that appear to be in Ponet's hand are scribbled in the volume, especially in the chapters dealing with navigation from Spain to the West Indies. Ponet referred to the *Decades* in his *Treatise*, and we know from Hooker that Ponet and Carew were in close contact in Strasburg in 1555. Given these facts, Garrett's surmise that Carew lent the book to Ponet before leaving for Antwerp seems logical. It requires a much greater leap to follow Garrett on her speculation about Carew's designs on the Spanish empire in America. The idea of sailing across an ocean to strange new lands would have been enough to engage Carew's attention. Ponet, in the midst of writing a work that encouraged further rebellion against Queen Mary, may have found more overtly anti-Spanish uses for Carew's book. Since Ponet died on 2 August 1556 but mentioned in his *Treatise* the 15 May kidnapping of Carew and Cheke, he must have been working on the book almost up to the day of his death, and well after Carew had left Strasburg. Garrett's reconstruction of Carew's thinking while in Strasburg is possible, but is by no means conclusively proved.[72]

Despite the favor of God and the company of Ponet, Carew apparently found exile in Germany no more to his liking than exile in

France or Italy. On 3 July 1555, Sir John Mason wrote from Brussels to Sir William Petre of the lamentable letters he was receiving from Carew. Carew expressed what Mason took to be genuine repentance for his misdeeds. Carew commended to Mason the goodness he had received in the past from Petre and asked Mason to write to Petre, requesting him to continue working in Carew's behalf until some good result had been achieved. Petre, as we have seen from Lady Tailboys's attentions to him, was a focus of the Carews' hopes for Sir Peter's restoration to favor. His connections with Carew came from his Devon family and his Edwardian credentials, having served as principal secretary to the Council during the previous reign. Mason, meanwhile, had been convinced to join Petre in the campaign to rehabilitate Carew by Carew's letters and by the future good service for England promised by Carew's ability and experience.

> He is not a man to be lost if he may be won unfeignedly, as by my troth I think he means none otherwise. This fall may be to him felix culpa, and the queen hath thereby occasion to win such a servant as for sundry qualities there be not money in the realm of England. I will adventure, at the first occasion that I shall have to write unto her grace, to make of him some mention; which, in good faith, I am moved the rather to do, for the gentle service I think he is able to do to his native land, than for any other private respect other than very pity.[73]

The service Sir Peter had loyally performed for Henry VIII and Edward VI spoke more eloquently on his behalf than did the man himself.

Having apparently spent the summer and early fall of 1555 in Strasburg seeking to work through friends and former colleagues for his pardon, Carew came by the end of October to Antwerp. Sir Peter journeyed to imperial territory upon notice from his wife that she was in Brussels to make suit for his pardon to King Philip. Lady Tailboys's efforts to have her husband pardoned and recalled had continued unabated almost since Carew's flight to France. Having, "but cold suits in England," Lady

Tailboys followed Philip to Brussels in the autumn of 1555, hoping to find there a warmer welcome for her cause.[74] Lady Tailboys asked permission of Philip for her long-suffering husband to return home, and presented the king with a letter from Carew. The letter audaciously declared that Carew had not lost favor with the queen "from any fault of his own" and, with Carew's usual heavy-handedness, told Philip that if Sir Peter's case was hopeless with the queen he would be compelled to accept service with the king of France, something Carew had heretofore chosen not to do.[75] This threat to enter French service proved to be effective, for, according to the Venetian ambassador in Brussels, Philip was willing to confer favor on any Englishman, no matter how ill-disposed, who could be profitably used in the service of the state.[76] Carew, despite his past treasons and the unfortunate tone of his letter, was a man with military experience and influential family connections in the seafaring West Country, traits that Philip needed on his side as he tried to fit England into Spanish foreign policy. Accordingly, Philip asked Mary, as a favor, to pardon Carew.[77]

On 22 November 1555, while awaiting the queen's answer to her husband's request, Carew met in Antwerp with the earl of Devon, who had been released from his second spell in the Tower and exiled in the spring of 1555. Devon was apparently well aware that Sir William Petre had been working in Carew's behalf. Devon wrote to Petre of the meeting the next day, indicating that he sought the interview with Carew to ascertain for Petre the genuineness of Carew's expressed desire to be reconciled with the queen. After speaking with Carew, Devon found in him "such a one for his body ready to the service of the King's and Queen's Majesties as you shall never repent the friendship you have showed him." But Carew was still in his conscience "led by his religion," and not fully conformable to the queen's doings therein; in the matter of religion, Petre still had "a piece of work for you to bring him to a more perfection." Devon, however, was confident that Petre could "do much with him, for without doubt, he reposeth his trust in you."[78]

Given Carew's experience with the earl in 1553-54, it is surprising that he should reveal to Courtenay any misgivings about serving the queen. If Carew had suspected that Devon was acting as an informer for the English government, he would likely have been less forthcoming with his religious feelings. Carew's expression of his religious doubts to Devon could be read as an indication of the depth of his commitment to Protestantism or as another example of his ineptness at intrigue and dissimulation. Or Carew may have been aware that Courtenay was friendly to his cause. Courtenay's letter to Petre, whom he clearly knew to be a Carew partisan, indicates this possibility. Courtenay was also in contact at this time with Sir Gawen Carew, who seems to have been acting as an agent for Courtenay's western interests while the earl was in exile. Devon wrote two letters to Sir Gawen on the same day he wrote to Petre of his meeting with Sir Peter.[79] These letters concerned Courtenay servants and some private legal matters, but the willingness to trust Sir Gawen exhibited in the letters could also betoken a willingness on Countenay's part to do what he could for Sir Peter. A final possibility is that Courtenay wanted to involve Carew in new plots to place the earl and Elizabeth on the English throne. One such plot was being hatched at this time in France by Henry Dudley, a cousin of the late duke of Northumberland. Kenneth Barlett proposes that Courtenay was himself on his way to Venice to take part in further intrigues against the queen being organised by English political exiles in Italy. He ascribes the earl's mysterious death in Venice in 1556 to poison administered on the orders of Peter Vannes,[80] whom we know from Carew's experiences to have been quite willing to use murder to further his queen's interests.

Two days after Carew's meeting with Courtenay, the queen told Philip that to gratify him she would pardon Carew. The Venetian ambassador in Brussels reported that Lady Tailboys sent word from there to Carew in Strasburg to come to Brussels to thank Philip for his favor.[81] Keeping track of the wandering Englishman was no doubt a full-time occupation, and the hardworking ambassador was probably incorrect as to Carew's whereabouts. Unless Carew returned immediately to Strasburg after his 22 November meeting with Courtenay in Antwerp, Lady Tailboys's happy message to her husband went to Antwerp and not Strasburg. Carew was in Brussels to express his gratitude to Philip by mid-December. On 9 December, Carew's pardon was enrolled in London, but actual copies of the document were not sent to Brussels until March. Carew was pardoned for all treasons specified in the London and Exeter indictments, for all attainders against him by act of Parliament, and for all offenses committed by him against the queen. The pardon restored to Carew all "lands and goods" forfeited by treason at the same rents and services owed before his attainder. A second pardon enrolled on the same date contained identical terms except that the regrant of forfeited possessions mentioned only goods and chattels, not lands.[82] Lacking any written pardon from the queen, Carew was expected to exercise prudence— something he was not noted for—and stay on the continent until he could accompany Philip to England on the king's return there, probably by February.[83] But Philip was still on the continent when Carew's written pardon arrived in Brussels on 16 March 1556. On that day, Philip wrote his wife acknowledging receipt of two pardons for Carew. Philip wrote that one pardon was to be given to Sir Peter and the other to be returned to England "that it may be canceled." Christina Garrett surmised that one document was a general pardon and the other a special license to return to England.[84] The two pardons were probably just copies of the two versions enrolled on 9 December. Philip also reported that Lady Tailboys was returning to England "to obtain the execution and fulfillment of that grace and mercy which your Highness has shown to her husband." Having secured pardon for the husband, Philip then asked the same for the wife, who, through Philip's delay in writing to the queen, had overstayed by "some days" the time prescribed in the queen's license for her return.[85]

The three-months' delay in sending the pardon, Lady Tailboys's need to ask the queen to fulfill her promise of pardon, and the generous restoration of property all suggest that Carew did not have forgiveness without conditions. Henry Dudley's wild plot to plunder the Exchequer and invade England with an army of mercenaries and English exiles was discovered in March 1556, about the time Carew's pardons were dispatched to Brussels. To illustrate his sincere repentance, Carew was expected to reveal to the government anything he knew about his fellow exiles' plans. Indeed, Carew did not return to England in March, but was still on the continent in May, when Giovanni Michieli, the Venetian ambassador in England, reported a series of arrests of western men in connection with the ongoing Dudley investigation. On 29 April, Sir William Courtenay, a Carew kinsman; Sir John Perrot and Sir John Pollard, two westerners; Sir Nicholas Arnold, one of Carew's co-conspirators in 1553; and John Chichester, who had been at least marginally involved with Carew during the Devon Christmas sessions of January 1554, were all imprisoned in the Tower. Michieli declared that the whole West was suspected and all the chief gentlemen of the region were being summoned to London. He further reported that Courtenay's arrest stemmed from an "evil letter" sent to Sir Peter Carew by certain of the Dudley conspirators. In the letter, the conspirators revealed their entire plan to Carew in hopes of drawing him into the plot because he was a man of ability with followers he could bring to the rising. Carew, who was still in Antwerp, had informed Philip of the letter, and Philip had sent Sir John Mason and Lord Paget to Antwerp to retrieve it.[86]

On 15 May 1556, just three days after the Venetian ambassador reported Carew's betrayal of the Dudley conspirators, Philip's provost marshal arrested Carew and Sir John Cheke as they were traveling together to Antwerp from Brussels. As an exile for religion in Germany, Cheke had been in Brussels at the invitation of his friends and former Edwardian colleagues Sir John Mason and Lord Paget, who had obtained for Cheke a safe-conduct from Philip. Carew, if Michieli was correct, had but recently met with the same two men in Antwerp concerning the Dudley conspiracy letter. Carew with his pardon and Cheke with his safe-conduct evidently felt secure in going to Brussels together to meet Mason and Paget. According to John Ponet, writing in Strasburg shortly after the event, Carew and Cheke were on their way back to Antwerp, after having conducted Paget a short way toward the coast on his return journey to England, when they were "taken by the Provost Marshall, spoiled of their horses, and clapped into a cart, their legs, arms and bodies tied with halters to the body of the cart, and so carried to the seaside."[87] On 17 May, the Venetian ambassador in Brussels wrote that the two were seized on Philip's orders for suspicion of involvement in new plots against the queen and himself. No one yet knew the whereabouts of the two men, although it was said they were being held secretly in Ghent and would soon be sent to England. The English in Brussels were surprised and troubled by the seizure, for Carew already had his pardon and Philip's talk of new plots was not believed.[88] Michieli echoed his continental counterpart's information two days later. Since Carew was thought to have revealed the Dudley plot to the government, his arrest was causing great astonishment in London. The ambassador could only speculate that the arrests were for religion, both Carew and Cheke having "very bad names in that regard." The two prisoners were still unaccounted for, although they were expected to be in London shortly.[89]

Hooker said that Carew and Cheke were in Brussels to greet Paget, "who seemed to accept in very good part, and gave them very good entertainment." The two gentlemen, "mistrusting nothing," intended to accompany Paget part way on his return journey to the Flemish coast, "but he would in no wise suffer them, but taking them very courteously by the hands, bid them both farewell." As they returned to Antwerp, Carew and Cheke were set upon by "the hired butcherly sheriff," who "entrapped and took them, and perforce, as sheep appointed to the slaughter, blindfolded them, and carried them to the sea-side, where, as was a Scallard fisher boat provided for them to carry them into England." Hooker also reported the unease of the English at Brussels over "such a disordered or traitorous kind of apprehension." The provost marshal was much blamed for the incident, but sought to absolve himself by claiming that he acted on Philip's orders, which were issued because both Carew and Cheke had involved themselves in new plots against the king and queen. Philip, when he heard of the marshal's claims, denied giving any such orders, "was very much offended, and would have delivered them if they had not been before carried away."[90] On 2 June, Michieli also reported that Philip was angry, but not about the arrest itself, only the manner in which it was undertaken. Philip reproved the provost marshal for not making the arrest quietly and not keeping it secret.[91]

Once on the coast, the two prisoners were again blindfolded and chained to opposite ends of a boat. They had no idea where they were or where they were going. Unable to see or move, their only comfort was in speaking to one another. Cheke, "although very well learned," was in much need of comfort, for he was "not acquainted with the cross of troubles" and was in "great despair, great anguish, and heaviness." He was fortunate in having Carew for his companion, for Sir Peter, "whose heart could not be broken, nor mind overthrown with any adversities," gave him much comfort and exhorted him "to be of good stomach, persuading him (as though he had been a divine) to patience and good contention." When the boat passed into the Thames and came up to the Tower, Carew heard the Tower bell and knew at last where they were. This small measure of certainty cheered them, for they had feared their captors meant to cast them into the sea so they should not be heard from again. Once in the Tower, the constable, according to his instructions, separated the two men and put Carew into "a close prison, and of small ease."[92]

For over two weeks, the whereabouts of the two men and the reasons for their seizure were a mystery. Philip's secretary, who had been sent to England to inform the queen of the incident, got only as far as Calais, where Paget, also on his way to England, sent the man back to Philip promising to himself "execute his entire mission."[93] On 26 May, rumors in London said Carew and Cheke would arrive there the next day,[94] but they did not come to the Tower until 1 June. The next day, Michieli was still uncertain as to why they had been arrested, but had at least learned that Cheke had been the real target and that Carew was taken only because he was in Cheke's company and because he and his servants resisted the marshal's men. The ambassador added skeptically that these reasons for Carew's detention were "but slightly verified," and Carew's servants were already at liberty while their master remained in the Tower.[95] In the next week, various comings and goings related to the two prisoners were noted, but exact details of the circumstances surrounding their imprisonment remained elusive. Michieli reported on 9 June that Cheke's case was serious if the government could successfully connect him to the overseas printing of numerous books against the king and queen being secretly circulated in London.[96]

Both Ponet and Hooker placed blame for the treacherous manner in which the two men were taken squarely on Paget. Ponet alleged that Carew and Cheke were waylaid according to a plan of "Mason's working and Paget's devising." Paget betrayed his involvement in the plan when he crossed paths with one of Carew's servants in Calais. This servant, on his way from England to his master, asked Paget how Sir Peter did, whereupon Paget smiled and said nothing but that "his master was in health." Ponet claimed that Paget needed to prove himself to Mary, who "suspected his religion." The queen supposedly promised "to set him aloft" if she could but perceive "his heart and mouth to agree together" in the matter of religion. To convince Mary of his right thinking on the subject, Paget crossed to the continent, ostensibly to take the waters for his health, but actually to capture through treachery the Protestant duchess of Suffolk, then in exile in Germany. When his plans to take the duchess miscarried, Paget turned instead to the capture of Cheke and Carew. As Ponet saw the incident, the two men were Protestant pawns to Paget's personal lust for power and position in Mary's government.[97] Since Ponet's account had to have been written before his death less than three months after the incident, its portrait of Paget as the villain and Carew as an innocent was probably the accepted version among the English Protestant community on the continent by the end of 1556.

When English exiles Robert Horn and Richard Chambers wrote to Henry Bullinger in Frankfurt in September 1556, they lamented the growing ferocity of the queen and her papist "pseudo-bishops," who, not satisfied with "domestic blood," were now seeking the destruction of innocent, godly men across the seas. The two exiles then related the treacherous seizure of Carew and Cheke, who, they reported, were carried before the queen and then thrown into prison. Rumors now declared that Carew and Cheke were soon to have their liberty, but only because both men had agreed to the "most iniquitous conditions." Horn and Chambers were clearly alluding to some heinous compromise of the reformed faith forced on the unfortunate prisoners by Mary's papist government. Cheke was indeed induced to recant, but no such pressure seems to have been applied to Carew, and the exiles' reference to "iniquitous conditions," in the sense in which they meant it, would seem to be more valid for Cheke than for Carew. However, by including Carew in their lamentation, Horn and Chambers showed themselves to be unaware of any treacherous practice on Carew's part with the papist regime.[98]

Hooker, without giving a precise motive, also ascribed the gentlemen's seizure to the treachery of Paget. Indeed, from some of Hooker's wording, it seems likely that Hooker followed Ponet's account to some extent when constructing his own. Neither man, wrote Hooker, suspected when they took Paget's hand in farewell that "under the fair green grass was hidden the venomous serpent." Paget had practiced with the provost marshal to have the two men "entrapped by the way" on the road to Antwerp, and taken to England as traitors.[99] Michieli said that an unnamed but important member of the Council had given him the information about the arrest warrant being only for Cheke, and that Carew was taken only because he was with Cheke and because he resisted. This man, whom the ambassador suspected of having arranged the whole incident, was likely Paget. The unnamed councilor then made a strange comment, saying that since "Carew is taken it would be desirable on several accounts to find him guilty of something, to have an opportunity of putting him out of sight, his presence here [London?] being of no profit."[100]

The meaning of this cryptic remark is hard to fathom. Christina Garrett argued that this "naive conclusion" by Paget merely showed his ignorance about what had really happened on the road to Antwerp. Garrett believed that the entire event was staged by Carew as a way to hide from his Protestant colleagues his betrayal of Cheke to the government. Having found Carew willing to betray the Dudley conspirators, the government imposed one more condition of pardon, requiring him to help trap Cheke, whose publishing activities on the continent were a sore irritant to the Marian regime. Carew could not allow his fellow exiles to know that he was betraying one of them to erase his own earlier betrayal of the queen, so he allowed himself to be taken, bound, and held for a spell in the Tower with Cheke, thereby convincing the Protestant world that Cheke was his fellow prisoner, not his victim.[101] If this theory is true, Carew's deception was successful, for the Venetian report of Paget's comment, as Garrett noted, was not known in England until the nineteenth century; Ponet's version of the story held the field in England and among the exile community in the sixteenth century. Samuel Rhea Gammon, Paget's biographer, conceded Paget's willingness to betray an old colleague, but found it highly improbable that he would do so mainly for religion. Cheke's treatment after his capture, which consisted of strenuous attempts to convert him to Catholicism, seemed to indicate that his symbolic status as a well-known Protestant and the propaganda points his conversion would win the government were the chief reasons the government wanted him. Gammon therefore found Paget's involvement in the seizure "not proven" and his remark about Carew as simply a politique's desire to make use of an unexpected opportunity.[102]

The betrayal of a friend and co-religionist would normally have been out of character for Carew. His usual way of operating, as shown by the way he conducted his part of the 1554 plot against the marriage, was direct confrontation and hasty action. Subtle plots and intrigues were neither to his tastes nor his talents. However, when a situation turned desperate and he was faced with severe personal consequences, as happened when the rising in Devon failed and the government proclaimed him a traitor, Carew showed himself capable of using others, such as his uncle Sir Gawen, and of much effective secret planning. His disillusioning experience in France, and the poverty and government harassment in Italy and Germany wore him down. Carew was already seeking means to return home in the summer of 1554, almost two years before his capture. Always in his past travels Carew had been engaged in some honourable service, had, as Hooker would put it, honourable "entertainment," whether with his father's French friend, his cousin John, the marquis of Saluzzo, and the prince and princess of Orange, or as a young gentleman of favor at Henry VIII's court. Masterless, stateless, aimless wandering without some service to perform or some goal to attain was not to Carew's liking; he found it tiresome and enervating. In such a state, Carew may well have been capable of the betrayal of Cheke, as he seems beyond doubt to have been of the Dudley conspirators. Carew's high spirits onboard ship with Cheke, which Hooker typically put down to Sir Peter's courage, perhaps owed more to Carew's knowledge of the security he had purchased with his services for the government. Also, the surprising failure of Queen Elizabeth to favor

Carew to the same extent she favored some of his fellow Marian conspirators and exiles may stem from a distrust born of knowledge of his activities for the Marian government in 1556. Although Carew's betrayal of Cheke to the government can be neither proved nor disproved conclusively, the weight of evidence marshaled by Garrett points to Carew's guilt.

The actual plan to have Carew seized with Cheke as a cover for Carew's actions may, despite Gammon's conclusions, have been Paget's idea. Aware of Carew's role in breaking the Dudley conspiracy and of his connections with the exiles in Germany, Paget would have found in Carew an ideal instrument for repairing his strained relations with the increasingly pious queen. Responsibility for the capture and conversion of Cheke—a high-profile Protestant—would have been an effective way for a distrusted minister to convince the queen of his Catholic zeal. Certainly such a ruse better fits Paget's character than Carew's. But Paget's strange remark about the desirability of finding Carew guilty of something now that he was in custody is hard to reconcile with knowledge by Paget of any betrayal of Cheke by Carew. If Paget had contrived that betrayal, it would seem the less said of it the better. The remark then can only indicate a cynical desire on Paget's part to dispose of his treacherous instrument, or a genuine belief that Carew's arrest was an unexpected windfall—an opportunity for a second chance to deal with a troublesome malcontent who had been undeservedly pardoned. Both interpretations are possible, although the former is given greater likelihood by Paget's activities in London after his return from Brussels. On 19 May, four days after the arrests, Paget spent over two hours closeted with the queen,[103] presumably executing the "commission" he had taken over from Philip's secretary, that is, reporting the capture of Cheke and Carew to the queen.[104] On 8 June, a gentleman of the queen's privy chamber visited an ailing Philip in Brussels and talked to him for some time of the two men, and especially of the strong evidence the queen had against Carew.[105] Convincing the queen to act against Carew, despite the pardon he had won at Philip's urging, would not have been difficult.

That some practice against Carew was being undertaken by Paget through the queen seems likely. Still, the entire episode is mysterious, and neither Carew's nor Paget's role in it can be clearly determined. Either Carew did not assist the government in seizing Cheke, or no word about his assistance ever leaked out, for Carew's high reputation in Protestant circles was unaffected. The inquisitive Hooker certainly knew nothing of it. Either there was nothing to know, or Carew's noisily contrived arrest on the road to Antwerp served its secret purpose well.

Lady Tailboys had no knowledge that her husband's imprisonment was but a cover. The news of his arrest threw her into despair and deep disappointment, for instead of an end to her husband's troubles there seemed now only "the beginning of new sorrows." But having worked so hard for her husband's pardon, she was not about to give up now. Seeing no other remedy, "she prepared herself to run into her old course of suits." Because Sir Peter lay in the Tower in what Hooker called "very extreme duress," unable to be seen by anyone, Lady Tailboys first petitioned the Council that he be provided with a "more convenient room" with a bed, and that he be allowed to have visitors.[106] These goals were accomplished by 7 July, when Michieli reported that Carew, Cheke, and Sir William Courtenay, the Carew kinsman imprisoned for the Dudley plot, were being given much liberty within the Tower. The wives of Carew and Cheke were allowed to pass freely and spend the night with them.[107] Lady Tailboys spent the summer making "earnest suit" that her husband "might come to his answer," and Sir Peter found himself during these months "sundry and oftentimes before the council." During these appearances, Sir Peter did "in such wise order, answer and acquit himself, that they could not justly charge him, or justify any matter against him." In the end, the only matter pressed against Sir Peter was the repayment of his lingering debts to the Crown, for "payment whereof his land was liable." All his troubles thereby "being brought to a money matter," Carew found means to make the payment "and so was released out of prison."[108]

Hooker's account implies that some attempt was made to proceed against Carew, but nothing of substance was found against him that fell outside the bounds of his pardon. Carew's unpaid loans were merely an afterthought, the promise of release being a good opportunity to force Sir Peter to finally retire this debt. But repayment of the debts appears to have been at least one of the government's objectives from the start. As early as 21 June 1556, the Council took recognizances from Griffin Ameredyth, Carew's frequent financial and business partner, and several others not to depart London until final order had been taken for Carew's debt.[109] While Carew was in exile, Ameredyth seems to have acted as his agent in the closure of previously agreed upon transactions. In January 1555, Ameredyth gave confirmation to Nicholas and Richard Parre of grants of certain lands in Mamhead parish made by Carew to the two men in 1552 and 1553.[110] Later in the year, he confirmed to Walter Baker a gift of lands made to him by Carew in July 1552.[111] After Carew's rehabilitation at the end of 1556, Ameredyth purchased part of the manor of Mamhead from Carew; this transaction occurred some time before 1 May 1557 when Ameredyth placed the lands in trust for his son Edward.[112] Six months later, on 20 November, Carew mortgaged part of the manors of Mamhead and Golmeton to Ameredyth for £355.[113] Since Carew had in November 1557 another 27 years to wait for the lapse of James Bassett's lease to bring him the reversion to Mohun's Ottery and the other ancient Carew manors, his financial needs at this time were probably great.

Carew's pardon of the previous December had restored to him all lands and goods forfeited by his treason, but, as Loades has noted,[114] the government seemed to treat the pardon as if it concerned only Carew's life. His properties were now looked into as if still forfeit. On 9 July, commissions were appointed in Devon and Somerset to examine all lands held in those counties by Carew, who, for "divers high treasons" committed against the queen, was outlawed and attainted.[115] Five days later, Michieli reported in disbelief a rumor that Carew would "adjust his affairs" with the payment of a fine, the ambassador having heard that Sir Peter had already paid £2000.[116] Although Carew remained in prison, conditions for his ultimate release had apparently been sufficiently fulfilled by September to settle the matter of his property. On 20 September, Carew received a detailed, formal regrant of all his lands. The park at Okehampton leased to George Jernigan, and the manors, including Mohun's Ottery, leased to James Bassett were granted in reversion; all lands still held by the Crown were regranted directly, at the same rents and services as paid and performed before Carew's treason.[117]

The patent of 20 September provides a glimpse into the state of Carew's holdings before his treason. The manors of Ashwater, Georgeham, Pykewell, and Weston Peverell had been the jointure of his late mother, Joan Carew. Stoke Fleming and the manor and borough of Southton at Dartmouth were the jointure of Sir George Carew's widow Mary, now the wife of Sir Arthur Champernon, who held the estates in her right. Carew and Lady Tailboys were also jointly seized of eight manors in Lincoln and two in Somerset that had originally been settled on Lord and Lady Tailboys by Parliament in 1539. These estates were held for the life of Lady Tailboys, and reverted on her death to the heirs of Lord Tailboys. On 24 March 1555, Lady Tailboys had successfully petitioned the Crown to lease these manors to Lord Willoughby of Param, who was later implicated in Carew's secret visit to Lincoln in the spring of 1555, and Sir Edward Dymmock; the two leasees were required to pay a yearly rent on the estates of £206 15s 2d to the Crown and £133 6s 8d to Lady Tailboys.[118] The patent reveals two important facts about Sir Peter Carew's lands: a sizable portion of the Carew estates had, until Joan Carew's death, been tied up in the jointures of his mother and sister-in-law, and the marriage to Lady Tailboys, besides bringing Carew a clever and energetic wife, had significantly increased his landed income. Carew's financial difficulties at the end of Henry VIII's reign, and his marriage at that time to Lady Tailboys, were surely more closely related than the account of this period by Hooker indicates.

Within a month of this grant, on 19 October 1556, Carew was released from the Tower, having compounded with the Crown for 2000 marks against his debt.[119] Carew petitioned the Council on 1 December for some action to be taken for repayment of his debt. In response, the Council ordered Carew to pay £300 by next Candlemas, £100 at the following Michaelmas, and £100 every half year thereafter until the total debt of £820 was discharged. The Council agreed to move the queen to accept this plan and ordered Carew to give the Crown sufficient sureties for his timely payment.[120] Since the Crown forgave Carew in 1552 for the outstanding balance on his grandfather's debt, the £820 must represent the unpaid remainder of the debts to the Crown that Sir Peter had himself incurred during the reign of Edward VI. According to the patent of December 1552, which reorganised this debt, Sir Peter owed the Crown over £2100[121]; this sum closely matches the £2000 which Carew either paid to the Crown or acknowledged as his total indebtedness to the Crown in the summer of 1556. The sum of £820 matches closely the £920 mentioned in the 1552 patent as owed to Henry VIII for 230 fodders of lead. This latter debt was still owing to the Crown in December 1553 when Mary's government took a recognizance from Carew for its repayment.[122] Since Carew went into exile within a month of this recognizance, further payments on the debt are unlikely to have occurred, thus leaving the full amount to be pressed upon Carew in 1556. It appears that most of Carew's Crown debt from the previous reign was still outstanding in 1556 and the government used this obligation to inflict on Sir Peter a monetary punishment in lieu of the stiffer punishments precluded by his pardon and perhaps by his services as an informant.

Upon his release, Sir Peter presented himself to the queen, who "gladly conferred with him of all his troubles, and seemed to be very sorry for the same." The queen promised to stand "his good lady and friend" and offered him some preferment, but Carew, "being contented after long troubles to live at some rest," declined these offers and remained "in private estate during all her reign."[123] Hooker's account of the cordiality shown to Carew by the queen may be questioned, but his assertion that Carew withdrew from public life for the rest of the reign is demonstrably wrong. On 22 May 1557, Carew was named to a commission charged with hearing a dispute concerning residents in the Scilly Islands, which lie southwest of England off Land's End.[124] In September 1557, Carew was part of an English army that Philip took over to France for the St. Quentin campaign.[125] A pay warrant dated 15 September lists 30 duckets paid to Carew for his services. In a strange irony, Carew, who had boasted while in exile in Normandy of his French heritage and railed against Spanish domination, now found himself fighting the French as a member of an English army lead by a Spanish king. Carew's presence in this army no doubt represented in part the fulfillment of Philip's desire to bring Carew back into the military service of the state. It probably also reflected the attempt of Carew and others implicated in the various rebellions against the Marian regime to demonstrate their newfound loyalty. Among those serving beside Carew were the rebel pirate Peter Killigrew and the Protestant earl of Bedford (son of Carew's friend John Russell, who had died in 1555). Also serving were the Dudley conspirators Sir William Courtenay and Sir John Perrot, and one of the 1553 London conspirators, Sir Nicholas Throckmorton. Philip did indeed seem willing to make use of anyone who could provide him with military service.

It is unclear how long Carew's service in France lasted. His September payment of 30 duckets was for a term of 30 days expiring at the end of the month. He does not appear in any other records of Philip's war, and is likely to have returned to England at the end of the campaign, before the fall of Calais to the French at the beginning of 1558. Carew spent the last year of Mary's reign "in private estate," figuring, as far as is known, in no further public service. With the death of Queen Mary in November 1558, Carew's prospects, and those of many other men of his views, outlook, and background, came full circle. Having lost much in power, wealth, and influence through the last change of monarchs, Carew and the others looked forward to having their losses restored with the next change of monarchs. Carew had greeted the accession of Queen Mary with caution and anxiety; he greeted the accession of Queen Elizabeth with hope and high spirits.

---

1   Dr. Nicholas Wotton to Queen Mary, 12 February 1554, PRO, SP69/3/74.

2   *Cal.SP Span.*, XII, p. 98.

3   Ibid., pp. 107-08.

4   Harbison, *Rival Ambassadors*, p. 159.

5   Queen Mary to Dr. Nicholas Wotton, 22 February 1554, PRO, SP69/3/98.

6   *Cal.SP Span.*, XII, pp. 131-32.

7   Captain Thomas Crayer to Lord Grey, 24 March 1554, PRO, SP69/3/123.

8   Harbison, *Rival Ambassadors*, pp. 161-63.

9   *Cal.SP Span.*, XII, p. 145.

10 Captain Thomas Crayer to Lord Grey, 24 March 1554, PRO, SP69/3/123.

11 Edgar Hornyold to Secretary Sir John Bourne, 28 March 1554, PRO, SP69/3/202.

12 *Cal.SP Span.*, XII, p. 153.

13 Ibid., p. 166.

14 Ibid., p. 171.

15 Ibid., p. 176.

16 Ibid., p. 188.

17   Harbison, *Rival Ambassadors*, pp. 163-64.

18   Dr. Nicholas Wotton to Queen Mary, 31 March 1554, PRO, SP69/3/210.

19   *Cal.SP Span.*, XII, p. 176.

20   Dr. Nicholas Wotton to Queen Mary, 17 April 1554, PRO, SP69/4/17.

21   *Cal.SP Span.*, XII, p. 224.

22   Dr. Nicholas Wotton to Queen Mary, 29 April 1554, PRO, SP69/4/63, 65.

23   Queen Mary to Dr. Nicholas Wotton, 29, April 1554, PRO, SP69/4/69.

24   *Cal.SP Span.*, XII, p. 264.

25   Queen Mary to Dr. Nicholas Wotton, 29 May 1554, PRO, SP69/4/105.

26   Dr. Nicholas Wotton to Queen Mary, 14 July 1554, PRO, SP69/4/140.

27   Dr. Nicholas Wotton to Queen Mary, 29 July 1554, PRO, SP69/4/187.

28   Sir Peter Carew to Dr. Nicholas Wotton, 11 July 1554, PRO, SP69/4/193.

29   Council to Dr. Nicholas Wotton, 22 February 1554, PRO, SP69/3/93.

30   *Chronicle of Queen Jane*, p. 66.

31   Dr. Nicholas Wotton to Sir William Petre, 23 February 1554, PRO, SP69/3/100.

32   Inventory of Mohun's Ottery, 2 February 1554, PRO, SP11/3/29.

33   Inventory of Sir Gawen Carew's House at Tiverton, 2 February 1554, PRO, SP11/3/27.

34   Indictment of 1553 Conspirators, 7 April 1554, PRO, KB8/29, r.2.

35   Howells, *State Trials*, I, pp. 869-902.

36   D.M. Loades, *Two Tudor Conspiracies* (Cambridge: Cambridge University Press, 1965), pp. 97-98.

37   *Chronicle of Queen Jane*, p. 65.

38   Indictment of William Thomas, 8 May 1554, PRO, KB8/30, r.1.

39   Loades, *Two Tudor Conspiracies,* pp. 96-98.

40 APC, IV, p. 403.

41 Ibid., V, p. 5.

42 Ibid., V, pp. 39-40.

43 Exeter Indictment of Sir Peter Carew and Others, 13 September 1554, PRO, KB27/1176, Rex III.

44 *CPR*, Mary and Philip and Mary, vol. II, 2 July 1555, pp. 291-92.

45 John Gough Nichols, ed., *The Diary of Henry Machyn* (London: Camden Society, 1848), p. 80.

46 APC, V, p. 90.

47 Dr. Nicholas Wotton to the Council, 27 January 1555, PRO, SP69/6/6.

48 APC, V, p. 131.

49 Ibid., p. 142.

50 *CPR*, Mary and Philip and Mary, vol. II, 2 July 1555, pp. 291-92.

51 APC, V, p. 10.

52 Exeter Indictment of Sir Peter Carew and Others, 13 September 1554, PRO, KB27/1176, Rex III.

53 *CPR*, Mary and Philip and Mary, vol. I, 13 June 1554, p. 274.

54 *Commons Journal*, p. 41; see also Loach, *Parliament and the Crown*, pp. 103, 123.

55 Loades, *Two Tudor Conspiracies*, p. 122.

56 Loach, *Parliament and the Crown*, pp. 102-03.

57 *CPR*, Mary and Philip and Mary, vol. II, 10 March 1555, p. 48.

58 APC, V, pp. 39-40.

59 Ibid., p. 75.

60 F.G. Emmison, *Tudor Secretary: Sir William Petre at Court and Home* (London: Phillimore, 1961), p. 189.

61 *Cal.SP Ven.*, V, p. 568.

62 Ibid., pp. 571-72.

63 Hooker, "Life," pp. 59-60.

64 Ibid., pp. 60-61.

65 Ibid., p. 61.

66 Kenneth R. Bartlett, "The English Exile Community in Italy and the Political Opposition to Queen Mary I" *Albion* 13, no. 3 (Fall 1981): 230.

67 Hooker, "Life," pp. 61-62.

68 APC, V, p. 114.

69 Action for Slander Brought Against Arthur Thimbleby by William, Lord Willoughby, 1556, PRO, KB27/1177, r. 170.

70 Hooker, "Life," p. 62.

71 John Ponet, *A Short Treatise of Politike Power* (1556); reprint, Facsimile Edition (Menston, England: Scolar Press, 1970).

72 Garrett, *Marian Exiles*, pp. 107-08.

73 Sir John Mason to Sir William Petre, 3 July 1555, PRO, SP69/7/3.

74 Hooker, "Life," pp. 62-63.

75 *Cal.SP Ven.*, VI, p. 227.

76 Ibid., p. 258.

77 Ibid., p. 227.

78 Earl of Devon to Sir William Petre, 23 November 1555, PRO, SP11/6/106.

79 Earl of Devon to Sir Gawen Carew, 23 November 1555, PRO, SP11/6/109, 109-10.

80 Bartlett, "English Exile Community," pp. 235-39.

81 *Cal.SP Ven.*, VI, p. 258.

82 CPR, Mary and Philip and Mary, vol. III, 9 December 1555, pp. 45-46.

83 *Cal.SP Ven.*, VI, p. 282.

84 Garrett, *Marian Exiles*, p. 106.

85 King Philip to Queen Mary, 16 March 1556, PRO, SP11/7/40, 41.

86 *Machyn*, p. 104; *Cal.SP Ven.*, VI, p. 446.

87 Ponet, *Treatise*, unpaginated.

88 *Cal.SP Ven.*, VI, p. 452.

89 Ibid., p. 454.

90 Hooker, "Life," pp. 63-65.

91 *Cal.SP Ven.*, VI, p. 475.

92 Hooker, "Life," pp. 65-66.

93 *Cal.SP Ven.*, VI, p. 456.

94 Ibid., p. 459.

95 Ibid., p. 475.

96 Ibid., p. 480.

97 Ponet, *Treatise*, unpaginated.

98 Robert Horn and Richard Chambers to Henry Bullinger, 19 September 1556, in *Original Letters Relative to the English Reformation,* ed. Hastings Robinson (Cambridge: Cambridge University Press, 1846), pp. 131-34.

99 Hooker, "Life," p. 64.

100 *Cal.SP Ven.*, VI, p. 475.

101 Garrett, *Marian Exiles*, pp. 106-07.

102 Samuel Rhea Gammon, *Statesman and Schemer: William, First Lord Paget Tudor Minister* (Hamden, Conn.: Archon Books, 1973), pp. 233-35.

103 *Cal.SP Ven.*, VI, p. 454.

104 Ibid., p. 456.

105 Ibid., p. 478.

106 Hooker, "Life," p. 66.

107 *Cal.SP Ven.*, VI, p. 510; HMC, Bedingfeld Manuscripts, *Third Report* (London, 1872), p. 239.

[108] Hooker, "Life", pp. 66-67.

[109] APC, V, p. 375.

[110] Manor of Mamhead Records, DRO, 484M, T15/1-T15/5.

[111] Ibid., T6/3.

[112] Ibid., F4.

[113] Ibid., T19/6.

[114] Loades, *Two Tudor Conspiracies*, p. 124.

[115] CPR, Mary and Philip and Mary, vol. III, 9 July 1556, p. 248.

[116] *Cal.SP Ven.*, VI, p. 524.

[117] CPR, Mary and Philip and Mary, vol. III, 20 September 1556, pp. 551-54. Although Bassett survived Mary's reign by only days, dying on 21 November 1558, he directed in his will that his leases in Devon be sold to pay his debts. See Bindoff, *House of Commons*, I, p. 393.

[118] CPR, Mary and Philip and Mary, vol. II, 24 March 1555, p. 268.

[119] *Cal.SP Ven.*, VI, p. 718.

[120] APC, VI, p. 27.

[121] CPR, Edward VI, vol. IV, 16 December 1552, pp. 398-400.

[122] Loades, *Two Tudor Conspiracies*, p. 124, n.

[123] Hooker, "Life," p. 67.

[124] APC, VI, p. 89.

[125] Warrant for Payment of English Nobles and Gentlemen in King Philip's Army, 15 September 1557, BL, Stowe MS 571, f. 85.

CHAPTER 9

THE DEVON GENTLEMAN

For both Sir Peter Carew and Princess Elizabeth, the years of Mary's reign were difficult and dangerous times. Both were in danger during those years of losing their lives, both spent a part of the reign imprisoned in the Tower, and both suffered official displeasure and suspicion. As a prominent member of the Marian opposition and of the 1554 rising to replace Mary with her sister, Carew was assumed to be in high favor with the princess. And as Mary's approaching death became increasingly evident, this assumption appeared to be true.

On 9 November 1558, Philip's emissary, the Count de Feria, landed in England to learn for his master whether the queen's illness was as serious as reported. He found Mary gravely ill, and informed Philip on 14 November that there was no hope of her life. The count then turned his attention to understanding who would be the important figures under the next queen and to currying support and favor among them for Philip and his policies. On 10 November, one week before Mary's death, the count visited Elizabeth and sought to discover her feelings and intentions. The count reported his interview with the princess in detail, and listed for Philip the men Elizabeth seemed to favor. Although not mentioned by Elizabeth herself, Sir Peter Carew was among those reported to the count by others as being "on very good terms" with the princess.[1] Others said to be in Elizabeth's favor were the earl of Bedford; Lord Robert Dudley, son of the late duke of Northumberland and future earl of Leicester; Sir William Petre, Carew's quiet champion during his exile; Sir Nicholas Throckmorton, Carew's fellow conspirator; and Sir William Pickering, another associate of Carew's, both in the plot of 1554 and in exile in France thereafter.

Mary died on 17 November, and in the first weeks of the new queen's reign both Sir Peter Carew was prominent in her service. On 28 December, the queen sent Carew to speak on her behalf with Count de Feria. Carew came ostensibly to inquire after the count's health and to thank him for his assistance in smoothing out the consequences of a recent disturbance at St. Augustine's church. Carew's real purpose was to ascertain Philip's likely reaction to any alteration of the Marian Church and to gauge how far Philip intended to stand by his alliance with England during peace talks with France. The queen's selection of Carew to undertake a mission requiring such subtlety and circumspection indicates how highly she favored him in the first years of her reign, and perhaps how little she as yet knew the man she was employing. Neither Henry VIII nor the Edwardian governments had used Carew on missions requiring diplomatic skills of such a high order. Henry VIII understood Carew's value as a soldier, sailor, and courtier, and employed him frequently on tasks requiring those skills, such as the naval campaigns of 1545 and the French embassy of 1546. When, in 1549, Protector Somerset sought to curb the incipient western rebellion through a policy of pacification, he soon discovered to his dismay how unsuited Carew was to carrying out such a policy. Those on the protector's Council who favored taking a harsher line with the rebels had little cause to complain of Carew's service in 1549. When Northumberland displaced Somerset, he used his former naval colleague to maintain the government's authority in the West and to grace the garter mission to France in 1551. Only after Elizabeth's accession did Carew find himself employed on service of a distinctly diplomatic nature.

The visit to de Feria may not have required diplomatic skills of a high order; perhaps the queen was more interested in sending a message than in gathering information. A memorandum in Cecil's hand written shortly after Elizabeth's accession listed Carew and Lord Robert Dudley, Northumberland's son, as possible messengers to bear official tidings of the queen's accession to the king of Spain.[2] Carew was known to Philip; the king had asked his reluctant wife to pardon Carew so he could acquire the troublesome gentleman's abilities and experience for his own military needs. Within a year of his release from the Tower, Carew was on the continent serving in Philip's campaign against the French. Sending Carew to Spain would serve notice on Philip that the talent and resources of England were no longer at his disposal, but under the direction and in the service of the new queen, who, despite her youth, knew how to use them. In 1558, Carew had recently suffered much in body and gained much in reputation through his efforts on Elizabeth's behalf against the discredited Marian regime. Carew's loyalty to Elizabeth's interest in the dark days after 1554 and his long record of honourable royal service before 1554 probably accounted in large part for the favor he enjoyed at the start of the new reign. But the talents he displayed in tormenting the Marian regime, talents that convinced Philip that Carew had to be restored to the queen's allegiance and the queen's service, made him a particularly good instrument for sending messages to the king of Spain.

Our only account of Carew's discussion with de Feria comes from the count's report of the meeting to Philip, which was written a day later, on 29 December.[3] Carew began by expressing the queen's concern over de Feria's health, citing the ambassador's failure to visit her. Carew then launched into the incident at St. Augustine's church, which involved an altercation started by a group of German Protestants who had broken into the church to preach their radical sermons. Carew described the queen's forthcoming proclamation against preaching, which, it was hoped, would prevent such occurrences in the future. Sir Peter offered to bring the count a copy of the proclamation. The count said he did not visit the queen because he had heard she was very busy and because he was not sure if a visit from him would be welcomed. He thanked the queen for her concern and for sending Carew to him to express it, and assured Sir Peter that he wished to do only what was pleasing to the queen. The count was eager to understand how Elizabeth intended to deal with religion, but did not want to show too much interest in the subject to Carew. Accordingly, he feigned disinterest in the proclamation, asking nothing about its particulars and declining Carew's offer to bring him a copy. He did, however, wish Carew to understand that Philip expected the queen to make little alteration in the English Church, largely because Philip believed the English people were satisfied with the Church as established by Mary. He therefore told Carew that the St. Augustine affair was scandalous, and expressed surprise that the queen would now issue an order contradicting her proclamation of the month before, which had called for no changes to be made in religion for the time being. The ambassador also expressed concern at the effect these diverging statements would have on public opinion, hinting that the English people would not be happy with any changes in religion. Beyond these statements, de Feria ventured no opinions, and, as he told Philip, maintained a reserved manner.

Carew responded that even the king of France had given Protestants a church in which to worship, but de Feria denied it. Carew persisted, saying the church was in Metz, but again de Feria denied it. The ambassador then conceded that if such a church existed in Metz, it would not be surprising. Metz was part of the empire and not part of the French king's domains; Henri kept only a defensive garrison there. There was no such church for Protestants in France. To end the fruitless debate, de Feria declared himself unwilling to pursue the matter further without instructions from Philip.

According to de Feria, the two men conversed for some time. Part of Carew's instructions were apparently to reassure de Feria that the English intended to remain on friendly terms with Philip and to determine if Philip meant to stand by his ally in the peace negotiations with France. At one point in the conversation, Carew told de Feria that he wished to God Philip had married Elizabeth and had children. The count said nothing about this wished-for marriage, but talked warmly of the good will Philip had for the queen and for England. Carew responded by speaking at length about the great obligation the English owed to Philip, a surprising statement from a man who had spent more than two years in exile for his strenuous efforts to keep Philip out of England. Talk then turned to the peace negotiations, and de Feria came away from the meeting convinced that the English accepted Philip as a true friend and believed that he would not "leave them in the lurch." Convincing de Feria of English friendship was probably the key message Elizabeth wanted delivered; by using such a well-known opponent of Spain as a messenger, Elizabeth hoped to give her assurances to Philip more believability and to hold Philip to his ally through the long peace negotiations. If such reassurance of English faith in Philip was indeed part of Carew's purpose, he had done his job well, despite the rather clumsy comment about the marriage.

Before closing the meeting, de Feria felt the need to impress Carew, and through him the queen, with the extent of Philip's wealth. He described the great treasure that came to Spain from the Indies, and told Carew he was certain the queen would rejoice at hearing of Philip's prosperity. If, as Christina Garrett has proposed, Carew spent part of his exile in Germany dreaming with Ponet of the wealth of the Indies and how best to intercept its flow to papist Spain, Sir Peter must have listened to de Feria's glowing descriptions with eager interest.

Count de Feria gave no indication of his impression of Carew, except to tell the bishop of Aquila early in the following year that he believed Carew, like Bedford, Throckmorton, and many other English noblemen and gentlemen, was pro-French.[4] The queen was apparently satisfied with the results of Carew's meeting with de Feria, for she employed Sir Peter on various assignments throughout the next two years. For example, within days of his meeting with de Feria, Carew was helping to oversee a general muster in the West of all men able to bear arms. The Council in this instance ordered Carew and his colleagues to take the unusual step of including the clergy in the muster, since the Council was reliably informed that many of the clergy had recently procured a good store of armor and weapons.[5]   Hooker wrote that Sir Peter resorted immediately to the court upon Elizabeth's accession, "and for that his former troubles were sustained partly for her sake, he was had in great favor, and in place to have been advanced to great honour and credit."[6]   With Elizabeth, however, high favor more often meant great opportunity for service rather than great advancement, and Sir Peter's next opportunity for service came just three months' after the meeting with de Feria.

In late March 1559, Carew and Sir William St. Lo, who was captain of the queen's guard, received a commission from the queen to survey the Tower.[7] St. Lo and Carew were ordered to ask the lieutenant and officers of the Tower whether the ancient orders for keeping the fortress were being observed, whether the Tower had a full complement of officers and how much and by whom each was paid, whether watch and ward was being duly kept, and whether the Tower was in a good state of repair. The commissioners found the ancient orders for keeping the Tower somewhat modified by the increased number of warders, but assured the queen that the modifications were necessary and made the keeping of the Tower stronger. The Tower was being kept in March 1559 by 21 yeoman warders and 17 gunners, all of whom were referred to as yeoman waiters of the Tower. Death had caused one vacancy among the 38 yeoman waiters, most of whom were appointees of Queen Mary. As to wages, the lieutenant had £100 per year, half for the diet of poor prisoners of short duration who could not afford their own keep, and half for his own diet. The 38 yeoman waiters had 8d per day, although several of them had patents for additional pay, such as Alexander Ames, who had another 4d per day out of the Exchequer by letters patent of Edward VI. The commissioners reported that watch and ward was being well and duly kept, the lieutenant having at the moment about 20 persons "mete to bear arms."

The commissioners' careful study of the physical condition of the Tower produced some interesting results and some practical recommendations for improvements. Carew and St. Lo concluded that the Tower was well suited for storing royal treasure, housing the mint, stockpiling artillery and ammunition, and keeping royal prisoners—all uses to which the Tower had been put for a long time. It was not, however, well prepared to stand as a defensive position in time of war. The commissioners, probably as a response to an expressed desire by the queen to save money, recommended several cost-cutting measures. If the queen were to reduce the number of yeoman waiters from 38 to 24, she could save £51 per year, plus, as the commissioners were careful to point out, an additional £71 per year in coats and liveries. The dismissed waiters could be pensioned off at 6d per day, saving the queen, at the death of the last pensioner, another £210. Carew and St. Lo recommended that this savings be used to increase the lieutenant's living and allow him to maintain always 16 yeoman of the guard. This plan would leave a staff of 40 in daily attendance at the Tower, with eight keeping ward each day. If the queen refused to increase the lieutenant's living, which, the commissioners reiterated, the queen could do without additional charge to herself, Carew and St. Lo suggested that a memo book containing the orders for keeping the Tower be drawn up, signed by the queen, and kept by the lieutenant at the Tower.

As to repairs, the commissioners identified several urgent problems. The hall was in great decay and would soon collapse if not repaired. The commissioners rather shyly suggested enlarging the hall and building a storehouse beneath it, but admitted that these alterations, though desirable, were not necessary. The constable's house and the privy bridge were desperately in need of attention, and certain leads needed repair. Another part of the fortress was "foul and loathsome" for want of a necessary house built over the water. The commissioners also noted the need for costly repairs to the Tower wharf and a great store of uncovered timber that needed to be moved out of the weather before it decayed.

The care and efficiency with which the Tower survey was executed is impressive, especially on Carew's part, since he was also sitting that spring as senior knight for the shire for Devon in Elizabeth's first Parliament.[8] In his last appearance in the Commons, in Mary's first Parliament in the fall of 1553, Carew had busied himself with more dangerous outside matters—the plot against the Spanish marriage. The 1559 session began in late January and ran until 8 May. During this session, Parliament once again, and this time for good, ended papal power in the land by restoring the Church of England to royal control with a new Act of Supremacy. A new Act of Uniformity imposed a Protestant prayer book on the Church and devised the religious settlement from which emerged the Anglican Church during the course of Elizabeth's reign. We may assume that Carew supported these measures, although the only definite evidence we have of his activities in this Parliament concerns another issue entirely. Hooker wrote that Carew incurred the queen's displeasure during the session for his support of a "bill put in concerning the motion of her marriage."[9] On 4 February, the Commons debated a motion that the queen be requested to marry, and in particular that she marry an Englishman.[10] Given Carew's unfortunate experiences with a queen who refused to marry within the realm, it is not difficult to understand why he would strongly support such a motion.

The accession of Elizabeth had restored the dominant position of the Russell family in the West. John Russell's son, the second earl of Bedford, was a strong Protestant, and under his influence Devon's parliamentary representation in the first Elizabethan sessions consisted of Protestant-leaning members of long-standing county families, like the Carews. Sir Peter had served under Bedford in the St. Quentin campaign of 1557, and after Elizabeth's succession had been named deputy lieutenant of Devon under Bedford's lieutenancy. Bedford's primacy in the West under Elizabeth promised a restoration of the influence Carew had enjoyed in Devon under the earl's father during Edwardian times.

Carew's selection as MP in 1559 was the first sign of this restoration. Oddly enough, Carew's parliamentary colleague in 1559 was Sir John St. Leger, the man who had tracked down most of the men implicated with Carew in the abortive rising of January 1554, including Sir Gawen Carew, William Gibbes, and Sir Arthur Champernon. The gentry leadership of Devon, which had been seriously divided and disrupted by Carew's activities in 1554, mended itself by 1559, accepting both Sir Peter and his associates back into the fold. The long association of Sir Peter Carew and his family with Devon evidently counted for more than passing political disagreements. Now that the government no longer considered Carew a traitor, his western neighbors, whatever their private feelings, allowed Sir Peter to slip back into his accustomed place in their ranks. Sir Peter's life and career is an excellent illustration of the flexibility and cohesiveness of the political grouping, the political family, of local gentlemen who ran the county for the monarch. Within the family, much could be accommodated and much could be adjusted.

Although the government no longer considered Carew a traitor, the law still did. The Marian bill of attainder against Carew was still in force, but did not keep him from sitting in Parliament. Sir Peter made no move to have the attainder reversed until the next Parliament in 1563. Although the queen may have been displeased with Carew's support for the parliamentary motion calling for her to marry, she did not withdraw her favor from him. A month after the end of the session, on 6 June, the queen granted Carew various lands in Somerset that had formerly been in the possession of the late duke of Somerset. Carew thereby acquired the site of Glastonbury monastery, the park at Wirral, the manor of Bryde, parcels of the lordship of Glaston, and various other lands in and about Glastonbury. Annual rents from these lands was put at over £50.[11] Carew already held land in Somerset by right of his wife, and this grant served to increase his influence in the county and in the West Country generally. In November, the queen appointed Carew to a post mortem commission in

Somerset charged with looking into the estate of one Grace Lyett.[12] The queen's generosity indicated her intention to make further use of Carew's services, and was perhaps an attempt to alleviate some of his lingering financial difficulties and allow him to remain at court and undertake that service. The lands and profits of Mohun's Ottery and the other manors granted to Bassett still lay beyond Carew's control under the weight of Queen Mary's 30-year lease, while Carew himself still lay under the necessity of paying off his heavy Crown debts, upon which his release from the Tower had been conditioned. What's more, since November Carew had incurred the expense of living near court. Hooker said that Carew "lay for the most part in the beginning of her [Elizabeth's] reign at London," and between the visit to de Feria, the session of Parliament, and the lengthy service at the Tower, Carew must indeed have spent the better part of 1559 in the capital.[13]

Carew's military experience was attractive to the new regime, then engaged in withdrawing from the French war and in removing the French from Scotland. The names of both Sir Peter and Sir Gawen appeared on a list "of such as have served on the seas" made by Cecil during the height of Anglo-French tensions over Scotland in 1560.[14] On 7 May, the military situation in Scotland deteriorated when the English forces in the country suffered severe losses in an unsuccessful assault on the strong French fortress at Leith. One reason for the disaster was dissension within the English leadership; Sir James Croft, one of Carew's co-conspirators against Mary in London in 1553, was even accused of treason for withdrawing his troops from the attack at a critical moment. Croft had quarreled violently with some of his fellow commanders before the battle. To understand just what was amiss with the army in Scotland, the queen dispatched Carew to Leith "with all speed" on 15 May.[15] Taking with him Cecil's detailed list of inquiries to be made at Leith, Carew was to discover the reasons for the failure of the 7 May assault, the numbers of Scots and English slain, the number of men serving compared to the number officially in the queen's pay, the quantity of victual on hand for the army, and the strengths and weaknesses of the French fortress and how it might best be taken. He was to gather the opinions of Lord Grey, Croft, and other army leaders as to the best way to surprise the French, and to confer with William Winter, the English naval commander in the Forth and another of the 1553 conspirators, as to the best use of the English fleet. Carew seems to have been given some measure of authority over army operations, for he was directed to put all things in readiness. Finally, Carew was to assure one and all that aid, money, and provisions were on their way, and to assure the Scots that Elizabeth would never give up the enterprise until she had her revenge on the French and Scotland had its liberty.[16] On 17 May, while Carew was making his way north, the queen wrote to the duke of Norfolk at Berwick directing him to look into the matter of Croft's behavior and to inform her of his opinion of the matter. For all other matters, the duke was to take his direction from Carew.[17] Sir Peter arrived at the camp before Leith by 24 May, for on that day Thomas Randolph wrote Cecil that the Scots lords were much encouraged by Carew's forceful declarations of the queen's determination to support them.[18]

On 25 May, the queen issued letters patent naming Carew to a commission charged with treating on all disputes with the French in Scotland; Carew's fellow commissioners were Cecil, Sir Ralph Sadler, Sir Henry Percy, and, interestingly enough, Dr. Nicholas Wotton, the Marian ambassador in France for whom Carew's activities in exile were such a trial.[19] On the same day, William Maitland of Lethington, one of the leading Protestant lords of Scotland, echoed Randolph's account of Carew's effectiveness in spreading assurance among the Scots. In a letter from the camp before Leith, Maitland thanked Cecil for the queen's "most comfortable" message conveyed to him by Carew. The queen's message was sufficient to recommend Carew to the whole Scots nobility, and Carew's obvious honesty along with Cecil's good report of him and friendship for him further increased his credit among the Scots lords. Carew had been briefed on the situation in Scotland and could supply Cecil with full information. In Carew's presence, the Protestant lords had taken order to bring into their camp the few Scots nobles who had refused to align themselves with either the pro-French or the pro-English party.[20]

By 28 May, Carew was back in Berwick drawing up his answers to Cecil's list of inquiries. He reported 2,300 soldiers still in Leith, as well as 2,000 citizens. The strongest part of the fortress was from Vaughan's fort to the sea; the weakest was the citadel, a mere mass of earth cast up to provide cover, but likely impervious to the use of a mine on account of the extreme hardness of the ground. The assault on 7 May cost 120 lives, one-third of them Scots. The assault failed because insufficient breeches had been blown in the walls, scaling ladders were too short by two yards, not enough arquebusiers were placed in the English trenches, and the artillery men were poorly placed and poorly instructed. Everyone agreed that the walls of the fortress could not be battered down with artillery and that only "sap or famine" could prevail. The soldiers had no meat, but were subsisting on bread, water, and one salmon among six men per week. The queen, however, was being "marvelously robbed," paying for over 8,000 footmen when Carew found not above 5,000 in the camp. As to the diplomatic part of his mission, Carew had comforted all with the queen's assurances of aid and had directed Norfolk and the other officers to put their forces in readiness. The lords of Scotland, meanwhile, were of good heart and most grateful to the queen for her assistance.[21]

Hooker made no mention of Croft or of the failed assault on Leith, but said that the queen sent Carew to Scotland to investigate and amend, if possible, a "jar" between the duke of Norfolk and Lord Grey, commanders of the English forces in Scotland.[22] Thomas Howard, fourth duke of Norfolk, was the grandson of the old Henrician courtier, who had finally died in August 1554, and the son of Henry Howard, earl of Surrey, who had been executed by Henry VIII in 1547. William, Lord Grey, had been, with Sir George Carew, one of the reformist minority on the Council of Calais in 1540, being described with Sir George as among those on the Council who "favor all such as love the word of God."[23] He had also served with Sir Peter in 1549 as one of Russell's lieutenants in the campaign against the prayer book rebels. Hooker, with typical exuberance, cast Carew's role in a more heroic light than the making of inquiries and the giving of assurance called for by his instructions. Hooker recorded how Carew, while in the camp at Leith, stepped in to further the queen's service when he realised that it was "like to be disorderly done" because of "the jars between these two noblemen." Hooker did not describe the particular "piece of service," but it was clearly military, for accomplishing it required Carew to "skillfully, and speedily, set the army in battle array." This was Hooker's description for what Carew himself described as conferences with Norfolk and the other commanders about getting the army into readiness for further action. Carew, continued Hooker, so successfully "took the matter in hand," that he not only furthered the queen's service but also managed to "appease the unquietness" and for himself "purchase great credit" and commendation as a skillful soldier.[24]

Carew spent the early summer of 1560 in Scotland with the English army. On 19 June, Cecil wrote the queen from Edinburgh, confirming for her that everything Carew had reported to her about military matters in his letters was "very true." Cecil sadly agreed with Carew's belief that Sir James Croft's neglect of duty was the chief cause for the costly failure of the recent assault on the French fortress at Leith.[25] The next day, Carew was himself in Edinburgh at Holyrood House, his first trip to the Scottish capital in 25 years.[26] On Carew's first visit, the 1535 presentation of the garter to James V, the young courtier had impressed the Scottish court with his command of the French language and French manners. Carew's inclusion in the 1560 mission was clearly due not to his talents as a courtier, but to his practical experience as a soldier. Sir Peter does not appear to have taken much, if any, part in the actual negotiations

that led in July to the Treaty of Edinburgh. His role was to investigate
and correct the dangerous disorders in the English military command and
to keep the queen informed and advised as to the military situation. In
early July, Carew's role shifted from advisor to the queen to confidential
courier for Cecil. Cecil wrote two important and delicate letters to the
queen on 8 and 9 July. The first, endorsed "viii July 1560. Lettres to the
Q. Majesty by Sir Peter Caroo," tells the queen of the proclamation of
peace and outlines for her the main points of the new treaty. The second
letter is headed "9 July 1560. My private lettre to the Q. Majesty for anwer
by Sir Peter Caroo" and answers an earlier letter of the queen's in which
she apparently expressed a willingness to break off talks over the issue of
Calais. Cecil in this letter carefully tells the queen that in his opinion
neither Calais nor further military adventures in France are worth the
queen's time or money. He ventures to predict that she will come to see
that it was a "good happ" that her letters about Calais did not arrive until
after Cecil had concluded the treaty.[27] Cecil must have dispatched Carew
to London almost immediately upon completing the second letter, for next
day, on 10 July, Norfolk reported to Cecil that Carew was come to
Berwick and would soon depart "to London wards."[28]

Conveying these letters to the queen may have been the only true
diplomatic mission Carew ever had to undertake, for the news and opinions
the letters contained could not have been welcome to Elizabeth. Perhaps
Cecil thought only an old soldier of Carew's experience could have braved
the queen's wrath. As it turned out, Carew was spared that wrath by a fit
of ague, which seized him at Darington on 11 July as he traveled "post
haste" toward London. In a letter from Darington, Carew told Petre that
he was sending the letters on by a servant and begged Petre to excuse him
to the queen for his indisposition and inability to deliver the letters in
person.[29] Petre apparently did his work well, for the queen graciously
thanked Carew for his good service when he returned to court, which must
have been in late July or early August. Indeed, Elizabeth seems to have

been in a rather playful mood, for she was "somewhat pleasant" with Carew and "thanked him for his letters of his own penning, commending him to be a very good secretary." Carew had written his letters to the queen himself, "fearing and dursting to commit" the details of the dispute within the army command to another person. Evidently acting as his own secretary was a difficult and unaccustomed undertaking for Carew, and not one that he attempted with much enthusiasm, being, as Hooker wrote, "a bad scrivener." Even in exile in France and Germany, Carew had made use of a secretary to write his letters. This lack of facility with a pen was the point of the queen's gentle joke; bad as Carew was at writing, he wrote his letters "with no more pain than she [the queen] had labor to read them: for as he spent a night in writing, so she spent a whole day in reading." [30]

Carew, shortly after his return from Scotland, "gave over London and came to his house at Mohun's Ottery, where, and at other places in Devon, he spent his time, to his great credit with her [the queen] and with the whole country." [31] As Hooker had noted, Carew lived mostly at London at the beginning of the reign. Carew's retirement to Devon may have been triggered by a grant made to him by the queen on 26 May 1560, one day after his appointment to the commission for treating with the French. This grant gave to Carew in fee simple the reversions of Mohun's Ottery, Stoke Fleming, Monckton, Weston Peverall, Ashwater, Georgeham, and the other Carew estates leased for 30 years to James Bassett by Queen Mary after Carew's attainder. [32] The grant described Carew's forfeiture of the estates through treason and their eventual restoration through the pardon of December 1555 and the grant of reversion of September 1556. [33] Bassett had died in November 1558, and his will directed that his leases of Carew lands be sold to meet his extensive debts, with first option on purchase of the leases given to James Courtenay, Bassett's nephew. [34] Courtenay does not seem to have exercised his option and the leases came into the possession of Henry Denny, who sold his interest in the lands of Mohun's Ottery, Stoke Fleming, and the other estates to Carew for £1000 in April 1562.[35] Thus Carew finally regained actual possession of the ancient family lands, but added substantially thereby to his burden of debt. In 1555, when the lease of Carew manors to Bassett was made, the Crown seems to have retained possession of the manor house at Mohun's Ottery, and the grant of 1560, besides confirming the Marian grant to Carew of the reversion of Bassett's lease, probably restored to Carew the possession of the house. Carew's attempts to make good the large sums paid and owing to the Crown under the terms of the 1556 agreement that secured his release from the Tower were hampered until 1562 by the loss of his lands and their profits to the Marian lease, and thereafter by the debt incurred to extinguish that lease.

Carew's virtual disappearance from court after 1560 is therefore not likely to have been caused by the queen's displeasure with Carew's out-spokenness in the 1559 Parliament, nor, as John Guy and Simon Adams[36] have suggested, by the taint of Carew's association with the radical and grasping Protestantism of Northumberland's regime, nor even, as Hooker stated, by Carew's desire to live quietly away from court, but rather by Carew's financial inability to maintain himself at court. Carew's employment on the Scottish service in the summer of 1560 disproves the theory that his stand on the queen's marriage in Parliament in the spring of 1559 denied him any further favor. Many closer associates of Northumberland, and indeed several of Carew's fellow conspirators from 1553, such as Throckmorton and Henry Killigrew, overcame their Edwardian associations to serve Elizabeth in various high positions for many years. Hooker alleged that at the start of Elizabeth's reign Carew was

> in place to have been advanced to great honour and credit, if he had been as ready to have received as she willing to have given; but, as the common proverb, is "he that will not open the bag when the pig is offered must needs go without it." Nevertheless, the queen considered him very liberally, and gave him very good things, and which was as liberally, if not wastefully, consumed.[37]

Like a moth, Carew had always been powerfully attracted to the flame of power and wealth that emanated from the monarch. If "the pig" was being offered to him, it is hard to believe that he would voluntarily do without it, although this may well have been the impression Carew wished to leave with Hooker. As Hooker once again complained, Carew was not the man to win his way out of debt by frugality and good management, and Elizabeth was not the monarch to shower rich rewards on a courtier. Heavy debts, a diminished income, and an inability to control spending simply put service at court beyond Sir Peter's means and forced him to retire to Devon.

If Carew could not serve at court, he could still make himself useful to the queen in the West Country. In October 1560, Carew and Thomas Williams wrote from Exeter to Bedford to make him aware of a serious state of affairs in the city concerning lack of public confidence in the teston, a Tudor shilling originally worth 12d.[38] The coin was heavily debased in the last years of Henry VIII and counterfeiting became a serious problem. Somerset's government called in the old testons and issued a new coin; the old testons remaining in circulation were given a value of 9d. On 9 October 1560, just two weeks before Carew and Williams wrote to Bedford, Elizabeth issued a proclamation fixing the value of testons at $4^{1}/_{2}$d and $2^{1}/_{4}$d, and ordering that the two values of genuine coins be stamped in certain ways[39] to make them distinguishable from the many counterfeits in circulation. Carew and Williams warned Bedford that because Exeter had neither received the stamps nor any information from the Council about when to expect the stamps, the citizens were "perplexed, and in some obloquy" about receipt of testons. This confusion was likely to increase because rumors were spreading that the coinage experts charged with the stamping were rejecting as counterfeits great quantities of coins brought to them. No one in Exeter would now accept an unstamped coin and the authorities dared "not use any enforcement to compel the people to take the testons lest the furniture of the markets might, perchance, by that means, be withdrawn." Carew and Williams persuaded those officials in the city responsible for collecting the queen's revenues to take unstamped coins in hopes of convincing others by their example to do the same. However, rumors of the recent arrival of stamps in Cornwall threatened to make the situation worse, and the two men urged Bedford to do what he could to hurry along the shipment of stamps to Exeter.

Three months after dealing with the coinage crisis, Carew received a further indication of the queen's favor. On 24 January 1561, the queen granted Carew a license for life to import at Dartmouth from friendly countries as much wheat, barley, and barley malt as needed to brew 1,000 tons of beer per year for export back to friendly countries.[40] The license allowed Carew to ignore the Marian statute prohibiting the export of beer. Carew was to record his imports and exports with the customer of the port, was to pay 18d per ton to the queen, and was not allowed to use any oak, ash, or elm in the making of beer casks or otherwise in the brewing process. If Carew's privilege was found to be prejudicial to any part of the realm, the Crown could revoke the license by letters patent. Carew likely did not himself engage in brewing beer, but instead sold his rights to do so to another for a handsome profit.

Brewing beer was far from being Carew's only activity in the years after 1560; he lived in these years the life of quieter but nonetheless important local service that had characterised his father and many of his fifteenth-century ancestors. In June 1561, Carew sat in Exeter Castle on a Devon commission of inquiry into the criminal activities of one John Pellowe of Modbury; the commission found sufficient evidence against Pellowe to lodge several indictments. Pellowe eventually had a pardon for his offenses, but he was apparently unimpressed with the working of local justice, for he involved himself in further difficulties in 1562, which required Carew to sit again as a royal justice in his case.[41] In September of the same year, Carew attempted to assist George Butsyde, a westerner who had been held captive in Ireland for a decade. Butsyde appealed to Thomas Randolph, Elizabeth's ambassador in Scotland for aid, telling Randolph that Carew could attest to his descent from "the best blood in Devon and Cornwall."[42] In February 1562, both Sir Peter and Sir Gawen were named part of the quorum of the Devon commission of the peace; Sir Peter was also appointed custos rotulorum for Devon.[43] The two men were reappointed to these positions in 1564, and Sir Peter was named as well part of the quorum for the Dorset commission.[44] A brief crisis in the spring of 1562 had the queen considering Carew as a replacement for Lord Grey, who was then somewhat out of favor, as governor of Berwick. Fearing that Mary of Scotland was about to open negotiations for a marriage with the king of Sweden, Elizabeth prepared to send ships, munitions, and money to Berwick with Carew to show her displeasure at the possibility of such a match. But news that Mary had shown herself unfavorable to the Swedish king's proposal kept both Carew and the ships from sailing.[45] In January 1563, Carew and Thomas Southcote, the husband of his niece Thomasine Kirkham (daughter of his sister Cecily), served together on a commission charged with levying 200 workers for the improvement of the harbor at Newhaven. The commissioners determined that tin miners were the best fitted for the work, but the terms of their commission did not allow them "to meddle" with the miners, so Carew and Southcote asked the Council for further instructions in the matter.[46]

In September 1562, Sir Peter found himself paired with John Chichester and Sir Arthur Champernon on an inquiry into the behavior of certain persons in Devon, against whom information had been laid with the Council.[47] Both Chichester and Champernon had been implicated with Carew in the abortive rising of January 1554; Champernon had suffered a brief spell of imprisonment in Exeter for his association with his cousin. This grouping by the Council once again illustrates the marvelous cohesion of the gentry leadership of the county. One may wonder at the state of

personal relations between Carew and Champernon; Sir Arthur had
abandoned Carew in 1554 when it became clear that the rising had failed
and Carew would receive primary blame for instigating it. Sir Arthur had
fallen all over himself in his attempts to distance himself from his cousin in
the days after his flight from Mohun's Ottery. Just as the accusations and
harsh words of 1549 had healed over in more stable times, so too the
divisions of 1554 fell away in the peaceful years of Elizabeth, or at least
were sufficiently buried to allow the long-standing gentry families to work
together in public to exercise their accustomed management of county
affairs. Carew and Champernon worked together, apparently without
difficulty, in June 1563 when Lord Admiral Clinton ordered Carew to
assist Champernon, then vice-admiral of Devon, in the taking of an
inventory of French ships that had been brought in to Devon ports as
prizes taken under letters of marque.[48] Carew also worked closely with
many other Devon gentlemen who had opposed him or abandoned him in
1554. This was particularly true of Chichester. In September 1564, the
two men were ordered to appoint searchers and keep watch on the coasts
of Devon and Cornwall for pirates attacking Spanish subjects; for this service,
which lasted 34 days, they were paid £40.[49] In the same month, they were
appointed with several other gentlemen to inquire into a complaint made
against one John Williams, and in January 1565 they investigated the case
of a suspected pirate being held in jail in Cornwall.[50] Six months later,
Carew and Chichester were again ordered to Cornwall, this time to sit with
two local justices at the assizes in examination of a dispute involving Sir
William Godolphin, Reynold Mohun, and Carew's old companions in
exile, the Killigrews.[51]

The outward calm and cooperation that marked Carew's relations
with the chief members of Devon's gentry leadership during the 1560s was
broken at least once, in the spring of 1567. On 31 March, the Council sent
letters to Carew and to Sir John Pollard ordering the two men to regard
the queen's peace and keep their recent dispute under control. Carew was

warned that he would answer at his peril if further disorder arose from his actions or from the actions of those incited by him.[52] The arrogant Sir Peter of Edwardian times seems for the moment to have submerged his less quarrelsome Elizabethan successor. The nature of the dispute that prompted these warnings is mysterious, but the Council's letter makes clear the seriousness of the matter and its potential for violence. It is tempting to suggest that the quarrel had something to do with Pollard's imprisonment in the Tower in 1556 for involvement in the Dudley conspiracy, the details of which had been revealed to the government by Carew as part of the price of his pardon. Such a suggestion, however tempting, would be mere speculation. Chichester, Carew's closest associate in county matters in the 1560s, had also gone to the Tower in 1556 on Carew's information, but there is no hint of friction between those two men over the matter.[53] Pollard and Carew had served together, apparently without difficulty, in the 1557 St. Quentin campaign, and the two men had served together again in the Parliament of 1559, Pollard sitting in that session for Exeter. Carew's role in uncovering the Dudley plot was probably unknown to the gentlemen he uncovered, and why the matter should erupt in 1567 after lying dormant for 11 years is difficult to explain. What's more, Pollard was a Protestant, a close associate of the earl of Bedford, on good terms with Cecil, and a friend of Sir Arthur Champernon, who was one of the overseers of Pollard's will.[54] In terms of politics, religion, and family, Carew and Pollard were cut from the same cloth. The dispute may have arisen out of the internal politics of Exeter, from some clash of the interests or influence the two men maintained in the city. Pollard and Carew were successively MPs for Exeter, Pollard in 1555 and 1559 and Carew in 1566. The dispute with John Trew (described below) was raging in Exeter at this time and certain disagreements between the city and the earl of Bedford were beginning; these tensions in Exeter provide the most likely cause of a dispute between two men so closely associated with the city's interests.

Whatever tensions existed between him and some of the members of the county leadership, Carew stayed in Devon throughout much of the 1560s and functioned as an important part of that leadership group. Only the meeting of Parliament called Carew back to London during the early and mid-1560s. When the first session of Elizabeth's second Parliament opened in January 1563, Sir Peter Carew was not a member of the Commons. Sir Gawen, who had attended the 1559 Parliament as member for the Devon stannery town of Plympton Earl, served in this Parliament as knight for the county with John Chichester.[55] In this session, Sir Peter petitioned for passage of a private act of restitution reversing his Marian attainder. After being brought from the Lords on 10 March, and read twice on the following day, Carew's bill of restitution passed the Commons on 12 March 1563, one of many such acts passed by the first two Elizabethan Parliaments to restore in blood former Marian rebels or their heirs.[56] In 1566, Carew became a member of the second session of this Parliament by being selected as MP for Exeter at a by-election held to fill the vacancy left by the death of Thomas Williams, Carew's fellow correspondent to Bedford during the coinage crisis in Exeter in 1560. Carew's selection was at his own request; he approached the mayor and city council, who elected burgesses in Exeter, and "made motion and request to be burgess." The mayor and council acceded to Carew's request on condition that he become a freeman of the city and that he "supply the office in his own person." If Carew would not agree to these terms, Mr. Periam was to have the seat.[57] Carew was apparently agreeable, for he was made a freeman by order of the mayor and council on 23 September 1566, one week before the opening of Parliament.[58]

During the session, Carew was named on 31 October to one of the committees dealing with the succession and the queen's marriage. The queen, to forestall a parliamentary petition on the succession, ordered 30 members of the Commons to appear before her on the afternoon of 5 November to hear her pleasure on the matter. Carew was one of the 30 appointed by the speaker to attend on the queen.[59] Although this was the second time Carew had been part of a movement in the Commons to meddle, as the queen saw it, in the marriage and succession questions, he must not have stood out on the matter as he did in 1559 when the queen took some offense at his activities. The queen was to be again angered by Carew in connection with Parliament, but not for his activities in the session of 1566. She was instead upset with his refusal to accept a seat in the Parliament of 1571, where, as she said, "he might have done her some good service."[60] The session of 1566 marked Sir Peter's last appearance in the House of Commons; for the remainder of his life, Carew's legislative and legal interests would be centered in Dublin, not in Westminster.

Exeter's acceptance of Carew as their Commons representative in 1566 illustrates the renewal of close relations between the Carew family and Exeter. Carew's plotting of rebellion in the city in 1554 had broken that relationship, causing the city authorities, like the Devon gentry, to quickly disassociate themselves from the traitor and his family. Carew's pension of £2 per year, which Exeter had granted him for his services in 1549, was immediately discontinued.[61] But the city was just as quick to restore its connection with Sir Peter when his pardon made it safe to do so. The city resumed Carew's pension in the last year of Mary's reign, and granted a gift of £3 3s 11d to Sir Peter and to his uncle George in the first year of Elizabeth's reign.[62] Given in consideration of the Carews' good will and favor, the gift reflected the assessment by the Exeter city fathers of the good will and favor Sir Peter and his uncle were likely to receive from the new queen. George Carew did indeed rise rapidly, being already a canon of Exeter at the time of the grant and soon to become dean, but Sir Peter's retirement from court after 1560 must have somewhat confounded those early expectations. Nonetheless, Carew made himself useful to Exeter in the 1560s in a most unexpected way—he helped to compose a pair of disputes in which the city embroiled itself.

The first of these incidents involved "the great troubles and suits" arising from the efforts at incorporation made by the company of Exeter merchants engaged in trade with France and Spain. This group petitioned Queen Mary for a charter in 1558, but the outcome of that suit is uncertain. However, in June 1558, the city of Exeter granted incorporation to all merchants in the city engaged "in the mystery and trade of transporting of wares and merchandise from beyond the seas."[63] But, as Hooker recorded, this incorporation "took no effect" because the merchants in the first month of the new reign asked the queen through Cecil for a new charter given under royal authority.[64] The queen answered this petition in late January 1559 by granting a company of 16 merchants a monopoly in Exeter on the sale of imported goods and on the export of domestic products. By the terms of this charter, no one outside the company could sell either at wholesale or retail any product of foreign manufacture; as MacCaffrey has noted, this "provision went far towards concentrating a great part of the commercial activity of the city in the hands of the company members."[65] When they became known, the terms of the charter aroused intense opposition among the members of the city's various craft guilds. Carew became involved in the matter when he was proposed by the merchants as a possible arbitrator. John Hooker was also heavily involved in the dispute on the merchants' side. Hooker composed the merchants' replies to their opponents' petitions and allegations, and the impressive volume and learned tone of these documents may have attracted Carew's notice.[66] When, several years later, Carew had need of assistance in framing weighty and persuasive legal arguments, John Hooker proved to be ideally suited for the job, thereby initiating the personal and professional relationship to which we owe so much of our knowledge of the life of Sir Peter Carew.

The second Exeter dispute involving Carew concerned the litigation arising out of the city's 1563 agreement with John Trew to improve the haven of the city by building a canal that would allow "boats and vessels laden with ten tons . . . at the least" to come and go at all tides "to and from the seas unto the city walls."[67] The work started well, but soon "by certain variances and the breech of covenants pretended great suits and controversies ensued and by that means the work very like to be clean overthrown, destroyed, and given over." [68] As with the dispute over the merchants' charter, Carew was not the only local worthy to intervene in the matter; the earl of Bedford, Sir Arthur Champernon, and several other gentlemen were all involved at various points in time. In 1567, Carew helped persuade the city to grant Trew more time to complete the project, and was for his efforts assigned with Champernon to judge whether or not Trew had fulfilled the terms of the contract when the additional time expired.[69]

With Bedford, the Carews, and other families of local influence and authority, the Exeter city government had to walk a fine line between cooperation and subservience. The city wished to make use of the "good will and favor" the leaders of such families exercised at court and in the surrounding county, but did not wish to lose their independence to these powerful figures in the process. These conflicting needs explain the city's acceptance of Carew as a burgess in 1566 but its insistence that he become a freeman and serve personally in Parliament. The city fathers wanted to gratify Carew but they did not want him serving as an election broker for Exeter seats in the Commons by appointing someone to sit in his place. As we have seen, Carew was involved in a number of quarrels with the city during his days of high favor under the Northumberland regime, but under Elizabeth Carew posed a threat to the city only in so far as he was a close associate of the earl of Bedford, who did attempt at times to bend the city administration to his will. Bedford inherited the commanding position in the county once held by the Courtenays, and he aspired also to the ascendancy the Courtenays had once held in Exeter. For instance, Bedford complicated the affair of John Trew and the canal by leasing from the queen the former Courtenay manor of Topsham, and thereby taking up the ancient claim of the Topsham men for goods bound to and from Exeter to be loaded and unloaded in their town.[70] The city, unwilling to exchange the Countenays for Bedford, vigorously fought the earl. Although Carew was not directly involved in this famous dispute, his long relationship with the Russells and his own and his family's connections at court and among the gentry leadership of Devon made the Exeter authorities anxious to please him and his uncles if at all possible. Thus in 1565 the mayor and city council made a cutler named Richard Collins a freeman of the city on Carew's request.[71] In 1562, they considered William Greenwood as keeper of the Cloth Hall on the recommendation of Sir Gawen Carew.[72] In 1574, they granted Sir Gawen the same freeman status and £2-pension held by his nephew.[73] Exeter's relations with the Carews, as with most of the city's relationships with local magnates and gentlemen in the Elizabethan period, were friendly and compliant on the surface, but cautious and tense underneath.

When not sitting in Parliament or concerned in Exeter affairs, Carew occupied himself in the proper ordering and directing of the county. For example, in November 1563, Carew wrote from Mohun's Ottery asking William Alley, the bishop of Exeter, to inquire into the conduct of John Parker, who lived outside Honiton and was a member of Carew's own parish of Luppitt. Carew complained to the bishop of Parker's "naughty and froward dealings toward his wife." During the subsequent inquiry, Parker fled the district for Exeter, prompting the bishop to ask the mayor and city council to seize him. Parker, wrote Alley, had "almost killed his wife diverse and sundry times" and had "been at no church almost these 12 months and regards neither God nor man."[74] Besides helping to punish the wicked, Carew also sought to help in rewarding the righteous. On 2 July 1568, shortly before Carew left for Ireland, no less a Protestant than Edmund Grindal, bishop of London and former Marian exile in Germany, wrote to Archbishop Parker of an application made to him on behalf of one John Wolton by his "very good friends" Sir Peter Carew and John Chichester.[75] The two western gentlemen supported Wolton's request for a dispensation for non-residence. Wolton, whom Hooker called "very godly and well learned and as great a politician as the like not to fore known in this Church," became bishop of Exeter in 1578.[76] Carew and Chichester assured Grindal that Wolton was a man of "very good conscience," and that Wolton did not mean to neglect his cure, but sought only opportunities to preach freely throughout the province of Canterbury and elsewhere. In these two episodes, Carew displayed a rather Puritan concern for public morality and for godly preaching, as well as solid connections with the higher levels of the ecclesiastical hierarchy, both in London and in Devon. Hooker made a point of describing Carew's respect for godly preaching. Sir Peter not only protected and promoted the preaching of Hayne and Alley in Exeter but maintained a preacher in his own household for the benefit of his family and neighbors.[77] By the 1560s, Carew was a convinced Protestant; and whatever his practice with the Marian government to secure his pardon, Carew's reputation in Elizabethan Protestant circles was high.

After 1563, Carew spent much time in efforts to suppress piracy along the western coasts. Hooker said nothing about Carew's actions against pirates in the 1560s; he merely summed up Sir Peter's life in Devon during the decade by saying that after his return to the county Carew "rested himself, attending such affairs of the commonwealth as the time required."[78] What the time required was safe western sea lanes, and the rest Sir Peter got while he attended to the matter was little enough. The queen initiated Carew's campaign against piracy with a letter of 29 September 1564 authorizing him "to cause one or two apt vessels to be made ready with all speed in the ports thereabout." Having heard that "pirates and rovers" infested the coasts of Devon and Cornwall and caused much injury to legitimate trade in the region, the queen thought first to send two of her own vessels to sea against them. Elizabeth reconsidered, however, when she learned how long it might take vessels from London to reach western waters; speed and secrecy were of the essence, and an expedition prepared in London might too easily lack the one and lose the other. The matter might, therefore, be better handled in the West by someone with naval experience and a familiarity with western coasts and waters. Carew seemed an excellent choice, and the queen, having supplied the what and the why, left the how entirely in Carew's hands. Except for a suggestion that Carew entice some of the pirates "with hope of our money to apprehend some of the rest of their company," Elizabeth promised to "leave the manner how herein to proceed to your policy, and shall allow anything that you shall put in execution to this end." Arrangements for how to pay for this expedition were similarly broad, with the queen assuring Carew that she would not fail to see all his necessary charges "readily paid and satisfied."[79] Some money was sent to Carew before the end of October, but he deemed the amount insufficient, asking to be advanced an additional £400.[80] This sum, accounting to a later accounting given by Carew to Cecil, was sent to Sir Peter through Sir William Damsell, a Devon man who was receiver general of the Court of Wards.[81] Secure in the queen's confidence and confident in the queen's assurances, Carew set about immediately to fulfill his secret commission.

The day after the queen wrote her letter to Carew, the Council directed him to arrest Edmond Coke of Plymouth and five other named individuals in various western ports on suspicion of victualling pirates. Coke and his fellow suspects were to be either bound over for their appearance before the Council or sent in custody to London.[82] Carew, meanwhile, responded promptly to the queen's letter, expressing his willingness to arm two ships for the venture and asking for more details as to how the expedition was to be financed. Carew asked if the sailors were to have wages and victual or victual only, leaving their wages to come out of the spoils taken from the pirates. The queen responded on 10 October by seizing enthusiastically on the suggestion of reducing her cost to victual only and allowing the pirates, through their lost goods, to involuntarily pay the sailors' wages. Lord Clinton agreed to waive his interests as lord

admiral in the pirates' vessels and goods, agreeing that any proceeds from
the spoils of the expedition should "remain to the takers." The queen
closed by urging speed and hoping "that we may hear of some good to be
done herein."[83] By December, Carew had, according to Guzman de Silva,
the Spanish ambassador in London, three ships at sea chasing pirates, and
in particular the notorious Thomas Stukeley, whose attacks on Portuguese
and Spanish merchants were of special concern in Spain. Cecil assured de
Silva that other vessels would join with Carew in the hunt for Stukeley;
Carew, de Silva explained to Philip, was "a person in whom much confidence
is placed."[84] On 23 December 1564, the Council responded to earlier letters
from Carew and Chichester that had enclosed a listing of suspected pirates
and others who had engaged in theft on the high seas. The two gentlemen
were ordered to assist the vice admirals for Devon and Cornwall in
apprehending these pirates.[85]

Carew reported the results of his pirate-hunting activities in a
letter to the Council written from Mohun's Ottery on 17 April 1565.[86]
After rehearsing the terms of his commission from the previous fall, Carew
wrote that he had sent two vessels to sea, along with another bark (thus
explaining de Silva's reference to three ships), for which he subsequently
obtained warrant from the Council. Finding no pirates along the west
coast of England, the little fleet sailed into Irish waters, where it came
upon a hulk belonging to the pirate Stukeley in Cork haven. Stukeley
being somewhere ashore, and the hulk being but lightly guarded, Carew's
mariners fired a few shots at the pirates, who promptly took to their long
boats and rowed ashore, allowing Carew's men to tow off the hulk without
further ado. After this success, the fleet sailed to Beerie haven, where it
encountered the ships of the pirates Laydon, Lysyngham, and Corbett
anchored off the castle commanding the haven. The pirate captains
trained their shore batteries and the guns of the castle on the English ships
and thereby prevented Carew's men from landing to assail them. Before
the castle, the pirates mustered 500 gallowglasses and kerns [heavily

armed Scots mercenaries and light armed Irish infantry], courtesy of the
Irish lord of the castle, who was Laydon's brother-in-law and who had
entrusted the castle to Laydon's keeping. To this force, the pirates added
another 200 of their own men. An artillery duel commenced between the
fleet and the pirate guns on shore, during which one of the pirate captains—
Carew thought Lysyingham—was slain. The duel continued from 10
o'clock in the morning until 4 o'clock in the afternoon, by which time the
fleet had sustained such damage as to make withdrawal necessary. With
one hulk and one drawn artillery fight the expedition's only results, Carew
apologised for the lack of success and fretted about what his commission's
dismal outcome would do to his standing at court, anxiously telling the
councilors, "I trust your lordships will conceive no other opinion of me."

Carew had good cause to worry about his standing, for the
expedition's lack of booty put him in a difficult position as to the mariners'
wages, and he needed the Council's good will and cooperation to extricate
himself from the possibly calamitous financial consequences. The queen
had agreed that the mariners should be paid out of the spoils taken from
the pirates, but the only spoil was the hulk taken from Stukeley. This was
little enough, but now the Council ordered Carew to deliver the hulk to
one John Petersen, a Fleming who claimed ownership. Carew warned that
the mariners, as soon as they saw the hulk restored, would "forthwith
make exclamation unto me for her majesty's wages." The three vessels had
carried 246 men who had agreed to serve for five or six months. If the
sailors demanded wages from the beginning of their service in the previous
fall, the sum demanded would exceed the value of the hulk. Carew
lamented that he had already attempted to satisfy the mariners "out of my
own purse," thinking to recover his outlay from the proceeds of the hulk.
He was now facing not only further demands from the sailors, but the loss
of the money he had already given them. Carew hoped that the lords of
the Council would advise the queen to satisfy the mariners' demands, and
so relieve him of a burden he could not sustain. Until he understood the

queen's pleasure, he would defer the restoration of the hulk to Petersen, but hastened to add that he was not and would not refuse to deliver the hulk should that be the queen's command.

To bolster his case, Carew wrote on the same day to Cecil, rehearsing again all the financial particulars of the expedition laid out in the letter to the whole Council, including the outlay of his own money. He made a personal appeal to Cecil for deferment of delivery of the hulk to Petersen; if Cecil could accomplish this, Carew would meanwhile dissemble the matter with the mariners until they were compounded with by the government for their wages. Since the queen would have the only spoil taken restored to its owner, Carew trusted that Cecil would do whatever he could to get the mariners wages for their service. Carew estimated the worth of the hulk at not over £210, which sum, he boldly assured Cecil, the mariners could be brought to accept as full payment for their wages. Carew thanked Cecil for his past friendship, and based his hope of speedy remedy in this matter on continuation of that friendship. If friendship would not expedite the matter, Carew planned, apparently, to fall back on persistence, assuring Cecil that the bearer of the letter, Carew's servant, would wait upon Cecil from time to time for satisfaction of the suit. Carew closed the letter by directing Cecil's attention to an enclosed brief of charges already dispersed to the mariners, and by telling Cecil of the good order he and Chichester had brought to the dispute between a Mistress Crudgie and one Drewe. The dispute involved a quarrel over the division of profits from a piece of property Drewe leased from Mistress Crudgie. Carew's main point to Cecil in this matter was how well satisfied the two parties were with the settlement devised by the two gentlemen. Carew could thus conclude his suit for the mariners' wages by describing a service he had performed effectively for the government.[87]

The brief of expenses enclosed with the letter to Cecil put the cost of victualling three vessels for six months, from 13 October to 9 April, at

£372. The three ships in Carew's fleet were the *Mary Bowes* at 200 tons, the *Mary Baxter* at 160 tons, and the bark *Peter* out of Dartmouth at 70 tons. With certain additional charges, the cost of victualling the fleet was put at £440 8s 11d. Toward this amount, Carew contributed £200. A separate hand noted on the brief the necessity of adding another £200 to the total cost of the expedition to cover the mariners' wages.[88] Another apparently earlier listing of expenses for the fleet is also preserved in the State Papers; it breaks down the charges for supplies for 246 men by particular items for the period from 12 October to 1 March. The fleet, for instance, used during that period three score hogsheads of beef at 43s 4d per hogshead, 108 tons of beer at 37s the ton, and an unlisted quantity of pilchards at 18s the hogshead. Also listed are large amounts of bread, four barrels of herring, supplies of wood and candles, and an unquantified amount of powder purchased from William Warde and Nicholas Holland of Dartmouth.[89]

The outcome of Carew's suit in this matter is difficult to determine. Another letter from Carew to Cecil, which concludes only with the date 18 May, is dated in the State Papers to 1570, but would seem from its contents to be better dated to 18 May 1565.[90] In this letter, Carew informed Cecil that he delivered the hulk to the Fleming before he received Cecil's letter of 11 April. Cecil's letter apparently gave Carew certain instructions for dealing with the mariners over their wages. Cecil's instructions on handling the mariners' wages may have crossed paths with Carew's suit on the same matter. In the 18 May letter, Carew informed Cecil that he had followed the instructions, found the mariners generally agreeable, and now hoped to discharge the queen of the wages for about £200, the amount subsequently noted for wages on the list of expenses Carew sent Cecil in April 1565. Carew promised to continue his negotiations with the mariners and make for the queen a better deal if possible, but he hoped the queen would be content to settle the matter for the £200. If she was not, Carew preferred to bear the cost himself rather than trouble Cecil further with the matter.

If the 1570 date is correct, the matter had indeed dragged on for some time, and Carew, newly returned to England from Ireland, had many important suits relating to his freshly reacquired Irish lands to put before Cecil and the queen. He may have been genuinely willing to settle the mariners' demands himself rather than exhaust the patience and good will of the queen and her minister on such an old matter when so many far more important new ones had lately arisen. If the date of the letter is really 1565, as seems likely, Carew's offer is better interpreted as a ploy to secure Cecil's best efforts in getting the queen to agree to the deal worked out with the sailors. Carew, for whom debt was a continual problem in this period, could have had no real desire to incur another large obligation, especially one that he felt to be rightly the queen's. This interpretation is supported by the letter's atypically profuse closing expressions of friendship and gratitude. Carew proclaimed himself more bold in suits for his "reasonable causes" with Cecil than with anyone else because he was so well assured of Cecil's friendship. Carew had such great cause to give thanks to Cecil that he stood more ready than any other to do the minister's bidding. These phrases ring more fulsome than sincere.

The results of Carew's expedition were likely as unsatisfactory to the queen as the queen's reluctance to pay his mariners was to Carew. The coasts of Devon, Cornwall, and Wales were thick with pirates during the Elizabethan period, yet Carew's fleet encountered no pirates at all in these waters and had to sail to Ireland to catch sight of some. Because of the nature of West Country piracy, this poor outcome of Carew's mission is not surprising. Western pirates were allied with, supported by, and employed by western gentlemen, many of whom, such as the Killigrews of Cornwall, were friends or associates of Carew himself. As one historian of Elizabethan piracy has noted, mobilizing the forces of the Crown against West Country pirates "was impossible. . .without arousing suspicion."[91] The pirates also had the use of privately owned havens up and down the coast. They could unload their cargos in these havens in secrecy and safety, and could hide themselves in them as well. No royal warships were stationed in the region, and occasional expeditions like Carew's were all the pirates had to fear. The queen's insistence on secrecy in her letter of commission was wise, but probably futile. As Carew set about his preparations, word of his commission spread among his fellow gentlemen, and from them to the pirates and rovers they supported and engaged. It would be a simple matter for the pirates to make themselves temporarily scarce as Carew's ships sailed by. A touchier question is whether Carew himself leaked information about his undertaking to friends he knew to be involved in supporting piracy. Of this there is no evidence. Carew would want the queen to be satisfied with his service, so it is unlikely he would deliberately sabotage his mission. He may, however, have trusted to Irish waters to give him the booty and success he needed to satisfy the queen—his fleet seems to have moved quickly westward when it did not immediately encounter pirates off the English coast—and to the time and activity needed to make his sailing preparations to warn any piratical friends of their danger.

Although not resident at court, Carew could and did use his connections in London on behalf of western interests. The Dartmouth city government, with which Carew had been on bad terms in Edward's reign, sought his help in November 1565 in persuading London to take steps to halt the recent alarming decline in shipping from the port. Dartmouth blamed the decline on the Elizabethan impost on wines, which had put many merchants out of business and ended most trading voyages out of the port. The mayor and council of Dartmouth sent Carew a list of 30 Dartmouth vessels, 2,570 tons of shipping, sold or lost since Parliament imposed the wine duty.[92] Carew, on 9 November, forwarded the list to Cecil with a letter of his own asking Cecil to look into what might be done to help the town. Carew assured Cecil that he did not by his request wish in any way to reduce the queen's revenue from the impost, but suggested that the town might have some relief and the queen continue to enjoy her accustomed revenues if a motion made by Cecil in the 1559 Parliament were revived and implemented. Cecil's proposal was for taverners to pay a portion of the duty for every ton of wine imported; this motion failed in the 1559 Parliament, even though Carew had supported it then and still thought it a good idea in 1565.[93] In August 1568, shortly before leaving for Ireland, Carew joined with his uncle Gawen and with Chichester to write again to the Council on behalf of West Country merchants. The three gentlemen made the Council aware of privateers operating in western waters under letters of marque from the king of Sweden. These privateers, who were authorised to attack Danish subjects and Hanseatic traders, were bringing their prizes into western ports and discouraging English merchants from risking trade with Denmark or northern Germany for fear of capture by one of these growing number of raiders.[94] In the 1560s, as these letters indicate, Carew's interest in and involvement with West Country trade and shipping became more frequent and more intense.

On 8 November 1565, Carew was commissioned with Chichester, Thomas Southcote, and Robert Carye to suppress piracy and other disorders on the coasts of Devon, and to look into the collection of customs and make a census of ships in county ports.[95] After this commission at the end of 1565, Carew seems to have been less frequently and less substantially employed by the government. Whether the unimpressive result of his expedition against pirates had anything to do with this is unclear. Whatever the reason, Carew found himself employed thereafter on such missions as inquiring into the idiocy of one Jerome Baker.[96] Carew was "now at some leisure," and so turned his thoughts to "such lands as he was persuaded he should have by inheritance within the realm of Ireland."[97] Apparently despairing of an heir and still in need of money, Carew had settled the future of his estates in Devon in 1563. On 2 July, Sir Peter sold his interest in his manors of Mohun's Ottery, Monckton, and Stoke Fleming, as well as in his lordship and manor of Southton in Dartmouth to Thomas Southcote, his niece's husband. For £2000, Southcote acquired future ownership of Carew's manors, lands, and properties in Devon. Southcote agreed to give Carew and Lady Margaret a life estate in the properties and to observe all leases either one made of the premises during their life times, except that Carew agreed not to lease the castle at Dartmouth for longer than the term of his own life and the house, park, and demesne lands at Mohun's Ottery for longer than his and Lady Margaret's lives. Lady Margaret's jointure in Mohun's Ottery and Monckton was to be observed, and the birth of an heir to Sir Peter, either by Lady Margaret or another wife, would, upon payment of £2500 to Southcote, abrogate the agreement and secure the inheritance of all the properties to Carew's heir.[98] With the ancient Carew estates in Devon poised to pass to the Southcotes after Carew's death, Sir Peter in his restless leisure after 1565 turned his attention toward the even more ancient Carew lands in Ireland, lands that had not been effectively held by a Carew since the end of the fourteenth century.

Impelled by a pride in family, a love of adventure, a lack of employment, and a need for money, Sir Peter Carew left England in August 1568 for Ireland, where he spent most of the next two years seeking to acquire at law and hold by the sword the vast lands his family had held in that island in the thirteenth and fourteenth centuries. The details of Carew's typically tumultuous exploits in Ireland in the years after 1568 are described in the following chapters. The rest of this chapter will concern itself only with Sir Peter's doings in England between his return there in 1570 and his second trip to Ireland in July 1573. Because much of his attention during these years was given to his continual suits and petitions concerning the newly reacquired Irish lands, Carew spent more time in London than he had between 1560 and 1568. Carew also found himself more heavily employed by the queen than he had been since 1565.

On 11 March 1572, Lord Hunsden wrote from Berwick to Cecil, now Lord Burghley, to marvel at the rumored possibility of Carew being named warden of the stanneries. Because the holder of that office supervised such a large number of men, Hunsden believed the post should go only to one "such as the queen has great cause to trust." The queen, Hunsden knew, had no such cause to trust Carew, but, he closed cryptically in Latin "*aliquid latet quod non patet.*"[99] Just what hidden things Hunsden wanted opened, and the cause of his hostility toward Carew, are difficult to know. Hunsden perhaps had some ambitions for the office himself and, as the queen's cousin and a privy councilor, did not relish being forestalled by Carew. His allusion to Carew's untrustworthiness may stem from the difficulties Carew had caused the queen and Council by his activities in Ireland in 1568-69.

If Carew's doings in Ireland were the source of Hunsden's remarks, the queen was less provoked by them, for she did not seem to share her cousin's dislike of Carew. In November 1569, shortly before Carew's return from Ireland, the queen reappointed him and Sir Gawen to the Devon commission of the peace. Sir Peter was also appointed to the Dorset commission and reappointed custos rotulorum in Devon.[100] In July 1571, the queen appointed Carew to a commission with the mayor and bishop of Exeter and several other gentlemen for levying in Exeter the subsidy granted by Parliament in the previous April.[101] Carew never had the wardenship of the stanneries, but in January 1572 Elizabeth made him constable of the Tower for the period of the duke of Norfolk's confinement there after his reinvolvement in Catholic plotting against the queen. In this grim role, Carew's chief duty was to see the duke safely and securely conveyed to his trial in Westminster Hall, or, as Hooker described it, "both to bring him and carry him back again from the Tower to Westminster."[102] Once at Westminster, Carew and Sir Owen Hopton, lieutenant of the Tower, led the prisoner to the bar, Carew holding the duke's left hand and Hopton his right. The chamberlain of the Tower went before the prisoner bearing the ax, the edge turned toward Carew.[103] In August, Elizabeth named Carew with Christopher Hatton, Henry Knevet, and John Mershe to a commission charged with looking into what had become of the Spanish ships and the ships of Netherlands merchants taken up by the queen's orders since 1568. Although the queen had directed all such vessels and their cargos to be held until she made her pleasure known, many of the ships and much of the cargo had been stolen, concealed, or sold by individuals seeking their own profit. The commissioners were to determine which ships were missing, what cargos they held, and who had taken them. They were empowered to seize all such ships and cargos when they found them and to arrest their unlawful possessors. They were to keep careful record of all goods and ships recovered, and were to have for themselves so much of the money and goods recovered as the legal owners were willing to assign them. Going through three years of records and accounts must have been long and tedious work, for the queen had to renew the commission in the following year.[104] Carew also continued with the less glamorous work of Devon administration; three weeks after his appointment to the commission with Hatton, on 22 August 1572, he was named to a commission with Sir Robert Dennys and two others to inquire in Devon into the lunacy of one Richard Drake.[105] In September, Carew was in London, for William Herlle, a servant of Carew's old companion in exile Sir Henry Killigrew, now Elizabeth's ambassador to Scotland, consulted with him there about the best way to deal with some Scotsmen being detained by the bishop of London for various offenses.[106]

Herlle found Carew in London because the queen had two weeks earlier given him another important commission. Perhaps remembering Carew's good work in connection with the Tower inquiry of 1559, Elizabeth appointed him to a second such inquiry on 16 September 1572. He and his fellow commissioners, Sir Thomas Wroth, Henry Knowles, and the recorder of London, were to inquire into the number, lodgings, keepers, servants, and degree of liberty of the prisoners currently being held. They were also to report on the Tower's state of defense, and its supply of ordnance and powder. The commissioners were also to implement certain reforms at the Tower. Only nobles and "men of special vocation" were to be assigned special keepers, and no prisoner committed for treason or suspicion of treason was to be allowed to meet or talk with any other prisoner. Access to the Tower by the wives of prisoners was to be more strictly controlled and access to the Tower wharf was to be denied to all except those who served in the Tower or had legitimate business there. The lodgings within the Tower of all those who served there were to be surveyed and any person dwelling within who did not serve in the Tower was to be removed. In general, access to the Tower was to be carefully regulated, and no "unmete person" was to be suffered to come into the place.[107] Increasing tensions with Spain caused this increased concern for Tower security. An anonymous letter of intelligence sent from London to the duke of Alva in the Netherlands in October described defensive preparations being made all over England, including the work of Carew and "other heretic gentlemen" at the Tower.[108]

The same Anglo-Spanish tensions gave Carew another commission for surveying defenses after the Tower assignment was completed. Over the winter of 1572-73, he surveyed the defenses of the ports of Devon and Cornwall. In March 1573, Carew gave a bond of £663 6s 8d to back his promise to return or pay for the ammunition delivered to him for the defense of certain western ports. Two weeks later, he gave another bond for the ammunition and supplies delivered to him for outfitting the royal ship *Primrose*.[109] In June, Sir Peter was once again at the Tower, this time to resolve a dispute between the imprisoned earl of Southampton and the lieutenant of the Tower over the earl's diet accounts. Carew's fellow commissioners were Wroth again and Sir William Pickering, a fellow conspirator and exile from 1554. The commissioners were to look into the matter and settle it themselves if they could; if they could not, they were to report to the Council with their recommendations.[110] A month later, Sir Peter left again for Ireland with the army of the earl of Essex. He may have returned briefly to England in 1574. Carew made his will, the contents of which will be described in Chapter 12, on 4 July 1574. He was definitely in Ireland in 1575.

Queen Elizabeth employed Sir Peter Carew many times in many different ways. His service for her was military, diplomatic, and administrative. For this service, Carew received neither the material rewards he had enjoyed from Henry VIII nor the increase in position and influence he had exercised under Northumberland. If Carew entertained hopes at the beginning of Elizabeth's reign of great favor and standing at court, he was disappointed. Although the queen looked on him, for the most part, with favor, neither his Edwardian background, nor his reformed beliefs, nor his opposition to Mary won for him any special position or influence with her. The effects of his own years of extravagance and the consequences of his rebellion and exile under Mary had left him in financial difficulties the queen was not disposed to rectify. If Carew could not maintain himself at court, the queen would use him where he could support himself—in Devon. When the naval expedition of 1564-65 failed to bag any pirates and ended in prolonged wrangling over the sailors' wages, the queen's use of Carew declined, and Sir Peter turned his attention and energy toward a new field of endeavor—Ireland. From 1568 until his death in 1575, Sir Peter Carew's service was often in his own behalf, seeking to restore his family's prestige and his own economic and social position by regaining the ancient Carew lands in the neighboring island.

1 "Count de Feria's Dispatch to Philip II, 14 November 1558," ed. M.J. Rodriguez-Salgado and Simon Adams, *Camden Miscellany XXVIII*, 4th series (London: Royal Historical Society, 1984), p. 332.

2 *Cal.SP For.*, Elizabeth, I, (Nendeln, Liechtenstein, 1966-69), p. 1.

3 *Cal.SP Span.*, Elizabeth, I, pp. 16-21.

4 Ibid., p. 34.

5 HMC, *Earl of Egmont's Manuscripts, Seventh Report* (London, 1879), p. 614.

6 Hooker, "Life," p. 67.

7 Warrant to Sir Peter Carew and Sir William Saint Lo to Survey the Tower, March 1559, PRO, SP12/3/145.

8 P.W. Hasler, ed., *The House of Commons 1558-1603*, vol. I (London: History of Parliament Trust, 1981), p. 541.

9 Hooker, "Life," p. 70.

10 J.E. Neale, *Elizabeth I and Her Parliaments 1559-1581* (New York: St. Martin's Press, 1958), p. 47; *Cal.SP Ven.*, VII, p. 28.

11 CPR, Elizabeth, vol. I, 6 June 1559, (Nendeln, Liechtenstein: Kraus, 1976), pp. 83-84.

12 Ibid., 4 November 1559, p. 147.

13 Hooker, "Life," p. 68.

14 HMC, *Salisbury Manuscripts, Ninth Report* (London, 1883), p. 52.

15 Maclean, *Life and Times*, p. 69 n.

16 HMC, *Salisbury Manuscripts*, App. 4, p. 220.

17 Ibid., p. 222.

18 Ibid., p. 226.

19 *Cal.SP Scotland*, I, p. 413.

20 Ibid., p. 412.

21 HMC, *Salisbury Manuscripts*, App. 4, p. 227.

22 Hooker, "Life," p. 68.

23 Henry Lacy to Thomas Cromwell, 26 October 1539, *Lisle Letters*, V, p. 694.

24 Hooker, "Life," pp. 69-70.

25 *Cal.SP Scotland*, I, p. 427.

26 Ibid., p. 430.

27 Ibid., pp. 445-46.

28 Ibid., p. 447.

29 HMC, *Salisbury Manuscripts*, App. 4, p. 248.

30 Hooker, "Life," p. 69-70. Anyone who has had occasion to read the extent letters in Carew's own hand can sympathize with the queen.

31 Ibid., p. 70.

32 *CPR*, Elizabeth, vol. I, 26 May 1560, pp. 469-70. See *CPR*, Mary and Philip and Mary, vol. II, 10 March 1555, p. 48 for the lease to Bassett.

33 See *CPR*, Mary and Philip and Mary, vol. III, 9 December 1555, pp. 45-46 for Carew's pardon and *CPR*, Mary and Philip and Mary, vol. III, 20 September 1556, pp. 551-54 for the Marian grant to Carew of the reversion to Bassett's lease.

34 Bindoff, *House of Commons*, I, pp. 393, 716-17.

35 Manor of Mamhead Records, DRO, 484M, T8/4.

36 John Guy, *Tudor England* (Oxford: Oxford University Press, 1988), p. 266; Simon Adams, "Eliza Enthroned? The Court and Its Politics" in *The Reign of Elizabeth I*, ed. Christopher Haigh (Athens: The University of Georgia Press, 1987), p. 65.

37 Hooker, "Life," p. 67.

38 Sir Peter Carew and Thomas Williams to the Earl of Bedford, 28 October 1560, PRO, SP12/14/57.

39 Coins valued at $4^1/2$d were to be stamped with a portcullis before the head of King Edward VI and those valued at $2^1/4$d were to be stamped with a greyhound behind the king's head.

40 *CPR*, vol. II, Elizabeth, 24 January 1561, p. 1.

41 Ibid., vol. II,14 July 1561, p. 16; 1 June 1562, p. 408.

42 *Cal.SP, For.*, Elizabeth, IV, p. 288.

43 *CPR*, Elizabeth, vol. II, 11 February 1562, pp. 435-36.

44 Ibid., vol. III, 1 June 1564, p. 21.

45 *Cal.SP Span.*, Elizabeth, I, p. 230.

46 *Cal.SP For.*, Elizabeth, VI, p. 57.

47 APC, VII, p. 132.

48 R.G. Marsden, ed., *Documents Relating to Law and Custom of the Sea*, vol. I (London: Navy Records Society, 1915), pp. 176-77.

49 APC, VII, pp. 151, 202.

50 Ibid., pp. 153, 189.

51 Ibid., p. 225.

52 Ibid., pp. 338-39.

53 Nichols, *Machyn*, p. 104; Cal.SP Ven., VI, p. 446.

54 Bindoff, *House of Commons*, I, p. 639; Hasler, *House of Commons*, III, pp. 229-30

55 Hasler, *House of Commons*, I, pp. 142, 538.

56 G.R. Elton, *The Parliament of England 1559-1581* (Cambridge: Cambridge University Press, 1989), p. 304.

57 MacCaffrey, *Exeter*, p. 223; Hasler, *House of Commons*, I, p. 541.

58 Margery M. Rowe and Andrew M. Jackson, eds. *Exeter Freemen 1266-1967* (Exeter: Devon and Cornwall Record Society, 1973), p. 87.

59 *Commons Journal*, pp. 75-76; Hasler, *House of Commons*, I, p. 541; T.E. Hartley, ed., *Proceedings in the Parliaments of Elizabeth I*, vol. I 1558-1581 (Leicester: Leicester University Press, 1981), p. 145-46.

60 Hooker, "Life," p. 70.

61 MacCaffrey, *Exeter*, p. 212.

62 Ibid., p. 213.

63 Hooker, *Description*, pp. 893, 917; MacCaffrey, *Exeter*, p. 136.

64 Exeter Merchants Petition for Incorporation, December 1558, PRO, SP12/1/23.

65 MacCaffrey, *Exeter*, p. 137.

66 For a detailed account of this dispute, see MacCaffrey, *Exeter*, pp. 136-148.

67 Hooker, *Description*, p. 908.

68 Ibid., p. 658.

69 MacCaffrey, *Exeter*, p. 213

70 Hooker, *Description*, pp. 658-59.

71 Rowe and Jackson, *Freemen*, p. 87.

72 HMC, *Exeter Records*, p. 49.

73 Rowe and Jackson, *Freemen*, p. 92; HMC, *Exeter Records*, p. 49.

74 HMC, *Exeter Records*, p. 24.

75 William Nicholson, ed., *The Remains of Edmund Grindal* (Cambridge: Cambridge University Press, 1843), p. 299.

76 Hooker, *Description*, p. 237.

77 Hooker, "Life," pp. 111-12.

78 Ibid., p. 71.

79 Queen Elizabeth to Sir Peter Carew, 29 September 1564, PRO, SP12/34/180.

80 *Cal.SP Dom.*, 1547-80, I, p. 246.

81 List of Charges for Sir Peter Carew's Ships, April 1565, PRO, SP12/36/83.

82 APC, VII, p. 154.

83 Queen Elizabeth to Sir Peter Carew, 10 October 1564, PRO, SP12/35/9.

84 *Cal.SP Span.*, Elizabeth, I, p. 397.

85 APC, VII, p. 180.

86 Sir Peter Carew to the Council, 17 April 1565, PRO, SP12/36/79.

[87] Sir Peter Carew to Sir William Cecil, 17 April 1565, PRO, SP12/36/81.

[88] List of Charges for Sir Peter Carew's Ships, April 1565, PRO, SP12/36/83.

[89] Charges for Victuals, March 1565, PRO, SP12/35/10.

[90] Sir Peter Carew to Sir William Cecil, 18 May 1570?, PRO, SP12/69/21. The strongest piece of evidence for dating the letter to 1570 is the fact that it was written from Collacombe, the Devon home of Edmund Tremayne, with whom Carew had worked in the previous year in Ireland. Despite this, the year 1565 seems a more likely date for this letter.

[91] David Mathew, "The Cornish and Welsh Pirates in the Reign of Elizabeth," *English Historical Review* 39 (July 1924), p. 337. Mathew's article (pp. 337-48) provides a detailed discussion of the nature of piracy in the Elizabethan West Country.

[92] List of Dartmouth Shipping Lost since the Impost on Wines, November 1565, PRO, SP12/37/183.

[93] Sir Peter Carew to Sir William Cecil, 9 November 1565, PRO, SP12/37/181.

[94] Sir Peter Carew, Sir Gawen Carew, and John Chichester to the Council, 1 August 1568, PRO, SP12/47/63.

[95] APC, VII, p. 283.

[96] *CPR*, Elizabeth, vol. IV, 2 May 1567, p. 131.

[97] Hooker, "Life," p. 71.

[98] *Calendar of Deeds and Documents*, Exeter City Library, DRO, #68402.

[99] *Cal.SP For.*, Elizabeth, p. 56.

[100] *CPR*, Elizabeth, vol. V, 4 November 1569, p. 222.

[101] *Calendar of the Archives of the City of Exeter*, DRO, p. 37.

[102] Hooker, "Life," p. 70.

[103] Howells, *State Trials*, I, p. 959.

[104] *CPR*, Elizabeth, vol. V, 2 August 1572, p. 438; *Cal.SP Dom.*, Elizabeth, I, p. 463; A.L. Rowse, "Sir Peter Carew, Soldier of Fortune," in *Court and Country: Studies in Tudor Social History* (Athens: University of Georgia Press, 1987), p. 129.

[105] *CPR*, Elizabeth, vol. V, 22 August 1572, p. 436.

[106] *Cal.SP Scotland*, IV, p. 404.

[107] Inquisitions and Orders for Things to be Done at the Tower, 16 September 1572, BL, Lansdowne MS 155, f. 313.

[108] *Cal.SP Span.*, Elizabeth, II, p. 421.

[109] *Cal.SP Dom.*, Elizabeth, I, p. 459.

[110] APC, VIII, p.111.

CHAPTER 10

THE IRISH ADVENTURE

"The last phase of Carew's career," wrote A.L. Rowse, "is not the least venturesome."[1] The activities and events of the years after 1568 are the part of Sir Peter Carew's life about which we know the most and for which Sir Peter is best remembered today. We have John Hooker to thank for this knowledge, as for so much else of what has come down to us about the life and career of Sir Peter Carew. Hooker's biography of Carew, when it reaches the year 1568, blossoms with great detail and rich anecdote. The reticence of Mary's years and the flatness of the early 1560s fall away from Hooker's writing when he begins to describe Carew's Irish adventure. The reason for this change is simple—after 1568 Hooker himself became a participant in and witness of the chief themes and events of Carew's life. Hooker's account of Carew's activities during these years is in part an account of his own activities, for some time in 1567 or early 1568 Carew persuaded Hooker to become his solicitor and agent in a great project he had decided to undertake during his years of semi-retirement—the recovery of the extensive estates the Carew family had once enjoyed in Ireland.

Sir Peter was himself partially responsible for the fullness of the record for this period. Recovery of his Irish inheritance became the all-consuming passion of the last years of his life. Carew had to overcome many obstacles, including some of his own devising, to achieve his Irish goals. In his typically single-minded pursuit of these goals, Carew bombarded the queen, the Council, and the Irish government with requests, proposals, complaints, and explanations. Most of these documents survive in the State Papers or in the preserved manuscripts of Sir Peter's cousin and ultimate heir, Sir George Carew, who eventually rose to the Stuart peerage as earl of Totnes.

Another mass of documents not only tells us something about Sir Peter Carew in Ireland, but a good deal about the role his ancestors had played in the island over 200 years earlier. Collected, transcribed, and ordered by Hooker, these ancient deeds, charters, grants, and wills—a Carew family archive apparently preserved in Devon since the fourteenth century—launched Sir Peter on his Irish adventure and brought Hooker into Sir Peter's life. These documents, together with the literary contributions of John Hooker, allow us to know more about Sir Peter Carew's last years than we know about any other part of his life.

Inactivity both offended Carew's nature and afflicted his purse. The debts that forced his retirement from court after 1560 continued to plague him in the years that followed. Burdened with this debt, and lacking a direct heir, Carew turned to the sale of land to meet his obligations. Besides selling a future interest in Mohun's Ottery, Monckton, Stoke Fleming, and Southton in Dartmouth to Thomas Southcote for £2000 in 1563,[2] Carew sold off various other family estates in the West Country in the 1560s. He sold to John Chichester the Devon manors of Ham, Nitherham, Spreycomb, Hole, Twangelegh, Prestlegh, and Sturdeton, the inheritance of his great-great-great-grandmother Joan Courtenay.[3] These lands had been in the Carew family since the 1430s. Sir George Cary of Cokington, a member of another prominent West Country family and kinsman of Carew's, purchased the manor of Ashwater,[4] which Carew's great-great-grandfather Thomas had acquired for the family in the 1440s by his marriage to the Carminow heiress. Gilles Balle, father of a future recorder of Exeter, had purchased various lands out of Carew's manor of Mamhead during the 1550s. In the next decade, Carew sold Balle the rest of the manor.[5] Mamhead went back in the Carew family to the late thirteenth century when Nicholas Carew had acquired it as a marriage gift from his new brother-in-law, Sir John Peverell.[6] The sale of these ancient family estates indicates the depth of Carew's need for money, which, in the 1560s, mingled in equal parts with Carew's need to be active. Sir Peter needed a project both engaging and profitable.

In the thirteenth century, Nicholas Carew, whose like-named son had acquired Mamhead and other lands from the Peverells, married the daughter of Richard Tuit, lord of Maston and baron of Idrone in Ireland. The extensive Idrone (also spelled Odrone or Hydron) estates were situated in the south central portion of the old Irish kingdom of Leinster, which occupied roughly the southeastern quarter of the island. The lands of the barony, which were traversed by the River Barrow, formed the western portion of County Carlow, running southeast along the border with County Kilkenny and touching in the east the border with County Wexford. The nearest towns to the barony were Carlow on the east, Kilkenny to the west, and Waterford to the south. The barony remained in the possession of the Carew family for over a century, until the reign of Richard II, when the Carews were "enforced to depart" by the Irish leader McMorough, who gradually extended his control throughout the region. Sir Peter's ancestor, Sir Thomas Carew, "repaired unto England" after the loss of Idrone and the name Carew was heard no more in Carlow until 1568, when Sir Peter decided that the recovery of Idrone was just the project to give him the adventure he craved and the revenue he required.[7]

Carew knew of Idrone from "sundry writings of evidences for the same" that he had in his possession in Devon. Being "unlearned" either in Latin or in the law, Carew could not read these old documents well enough to know if he still had a valid claim on his family's Irish lands. If he were to undertake the recovery of those lands, he needed the instruction and assistance of someone skilled in understanding old legal records. John Hooker described how this need brought him into Sir Peter Carew's affairs and life.

And having continual speeches thereof unto his friends and acquaintance, bemoaning, as it were, the want of some expert and skillful man to instruct him, it was, at length, advertised unto, that the writer hereof, being to him then unacquainted, was a man greatly given to seek and search old records and ancient writings, and

was very skillful in reading of them, and that he was best able of any in the city of
Exeter to do him pleasure in this behalf.[8]

Carew, "being very earnest and desirous to have his humor to be satisfied,"
had himself introduced to Hooker, and began immediately to tell his new
acquaintance about his plans, showing him several sample documents from
his family archive. The samples illustrated Carew's problem perfectly; one
document was "very old, and had been trodden under the foot, and by that
means the letters were almost worn out." But Hooker did not disappoint;
he was able to read the documents "and declare the effect of them unto
him." Carew was so pleased with Hooker's talents that he "committed
unto him the view and search of all his evidences." Hooker, whose passion
for ordering and arranging written records is still testified to by his work
with the Exeter city archives, began by extracting from the mass of Sir
Peter's materials those documents which pertained to Idrone and the family's
other Irish lands. He then transcribed these relevant items into what he
called "a fair book," which is today preserved among the Carew Papers.[9]
From this selection of evidence, Hooker untangled Carew's "pedigree and
descent" and satisfied Sir Peter as to the validity of his title to various Irish
lands. Hooker then advised Carew to lay his title before the queen and
seek her permission to begin recovery at law of the lands in question, which
an excited Carew proceeded to do.

The queen and Council granted Carew's request for permission to
travel to Ireland and begin legal action for recovery of the lands. Hooker
wrote that they "seemed to be glad" of the request, and even sent letters
on Carew's behalf to the lord deputy and chief officers of Ireland. Upon
his return from London to Devon, Carew sent for Hooker and conferred
with him on the best way to proceed. The two men decided the most
prudent plan was to first make certain Carew had a good chance of success
before he undertook difficult and costly legal action. Such certainty
required research in the archives in Dublin Castle for any "attainder,

statute, or alienation" by which one of Carew's ancestors might have extinguished the family's rights to its Irish possessions. There was no sense in Carew beginning legal proceedings until the possibility of such a bar had been eliminated. Carew credited Hooker with "the whole success" of his venture up to this point, and he could think of no one more mete for the business than his trusted advisor. He therefore entreated Hooker to become his advance agent in Ireland and to undertake the requisite research. Hooker claimed that he was "very loath" to accept the offer, but "at length . . . yielded thereunto," and in early May 1568 took ship from Ilfracombe for Waterford.[10]

On 26 May 1568, Hooker wrote Carew a long letter from Dublin reporting on all his activities and discoveries since arriving three weeks earlier. From Waterford, Hooker set out for Dublin by way of Idrone, stopping at the house of Henry Davells, a Devon man who lived on the borders of the barony. Davells gave Hooker a tour of the barony lands and promised Hooker "his friendship and help to the uttermost of his power" in Carew's undertaking. Once in Dublin, Hooker delivered letters from Carew to Lord Chancellor Robert Weston and Henry Draycott, the master of the rolls. He found both these men "as friendly as I can wish." Hooker lodged with Weston and worked daily with Draycott in the castle archives, to which he was given full access.[11]

Whether part of his agreed upon duties or not, Hooker spent much time during his first weeks in Ireland promoting Carew's cause among important officials of the Irish administration. He traveled, for instance, to the home outside Dublin of ailing Lord Justice Sir William Fitzwilliam to discuss Carew's affairs with him in detail. Fitzwilliam was brother-in-law to Lord Deputy Henry Sidney and an influential man in the Irish government. Hooker sat with Fitzwilliam in his bedchamber and secured from him promises of friendship and help. Fitzwilliam urged Hooker to come to him whenever he needed advice and pledged that

Hooker should never "want horse, men, or money" in his efforts to further Sir Peter's business. Hooker also expanded the scope of his advice to Carew beyond mere documentary matters. He promised to reward Master Draycott for "his pains and courtesy," but told Carew that he could not as yet come up with a good way to do so. In the meantime, he advised Carew to commend Draycott to Cecil and to make sure Cecil was fully aware of how helpful Draycott was being. Draycott, Hooker had discovered, was so eager for favor with Cecil, that "to satisfy his [Cecil's] request no pains are too hard for him." There was no better way for Carew to retain Draycott's favor than to help him win favor with Cecil.

Hooker's consultation with Fitzwilliam bore immediate fruit. Carew's claims to estates in Ireland involved far more lands than those comprising the barony of Idrone. The Carew family had once held lands in County Meath northwest of Dublin, and in the ancient kingdom of Munster in the south of Ireland. The Munster lands had been particularly extensive. A fifteenth-century letter from the citizens of Cork, which Thomas Wadding, another of Carew's agents, later uncovered, mentioned the lord marquess Carew as having once been the chief landholder in the region with an annual revenue of £2200.[12] Even if this figure was exaggerated, as is likely, the extent and value of possible Carew lands in southern Ireland were great. But, as Fitzwilliam pointed out, the more of these lands Carew laid claimed to, the more current landholders he discomfited and the more resistance he would face. Carew would be best served by focusing his efforts on those estates he had the best claims to and the best chances of actually obtaining. The lord justice advised Hooker to abandon his search for evidence supporting Carew's claims to lands "holden of the Castle of Trymme," part of the Meath claim, for these lands, although rich and profitable, all lay within the English Pale in the long-standing possession of gentlemen "of worship and of great wealth." Because these gentlemen would be understandably "loath to yield and forego the same now," any attempt to reassert Carew's claim to these lands

would be "painful, troublesome, and. . .a suit infinite." Hooker was quickly
discovering that Sir Peter's Irish land claims had a potentially explosive
political component.[13]

Hooker was already finding research into the Meath lands difficult
because all the "old and ancient names" had been changed, making original
ownership almost impossible to trace. The only former Carew holding in
Meath that Hooker could verify was Maston, "a strong and fair castle"
presently held by Sir Christopher Chivers. News of Hooker's mission had
caused Chivers "to fear and quake at the matter," a reaction shared by
numerous other Meath land owners who worried that Carew's claims could
dispossess them as well. Hooker told Carew that he planned shortly to
travel into Meath and make search into Sir Peter's titles, a task that would
likely "require a long time" because of the reluctance of the current landholders to assist in any way in such an effort. Despite this resistance,
Hooker had good hopes of success for his trip because of the offers of
friendship from "sundry gentlemen of England dwelling in those parts,
who, some of them for acquaintance of you, and some of them for your
name's sake, do wish you good success." Almost from the day of Hooker's
arrival in Ireland, Sir Peter's land claims found as much favor among
Englishmen living in the island as they found hostility from the Irish and
Anglo-Irish landholders they threatened to evict.[14]

By late May, Hooker had found nothing to prejudice Carew's
claims in Meath except a document stating that Maston was resumed into
the king's hands in 6 Henry VI. This resumption appeared upon further
research to be merely a temporary attachment for debts owed and later
discharged by Carew's ancestors. Therefore, the matter now rested with
Chivers, who had to "declare and show" how he came to hold the property.
If Chivers would do this "with courtesy," the whole business would be
easier both for him and for Carew. Nonetheless, Hooker, on the advice of
friends, would "forbear to deal with any [landholder] in this country of

Meath" before Carew himself came to Ireland. Hooker would in the meantime endeavor to learn all he could about Carew's lands in Meath and their present occupiers.[15]

As to the Munster lands in County Cork, Hooker discovered that the Caringdoms, senechals to Carew's ancestors, had intervened in a dispute between two Carew brothers in the fourteenth century, had slain the brothers, and then had seized the lands.[16] The present occupiers, descending from the Caringdoms, had thereby "no good title." Hooker promised to go to Cork and assess the value of these lands as soon as "I have viewed and surveyed the county of Meath." Hooker assured Carew that recovery of the Cork lands was beyond doubt, and would be "as easy as the recovery of your barony of Idrone." The greater part of the barony was currently held by "a certain sort called the Kavanaughs," who traced themselves back to the McMorough who had seized the barony at the end of the fourteenth century. The Kavanaughs were men "of stout stomach and courage,"[17] but had been held in check and quiet by the former constable of Carlow, Sir Nicholas Heron, and by the current constable, none other than Thomas Stukeley,[18] the former pirate from whom Carew's sailors had seized a vessel in Cork harbor in 1565. Stukeley's headquarters was at Leighlin, a fortress, now in the queen's hands, that had been converted from a dissolved monastery founded by one of Carew's ancestors in the thirteenth century.[19] Stukeley and Davells were in such favor of Carew's undertaking, and the Kavanaughs' title to Idrone was so weak, that Hooker believed the Kavanaughs would not be "able to withstand you, nor such your friends as you have here: nor shall you be in danger or peril for the attaining unto the same, or for the keeping thereof." Stukeley offered Hooker immediate possession of Leighlin in Carew's behalf, but Hooker thought it best to leave such a transfer until Carew could take personal possession. Stukeley proclaimed himself much bound to Carew, because, as Hooker told Sir Peter, "when all men did report evil of him, yet you gave good report, and spake in his defense, which he will not fail to consider with the uttermost of his power." To prove his gratitude, Stukeley offered his house in Dublin for Carew's use, and so impressed Hooker with his good will that Hooker declared him to Carew to be the "one man in all Ireland of his degree which can do you more pleasure than which he will not fail to, as you shall well perceive at your coming."[20] But within a month Stukeley was to lose his constable's office, and within a year he would be imprisoned in Dublin Castle on a charge of treason.[21]

Thanks to Davells, Hooker had seen the lands of Idrone, and could describe them in detail to Carew.

> The soil and country of that barony is very large and great, and in all Europe not a more pleasant, sweeter, or fruitfuller land; the same being referted with all things necessary for man in any respect, serving for pleasure or need, for hunting the stagg, the hare, the fox, the wolf, for your pleasure at will; for hawking with all kinds of hawks, at partridge, rayle, pheasant, crane, bittern, and a number of other fouls, as much as can be wished, and desired. For fishing, there is much as any freshwater can give; the seas are somewhat distant from this country of Idrone, but yet, on the one side, a goodly river called the Barrow fleets through the whole country, and this so serves the country that upon it they do convey all their commodities and merchandise from the seas, of from Waterford, even to the house of Leighlin; which stands full upon the said river.[22]

Hooker found Leighlin to be the ideal residence for Carew in Ireland. Carew's furnishings could easily be conveyed to it up the river, it was near to Idrone, and living there would be cheaper than living in Dublin. Still, a house in Dublin was necessary, and the efficient Hooker had found one for Carew's use. If Carew decided to make "a summer journey" to Dublin, which Hooker pronounced "very requisite and necessary," he would find the house ready for himself and his company when he arrived.

Hooker also assured Carew that the prospects for a successful conclusion to his suit were excellent. Upon his arrival in Ireland, Carew should repair immediately to Dublin to confer with the lord deputy and with others who were friendly to his cause. When not combing through old records, Hooker had been busy winning friends and cementing support for Carew among English gentlemen resident in Ireland and among members of the Irish government. Hooker had gone about to make the acquaintance of gentlemen who had long lived in Ireland, who were familiar with its ways and customs, and who were acquainted with the lands Carew sought and the basis of his claim. These gentlemen proved so friendly and favorable to Carew's suit that they offered Hooker any assistance within their power toward accomplishing it. With this support, Hooker was confident that Carew would have his lands, both in Idrone and in Cork, for, he assured Carew, there had never "been a better opportunity offered for the recovery thereof then now is."[23]

Hooker was also anxious that his optimistic report not breed unreasonable expectations in Sir Peter. He therefore hastened to warn Carew that Ireland was not England.

> And, albeit, this may seem very comfortable and pleasant unto you. . . yet do not you make your account of a more gain and profit than you shall find, for though a great country of land may happily fall into your hands, yet there grows not thereby such benefit or gain as in other countries, a great deal of land here being set to a small price, and yet the same rents not paid in money, but in corn and cattle; serving for the maintenance and keeping of the Lord's houses, who, if he have not other means for money, he shall not be able to maintain his state in worship, and keep his people in subjection, unless he will yield to live after the savage manners of the Irish.[24]

Hooker was particularly struck by the cost of things in Ireland, telling Carew that prices of basic commodities in Dublin were double what they were in England. Carew, he warned, must come "furnished with store of money," for "if you have it not of yourself it is not here to be had." To meet the expenses he expected to incur in Carew's behalf, Hooker had been forced to ask Fitzwilliam for a loan of £40, of which the lord justice had so far been able by great travail to raise only half. Hooker could wait for the rest, having no need for the money at the moment, but great sums would be required to travel about surveying Carew's lands and to make preparations for Carew's arrival. Hooker had to have money in readiness for these needs, for Ireland was "of money and good people. . .very barren." Carew should therefore make arrangements to promptly repay Fitzwilliam and should give Hooker plenty advance notice of his coming. He also advised Carew to bring with him "spice, sugar, and such other foreign wares and merchandise," which were not to be had in Dublin, where "all things are at a hard hand."[25]

Hooker, calling himself "a bad steward," promised to do his best in securing all the supplies Carew needed to keep house in Dublin; yet, he advised, it would be best for Carew to find "an expert man in these things" to run the household once it was established. As it happened, Hooker had just the man in mind—his brother, Roger Hooker, who is remembered today as the father of the famous Anglican apologist Richard Hooker. John Hooker called his brother "a man very expert and skillful" and of great profit as steward to his past masters, who included Sir Thomas Chaloner, English ambassador to Spain. Roger was currently in the employ of "the old Lady Mountjoy," but Hooker anticipated no difficulty in persuading either Roger or Lady Mountjoy to terminate that arrangement should Carew be agreeable to taking Roger into his service. Indeed, Hooker was so sure of the agreement of all parties that he had already told his wife to send for Roger. "I trust," Hooker wrote Carew," "he shall like you both in such sort as to your contents."[26]

Hooker closed his long report by asking if his wife might send

along some of his furnishings in Sir Peter's bark, for he expected the
following of Carew's suits to "require a time before they can be brought to
their full effect." He passed along to Carew the commendations of
Fitzwilliam, Draycott, and others, and sent along his own respects to Lady
Tailboys, Bishop Alley of Exeter, and the mayor and council of Exeter,
excusing himself to the latter for his absence "until I have . . . brought to
effect, your matter and cause, now taken in hand." He reminded Carew
to bring with him his two physicians, "Mr. Welton and Narcissus," whose
presence in Ireland Hooker had already longed for to do pleasure to the
still ailing Fitzwilliam and others of Carew's friends. Finally, if Sir Gawen's
cook were to leave his service, Carew was to speak with Richard Tremayne,
treasurer of Exeter Cathedral, about taking his cook Nicholas along to
Ireland; Hooker did not believe Tremayne would deny him to Carew for "a
summer's voyage."[27]

Hooker apparently spent a long time at his writing on 26 May,
for he addressed a second letter to Carew at Mohun's Ottery on the same
day. With this letter, Hooker enclosed a copy of a statute from 28 Henry
VIII concerning the resumption of lands in Ireland into the king's hands,
as well as "copies of certain records which I have selected, chosen, and
gathered, out of the records in the Castle of Dublin." The documents
proved that Carew's ancestors "possessed. . . sundry seignories within this
realm," none of which were now in the queen's hands except for Leighlin.
Hooker assured Carew that neither the queen, nor the Council, nor anyone
else, "saving they which, perforce, do withhold it," could deny his title.
Indeed, the queen would greatly benefit by Sir Peter's restoration to his
lands; she would no longer be defrauded of the rents and services Carew's
ancestors had rendered to hers, and she would be relieved of the "great
charges" for "repressing of these rebels and wild lawless kerns." Although
Carew might initially be put to some trouble and cost to attain his ends,
yet the ultimate benefit to himself and the queen would be great. If Carew,
after considering the matter, should decide "to take the opportunity now

offered," Hooker urged him "to accelerate and hasten your repair hither, and not to lose this summer." And he again told Carew to give him good notice of his coming, so "that I may provide and set all things in order accordingly."[28]

Carew wasted little time in acting upon his agent's advice. He left England in early August and landed at Waterford, where he sent immediately for Hooker, who had been staying at Davells's house near Idrone. Hooker came quickly to Waterford, followed closely by Davells and the unctuous Stukeley. Once horses had been obtained for the company, Stukeley conducted Carew to Leighlin, which was apparently still in Stukeley's hands despite the queen's decision in June to disallow his purchase of the constableship. While enjoying the "very liberal and honourable entertainment" of Stukeley, Carew received a number of the Kavanaughs who occupied barony lands and explained to them his plans to reclaim the barony. Although Hooker claimed that Carew spoke reasonably to them, the Kavanaughs found what Carew had to say hard to take. After surveying the lands of Idrone, Carew and his whole party traveled to Dublin, where Sir Peter waited for the return of Lord Deputy Henry Sidney from England before taking any legal action.[29]

In Dublin, Carew caused a sensation. He resided at a house called St. Mary Abbey, where Hooker, with less disapproval than usual, said Sir Peter kept a "very liberal and bountiful house," which won him "great admiration" from the citizens. Large numbers of people came to the house each day, apparently simply to see the English gentleman who had the will and audacity to claim "such great lands as was thought would never have been claimed." According to Hooker, everyone knew that the Carews, "in their language, 'Carones,'" had once been great landholders in the island; many people with the name still lived throughout the island. But the ancient landholding family was thought to be extinct, and no one realised until Hooker's arrival that an heir to the name Carew still lived.[30] To

illustrate the effect of Carew and his suit on Dublin, Hooker told the story
of an old gentlewoman who watched Carew ride by one day as she sat by
her door.

> [T]alking with one of her neighbors, [she] said: "You have heard that it is an old
> saying that a dead man should rise again, and lo," said she, pointing her hand to
> Sir Peter, "yonder he is; for his ancestors were great Lords, and had great possessions
> in this realm, but having not been heard of these two or three hundred years, it was
> thought they had been all dead, and none left alive to claim the same, but now this
> man is risen as it were from the dead, and is awaked and minds to *stir* them out of
> their nests, which thought to lie all at their rests."[31]

The woman's sentiments were shared by many, rumors of Carew and his
intentions having spread from Dublin throughout Ireland. Hooker
believed that "the most part, generally, were glad, and rejoiced that so
noble, so worthy, liberal, and valiant a gentleman, and sometimes of their
own nation, was come to dwell again amongst them."[32] Although the
placing of Irish lands into the possession of a sober, proper English gentleman
was clearly a good thing in Hooker's eyes, the "most part" of Ireland would
not look upon Carew as one of their own, and came to view his extravagant
land claims with even less favor.

Sidney returned to Ireland in September.[33] While waiting for the
lord deputy, Carew immersed himself in current Irish politics, and gave
Sidney, once the deputy was back in Dublin, the full benefit of his newly
acquired expertise on the subject. On 2 November, Carew wrote a letter
to the English Council describing in detail the state of various rebellions
and disputes around the island and the lord deputy's actions in each case.
He highly commended the lord deputy for containing the spread of a rising
in Ulster, a policy he estimated saved the queen £100,000 that would have
been needed to suppress "the wicked lot." He also endorsed the plan for
regional presidencies then under discussion as a definite advancement of

good government in Ireland. Carew concluded with news of his own affairs, telling the Council that he was being well served by the ancient records in Dublin Castle, and that he hoped to finish his business within 14 days.[34] But at the end of two weeks, on 16 November, Carew seemed far from completing his business, and was writing to Cecil beseeching the secretary to revoke the appointment of William Peryam to be a justice in Munster under the newly appointed lord president, Sir John Pollard. Peryam was a London lawyer who haled originally from Crediton in Devon, and whom Carew had persuaded to accompany him to Ireland as legal advisor. Pollard was the gentleman with whom Carew had clashed in 1567, in a mysterious dispute that was violent enough to attract the disapproval of the Council. Carew and his friends had apparently had much ado convincing Peryam to come to Ireland, and now the Munster appointment threatened to undo everything. Peryam's legal expertise and learning were vital to Carew's cause, and Carew hoped Cecil could do something to keep him from losing Peryam's services.[35]

Carew felt the possible loss of Peryam so deeply because he had, with Peryam's assistance, just undertaken legal proceedings for the recovery of Maston from Sir Christopher Chivers. While waiting for Sidney, Carew had considered which of his claims to pursue first. The Munster claims, because they were so extensive and involved so many people in a politically unstable region, seemed best put off, and Carew decided to pursue either the Meath claims or Idrone. Although leaning toward Idrone, he sent for Chivers, whose manor of Maston, situated some 15 miles outside Dublin in the Pale, was the centerpiece of the Meath claims, and exhibited to him the documents that proved the house and lands of Maston to be rightfully his. Carew apparently had some hope that Chivers, seeing the strength of Carew's claims, would come to some settlement and relieve Carew of the need to try the case at law. Although "astonished" by these evidences, Chivers calmly asked Carew for time to consider the matter, which Carew granted. When Chivers answered that he would not deal with Carew until

Sir Peter had recovered the lands at law, Carew determined to start his legal actions with the recovery of Maston. Sir Peter thought Chivers might serve as a good example to the other occupiers of Carew lands in Meath. Because Chivers was "a gentleman of good countenance and wealthy, and well allied, especially with lawyers," Carew would start with him, being "the best, and, if he did prevail against him, then the residue would the sooner yield."[36] Carew clearly believed that if he could prevail against the English gentleman, he would have no difficulty in triumphing over the Kavanaughs.

But for all his high hopes, Carew soon discovered the frustration of being the outsider. The landholders of Meath so rallied around Chivers that Sir Peter could find no lawyer in Ireland who would take his case. Carew was now faced with the same impenetrable shield of local power that had kept Robert Warren from proceeding against Carew himself in the common law courts of Devon in the debt action of 1550. Carew, it will be recalled, simply instructed the jury to find against Warren, who had to take his case to Star Chamber to have it heard.[37] His inability to obtain the services of legal counsel in Ireland had forced Carew to seek out Peryam, who drafted and submitted to the lord deputy on 29 October a petition asking the deputy and Irish Council to hear the case. The petition argued that Carew could have no remedy at common law because Chivers was "of great power and strength within this realm; and greatly allied and friended," and Carew could therefore expect in the ordinary courts no "indifferent and lawful trial." The prejudicial atmosphere of the courts was being used by Chivers "to defraud the said complainant of his just and lawful inheritance." Carew had no recourse but to ask that the case be decided by the deputy and the Irish Council, and to request them to summon Chivers to answer to the complaint. In reply to this petition, the Irish Council sent out an immediate summons to Chivers to appear before its members in Dublin on 3 November. One councilor, Sir Thomas Cusak, refused to sign the warrant because Chivers was his good friend and neighbor.

The Council entrusted delivery of the warrant to one William Goodall, who gave it to Chivers at Maston on 1 November.[38]

    Chivers appeared "very unwillingly" on the appointed day with eight counselors. He responded to the lord deputy's demand for an answer to Carew's petition by asking for one more day before replying. The lord deputy, having other matters to attend to on the following day, which was Thursday, commanded Chivers to appear then before Lord Chancellor Weston to answer the matter. Chivers came next day as ordered, but only after being called several times. He declined to answer the petition directly, declaring that the deputy and Council were not competent to decide the case since the common law courts, the ordinary courts for judging land disputes, were open and functioning, and no subject ought have his right to a hearing at common law abridged. Chivers had, therefore, on the advice of counsel, determined not to answer in the matter before the lord deputy and Council. When the two chief justices agreed with Chivers, the chancellor declared that he would bring the whole question before the lord deputy and full Council on the following day, Friday 5 November.[39]

    When the deputy and Council had assembled on Friday, Mr. Peryam responded to Chivers by stating that the queen, "by her prerogative, might and did use to call before her all matters whatsoever depending in any court."[40] He cited a recent dispute over an Exchequer office that had been settled by the queen personally. The lord deputy, having "under her majesty full power and authority in this land may do the like." What's more, any man who could for whatever reason not obtain a fair trial at common law might bring his matter before the Court of Chancery or before the queen's Council. Finally, Peryam declared himself ready to lay before the Council numerous examples of cases in Ireland brought in the past before the lord deputy and Council for judgment. Lord Justice Dillon then answered for Chivers by essentially repeating the arguments of the previous day. The arguments of Chivers and Peryam had transformed a land dispute into a debate on the extent of the royal prerogative. With the matter touching the queen so closely, Sidney was unwilling to proceed any further until the two justices, Sir Robert Dillon and Sir John Plunket, could, with Sir Thomas Cusak, "look upon the books and . . .give an answer" as to the deputy's competence to decide the case. If, declared Sidney, they determined he could not judge the case, he had no mind "to meddle in any such matter henceforth until the Queen and Council be further advised." He then ordered the justices to return on the following Monday, 8 November, to give their answer.[41]

On Saturday 6 November, Justices Plunket and Dillon assembled after dinner all the gentlemen and students then present at the Inns of Court in Dublin, and put to the assemblage the question of whether or not the deputy could deal in the Carew-Chivers case under the royal prerogative. Chivers was also present at the meeting. One Talbott, justice of the Common Pleas, stood up and said the deputy and Council might hear and determine any matter in law. This declaration and its favorable reception by the bulk of the assembly alarmed Dillon and the baron of Bath's son, both partisans of Chivers. They took Sir Christopher aside and told him point blank that if the deputy and Council decided his case, he would be "shrewdly shaken."

"God forbid," said Sir Christopher. "Yes," said he [Bath], "and if you have not the better charts you may happily be shaken out of great piece of your land." "No," said Sir Christopher, "I would rather spend £10,000."[42]

Based on the impromptu debate at the Inns of Court and on their research, Dillon and Plunket informed the deputy and Council in secret on 9 November that they might proceed in the matter and come to a determination. Since Carew could not have fair trial at common law, he was within his rights to lay the matter before the deputy, who, with the Council, might give judgment.

Having failed to return the case to the common law courts, Chivers and his counsel now tried to delay judgment. They declared themselves unable to answer Carew's petition because they could not understand it, and repeated again their contention that the case could only be heard at common law. After several continuances, the Council declared these answers to be "frivolous" and cut short "all such dilatories as [Chivers's] counsel learned were minded and might have used at the common law,"[43] and ordered him to give answer before the deputy on 20 November. In his answer, Chivers again denied the competency of the deputy to sit on the case, citing not only several Elizabethan statutes, but Magna Carta itself, as proofs of his contention. Brought at last to give answer to the particulars of Carew's petition, Chivers attempted to show that it was untrue and inaccurate, but was able to prove good title only to a tiny portion of the land claimed by Sir Peter. In the end, he was forced to admit that he did not possess the freehold of most of the land in question.[44]

The deputy "marvelously misliked" Chivers's answer because it derogated the queen's prerogative. He angrily reproved Chivers and his advisors "for so slanderous a bill, contrary to the order of the council."[45] The case dragged on for some time longer, but by the end of the year Chivers sued Carew for a compromise, "alleging the undoing of himself, his wife, and children, if the land should be evicted of him."[46] Carew agreed to arbitration, the outcome of which Hooker related with some disapproval at what he saw as Sir Peter's excessive generosity.

[T]he arbitrators finding that Sir Christopher had nothing to show for his title, but only a lease for some parcel of land whereof were a hundred years then to come, they set a price between them, which, albeit it were nothing in respect to the value of the land, yet a great deal more than it was for Sir Christopher's ease to pay; wherefore, submitting himself wholly to Sir Peter's devotion, he so entreated with him, and by entreaty so prevailed with him, that in the end, he had the whole land released unto him almost for nothing, saving a drinking "nutt" of silver worth about twenty pounds, and three or four horses, worth about thirty pounds.[47]

According to Hooker, Carew declared himself more interested in his victory over Chivers and his success in getting Chivers to admit his lack of title than he was in the value of the land.

Sir Peter, in a letter to Cecil written the day after Christmas, showed himself more interested in money and better recompensed by Chivers than Hooker had indicated. Chivers agreed to refer the matter to the "judgment and determination" of Sir Thomas Cusak, with both Carew and Chivers giving bonds of £2000 to accept Cusak's decision. Chivers then produced a document by which Sir Nicholas Carew supposedly conveyed Maston to Chivers's ancestor in 1444. But the "ink, parchment, and wax" clearly showed the document to be nowhere near that old, and Chivers was left with nothing to counter Carew's mass of documentary evidence. Chivers thereupon offered Carew 18 years purchase for Maston and all the lands in question to which he was unable to show good title. Carew accepted 15 years purchase, the lands to be "viewed and rated by indifferent persons" chosen by both parties.[48]

While winning his case against the Englishman Chivers, Carew also pursued his suit against the Irish occupiers of Idrone—the Kavanaughs. Peryam submitted a petition asking the deputy and Council to hear the Idrone suit on 29 October, the same day he submitted the like petition for Maston. Peryam once again asked for a hearing before the deputy, alleging as before that Carew could not have a fair trial at common law because the defendants were born in Ireland, were many in number and kindred, and were "greatly friended and allied" with the gentlemen and freeholders of Carlow. The five members of the Kavanaugh clan mentioned in the petition were summoned to answer the petition before the deputy and Council on 10 November. The three members of the clan from whom the rest held their lands appeared on the day appointed. They were handed a copy of Carew's complaint and ordered to give answer on 19 November. As with the Maston suit, the case was continued several times; the Kavanaughs also attempted to argue that the deputy and Council had no right to hear the case, but in this contention they had no more success than Chivers. At length, the Kavanaughs were forced to base their claim on their descent from Dermond Gulde McMorough, who had been king of Leinster before the Norman conquest of Ireland.[49] This claim carried no weight with the Englishmen on the Council, who considered it voided by the conquest. What's more, they considered the claim untrue. Dermond's only child, a daughter, had married one of the leaders of the Norman conquest, Richard de Clare, earl of Pembroke, known as Strongbow; the descendants of this match included numerous English noblemen and gentlemen, including the Carews. The Kavanaughs were "a wild Irish race and kindred sprung up since within the realm." Carew could claim descent from Strongbow and could show that many of his ancestors were seised and quietly possessed of the barony of Idrone until the McMoroughs, "a rebellious nation of Irish people, in time of common rebellion, wrongfully and by force seized the barony and the lands, and with the strong hand, and without right or title maintained it."[50] The Kavanaughs and their ancestors had been on the land before, during, and after the conquest; they had submitted to any Norman or Englishman who was strong enough to make good his claim to overlordship, and had re-emerged to hold the land in their own right whenever that strength weakened or disappeared, as had happened to the Carew claim in the fourteenth century. But as Hooker told Carew, the Kavanaughs had no claim to Idrone except prescription, "which in that land holdeth not."[51] In English eyes, almost 200 years of quiet use and enjoyment by Irishmen meant nothing next to the musty papers of a well-connected English gentleman. If the conquerors of Dermond's kingdom could by their conquest extinguish the claims of previous landholders, why did not the fourteenth-century expulsion of the Carews extinguish their claims? Apparently, because the conquerors in the fourteenth century were Irish.

On 7 December, the chancellor and the Council, the deputy being then on progress, gave judgment for Sir Peter Carew, decreeing that Carew should be put in possession of the barony and ordering the Kavanaughs to quietly allow him to take possession.[52] After the Kavanaughs failed to appear as ordered on 17 December to give further proof of their title, Sidney confirmed the judgment on 22 December,[53] by which time Davells, sheriff of Carlow, had already put Carew in full possession of Idrone.[54] The Kavanaughs made suit to the deputy for a stay in executing the judgment for Carew and for an order to him "to cease to vex them any further." They wanted more time to make their case, blaming their earlier failure to appear on an unfortunate fall taken by their legal counsel from the back of his horse during "evil weather." This tale of misfortune won them a new hearing before the Council in January, but since they had no further evidence to support their title, the decision for Carew stood.[55] Carew proudly informed Cecil of the success of his suit, and took time to praise Sidney for being "vigilant and careful" in maintaining order. He particularly commended Sidney for executing numerous rebels in Kilkenny and Waterford "by verdict of twelve men, orderly," not "by martial law." He also noted that good order and quiet prevailed in "all the countries where our own countrymen are either senechals or sheriffs."[56] All in all, the year 1568 ended most satisfactorily for Sir Peter Carew, and the year 1569 promised even better things for the future.

---

[1]   Rowse, "Sir Peter Carew," p. 121.

[2]   *Calendar of Deeds and Documents*, Exeter City Library, DRO, #68402.

[3]   Pole, *Collections*, p. 398.

[4]   Ibid., p. 352.

5 Manor of Mamhead Records, DRO, MS 484M, T1/1.

6 Ibid., T8/1.

7 Thomas Wadding to Sir George Carew, 12 March 1603, Lambeth, Carew MS 605, f. 242.

8 Hooker, "Life", p. 71.

9 Ibid., pp. 71-72. This "fair book" of evidences is part of Carew MS 606 in the Lambeth Library. The documents collected here date back to the late thirteenth and early fourteenth centuries, and are of many kinds. For instance, a document dated to 1334 (f. 1) releases to one David of Carew and his heirs the manor of Mastin-Tuit, and, like so many of the documents, is accompanied by an English description of the Latin text supplied by Hooker. Folio 19 contains a genealogical tree of the Carew family descent in the fourteenth century, drawn by Hooker probably as an aid in understanding who was who—a good idea given the number of Carews named either John or Nicholas in the fourteenth century. If these selected samples are any indication, the mass of Carew documents through which Hooker had to work must have been impressive.

10 Ibid., pp. 72-73.

11 John Hooker to Sir Peter Carew, 26 May 1568, Lambeth, Carew MS 605, f. 5; see also Hooker, "Life," pp. 73-74.

12 Thomas Wadding to Sir George Carew, 12 March 1603, Lambeth, Carew MS 605, f. 241.

13 John Hooker to Sir Peter Carew, 26 May 1568, Lambeth, Carew MS 605, f. 5.

14 Ibid.

15 Ibid.

16 The identity of these two Carew brothers is an interesting mystery. It is hard to fit them into the Devon branch of the family, so it is likely they were the descendents of a collateral branch, perhaps descending from the brothers of the Nicholas, baron of Carew, who died about 1286. Nicholas's brother Robert, for instance, died at Kilkenny near Idrone and so was resident in Ireland. He or another brother may well have left issue who inherited lands in Munster. Another possibility is Thomas Carew, brother of the John, baron of Carew and Idrone, who died in 1324. We know that Thomas was sheriff of Cork and a landholder in the region in the 1320s. We know also that he contended with his nephew John Carew for possession of the family's estates in Wales and England, and it is tempting to see the Caringdom episode as the culmination of the Irish phase of that dispute (see Chapter 1). For this specula-

tion, however, we have no evidence, and the unfortunate victims of the Caringdoms were most likely Thomas Carew's sons or grandsons.

17 John Hooker to Sir Peter Carew, 26 May 1568, Lambeth, Carew MS 605, ff. 5-6.

18 Stukeley had an even more adventurous and decidedly less reputable career than Carew. In 1563, he sailed from England with six vessels on a colonizing expedition ostensibly bound for Florida. Unbeknownst to the queen, who supplied one of Stukeley's ships, the expedition's real purpose was to replenish Stukeley's squandered fortune by acts of piracy. Stukeley preyed on Spanish, French, and Portuguese ships alike, and the resulting outrage of the concerned governments forced Elizabeth to take action and led in part to the commissioning of Carew's expedition in 1564. The expedition's seizure of Stukeley's vessel in Cork in the spring of 1565 came only after the pirate leader had landed and surrendered himself to Irish authorities. Stukeley spent some months in prison, but was released on recognizances in the fall of 1565. He then took himself to Ireland and purchased for £3000—probably derived from piracy—the Irish lands and marshalcy of Sir Nicholas Bagenal. The queen disallowed this transaction, and Stukeley next sought to purchase the Irish offices of Sir Nicholas Heron, including the constableship in Carlow. In June 1568, only weeks after Hooker wrote to Carew of Stukeley, the queen quashed this second transaction and Stukeley found himself again without Irish office, which was the queen's intention. Stukeley was in the next year accused of treason and spent time imprisoned in Dublin Castle. He avoided conviction on this charge through lack of evidence, but his imprisonment decided him on practicing treason for real, and in 1570 he fled to Spain and placed himself in the service of Philip II, upon whose ships he had preyed unmercifully only five years earlier. After many further adventures, including a planned piratical raid on Ireland, he died in battle in 1578 while taking part in the Portuguese king's campaign in Morocco (*DNB*, pp. 124-25).

19 Snow, *Holinshed's Chronicles*, VI, pp. 207-08. The Carews had built a house of grey friars next to an ancient castle by the Barrow that was part of their barony of Idrone. After the dissolution, the Crown detached the site from the barony and converted the friars' house into a fortress meant to keep a perpetual garrison. Because a bridge spanned the Barrow at the site, the fortress was called Leighlin Bridge to distinguish it from the nearby town of Leighlin, where was located the cathedral church for the diocese of Leighlin.

20 John Hooker to Sir Peter Carew, 26 May 1568, Lambeth, Carew MS 605, f. 7.

21 "Thomas Stucley" *DNB*, p. 125.

22 John Hooker to Sir Peter Carew, 26 May 1568, Lambeth, Carew MS 605, f. 6.

23 Ibid., ff. 6-7.

24 Ibid.

25 Ibid., f. 7.

26 Ibid.

27 Ibid.

28 John Hooker to Sir Peter Carew, 26 May 1568, Lambeth, Carew MS 605, ff. 9, 9a. This is a second letter to Carew written by Hooker on 26 May.

29 Hooker, "Life," pp. 75-77. Sir Henry Sidney was the father of Sir Philip Sidney and a kinsman of Charles Brandon, the late duke of Suffolk and friend of Henry VIII. See "Sir Henry Sidney," *DNB*, pp. 210-17.

30 Hooker, "Life," p. 77.

31 Ibid., p. 78.

32 Ibid.

33 Snow, *Holinshed's Chronicles*, VI, p. 340.

34 Sir Peter Carew to the English Council, 2 November 1568, PRO, SP63/26/56.

35 Sir Peter Carew to Sir William Cecil, 16 November 1568, PRO, SP63/26/84. For more on William Peryam, see Hasler, *House of Commons*, III, p. 209. For Carew's dispute with Pollard in 1567, see APC, VII, pp. 338-39.

36 Hooker, "Life," p. 79.

37 Court of Star Chamber Records, Edward VI, PRO, STAC 3 4/23.

38 John Hooker's Notes and Transcriptions of Documents Relating to the Maston Suit, Lambeth, Carew MS 606, ff. 47-48.

39 John Hooker's Notes and Transcriptions of Documents Relating to the Maston Suit, Lambeth, Carew MS 606, f. 48; see also Hooker, "Life," p. 80.

40 Hooker, "Life," p. 81.

41 John Hooker's Notes and Transcriptions of Documents Relating to the Maston Suit, Lambeth, Carew MS 606, f. 49.

42 Ibid.

43 Hooker, "Life," p. 82.

44 John Hooker's Notes and Transcriptions of Documents Relating to the Maston Suit, Lambeth, Carew MS 606, ff. 50-51.

45 Ibid., ff. 51-52.

46 Hooker, "Life," p. 82.

47 Ibid., p. 83.

48 Sir Peter Carew to Sir William Cecil, 26 December 1568, PRO, SP63/26/124. Carew enclosed with his letter a copy of the order taken by the chancellor and Council and confirmed by the lord deputy. This enclosure is preserved in the Public Record Office as SP63/26/123.

49 John Hooker's Notes and Transcriptions of Documents Relating to the Idrone Suit, Lambeth, Carew MS 606, ff. 53-56.

50 *Calendar of Patent and Close Rolls of Chancery in Ireland, 5 Henry VIII to 18 Elizabeth.* vol. I (Dublin, 1861), p. 520.

51 Hooker, "Life," p. 75.

52 *Calendar of Patent and Close Rolls of Chancery in Ireland*, I, p. 520; John Hooker's Notes and Transcriptions of Documents Relating to the Idrone Suit, Lambeth, Carew MS 606, f. 56.

53 *Calendar of Patent and Close Rolls of Chancery in Ireland*, I, p. 550; Order by Irish Council and Deputy Confirming Sir Peter Carew's Possession of Idrone, 17 December 1568, PRO, SP63/26/123.

54 Hooker, "Life," p. 84.

55 John Hooker's Notes and Transcriptions of Documents Relating to the Idrone Suit, Lambeth, Carew MS 606, f. 57.

56 Sir Peter Carew to Sir William Cecil, 26 December 1568, PRO, SP63/26/124.

CHAPTER 11

THE BUTLER WARS

The year 1569 began as well for Sir Peter Carew as the year 1568 had ended. On 10 February 1569, the queen accepted Sidney's recommendation to appoint Carew a member of the Irish Council, telling Sidney "we think him very able and mete for many respects which we would have you declare unto him."[1] Carew was sworn of the Council on 12 March.[2] Carew's enjoyment of this rare and valuable compliment from the queen was cut short by uncertainty over the status of the house at Leighlin. The lord deputy, seeking to reduce the government's expenses and find funds to support the new lord presidencies, of which plan the queen had reminded him the previous November,[3] offered to turn Leighlin over to Carew if he would agree to maintain order in the region at his own charge. The queen would thereby be saved the 800 marks required to maintain the garrison at Leighlin for the cost of seven nobles, the yearly income from Leighlin, which would be given to Carew.[4] Carew readily accepted this arrangement, whereupon the deputy discharged the unfortunate Stukeley and disbanded the garrison. Carew had apparently just taken possession of the house when Sidney received orders from the queen to hand all Stukeley's offices, including the keeping of Leighlin, over to Nicholas White. Carew wrote to Cecil from Dublin on 23 February asking that he be allowed to keep Leighlin. Carew argued that to remove him from Leighlin now, when all his lands round about the house were in "good and quiet estate," would cause many to "think the Queen's highness did not stand my good Lady." The revocation of the arrangement with Sidney would bring some "discredit" on the deputy and "must needs be a great reproach" to Carew, who would thereby be at some "danger and hazard" should "the fickle people, now quieted and in stay, upon change, seek to be at liberty." Carew wisely followed these reasons for upholding the deputy's actions, which, after all, largely reflected only his need to solidify his hold on his new estates, with reasons better calculated to capture the queen's attention. Carew declared himself the only man in Ireland who could hold Leighlin and save the queen the cost of the garrison. Anyone else would require the queen's "entertainment" and would also need to exact supplies from the country round about, that is, from Carew and his new tenants. The queen and England would in time derive other great benefits from Carew's continued possession of Leighlin and of Idrone.

> The order devised and purposed for the planting of Englishmen in this country, for the making and building of towns which shall be replenished with all sorts of English artificers, and many other things purposed and appointed for the good government, quietness, and stay of this country, shall, by sequel of my doings, and in time, appear to the acquittal of my faith and truth in her highness service, and to the benefit of this commonwealth.[5]

More Englishmen—that was Carew's prescription for order and good government in Ireland. By looking at the outcomes of the Maston and Idrone cases, the Anglo-Irish landholders of Ireland had an inkling of the Irish future envisioned by Carew and by many other Englishmen now coming from the neighboring isle, especially from the West Country. By looking at what Sir Peter was about to do at Leighlin and on his Idrone lands, the Irish had a glimpse of the future Ireland transplanted Englishmen like Carew sought. By pursuing both visions in his typically heavy-handed and self-righteous manner, Carew was instrumental in accomplishing a most difficult and unusual feat—frightening ancient enemies into taking up arms together against a common threat, against himself and the government that seemed to be supporting him.

Hooker described both Carew's doings and the reaction of some thereto in detail. At Leighlin, Hooker claimed Carew was noted for three things: his generous hospitality, his upright conduct of local government, and his fair dealing with tenants. Sir Peter maintained a household of 100 persons, always went about with 40 horsemen, and maintained a body of footmen and Irish kerns besides. These retainers were needed in part to replace the local security once offered by the disbanded royal garrison—something the queen insisted on—but Carew used them also to closely guard the borders of his barony, although Hooker said any transgressor could have mercy if he submitted to Sir Peter.[6] Carew was, however, much interested in reducing the unacceptedly high level of disorder in Ireland. On 3 March, he wrote to Cecil on behalf of the bearer of his letter, one Richard Lucar, who had impressed Carew by reducing Waterford to unprecedented order and quiet; travelers to the town could pass without danger and cattle were now left safely in the fields all night.[7] In his own county, Carew drove out all "oppressors, kerns, and other loose people, which lived upon the spoil and rapine of others." For this work, he was "marvelously beloved" and known throughout Ireland. As to the Kavanaughs, Hooker conceded that "it were some grief unto them to be dispossessed of the possessions which on long time they had held and enjoyed," but Carew's liberal treatment induced them to "most gladly serve him, and. . . be his tenants." Carew parceled out the barony "by writing [leases] as pleased him to devise unto them, yielding such rents, duties, and service, as it pleased him to reserve." He also set up courts baron "according to the laws and usages of England, which to them, before that time, was not known." By means of these new courts, Carew maintained law and order on his lands and further extended his name and fame throughout Ireland.[8]

Most people, wrote Hooker, were content with Carew's doings and happy that he had chosen to dwell in Ireland, but some who were "accustomed to reap what other men do sow, and to spend what other men do get," were somewhat less pleased to have Carew living among them.[9] Failing in attempts to discredit Carew's name, this ill-disposed sort then sought to take his life. To illustrate his point, Hooker told of an ambush planned by Carew's enemies to catch Sir Peter unawares as he traveled the highway between Dublin and Leighlin. Horsemen and kerns were hidden along the road at a spot called Black Raghe, where the road crossed Bolton Hill, a high spot from which travelers could be espied a long way off. Carew had been warned of possible danger at Bolton Hill, and apparently did a little spying of his own to confirm the information. Having already cheated death at the barricades of Clyst St. Mary in 1549 and the cross-roads of *ruga causa* in Venice in 1554, Carew took no chances this time and gave Bolton Hill a wide berth, and so came home safely to Leighlin. Somewhat belying his earlier contention that Carew's doings were widely approved of, Hooker admitted that such conspiracies against Sir Peter were numerous, "and daily . . . contrived against him." In Hooker's opinion, all these wicked and misguided attempts were directed at Carew for one reason.

[F]or no other cause but because he did not only abolish in his own country, but also inveighed against the wicked and detestable usages of the Irishry, in coyne, and livery, in cessheries, and cesses, and such other Irish customs, the same being but the spoiling of the honest subject and the laborer, and the maintenance of thieves, murderers, and all loose and disordered people.[10]

Suddenly dispossessed of their ancient lands by a foreigner who then imposed upon them alien and unfamiliar customs, claiming thereby to have rescued them from the barbarism of their own traditions, the Kavanaughs can perhaps be excused for their actions, and can certainly be understood for their feelings. What was for Carew and Hooker the spreading of a superior culture to an inferior people, was for the Irish nothing less than the destruction of a way of life.

Sir Peter's personal gain was caught up with the benefits of English culture. Carew wrote to Cecil on 28 March proposing that the queen grant him the fee farm of Leighlin for himself and his heirs in return for his pledge to pay for the rebuilding and fortifying of the house at Leighlin, and the building of a town to be peopled with "all sorts of artificers." Carew affirmed his determination to stay in Ireland until he had set all things "in good and quiet stay." He apparently expected this to take some time, for he had recently sent for Lady Margaret to come over from England. He commended Sir Thomas Cusak to Cecil, describing the fair and indifferent judgment Cusak had rendered in the Chivers case. Cusak would, suggested Carew, be most gratified by letters of thanks from Cecil. He then strongly commended to Cecil the bearer of his letter, who was none other than John Hooker.

> The bearer hereof is my dear friend, and he who hath travelled in all my causes in this land, and presently hath certain matters to move to you concerning the commonwealth of this realm, which he will break unto you. I am so bold to commend him unto you, praying that he may have your best furtherance and friendship, with dispatch, that he may return hither, as he hath appointed: for I shall think it long or he do come.[11]

The queen responded to this request for Leighlin in June by telling Sidney that Carew might have an estate in the house provided he paid the accustomed rent and kept "the like number of sufficient persons for the warding of the same as we did lastly allow before you did discharge the same."[12]

Hooker's "matters" probably concerned the solicitor's license from the lord deputy and Irish Council, issued on 20 March, for the sole right to print the statutes of the Irish Parliament, both those passed in previous sessions and those to be passed during the next 10 years. A session of the Irish Parliament had just been held in January and February 1569; the license to Hooker grew out of a request from the speaker of that session to prevent loss of statutes (as had happened in the past) through lack of printing.[13]

As Carew knew, Hooker was the ideal choice for a task requiring the collection and ordering of old documents.

Hooker, through his presence in the recently concluded Parliament, had made himself almost as well known and liked in Ireland as Sir Peter. Hooker sat for the town of Athenry, his presence helping to bolster a pro-government party within the House. Sidney had apparently made some attempts to influence the election of members to this Parliament by supporting the election of a number of non-resident Englishmen such as Hooker. From the Irish perspective, the election of Sir Peter Carew's solicitor to Parliament was ominous. The native landowners, whether Anglo-Irish or Irish, were already suspicious of the way Sidney had intervened on Carew's behalf to circumvent the common law and overthrow the titles of long established landholders. The presence in Parliament of Hooker and of other West Country Englishmen (Sir Humphrey Gilbert may also have been an MP) gave further alarm.[14] Was the government embarking on a policy designed to legally confiscate lands from their current holders and give them to Englishmen pledged to impose English customs and settle English colonists? Were the circumventing of the common law and the suborning of Parliament the key steps in this policy? Was Carew merely the first of many Englishmen to become colonial proprietors of Irish lands? Recent events seemed to point in that direction. The list of bills to be presented for consideration in the session only added to Irish suspicions: abolition of coyne and livery, temporary repeal of Poynings Law,[15] shiring of new territory, and imposition of new taxes.

Tension was therefore already thick when the Parliament met in January 1569. The session opened with members of the anti-government party, whom Hooker called in his diary simply "the Irish," demanding that sheriffs who had returned themselves and Englishmen, like Hooker, who were not resident in the towns they sat for, should be barred from serving. This would have greatly reduced the pro-government party, whom

Hooker called "the English," and jeopardised the government's legislative program. After long and angry debate, the deputy settled the matter by ordering the self-returned sheriffs to be dismissed and the non-resident Englishmen to be admitted. The "Irish" and the "English" continued to clash, and several of the government's bills were lost, including the vital suspension of Poynings Law.[16] The hostility toward the lord deputy of some of the anti-government leaders was great.

Hooker spoke for the first time on 9 February in support of the impost on wine. The description of the speech in his diary is deceptively matter of fact: "this day I spoke on the bill of impost and made an oration . . . describing the office and authority of a prince, the duty of a judge, etc. which was well liked but by some misliked."[17] In his edition of Holinshed's *Chronicles*, Hooker described the content of his speech in more detail. He had not intended to speak, but the opponents of the measure were "very froward and so unquiet, that it was more like a bear-baiting of disordered persons, than a parliament of wise and grave men." Hooker began by scolding the "Irish" opposition for their ingratitude and disobedience to the queen; "for her great expenses spent for their defenses and safeties they ought to have yielded to her." He then chastised them for their perverse refusal to repeal Poynings Law for the session and for their attacks on the wine impost. These bills were meant for their benefit and the queen had only asked for their consent to the measures "that she might thereby have the better trial and assurance of your dutifulness and good will towards her." The queen, "of her own royal authority, might and may establish the same without any of your consents, as she hath already done the like in England." Having declared the House's deliberations unnecessary and a mere favor conferred by the Crown, Hooker next denounced the opposition's attacks on the deputy, characterizing the members' offensive behavior with various biblical and classical allusions.

[H]e [Lord Deputy Sidney] hath deserved more than well at your hands: yet as the unthankful Israelites against Moses, the unkind Romans against Camillus, Scipio, and others: and as the ungrateful Athenians against Socrates, Themistocles, Meltiades, and others: you have and do most ungratefully requite and recompense this your noble governor: against whom and his doings you do kick and spurn what in you lieth. But in the end it will fall upon you, as it hath done unto others to your shame, overthrow, and confusion.[18]

After this string of slights, Hooker finally proceeded to speak upon the merits of the impost bill. Hooker spoke at some length, not concluding until two o'clock in the afternoon. The speaker, once he heard the tenor of Hooker's remarks, ordered the doormen to close the doors of the House and allow no one to enter or leave until Hooker was finished. Immediate attempts to answer the speech were cut off by the speaker, who, because of the lateness of the hour, adjourned for the day. The opposition, having been forced to listen to Hooker and now denied opportunity to respond (and having missed their mid-day meals as well), began to threaten and abuse Hooker so violently that a group of pro-government gentlemen took it upon themselves to conduct him safely to Carew's Dublin residence.[19]

Hooker's anti-Irish diatribe had a number of important results.[20] Of most immediate consequence to Carew was the effect Hooker's words had on Sir Edmund Butler. Butler was the younger brother of the earl of Ormond and a member of a powerful Anglo-Irish family distinguished for its loyalty to the Crown. As one of the leaders of the anti-government party in the 1569 Parliament, Butler believed Hooker's reproaches were aimed particularly at him. Two days after the speech, Butler rose in the House "in a coller" and declared that if Hooker's words "had been spoken in any other place than in this house there be a great many here that would rather have died than to have suffered it."[21] Butler was already in great disfavor with the deputy for his conduct during the session, and he left Dublin quickly after the end of the session to avoid the consequences of

Sidney's displeasure. Butler's disaffection was a potentially serious matter for Carew because a large part of Butler's landholdings consisted of the Dullogh, the western portion of the barony of Idrone. The Dullogh had been awarded to Carew in December along with the Kavanaugh-occupied eastern part of the barony.[22] Butler was therefore only six weeks past having the bulk of his property handed to Carew by the deputy when he was forced to listen to Carew's solicitor berate him for ingratitude to the deputy and reduce his voice in Parliament to irrelevance.

Sir Edmund's title to the Dullogh was no better than the Kavanaughs' titles to their lands, for Sir Edmund's father had originally acquired the property by taking it from the Kavanaughs. After the Council's judgment in his favor, Carew had conferred several times with Butler about the Dullogh. Butler's brother, the earl of Ormond, was in England at the court in high favor with his distant cousin, the queen; Carew had to proceed much more cautiously with Butler and his Anglo-Irish pedigree than with the "mere Irish" Kavanaughs. Sir Peter agreed to allow Butler to remain in undisturbed possession of the Dullogh until the matter could be laid before the earl of Ormond on his return from England. If the earl decided his brother's title was sufficient, Carew would leave Sir Edmund in peace; but if the earl decided for Carew, Sir Peter agreed to deal fairly and justly with Sir Edmund to reach a mutually agreeable settlement. Although this arrangement may have seemed fair to Carew, Butler was anything but satisfied, especially in light of what he saw as the high-handed way Carew had collaborated with the lord deputy to take away his rights at common law and establish a claim to his property. Hooker, of course, saw Butler's reaction to Carew's offers from another perspective: "Sir Edmund. . . could not brook Sir Peter, nor digest his manners, nor allow of his offers, but, as one maligning at his good success, and envying his government, did what he could to supplant him."[23] For Butler, the matter was personal. He hated the man Carew as much as he hated the smug sense of English superiority Carew represented.

Butler's hatred lay behind several further attempts against
Carew's life. On one occasion, Butler and a group of horsemen blocked
Carew's passage through the town of Thomastown as he returned from
Waterford to Leighlin. Carew, accompanied, as always, by his band of
horse, made for the open fields where he commanded his men to form up
and prepare to receive Butler's attack. Butler apparently had no stomach
for a pitched battle this day, for he led his men away allowing Carew to
proceed without further hindrance. On a second occasion, Butler learned
when Carew was expected to end a visit to Dublin and return to Leighlin.
Sir Edmund then conspired "with certain Englishmen," who disliked
Carew because "he sought that general reformation, as which if it might
take effect a great part of their gain would be cut off." The conspirators
set yet another ambush along the road for Sir Peter "to entrap him" and
"to make an end of him." Carew foiled this attempt by changing his plans
and not leaving Dublin on the appointed day. Fearing that they were
discovered, the conspirators gave up the attempt and went home. Carew
did not learn of the attempt until later when Butler's English henchmen
fell out among themselves and some of them disclosed the details to him.[24]

Butler's dissatisfaction with the way Sidney and Carew had dealt
with him drove him to make common cause with James Fitzmaurice, a
member of the family of Fitzgerald, ancient enemies of the House of
Butler. Fitzmaurice acted as leader of the Fitzgeralds while the earl of
Desmond remained a prisoner in the Tower. Fitzmaurice rose up against
the government in the late spring of 1569, as did various other Irish lords
and clans alarmed by Sidney's administration, which they believed was
bent upon anglicizing and protestantizing Ireland through the extension of
royal authority throughout the island. The actions of Carew and other
newly arrived Englishmen were certainly one cause for this alarm, but fear
of Sidney, of a stronger royal government in Dublin, and of the destruction
of Irish Catholicism lay at the heart of most of the 1569 risings. In Cork,
Fitzmaurice called for the restoration of the old religion and the expulsion

of all Huguenots. He also practiced with Philip II to bring in Spanish troops to assist him in overthrowing the Church of Ireland as established by Parliament. Sir Edmund Butler's involvement with Fitzmaurice and the other rebels was motivated solely by his quarrel with Carew; with the Catholic and Spanish agenda of Fitzmaurice he had no sympathy.[25] The disturbances that wracked Carlow in 1569, which Hooker termed "Butler's wars,"[26] stemmed almost completely from the fear and disaffection generated by the land suits and anglicizing activities of Sir Peter Carew.

The trouble began in Carlow in June. Sidney had expected trouble from Butler ever since the latter's departure from Dublin in the spring. Accordingly, he dispatched a messenger named John Devawe to Sir Edmund and his brother Sir Edward with letters requesting their presence in Dublin. After many adventures, Devawe finally tracked down Sir Edmund and delivered the deputy's messages. Butler refused to come to Dublin without the deputy's "pardon," by which he probably meant a safe-conduct. He complained to Devawe that the deputy was surrounded by "such a sort of flattering knaves. . .which doth inform him of as many lies and tales as they can hear of me, that I dare not come in his sight." If he were to go to Dublin, Butler would demand the deputy's permission to "combat. . .against Sir Peter Carew, for that Sir Peter said he was a traitor."[27] Concerned to prevent Butler from joining the other rebels and hesitant to declare the earl of Ormond's brother a traitor, Sidney tried again to dissuade Sir Edmund from his course. This time Sidney's messengers were Roland, Lord Baltinglass, Butler's father-in-law, and Richard Shee. The instructions given to these two men on 17 June charged them to warn Butler of the consequences to himself and his house of continued disobedience and to inform him of the deputy's intention to declare him a rebel if he did not comply. Once this occurred, "it would be all too late to hope or crave favor." Sir Edmund responded by making a distinction between royal troops led by the deputy himself, which he would never oppose, and the same troops under another commander operating on behalf of his enemies, especially Sir Peter Carew. In the latter situation, Butler would bitterly oppose any troops sent against him. In a rage, Butler ordered the two messengers to tell Sidney that Carew was not so true a servant of the queen as he was, and that Carew "had bred such a stir in Ireland, as [he] will never well redress." But if the deputy would grant him protection and pardon, he would serve in the queen's wars without pay, unlike Carew, who served only for wages.[28] This was the answer the two messengers brought back to Sidney on 19 June.

Two days later, Captain Nicholas Malbie informed Cecil that "Sir Edmund Butler hath gathered a great company, and with fire and sword spoils Idrone and adjoining lands. He hath taken one Robert Manaring, an English gentleman, and leads him up and down in a halter."[29] The English-Irish hostility that underlay Butler's rising was intense. Butler told another of Sidney's messengers why he took up arms: "I do it not to make war against the queen, but against those that banish Ireland and mean conquest."[30] Hooker, with evident disgust, described Butler's methods and motivations as he perceived them.

Sir Edmund Butler. . . who little accounting that he was an Ireland man and descended of an honourable parentage [i.e., English], was entered into such a folly, or rather a frenzy, that he became not only a mere Irishman, but also an Irish kern, in apparel, behavior, and all other savage manners of Irishry; and being altogether carried and led by them, he ranged and spoiled the whole countries with sword, fire, and, all hostility. His colored excuse, and false pretence was because Sir Peter Carew did make claim to some part of his land. . .but true it is, a general conspiracy was made, and had been working a long time, to have prevented and withstood the general reformation which was supposed should have been established throughout the whole land, for the suppressing and reforming of the loose, barbarous, and most wicked life of that savage nation.[31]

Hooker's "general reformation" was Butler's banishing of Ireland through conquest. What one would struggle to bring about, the other would fight to prevent. These were the deep seated cultural conflicts that Sir Peter Carew's Irish land claims brought to violent life.

By the end of June, Sidney responded to Butler's disorders by waving a flag in front of the bull; he dispatched Carew's kinsman Humphrey Gilbert, the future explorer of Newfoundland, to Carew at Leighlin with 300 or 400 of the queen's horse. Hooker described what happened next. Carew took command of the troops and dispatched one of their number to Butler's seat at Clogrennan Castle, which was only about three miles from Leighlin. The messenger demanded the castle's surrender, but found Butler absent and the defenders under orders not to yield the castle to anyone. The defenders' defiance convinced Carew to lay siege to the castle. Clogrennan was a small, square pile of stone, and the defenders had blocked up all windows and openings in the walls except four "small loops" at the corners out of which the defenders fired down with their guns upon Carew's men. Carew had his men concentrate their own fire on the loops "and by that means so dogged at those loops, that sundry of them within were slain." The execution at the loops was so severe, no defender would dare attempt to fire a shot or even look out the openings. Having stilled the fire from the castle, Carew sent forward men with hurdles on their backs to begin undermining the walls. Upon realizing what the soldiers were doing, the defenders called down and asked if they could send out a representative to talk to Carew. This Carew allowed, but the talks came to nothing, and the defender turned to go back to the castle. As he was about to fasten the iron outer door, one of Carew's soldiers named Baker rushed up and thrust a great block of wood between the outer door and the inner door, thereby preventing the outer door from closing completely. By means of this breech, Carew's men forced their way into the castle and overpowered the defenders. Carew took possession of Clogrennan for the queen, and the soldiers were allowed to loot the contents of the castle.[32]

The storming of Clogrennan affords a rare opportunity to compare Hooker's account of an event in Carew's life with an account of the same event from a source unsympathetic to Carew. Sir Edmund Butler is hardly an unbiased source for the events at Clogrennan, but the tale he told of the castle's fall contains a number of elements not found in Hooker's account. At the end of August, Sir Edmund wrote to his brother the earl, then newly arrived in Ireland, of the capture of Clogrennan. Before leaving the castle, Sir Edmund ordered his men to give up the castle only to the lord deputy. This accorded with the policy Butler outlined to his father-in-law in mid-June: he would not oppose the deputy personally, only those, like Carew, whom he deemed to be his enemies. The defenders, seeing a great number of soldiers surround the castle, shouted down to know if the lord deputy was present. The besiegers answered that he was. Assured of a safe-conduct, Butler's man agreed to come down and surrender Clogrennan according to his master's orders. But when he came outside the walls, Butler's servant was led to Carew and given to understand that the deputy was not present. The dutiful servant then asked for safe-conduct back to the castle, saying he had no authority to surrender Clogrennan to anyone but Sidney. As he was being escorted back, apparently under a promise of safe-conduct, one of Carew's men "did murder him in the door with a dagger (which was thrust into his back)." Fighting now raged in the castle, and Carew lost some men, but eventually secured Clogrennan and spoiled Butler of all his "plate, household stuff, and evidence," meaning all evidence supporting Sir Edmund's title to his lands. Why, wondered Sir Edmund bitterly, had Carew bothered to destroy these evidences, for "Sir Peter needed not my evidence, seeing he doth win land by the sword."[33]

A month earlier, on 24 July, the earl of Ormond, hurrying to Ireland to save his brothers, wrote an even more horrific account of the fall of Clogrennan to Cecil. While waiting in Bristol for passage to Ireland, the earl had encountered two of his servants just arrived from Waterford with news of his brothers. They told him that Carew had assaulted Sir Edmund's house, which was defended by only eight men, with a great company while Sir Edmund was away. Upon capturing Clogrennan, Carew executed not only the eight defenders, but also all the women and children in the castle, including the innocent three-year-old son of a neighboring gentleman. Ormond took a grim pleasure in reporting that Carew's men, despite their numerical advantage, went not unscathed in their "evil enterprise," for some were lost whom Sir Peter "doth lament." The earl also reported an earlier encounter between his brother and Carew. About 9 July, Carew sent some of his horsemen to take hay from one of Sir Edmund's meadows. Butler, upon hearing of the trespassers, charged the meadow with 20 horsemen and slew 14 of Carew's men in the fight.[34] Carew, meanwhile, reported to Sidney from Carlow on 12 July of his loss to the rebels of all his cess cattle from the Idrone lands.[35] The loss left Carew and his company in want of provisions, and may have contributed to his decision to take the troop to Kilkenny in search of Butler when word came shortly thereafter that Butler was near the town.

At Kilkenny, an even bloodier encounter occurred between Carew and the Butler forces, which an outraged Ormond related to Cecil. Carew and Gilbert sallied out of Kilkenny with 200 horse and set upon some 400 galloglasses in Butler service; 80 of the Irish foot were slain, including two captains "that were tall fellows," and had long been in the earl's service. Carew suffered losses among his horsemen as well.[36] Sir Edmund later confirmed for his brother the loss of the two galloglass captains and 80 others with them in the fight with Carew's men. Carew with 300 men fell upon the galloglasses suddenly and caught them unarmed. The Butler men foolishly tried to make a stand in a field against the cavalry charge, which accounted for the high losses. Thirty of the slain were the earl's men. If he had been with his men, lamented Sir Edmund, Carew "might have lost his better eye."[37] Sir Edmund had heard how Carew boasted of the men he had slain, declaring in letters that the number was far higher than 80. Butler denounced this claim as "most untrue," and added sarcastically that Carew was wise to leave out of his letters details about all the men who were slain in the fight on his side. The dead galloglasses had done better service for the queen under the earl's leading than ever Carew had done.[38]

Hooker's account of the fight with the galloglasses again differs from the Butler versions in some important particulars. After the capture of Clogrennan, Carew learned that Butler was near Ormond's town of Kilkenny and marched there straightaway. The town was sympathetic to the Butlers, but unwilling to turn away the queen's captain, so Carew and his men were allowed to enter and lodge in the town. Carew sent out scouts who discovered Butler's galloglasses in a field two or three miles outside Kilkenny. Leaving their horseboys behind to ensure secrecy, Carew's party crept up on the galloglasses and fell upon them totally unawares. Henry Davells led the charge, in which almost all of the estimated 200 galloglasses were killed. Carew charged into the battle brandishing a brace of pistols which he discharged into two of the galloglasses and then threw at two others, unhorsing both. He then fought valiantly with his sword, and earned the praise of the entire company both for his leadership and for his bravery. To celebrate their victory, every man of Carew's company picked up one of the axes for which the galloglasses were known and feared and carried them back into Kilkenny.[39]

In his narrative of the battle for Holinshed's *Chronicles*, Hooker put the total number of Butler's force, including horsemen and kerns, at 2,000, and the number of dead, mostly among the heavily armed galloglasses, at 400 or more. The more mobile horseman and lighter armed kerns escaped Carew's men by fleeing into the mountains. Carew's force had none killed and only one of Captain Malbie's men wounded, an absolute contradiction of the Butlers' claims that would not have surprised Sir Edmund had he read it. Having doubled the number of dead galloglasses in this account, Hooker also doubled the number of captured axes, claiming each soldier and captain paraded into a dismayed Kilkenny bearing two axes.[40]   In each account, the joy of Carew's men at their triumph is reported as nothing unto the sorrow of Butler at the overthrow of his men, for in the galloglasses "did consist his chiefest hope and force."[41]

Feeling against Carew in Kilkenny ran high. A servant of the earl of Ormond, observing that Carew liked to walk each day in the earl's garden next to the castle, provided himself with a pistol and set watch at a window with a good view of the garden, intending to shoot Sir Peter at the first opportunity. Nothing came of the servant's first two attempts because the powder failed to light. On the third day, however, the gun discharged, and Carew was only saved by the intervention of William Stapleton, the dean of Cashall and chaplain and steward to the earl of Ormond. Stapleton came upon the would-be assassin just as he was about to shoot, and knocked the gun aside at the last moment, sending the ball wide of its mark. For Carew, no stranger to ambushes and assassination attempts, this was the closest call yet. Carew thanked God yet again for a miraculous escape, and was, wrote an approving Hooker, not disposed to take vengeance upon a man so obviously ready to take vengeance on him.[42]

Hooker's accounts of Carew's actions against the Butler rebels described honourable combat, with heavy Butler battle losses and little or no loss to Carew's company. Although Hooker said Carew allowed his soldiers to spoil Clogrennan, he made no mention of putting the defenders to the sword, much less of executing women and children. Even the fate of the Butler servant who came out of Clogrennan to parlay is unrecorded by Hooker. The action outside Kilkenny is in Hooker's account a much more one-sided affair than the stiff fight described by the Butlers. Hooker's accounts, untroubled by any need to understand the Butlers' point of view, and concerned, as always, to portray Carew as the valiant warrior and generous foe, most likely ignore Carew's reverses and understate his losses. The earl of Ormond, attempting to deflect blame from his brothers and fasten it upon Carew and Lord Deputy Sidney, may not have been careful in verifying tales of Carew's atrocities before passing them on to the English court. In his description of the fall of Clogrennan, Sir Edmund seemed most distressed by the loss of his papers—the documentary evidence supporting his land titles. Tales of the slaughter of innocents at Clogrennan came to Ormond not from his brother, but while he was yet in England via servants who fled the general rebellion in the south of Ireland and who do not seem to have been eyewitnesses to the fall of the castle. Sidney, of all people, confirmed the Butlers' claims of hangings at Clogrennan by telling Sir Francis Walsingham in 1583 that Clogrennan fell to Carew "after a bloody bickering and slaughter" of Sir Edmund Butler's men. Sidney also added that Carew "hanged the ward" after the castle fell.[43] That Carew executed the defenders of Clogrennan is sure; that some unnecessary death and destruction accompanied the sacking of Clogrennan is most likely; that Carew ordered the executions of noncombatants within the castle is less likely, and is certainly unproven.

The tales the Butlers' told of Carew, however inaccurate, served their purpose well. While Carew was faring well in the war of shot and steel in Carlow, he was suffering defeat in the war of words and opinions taking place across the Irish Sea. And defeat in the one was more serious than victory in the other was beneficial, for the gain of a thousand Clogrennans was nothing beside the loss of the queen's favor. The queen was already alarmed by reports coming to her from Ireland when she wrote to Sidney on 2 July.

We be also informed that of late you should by some decree in our council there order Sir Peter Carew to have the possession delivered to him of certain castles and lands which Sir Edmund Butler, Knight, has of long time quietly possessed and that the title and right thereof was not heard and determined by the course and order of our laws. Wherein (if the information should be true) the said Sir Edmund may colorably allege some lack of indifferency towards him. And therefore we require to understand certainly the manner of your proceedings in this cause and do think it mete except there be some more necessary just cause to the contrary than we yet understand that Sir Edmund Butler be not removed from his ancient possession by any private order or decree taken there in our privy council until the right may be heard and determined by judgement in some of our courts of record according to the laws of that our realm.[44]

The queen's letter, coming before the events at Clogrennan and Kilkenny, was a response to letters from Cork describing the outrages committed in the region by Fitzmaurice. Inclusion of a passage on the Carew-Butler dispute indicates how strong was distress in Ireland over Carew's land claims, the anxiety having already made itself felt at the English court. The queen concluded her letter with a demand for more information; the whole Irish situation was being confused in England by contradictory rumors and reports, and the queen found herself "drawn into doubtfulness of opinion what to determine."

On 9 July 1569, the queen wrote again to Sidney to tell him that she had given an anguished Ormond leave to return to Ireland and persuade his brothers to submit. The lord deputy was to "use him honourably," for he was a great noble and had the queen's trust. She also reproved Sidney for proclaiming the earl's brothers rebels with Fitzmaurice and others of his ilk. In the detestable rebellion of Fitzmaurice "no spark of grace has appeared," but Sir Edmund Butler believed himself unfairly treated because the deputy was "incensed against him by some that he thinks his adversaries for title of land and government." The queen had heard that Sir Edmund wished to appeal his case directly to her; she had disallowed this for she would have her deputy obeyed. But the queen's meaning is too clear for Sidney to miss: he is to take great care how he proceeds against the Butlers and to preserve "the credit of this house of Ormond in respect of the good services done and to be done by it to our crown."[45]

Secure in the queen's favor, Ormond began the drumbeat against Carew in late July while still in England. While awaiting passage from Bristol, he described for Cecil the consequences to the queen's Irish realm of Carew's "rash dealings in matters of land."

This [the alleged executions at Clogrennan] is the order now a days to come by the possession of my brother's lands, and to make the better quarrel to his living my lord deputy proclaimed him rebel. I hope the queen's majesty, of her gracious goodness, will think of this manner of dealing with her subjects. Now, sir, mark the mischief happened in this time, my country is invaded by the traitors James Fitzmaurice and Macarthy More. . . . They have utterly spoiled my country of corn, cattle, and all I have, so there is not one plow going in the whole county of Kilkenny, nor any living creature remaining in it. . . . I assure you, Sir Peter, dealing for his land, hath made all the ills, and men of living, dwelling out of the English pale, think there is a conquest meant to be made of all their countries.[46]

Ormond reported his brother to be "in very ill case," believing rumors that the queen had been poisoned, which, if true, destroyed his one hope of deliverance from the plots of Carew and the deputy. Sir Edmund ate and slept little, but talked incessantly, especially of the queen's death, "saying if she were alive he should not be thus used." His men feared for his life, for he was given to riding about wildly with but three or four servants seeking to encounter with Carew. The earl closed by begging Cecil to get the queen to give him some English soldiers to try and put right the consequences of Carew's actions.

In Ireland, meanwhile, Sir Edmund had joined with Fitzmaurice in besieging Kilkenny. The town, despite its Butler sympathies, wanted no part of Fitzmaurice and the terrors he had visited on Cork. The townsmen stoutly defended themselves against the rebels, and by early August the siege had failed. The main efforts of the Butlers, however, continued in Carlow, where about 3 August, Piers Butler, another of Ormond's brothers, spoiled the town of Leighlin. Indeed, the Butler rage against Idrone was characterised by the Irish annalist Thaddy Dowling as "Diaboli contra Petrum Carew."[47] The raid on Leighlin was reported to Dublin by Hooker's brother Roger, whom Carew had apparently left in charge at Leighlin when he followed Sir Edmund to Kilkenny. Roger Hooker reported that Piers Butler burned 70 houses, killed nine men, wounded three or four others, and burned four children. With Carew in Kilkenny, the house at Leighlin was kept by 12 men, an insufficient force to hold it in case of siege, which the Butlers threatened every day. Hooker believed an attack was imminent, and begged the chancellor, who was in charge in Dublin while the deputy was in the west dealing with rebellion, to "consider our estate here, and send us your men that are there." With a concern appropriate to an experienced steward, and reminiscent of his brother, Roger promised that any troops sent would be well provided with food and supplies.[48]

Sir Edmund made clear to the deputy that his anger over Carew's claim to his land lay at the root of his alienation from the government. In a letter preserved in the Carew Manuscripts, Sir Edmund complained to Sidney (the letter is mis-addressed to Sir William Fitzwilliam, Sidney's successor as deputy) that Carew had slain a great number of his men on the past Sunday, which he called 3 July. This date is too early in the month to be the fight at Kilkenny, and may refer to the capture of Clogrennan—Butler's imprecise description may apply to either episode—or to another encounter entirely. Butler claimed that Carew slaughtered his men without rhyme or reason, putting to the sword even those he took prisoner. "The Turk could not show more extremity," wailed Sir Edmund. Carew's cruelty left Sir Edmund no choice but to seek revenge for the murder of his men. What's more, Carew, claiming descent and inheritance from ancestors "five hundred years agone," was seeking to take Sir Edmund's lands illegally under an order he had obtained of the deputy. Sir Edmund declared himself willing to surrender the lands if Carew recovered them by law, but not otherwise. Carew, he charged, was also threatening "to have my head, in calling me traitor, rebel, saying many other uncourteous words not fit for gentlemen to use, which I leave unwritten." He warned the deputy that whatever actions he would take from now on were done solely to save his life and to gain revenge for Carew's cruelties, "seeing no punishment is done to Sir Peter Carew, or his partners in this cruel murder." Ireland, he concluded, would have been better off had Carew "never been born than come to this realm."[49]

On 24 August 1569, Sir Edmund wrote to his brother the earl to explain his actions. He denounced Sidney for using the law and the queen's army to aid Carew in dispossessing him of his living. He rehearsed his request to lay his cause before the queen and his offer to serve the queen anywhere in Ireland that the deputy willed him to go. When Sidney spurned these efforts and sent Carew to attack him, Sir Edmund decided to join Fitzmaurice "to make me the abler to revenge my cause upon Carew." The greatest injury done to him, Sir Edmund argued, was the deputy's claim "that I am the chief maker of these wars in Ireland." This lie was being told only to hide Sidney's own guilt. "Indeed, his government had need of some color to cloak his doings, for now he makes Peter Carew's cause the queen's Majesty's quarrel." Sir Edmund had served the queen too long and suffered too much in her service to turn traitor to her now. He had turned to Fitzmaurice only to deal with Carew, and had utterly rejected Fitzmaurice's attempts to bring in the Spaniards and alter religion as established by the queen. He had refused to make open war on the deputy for the queen's sake, "and not for any love I bear Sir Henry Sidney, or Peter Carew; for I protest to God, I could be content to die to be revenged upon them, so it were no offence to the queen nor peril to her state." If only the queen knew how her business was mishandled and her treasure consumed "by such cormorants as serve more to enrich themselves by her than for any quiet or good order they devise for the state of the land." Sir Edmund railed on at length against the deputy and declared that Ireland would "never be in quiet while he governs, Sir Peter Carew being one of the council." To prove to the queen that his quarrel "was against Carew and others for my living," Sir Edmund had challenged to combat Carew, Gilbert, and other enemies "who persuaded my Lord Deputy thus to deal with me, and upon their ale benches betraitor me at their pleasure." Sir Edmund closed his diatribe with a promise to come to the earl at any place of his choosing, so long as the lord deputy was not present.[50]

The two brothers met on 1 September outside Kilkenny. Six days later the earl forwarded a summary of his brother's comments at the meeting to Cecil. In his covering letter, the earl made clear to Cecil where he and his brother felt the blame belonged for the recent upheaval. Sidney's proclamation declaring the Butlers rebels was merely "a cloak for Sir Peter's enterprises." Few landowners in Ireland, claimed the earl, did not think that Sidney was out to take their lands from them by the sword. If they were not convinced otherwise, there would be great disquiet in Ireland and great charge thereby for the queen. Carew was the only author of all the Butlers' troubles, and Sir Edmund was constrained from dealing with him as an enemy by the high position he held with the lord deputy. If Cecil but knew the claims and challenges Carew made to the lands of many nobles and gentlemen in Ireland, he would have no need to marvel at the great mischief Carew's presence in Ireland was causing and would continue to cause. Ormond closed by proclaiming himself more willing to lie in the Fleet than to serve in Ireland at this time with men whose good will toward him and his family he doubted.[51]

The summary of Sir Edmund's words at Kilkenny struck the same note. Sir Edmund complained bitterly to his brother that the deputy and

Carew were out to spoil him of his lands and living without any order of law, and had done all they could to take his life and to destroy his good standing with the queen. He had refused the deputy's summons to Dublin because he feared Sidney would imprison him until he agreed to surrender his land to Carew. He rehearsed again the slaughter of the galloglasses outside Kilkenny and explained his refusal to make active war on the deputy because he was the queen's representative. Sir Edmund's only aim had always been to avenge himself on Carew, who had stolen and continued to hold his lands. The summary closed with Sir Edmund's submission.

> And for such hurts and offences as by occasion of my Lord Deputy and Sir Peter Carew's said dealings he was driven to do and commit to others of the queen's majesty's subjects, he most humbly and lowly submitted himself to the queen's majesty's mercy, and promised to me [Ormond] to keep her majesty's peace from henceforth.[52]

Carew had once again become a magnet for blame, just as he had been in January 1554 when the Devon rising against Mary had collapsed amidst fear and recrimination.

On 19 July, in the midst of the Fitzmaurice and Butler risings, the queen issued a commission to Carew and Henry Davells to take charge of the defense of the Pale while the deputy was in the field against Fitzmaurice and other rebels.[53] In the crisis of the summer, Carew's military experience was still valued, but in the autumn, when the crisis had passed and the Butlers' serious and repeated accusations had made their way to London, Carew's standing with the queen had fallen sharply. On 27 October, one day after the Irish Council forwarded his name to London as one deserving of thanks for his role in putting down the summer rebellions,[54] Carew wrote a plaintive letter to Cecil defending that role. Sir Peter denied disturbing Sir Edmund Butler in the possession of his lands until he was appointed to repress Butler's "disorderly proceedings." All his adversaries in Ireland, lamented Carew, believed him to be in disgrace with the queen and were mightily encouraged thereby to act against him. He humbly desired that the queen continue to look upon him with favor, or all his efforts in Ireland would be undone.[55]

The situation depicted in Carew's October letter does not accord well with Hooker's description of Carew's position in Ireland in the last months of 1569. With the end of the Butler disturbances, wrote Hooker, Carew returned to Leighlin and his barony of Idrone. This is confirmed by a letter of 27 December from Sidney to the Council in England, in which the lord deputy announced Carew's final reduction of the Kavanaughs and his restoration of quiet and order to Idrone after the disturbances and disorders of the summer.[56] But Hooker, far from describing the exaultation of Carew's enemies at his disfavor with the queen, described instead the willingness of landholders in Munster to submit themselves to Carew and to come to some accommodation with him over the lands he claimed from them. Such important Anglo-Irish lords as Lord Courcy, whom Henry VIII had knighted at the siege of Boulogne, and such Irish families as the O'Mahones and the O'Driscolls wrote in both Irish and English to invite Carew to come to Cork and settle with them. These offers were not made simply because the gentlemen believed they could now get advantageous terms from the disgraced Carew, but, according to Hooker, represented a complete submission to Carew's claims of ownership. Courcy and the others agreed to "become his tenants for all such lands as they hold, and whereof he was their lawful and rightful lord, and would also give unto him those rents and services as their predecessors did, and were wont to pay and yield to his ancestors."[57]

One reason for these generous offers appears in a memorandum in the hand of Sir Francis Walsingham dated to the fifteenth year of Elizabeth (1573-74). The memorandum assesses the then current state of Munster by examining the Carew claims to lands there. After tracing the Carew title in some detail from the time of Henry II, the memorandum identifies the earl of Desmond as the chief holder of former Carew lands. Desmond's exactions of coign and livery and other Irish impositions was ruthless, and generated great resistance from his tenants, thereby keeping Munster in continual strife and turmoil. Of these tenants, the "meaner sort," not being well able to resist Desmond, offered to yield themselves to Carew if he promised to defend them from Desmond. Such a promise, the memorandum concludes, Carew cannot keep without peril to the state and everlasting continuance of wars and quarrels in Munster. No wonder the queen was unwilling to allow Carew to proceed with his Munster claims, even after she had forgiven him the Butler wars. The memorandum hints at the ultimate desirability of Carew displacing Desmond as chief landlord in Munster, but realistically assesses the difficulties in the way of achieving such an end. To make good and maintain his claims in Munster, Carew needed to be "of a great countenance, power, and ability, as also bounteous and liberal." The detail of this document,[58] and of a second document listing all the Carew lands in Munster and their current holders,[59] indicates how concerned the government had become by 1573 or 1574 over the possible impact the pressing of Carew's land suits would have on Ireland in general, and on troubled Munster in particular.

Despite the responsibility the Munster offers entailed, Carew accepted them, although he could not finalize arrangements until he had obtained the queen's permission to proceed with these claims. Either Carew's original permission to come to Ireland had encompassed only his claims to Idrone and the Leinster lands, or permission to deal in the Munster lands had since been withdrawn, perhaps as a result of the queen's 2 July letter to Sidney essentially forbidding further use of the Irish Council to decide land suits in Carew's favor.

In any event, by the end of 1569, it was clear to Carew that preservation of all he had gained at law in 1568 depended on regaining the favor of the queen, which had been seriously eroded in the last half of 1569 by the anti-Carew attacks of the Butlers. Because he could do little to repair his position with the queen while he was in Ireland, Carew returned to England early in 1570. He would spend a good part of the remaining years of his life at court attempting to regain the queen's trust and good will, essential prerequisites to consolidating his position and authority on his newly won but shakily held Irish estates.

---

1   Queen Elizabeth to Sir Henry Sidney, 10 February 1569, *Sidney State Papers 1565-70*, ed. Tomas O'Laidhin (Dublin: Irish Manuscript Commission, 1962), p. 103.

2   John Hooker's Diary for the 1569 Irish Parliament, Cambridge University Library, MS Mm.1.32.

3   Queen Elizabeth to Sir Henry Sidney, 4 November 1568, "Additional Sidney State Papers 1566-70," ed. D.B. Quinn, *Analecta Hibernica* #26, Irish Manuscript Commission (1970): 97-98.

4   A mark was valued at about 13s 4d, thus the queen's charge for Leighlin was about £550. The noble was valued at about 6s 8d, thus the queen's loss of revenue to Carew was only something in the neighborhood of £2 3s.

5   Sir Peter Carew to Sir William Cecil, 23 February 1569, PRO, SP63/27/77.

6   Snow, *Holinshed's Chronicles*, VI, p 377.

7   Sir Peter Carew to Sir William Cecil, 3 March 1569, PRO, SP63/27/89.

8   Hooker, "Life," pp. 85-86.

9   Ibid., p. 86.

10 Ibid., p. 87. Coyne and livery referred to various Gaelic exactions in goods and services that arose out of the clan chief's right to billet his retainers upon the countryside. Cess referred to various impositions in goods and services levied by the

Irish government; these included levies of food for royal garrisons, of carts and horses for transport, and of labor for building projects. Carew was to spend much time wrangling with both the Irish and English governments for the lifting of traditional cess obligations from Idrone.

11 Sir Peter Carew to Sir William Cecil, 28 March 1569, PRO, SP63/27/154.

12 Queen Elizabeth to Sir Henry Sidney, 6 June 1569, *Sidney State Papers*, p. 110.

13 License to John Hooker to Print Irish Statutes, 20 March 1569, Lambeth, Carew MS 605, f. 3.

14 For more on the Irish Parliament of 1569-71, see Victor Treadwell, "The Irish Parliament of 1569-71," *Proceedings of the Royal Irish Academy* 65, sect. C (1966-67): 55-89.

15 Poynings Law was enacted by the Irish Parliament in 1494 during the deputyship of Sir Edward Poynings. The statute stipulated that acts passed by the Irish Parliament only became valid when approved by the English Parliament. Following the queen's instructions, Deputy Sidney planned to expedite the government's legislative program by temporarily suspending Poynings Law for all public bills. The opposition to Sidney in this Parliament could wreck the government's entire program by refusing to suspend Poynings Law, which is what they did by four votes. For more on this Parliament and the procedural device of suspending Poynings Law, see Steven G. Ellis, *Tudor Ireland: Crown, Community and the Conflict of Cultures 1470-1603* (London: Longman, 1985), p. 258.

16 John Hooker's Diary for the 1569 Irish Parliament, Cambridge University Library, MS Mm.1.32. Hooker's diary is printed in C. Litton Falkiner, "The Parliament of Ireland under the Tudor Sovereigns: With Some Notices of the Speeches of the Irish House of Commons," *Proceedings of the Royal Irish Academy* 25 (1904-05): 563-66.

17 Ibid.; also Falkiner, "Parliament of Ireland," p. 565.

18 Snow, *Holinshed's Chronicles*, VI, p. 344.

19 Ibid., p. 345.

20 For one thing, the speech sank the impost bill, which was heavily defeated three days later. For another, it led to the composition by Hooker of a brief treatise on the way parliaments were conducted in Elizabethan England. "The order and usage how to keepe a parlement in England in these daies" was written from Hooker's experience as a member of the English Parliament in 1571, but the notion of such a document arose from a motion made to the speaker of the Irish Parliament in 1569 to "reform those abuses and disordered behaviors" of the Irish members. Hooker agreed to prepare a "book of the orders of the parliaments used in England" as a blueprint for

future Irish parliaments to follow. In doing so, he also prepared a valuable historical source for the functioning of Elizabethan parliaments. "The order and usage" is printed in Snow, *Holinshed's Chronicles*, VI, pp. 345-62; it has also been printed in Vernon F. Snow, *Parliament in Elizabethan England: John Hooker's* Order and Usage (New Haven, Conn.: Yale University Press, 1977). See also Treadwell, "The Irish Parliament," pp. 70-71.

21 John Hooker's Diary for the 1569 Irish Parliament, Cambridge University Library, MS Mm.1.32; also Falkiner, "Parliament of Ireland," p. 565.

22 Hooker, "Life," pp. 87-88.

23 Ibid., p. 88.

24 Ibid., pp. 88-90.

25 For more on the wider causes of Irish rebellion in 1569, see James Hughes, "Sir Edmund Butler of the Dullogh, Knight," *Journal of the Royal Society of Antiquaries of Ireland* 11 (1870-71): 153-92, 211-31 and Ellis, *Tudor Ireland*, pp. 259-60.

26 Hooker, "Life," p. 90.

27 Deposition of John Devawe, 16 June 1569, printed in Hughes, "Sir Edmund Butler," p. 177.

28 Deposition of Roland, Lord Baltinglass, and Richard Shee, 19 June 1569, printed in Hughes, "Sir Edmund Butler," pp. 179-80.

29 Captain Nicholas Malbie to Sir William Cecil, 21 June 1569, PRO, SP63/28/102.

30 Deposition of William Sweetman, 27 July 1569, printed in Hughes, "Sir Edmund Butler," p. 181.

31 Hooker, "Life," pp. 90-91.

32 Ibid., pp. 92-93.

33 Sir Edmund Butler to the Earl of Ormond, 24 August 1569, PRO, SP63/29/80.

34 Earl of Ormond to Sir William Cecil, 24 July 1569, PRO, SP63/29/47.

35 Sir Peter Carew to Sir Henry Sidney, 12 July 1569, PRO, SP63/29/15.

36 Earl of Ormond to Sir William Cecil, 24 July 1569, PRO, SP63/29/47.

37 Just what Sir Edmund meant by this remark is unclear. Hooker left a detailed physical description of Carew, but made no mention of an eye problem, and we have

no other evidence of Sir Peter having suffered an eye wound, although such an injury would not have been impossible either during the course of Carew's active, martial life or as a result of the fighting in 1569. Hooker's failure to make mention of such a blemish would also not be surprising.

38 Sir Edmund Butler to the Earl of Ormond, 24 August 1569, PRO, SP63/29/80.

39 Hooker, "Life," pp. 94-95.

40 Snow, *Holinshed's Chronicles*, VI, pp. 362-63.

41 Hooker, "Life," p. 95.

42 Ibid., pp. 95-96.

43 Sir Henry Sidney to Sir Francis Walsingham, 1 March 1583, Lambeth, Carew MS 601, f. 89.

44 Queen Elizabeth to Sir Henry Sidney, 2 July 1569, *Sidney State Papers*, p. 114.

45 Queen Elizabeth to Sir Henry Sidney, 9 July 1569, *Sidney State Papers*, pp. 115-17.

46 Earl of Ormond to Sir William Cecil, 24 July 1569, PRO, SP63/29/47.

47 Maclean, *Life and Times*, p. 222, n.

48 Roger Hooker to Lord Chancellor Weston, 10 August 1569, PRO, SP63/29/65.

49 Sir Edmund Butler to the Lord Deputy [Sir Henry Sidney], Undated, Lambeth, Carew MS 605, f. 22. The letter bears the annotation, possibly in Carew's own hand, "1571 vel 1572," but 3 July fell on a Sunday in 1569 and the tone and the content of the letter also date it to that year, probably some time in the middle or end of July.

50 Sir Edmund Butler to the Earl of Ormond, 24 August 1569, PRO, SP63/29/80.

51 Earl of Ormond to Sir William Cecil, 7 September 1569, PRO, SP63/29/105.

52 Words of Sir Edmund Butler to the Earl of Ormond, 1 September 1569, Lambeth, Carew MS 611, f. 95.

53 Commission to Sir Peter Carew and Henry Davells, 19 July 1569, Lambeth, Carew MS 605, f. 15.

54 *Cal.SP Ireland*, vol. I (London, 1860-1912), pp. 421-22.

55 Sir Peter Carew to Sir William Cecil, 27 October 1569, PRO, SP63/29/154.

56 Sir Henry Sidney to the English Council, 27 December 1569, PRO, SP63/29/185.

57 Hooker, "Life," p. 96.

58 Notes of Sir Francis Walsingham on the State of Munster, 1573-74, BL, Cotton MS, Titus B XII, f. 158.

59 Notes on the Ancient Lands of Carew in Ireland, Undated, BL, Add. MS 4797, ff. 61-62.

CHAPTER 12

THE FINAL YEARS

Carew left Ireland for England in early 1570, determined to restore his position with the queen. He stopped briefly at Mohun's Ottery, but his real destination was the court, where he planned to seek "leave to prosecute his suit for the recovery of his lands and title in Munster."[1] Although Hooker gave us no dates for Sir Peter's return trip and no details as to his movements in the early months of 1570, we know he was at court in mid-May 1570 from the queen's letter of 17 May to Sidney, in which she mentioned having heard from Carew about the lord deputy's plans for naval action in the Irish Sea to prevent the troublesome Scots from landing in Ireland. In the same letter, the queen cleaned up the lingering consequences of the Butler rising. Sir Edmund and Piers had made formal submission to the deputy in February and were now in prison awaiting the queen's pleasure. Sir Edward Butler remained at large, much to the queen's displeasure. Elizabeth disagreed with Sidney's desire to send the Butlers to England, thinking their great fault might thereby seem to gain some favor. Instead, she ordered Sidney to capture Edward and then arraign and indict all three together. They were to be induced to confess their treason and to offer to surrender their lands and goods to the Crown. Once they had done this, Sidney was to suspend judgment and await the queen's further pleasure. If they refused to confess and surrender their property, Sidney was to proceed to judgment, but was not to impose the death penalty until he had heard from the queen.[2] With the Butler affair fresh in her mind, the queen was not disposed to look kindly upon Carew; Sir Peter found the queen "not. . . favorable unto him, for that she, upon advertisement made unto her, did conceive, and also charge him, that he should be the cause and occasion of the Butler's wars and rebellion, and therefore he durst not to enter his suit until she was persuaded and resolved of the truth."[3] The queen meant to keep Carew in England and prevent him from making further attempts to recover lands in Ireland.

Sidney, in a friendly and comforting letter to Carew on 28 May 1570, thanked Sir Peter for "how careful and friendly you have been for me in all places where your word or deed could stand me in stead." The disorders of the previous year and the hostility of the Butlers had put both Carew and Sidney in a bad odor, and cemented their friendship. Understanding that Carew would not return to Ireland in the summer, Sidney accounted the lack "of so good a companion, and so faithful an assistant" one of the greatest of many "discontentions" he suffered in Ireland. If it were not that the queen needed Carew for service in England, Sidney would think that by keeping Carew from Ireland the queen "did both much hinder yourself thereby, and her own service in this country." After catching Carew up on the current state of affairs in Ireland, the deputy offered some advice to his friend on the following of his own suits.

> [F]or your own cause, you shall never find any that shall be able, though he were never so willing, to do for you that that you should do for yourself. . . . And, therefore, if you will follow my advice, never yield that your turn can be served here by any attorney, for you shall, thereby, both prolong your coming, and do your cause no good, but rather lose that you have won.[4]

Sir Peter took Sidney's advice to heart, employing the persistence that won Henry VIII's permission to travel the continent and Lady Margaret's reluctant hand. Over the next three years, Carew bombarded the queen and the Council with all manner of petitions, requests, and offers relating to his Irish claims.

Carew began his campaign in the summer of 1570 by requesting that his attorneys and agents, through whom he must administer his Irish

estates during his enforced absence, be favorably treated by the deputy and
Irish Council. The queen, noting that the planting of good English subjects
in Ireland was "very profitable," and wishing to oblige a man who "has
always deserved favor in his just and reasonable causes," ordered the
deputy to show such favor so long as it was "agreeable to justice and the
laws of our realm." Next, Carew sought to renegotiate the status of the
house at Leighlin. He asked for the house and for adjoining lands worth
£40 6s 8d to be given to him and his heirs in fee simple, or else to be totally
discharged of the house and his expensive garrison obligation, with some
reimbursement for his costs in garrisoning Leighlin for the past year and a
half. The queen, advised of the need to maintain a garrison, but unwilling
to reassume the cost of such a garrison herself, dropped the matter into the
deputy's lap. She ordered Sidney to find a way to garrison Leighlin without
increasing her own charges and without unduly burdening Carew. Finally,
Carew asked that if Leighlin be returned to the queen, Idrone be freed of
all cess obligations except the need to support the Leighlin garrison. If this
petition was granted, Carew offered to maintain a troop of horse in Idrone
at his own charge to be at the service of the captain of Leighlin whenever
needed. Again praising Carew's "sufficiency and ability to serve,"
Elizabeth deferred a decision until the deputy could advise her on how best
to handle the royal cess obligations on Idrone.[5] By the end of June 1570,
the queen seemed cautiously willing to favor Carew if his suit would not
cost her money or cause more trouble in Ireland. For Carew, these petitions
were just a first step on the road to eventual return to Ireland and full
resumption of his land suits.

In 1571, Carew laid a whole series of petitions and offers before
the Council. He began by asking again for permission to return to Ireland
to "bring his lands to perfection." Idrone, although recovered, remained
unbounded and largely unleased and his profits from the barony remained
small, far less than the cost of recovery. He complained again of the burden
of cess and coign and livery, and offered the queen 100 marks (about £70)

a year out of the barony in return for abolition of all exactions. Carew even went so far as to suggest that the order and prosperity resulting from a ban on all such exactions throughout Ireland, and their replacement with similar assessments on all the baronies of the island, would give the government more than sufficient revenue to support the entire English garrison. If the queen did not share his enthusiasm for that plan, Carew asked that the cess be at least rated at an indifferent and certain amount, rather than being subject to the whims of the commander at Leighlin, and that collection in Idrone be left up to him and not to the soldiers of the Leighlin garrison. Carew's last petitions were apparently based upon a belief that his favor with the queen had revived, for Sir Peter concluded by asking for the Dullogh and permission to proceed with his Munster claims. While Butler languished in an Irish prison and Carew in English exile, the Dullogh remained in the queen's hands. Carew asked that the queen's legal counsel view his title to the property and give judgment as to his claims. As to Munster, Carew promised to proceed with "the quietest means that may be devised for view of the titles on both sides," and to submit all his claims to arbitration in an effort to avoid any repeat of the Butler disorders.[6]

The queen, not wishing to set any dangerous precedents, and being informed of the necessity of the Leighlin garrison and the difficulty of supplying it by any means but from Idrone, refused Carew's petitions. Sir Peter then tried a different tack. He complained to the queen of various abuses in rating and collecting the cess which both impoverished Idrone and starved the Leighlin garrison. The queen thought the complaints serious enough to warrant an investigation by the Irish Council, which she ordered in February 1572.[7] The Council completed its investigation a year later, issuing orders based on its findings on 16 February 1573. They granted Carew's request for more equitable, rational rating of cess, and set up procedures giving Carew and future lords of Idrone more say in the rating process. The Council, to end the violence that had often accompanied collection of the cess in the past, and which had formed the basis of

Carew's complaints, gave responsibility for collection in Idrone to Carew. It utterly rejected, however, Carew's offer of 100 marks instead of cess as "neither reasonable nor indifferent" for either the queen or the Leighlin garrison, implying that the chief advantage in the plan would be Carew's. What's more, the queen's constable was given power to adjust the assessment rate if he should not be satisfied with the "conditions or goodness" of the Idrone supplies, and according to large rises or falls in the Irish market for a particular item. If the deputy felt it necessary to increase the garrison above its normal size of 20 horse and 10 foot, Idrone would be liable to supply the additional troops as well. Carew, as lord of Idrone, was to have more say in the rating and collection of cess in the barony, but the needs of the royal garrison remained paramount and Idrone would not diminish or escape its cess obligation. This obligation was for the time being somewhat mitigated, for Carew himself remained the constable of the Leighlin garrison in 1573.[8]

Because Carew was an absentee constable, as well as an absentee landlord, Robert Tallon, one of his disaffected tenants in Idrone, was emboldened to turn the tables and exhibit a complaint against Carew in Star Chamber in November 1570 for wrongful dispossession of a town called Nourney. Sidney and the Irish Council decided that they could not act in the matter because neither Carew nor a sufficiently instructed representative of his was then in Ireland. They therefore ordered the town to remain in Carew's possession until Easter term, when it would be handed over to Tallon if neither Carew nor his representative appeared to answer the complaint. When Tallon asked for execution of this order in May 1571, the Irish Council (Sidney having been recalled) feared that Carew was unaware of the complaint and ordered that letters be sent to him apprising him of it. The Council thereupon gave Carew until Michaelmas term to respond before turning Nourney over to Tallon. The case dragged on into 1572, with both Thomas Wadding and Hooker appearing as attorneys for the absent Carew.[9] The suit was removed from Star Chamber in November and placed directly before Lord Deputy Fitzwilliam and the Council. Hooker, who had returned to Ireland as Carew's agent in the spring of 1572, summarised the case for Carew in January 1573.

> Your suit against the Tallons. . .is removed from the Castle chamber: and, as I remember, I sent you both the petition and the answer. I would, gladly, quietly have compounded with them, but they, standing in the trust of their cause, and relying themselves upon some which are in authority, will yield to nothing; thinking to have their purpose: but if they have no better proof than I do yet know of, and do prevail, as I hope I shall, against them, be they assured I will keep promise with them for my own part; and small shall be the courtesy which I will show them, trusting that you, of your wisdom, will consider of them according to their deserts.[10]

Proceedings in the case continued through 1573, with the Council examining both the Carew and Tallon ancestries back to the fourteenth century. In May 1573, each side presented the other with a list of interrogatories. A final hearing was called for 21 May 1574 in Dublin Castle, but neither Hooker nor the proceeding records give us a final outcome.[11] It may be that by 1574 Carew, turning his attention to Munster, was ready to compound with Tallon for the best terms he could get. In any event, the final result is less important than the clear picture the long drawn out case gives us of how difficult and frustrating Carew's Irish affairs became when he was prevented from being in Ireland to pursue them himself. Neither the legal training of Wadding nor the research expertise of Hooker were any substitute for the energy of Carew.

Hooker, to be sure, did his best to advance Carew's interests, but Sidney's words proved true: no agent, however willing, could prosper the master's affairs as well as the master himself. Hooker, in a letter addressed to Carew in London on 23 October 1572, made plain his utter agreement with this sentiment.

Your tenants do verily refuse to take any estate at all other than at your own hands,
partly because the more desirous they are of your coming the more they doubt
thereof; partly because they are informed that you do mind and intend to sell or
convey the same to some one of the earls of this land, which, if you should so do,
then, besides the rents which you compounded, they shall stand at such devotion
as which they do curse the time to think upon: Again some do formerly persuade
them that you mind not to come at all but have sent me for a color and shadow,
which they partly crediting do determine to save that they have, and keep it as well
as they can, but, assuredly, if you mind to come over yourself you shall be assured
to set the same at such rate, price, and rent as you will yourself: for so they may
have you to be their defender, and to be free from such governors as whom they do
fear to offend, they care not how far they do strain themselves. Surely there was
never man more desired and wished for than yourself, not only among them, but,
generally, of all others within this land. To travail, therefore, herein it is but lost
labor, for, as I have said, only you, and you alone, must be the doer thereof.[12]

Hooker further described his difficulties in collecting the rents Carew set
before he left, as well as outstanding cess payments. Part of Idrone lay
waste, generating no rents at all; neither the letting of these empty lands
nor the proper collection of rent would go forward until Carew could take
the matter in hand himself. As to the Munster claims, Hooker had
researched Carew's title and was sending a copy of his findings. He urged
Carew to have the document reviewed by legal counsel and to return it to
Ireland as quickly as possible. Hooker had retained six legal advisors in
Ireland, "the best which I can get," to direct Carew's burgeoning legal
affairs, and expected good success from the labors of this team. Hooker
closed by describing his efforts to rent Carew a house in Dublin, and to
stock it with supplies. Hooker declared his intention to return to England
on the conclusion of this business unless Carew objected. He ended the
letter by reiterating his main point: "If you do mind to save that you have
purchased, and to keep that you have gotten, you must determine to come
over yourself."

Despite his desire to come home, Hooker was still in Ireland on 20 January 1573, when he responded to Carew's newly arrived letters from the previous October. The letters found Hooker at Leighlin, and apparently asked for a full report on Carew's affairs. Hooker considered that his reports of the previous months had been so frequent and so complete as to constitute "a full answer to these your letters."[13] However, some of the issues Carew inquired about, being newly concluded, required updating. One of these issues was the surveying of Idrone, the report of which had been issued on 6 October 1572. The Council had ordered the lord deputy to appoint a commission to conduct the Idrone survey back in March 1571,[14] but no action was taken on the matter until September 1572 when a commission was appointed for the purpose by letters patent. The commission included the ubiquitous Henry Davells and various other English and Anglo-Irish gentlemen; the commissioners were to determine "the old, true, and ancient limits and bounds of the said Barony of Odrone" by summoning to Leighlin all "ancient and expert" gentlemen, freeholders, and other inhabitants of Idrone who could declare what the true boundaries were.[15] The commission was executed at Leighlin on 3 October, and determined the barony to contain, exclusive of the Dullogh, 53 marts of land, which amounted to something between 6,000 and 7,000 acres. Close examination of over 20 local gentlemen and residents established the exact boundaries of the barony, which were described in detail by such landmarks as "the middle of the black bog. . .which runs westward into the Barrow. . .unto the ford of Rowse, and there is, as it were, a ditch which mears between the Bishop's lands and the lands of Odrone."[16] Hooker made a copy of the survey, "dursting not to send the original for doubt of some mischances,"[17] and sent it to Carew shortly after its issuance.

Hooker had returned to Ireland as the bearer of a royal letter to the lord deputy and Council on Sir Peter's land suits.[18] The queen had continued to deny Carew permission to return to Ireland, but on 3 May 1572 she took cautious steps toward permitting Carew to proceed with his

Munster claims. The queen acknowledged that Carew "has of long time been a humble suitor unto us," but she had "not hitherto thought it convenient to grant him his suit so fully as his request was." She had now, however, "condescended to his suit thus far, that the said Sir Peter Carew shall cause declaration to be made unto you . . . of all the titles and interest that he pretends to those said lands." The deputy and Council could then, at their discretion, have the titles declared to the landowners involved. They were to choose who was approached, and when and how they were approached. Every effort was to be made to persuade the landowners to come "to some reasonable composition and agreement with the said Sir Peter, so as the trial of law may be avoided." If any landowner utterly refused to compound, the Council was to forbear for the time being, report the landowner's answers to England, and render their best advice as to how the case should be handled. In short, the queen was allowing Carew's Munster suits to go forward, but entirely in the manner and at the speed dictated by the Irish government.[19]

The deputy and Council disliked having Carew's troublesome causes dumped on them. Munster was just settling down after the lingering aftereffects of Fitzmaurice's rebellion in 1569-70, and no one was anxious to stir things up again. In February 1573, Deputy Fitzwilliam, "considering the jealous nature of the Irishry, and the unaptness of this stirring time for the preferring of such titles," sent both a copy of the queen's letter and Hooker to John Perrot, the lord president of Munster, essentially throwing the whole question into his lap. The deputy was sure that Perrot, being more familiar with current conditions in Munster, would be better able to decide who should be approached about Carew's claims, and when and how it would be best to do so. Perrot was left "without further direction to your own good discretion" to find the best way to advance Carew's claims "without danger to increase the stirs that be, or to raise any." The deputy was supported in this plan by Hooker, who said he had already dealt with Perrot and found him agreeable to Carew's cause. Fitzwilliam closed by recommending Hooker to Perrot as a reliable advisor in the case.

The bearer's conference we think your lordship may safely use, for that how well soever he wishes to the cause, yet we take him to be so discrete and dutiful that he would have no more haste therein than may stand with the good speed and quiet of the state.[20]

Hooker's earlier meeting with Perrot had occurred at Waterford just before Christmas 1572. He described for Perrot the entire history of Carew's Irish proceedings, about which Perrot had known nothing. Hooker assured Carew that the lord president "gave me very good words, and seems to tender your cause very much."[21]

Sir John Perrot was reputed to be an illegitimate son of Henry VIII because his mother had briefly been a royal mistress and his physique and coloring strongly resembled the late king's.[22] In April 1556, Perrot was arrested on suspicion of being involved in the Dudley conspiracy, a result of information passed on to the Marian government by Carew. Perrot was released within a short time, the government being unable to proceed against him for lack of evidence. He had been serving as lord president of Munster, with headquarters at Cork, since February 1571. Hooker reached Cork on 15 March 1573 with the lord deputy's letter of the previous month and a copy of the queen's letter from the previous May. Four days later Perrot replied to the deputy and Council concerning the advisability of proceeding with Carew's land claims in Munster. Perrot began by noting that the queen's letters were directed to the deputy and not to him, and asked, therefore, that the deputy "pardon me from dealing in a cause of such importance." Perrot would carry out any orders the deputy cared to give in the matter, but was no more willing than the deputy to be responsible for Carew's proceedings. Perrot was, however, willing to give Fitzwilliam his opinion about proceeding in the matter.

I. . . put you in remembrance what stirs grew upon the like occasion offered in the late L. Deputy Sir Henry Sidney's time (yea, by such a one as was civilly brought

up, having great friends and other means to tie him to obedience) when that title
was had in question, the flame of which fire could never be quenched until within
these xiii days. What should I recite unto your L. what hazard the state was
brought unto by the same, when the said Sir Henry had for every soldier your L.
has iii, or to declare what charge her Majesty was put unto by reason thereof. . .and
yet there was at that time dealing but with one, being a civil man, where now most
of the wildest and strongest in Munster should be touched therewith; being men
that have been without law, and never obedient unto the same. . .who tasting such
sour medicines at the first may . . trouble your L. and loath justice from hence
forward.[23]

To begin with any one of the Munster landowners, continued Perrot, was
to alert all of them that Carew's claims would affect them in time. The
lord president then rather plaintively asked Fitzwilliam to consider "with
what difficulty, what trouble of body and mind, what hazards of credit, and
what wants I have sustained in the service past to bring this state to the
quiet it is now at." If Perrot should disrupt this hard-won peace by meddling in Carew's affairs, he would be "compared to the cow, that yielding
great store of milk, overthrows the same with her heel." But Perrot understood the lord deputy to be convinced of the justice of Carew's claims, and
had no wish to see Sir Peter kept from the enjoyment of his rights. Perrot
concluded by offering the deputy his best advice on how to resolve the
dilemma.

Wherefore, to conclude, my opinion is, that it were much better her Majesty
should take his title into her highness's hands, giving him some piece of land in
England, or otherwise to consider of him, than by meddling therewith . . . . And
weighing that all Ireland enjoys not thorough quiet, and that neither between us
and Spain, nor France. . . is perfect amity, I would wish this matter to proceed no
further til time might more aptly serve.[24]

On 10 June 1573, the deputy and Irish Council wrote to the queen about what they had done in the past year concerning Carew's case. They excused themselves for their delay in responding by pleading the aftereffects of Fitzmaurice's rebellion on Munster as reason for waiting to take up Carew's cause there. They also enclosed a copy of Perrot's letter both to support this excuse and to endorse his advice for resolving the matter.

> Since, therefore, it is no safe meddling with the first direction of your Majesty's letters for discovery of the title to this people that account possession and one or two descents such a right as is not to be called in question, we must, of consequence, leave all the other directions unmeddled withal. . . . Which way else soever Sir Peter is to be contented we humbly leave to your Majesty's gracious consideration, but surely this matter is this way no further to be dealt withal without present and apparent peril of stir, which would not be appeased but with so great a charge as we would not wish your Majesty should enter into for any private man's title or interest.[25]

The deputy and Irish Council wrote on the same day to the Privy Council rehearsing in part what they had told the queen, and requesting the Council in London "to be a mean that such way may be taken therein to content or stay Sir Peter, that for fear of reviving further stirs here, those titles be no further revived."[26] However good Sir Peter's titles to the Munster lands were, no one in the Irish government was willing to risk a repeat of the trouble and expense the Carew claims had caused in Carlow. Sir Peter's Irish opponents had found a way to beat him; they might not be able to prevail at law, but their threats of rebellion could scare off official favor and support, without which implementation of Carew's claims became impossible. With the arrival of the 10 June letter in England, Hooker noted glumly that Carew's suits for Munster "took small effect."[27]

Throughout 1572 and 1573, Hooker's reports to Carew grew more agitated and alarming. On 20 January 1573, Hooker wrote from

Leighlin to warn Carew that neither Fitzwilliam nor Perrot seemed in favor of proceeding with the Munster claims for fear of renewed rebellion. Idrone, however, was quiet, both Hooker and Davells, who was in charge at Leighlin, had settled some disputes among the Kavanaughs. Hooker had been put to much trouble placating the otherwise faithful Davells, who believed Lady Tailboys had some grievance against him stirred up by one Thomas Jakeson, a troublesome servant of Carew's. This interesting broil somehow involved a woman, for Hooker complained that he could not talk any sense into Jakeson, for such was "the nature" of Ireland that "young men. . .far from their masters, and carried with women," were not to be reasoned with. Hooker had also talked with Chivers about the payment of his debt to Carew; Chivers gave "good words," but "the matter proceeds no further," Sir Christopher apparently feeling no great urgency to pay during Carew's prolonged absence. Carew had expressed in a recent letter some dissatisfaction with the rents being received from his Irish lands. In answer, Hooker warned Carew that if he did not return soon to look to his own affairs he could expect no better return; Hooker then erupted in frustration, using, typically, a classical allusion: "I am not that great Atlas which can carry the heavens upon my shoulders, nor yet bring that to pass which is above my reach and power, and, therefore you must pardon me therein."[28]

Hooker followed this outburst with a promise to secure Carew an Irish hawk, and the welcome news that he and Davells had custody of the Dullogh while the queen decided what to do with the property. He advised Carew to make immediate petition to the queen for it. Another parcel of Idrone, called Clogney, was still being held by Mr. Harepool, who claimed Carew's permission to retain possession under an improved lease. Sir Humphrey Gilbert and Jacques Wingfield both backed Harepool's claim, so Hooker declined to deal in the matter until he heard more about it from Sir Peter. Hooker declared his intention to leave Leighlin soon for Dublin and the new court term, and reminded Carew of the wisdom of

sending letters of thanks to the lord deputy and to Davells for their past
assistance and to ensure their future favor. Collection of rents was proceeding, but times were hard and money was scarce, and the collection
process was "both troublesome and with great pains both to the receiver
and the payor." He concluded by emphasizing again that Carew's return
was daily looked for and would greatly profit Carew's affairs. Blame for
the consequences that would attend his continued absence "must needs
rest upon yourself."[29]

Hooker's next letter to Carew was written on 8 March 1573, as
Hooker made his way to Cork with the deputy's letter to Lord President
Perrot. Ironically, a disruption had arisen in Idrone over a land claim
being made by another English gentleman. Anthony Colcloghe from
Shropshire was claiming the barony of St. Molyn, which was also claimed
by a branch of the Kavanaughs. This further claim on Kavanaugh lands
caused great unrest among the Idrone branch of the family, from which
Hooker feared "great mischief" for Carew and "the utter spoiling of me,
because your Kavanaughs, being desirous and having will to recover themselves to their old wonted liberty," were eager to rise in rebellion with their
St. Molyn relatives. Hooker had rushed back to Dublin to inform the lord
deputy, who apparently stayed Colcloghe's proceedings and so calmed
matters for the time being. But the Kavanaughs were still "buzzing
abroad" as a "sort of buzzing flees" complaining that Carew would never
come back, an opinion given unfortunate support by the recent pessimistic
report on Carew's situation given by Carew servant John Dodd. The
Kavanaughs grew so obstinate that soon Hooker would be "able to do no
good at all." What's more, unless Carew "set aside delays" and came
quickly to Ireland, the release of cess on Idrone, which Carew had requested,
could not take effect.[30] Hooker was also awaiting further documentary
evidence to be submitted in support of Carew's land titles in the next court
term in Dublin. If these documents did not arrive soon, Carew could
"impute it to [his] own folly." Tired and frustrated by his inability to settle

anything, Hooker allowed himself another outburst: "I can do no more for my part than I have done. I have so often written to you herein that I am both weary and ashamed thereof." Hooker closed with a warning. Many landholders in Munster, whose lands Carew claimed, were surrendering their titles to the queen and then leasing the properties back. One Fyon O'Driscoll was then in Dublin to accomplish such a deal. "They think," warned Hooker, "by these means to avoid you, wherefore you may take advice."[31]

Most of Hooker's letters during this period were addressed to Carew "at the great St. Bartholomew's in London," not to Mohun's Ottery, indicating Sir Peter's almost continual presence at court in these years as a suitor in his Irish causes. Perhaps stung by Hooker's January letter pleading for his presence in Ireland, Carew obtained a letter from the queen on 15 March 1573 ordering the lord deputy and Irish Council to inform Carew's Idrone tenants that his stay in England "has been by our commandment for some respects of service." The Dublin government was ordered to assist Carew's agents "to have care to see his tenants to be well used, to enjoy their estates, and to be defended in their rightful causes." The queen also pointedly reminded them that she had "heard not yet what order you have agreed upon" concerning the handling of Carew's Munster claims, as outlined in her letter of the previous May.[32] Although the queen did make use of Carew's services at the Tower and during the 1572 trial of the duke of Norfolk, her fear of the disruption and expense Sir Peter's personal pursuit of his claims would cause remained the chief reason for her refusal to sanction his return to the neighboring island.

Carew admitted the real reason for the queen's continuing refusal to allow him to return in an undated letter to the lord deputy that probably belongs to 1573. "I fear me," wrote Carew, "those untrue reports that were made of me unto her highness for being the occasion of the first rebellion when I was in Ireland is not yet out of her Majesty's head."

Carew estimated that pursuing his Irish suits had to date cost him "six thousand pounds at the least," which could not be recouped because his tenants in Idrone refused to compound with his agents, thereby making his return to Ireland ever more urgent. Carew declared himself happy that he was not in Ireland when the most recent rebellions began, and even happier that none of his tenants had taken part in those risings, thereby proving "that they are well contented with myself and my doings also." He protested that he wanted nothing from the queen but her favor in his "just and righteous causes." Carew then toted up his financial losses of the last two decades, claiming to have lost £8000 "in value at the least" in Mary's reign and to have been forced to sell lands worth 300 marks (about £200) since Elizabeth's accession. After all this loss in the queen's service and at her sister's hands, Carew found himself denied "the benefit of a poor subject." He considered himself "the most unfortunate man living, being such a corrosive unto my heart as yet never heretofore I received the like in all my days." Before closing, Carew explained for the lord deputy why he believed English settlement in Ireland had to go forward.

> But to be bold to trouble your L. with my simple opinion concerning persuasions that are made, why our countrymen should not be permitted to inhabit within that land, surely her Majesty shall never be thoroughly known there so long as her own laws are not current, and her own sword be not the minister of justice, and those Regali are under kings not suffered to have the administration of laws and justice at their wills and pleasure. Thus I am bold to trouble your L. with my opinion herein.[33]

Carew concluded by referring the deputy to an enclosed set of petitions and offers concerning his Munster claims that he had submitted to the queen. He hoped that the petitions would be speedily answered, for "being now well grown in years. . . the loss of a little time is much." Although weary and disappointed, Carew was far from ready to give up his Irish claims.

The enclosed offers were extraordinary, simultaneously exhibiting Carew's weary frustration and his dogged persistence, as well as his financial desperation. If the queen allowed him to return to Ireland to pursue his land titles in Munster, Carew promised to settle 1,000 Englishmen in Munster within one year, by the following Michaelmas. If Carew failed to do this, he would forfeit all his land titles in Munster to the queen. If the Irish raised any rebellion within Munster because of Carew's activities, so long as there was no involvement by a foreign power, Sir Peter undertook to put down the rebellion at his own charge with only the aid of friends. If Carew failed to keep this promise, he would likewise forfeit all his Munster interests to the queen.[34] The constant drain on Carew's financial and other resources that began with the failure of the marriage plot in January 1554 had taken a severe toll. Sir Peter had withdrawn from court after 1560 because of it, and had begun his Irish projects, in large part, to repair it. Now that the Irish hopes seemed about to disappear, Carew made a last attempt with these radical proposals to save the Irish venture and restore his position.

Carew never had to live up to these pledges, for about the time they were made, Carew finally found a way to get back to Ireland. Walter Devereux, earl of Essex, contracted with the queen to undertake an expedition leading to the settlement of Englishmen in Ulster in northern Ireland. In exchange for agreeing to bear the lion's share of the cost for the expedition, Essex was given an extensive grant of land and named Captain-General of Ulster. He pawned lands worth £500 with the queen for a loan of £10,000 to start the venture. From the beginning, Essex was bedeviled by enemies, such as Lord Deputy Fitzwilliam, who resented the threat Essex's position presented to his own, and the earl of Leicester, who initially promoted the project to remove Essex's influence from the queen, but then worked behind the scenes for its failure to discredit and ruin Essex. Many noblemen and gentlemen accompanied Essex as volunteers when his army left Liverpool on 16 August 1573.[35] Among those volunteers was Sir Peter

Carew, who, if not exactly free to pursue his own claims, was at least returning to Ireland.[36] On 16 September, Carew wrote to Burghley to report on the progress of the expedition. Already there were problems. Carew praised Essex as noble in mind and able in body, with sufficient force to reduce all of Ulster, but so slenderly authorised by the queen's commission that he could not properly govern his soldiers.[37] Two weeks later, Carew wrote again to Burghley to complain of the treachery of the Ulster Irish and of the earl's need for authority from the queen to execute traitors and rebels.[38]

Carew soon grew weary of the trouble and hardship that attended the Ulster enterprise, and considered Ulster, though a fertile land, too "savage, wild, and desolate," and too full of "deadly enemies" to be worth all the hardship required to subdue it. According to Hooker, Carew's thoughts naturally turned to his own Irish lands, so in need of attention, and he therefore took the first opportunity that came his way to leave Essex and to travel to Leighlin.[39] Essex himself told a somewhat different story of Carew's departure in his letter to the Council of 2 November 1573. Carew had served as the marshall of Essex's army, but that office being "more painful than is mete for his years," Essex persuaded Carew to withdraw to the Pale. The earl advocated Carew's departure because Carew's health was bad; he had "great pain in one of his legs," which complaint was not likely to improve in the cold climate of Ulster. Essex had also released his marshall because he understood from letters Carew had received from his tenants in Idrone that the barony was "greatly wasted," both from raids by the neighboring O'Mores and by dissension between the constables of Leighlin (Davells) and Carlow (Robert Harepool). Before leaving, Carew had made "firm promises" to Essex that he would not deal in his Munster titles unless by composition. If the Council could assist Carew to profit from his lands, either by exchange or otherwise, "it were a benefit well employed upon a servant of so long continuance, and a gentleman of so good desserts."[40]

Carew spent the winter of 1573-74 in Ireland, mainly at Dublin and Leighlin. On 6 February 1574, he wrote from Dublin to fellow Devon man Edmund Tremayne, clerk of the Council and, like Carew, an old Marian dissident.[41] Carew lamented the miserable state of Ireland, which, "without some speedy redress," was about to fall to ruin. Every county, even in the Pale, was greatly wasted. In Munster, all the good work of Perrot, the former lord president, was being undone by the disorderly earl of Desmond. Carew then went into a detailed description of all the Irish and Anglo-Irish rebels then in action and all the trouble each was causing. He had particularly harsh words for the Anglo-Irish earls, such as Kildare and Ormond, whose countries were especially misgoverned, there being "no Englishmen. . . amongst them." Earls, declared Carew, were "dangerous men to be dealt with here." If the earls would assist the queen in governing Ireland, the island "would not be as it is now, nor the Queen's Majesty at such charges," although Carew asked Tremayne to keep this opinion to himself. The only good thing currently afoot in Ireland was the Essex venture, which Carew had no doubt would come "to good pass and prosperous success."

Idrone was not so well as Carew could wish, but still quieter than many parts of Ireland, thanks in part to Davells and his troops at Leighlin. Carew had every hope of making "a very good rent" out of Idrone. Carew understood from Tremayne's last letter that Sir Thomas Smith, the secretary of state, had conceived a "great jealousy" of him. Carew assured Tremayne that Smith's opinion was not new, and was truly without cause. Carew closed the letter by asking Tremayne to do whatever favors he could for Davells, who would soon be coming to England.[42] A month later, on 6 March, Tremayne ignored Carew's desire for secrecy and sent the letter to Burghley, thinking Burghley would find Sir Peter's assessment of the state and needs of Ireland useful. He told Burghley that he had advised Carew to make amends with Secretary Smith and to work to mediate the growing dispute between Essex and Lord Deputy Fitzwilliam.[43]

Whether Carew returned to England in 1574 or remained in Ireland until his death in late 1575 is unclear. Hooker said nothing of a return to England, but wrote instead that Carew began to pursue his Munster claims immediately upon arrival at Leighlin from Ulster.[44] If this is true, Carew apparently forgot his "firm promises" to Essex not to meddle in Munster. We know that Carew was still in Dublin on 8 March 1574, for on that day Essex laid his plans for an expedition into Tyrone before Sir Peter, the lord deputy, and other members of the Irish Council.[45] We next hear of Carew in April 1575, when the queen sent Nicholas Malbie into Ireland with instructions for Essex and the lord deputy. In her instructions, the queen indicated her intention to order Sir Peter to accompany Essex into the north as his lieutenant, to provide the earl with advice, assistance, and comfort. She considered Carew ideal for this appointment, being "a person for his wisdom, discretion, reputation, and for his affection to the Earl, most mete." So that Carew might exercise his new office without charge to himself, the queen planned to allow him 10s per day and 20 horsemen with pay, as well as command of another 100 horse and foot.[46] Malbie's instructions imply Carew's presence in Ireland, and the letter of appointment Elizabeth wrote to Carew himself on 12 April is merely addressed "To Sir Peter Carew," with no indication of whether he was to be found in England or Ireland. The queen ordered Carew to repair to Essex with all speed, for the earl had great need of "such a friend and assistant unto him as you are"[47]; once again the implication is that Carew was already in Ireland and could quickly come to the earl. The weigh of evidence argues for Carew's continued residence in Ireland throughout 1574 and 1575.

The one contrary indication is provided by Sir Peter's will, dated 4 July 1574, which may indicate at least a brief trip back to Devon in the summer of that year. Since Carew had transferred a future interest in Mohun's Ottery and the other Devon properties to Thomas Southcote in 1563, the will of 1574 dealt primarily with the barony of Idrone. The will describes Carew's settlement of Idrone on his trustees by a deed dated 24 June 1574. The eight trustees included Hooker, Edmund Tremayne of Devon, Lady Margaret's brother Henry Skipwith, Jacques Wingfield of Dublin, John Harrington of Essex, John Wood, and George Harvey and Jasper Horsey of Dublin, all Devon men or men with Irish connections except for Skipwith and Harrington. The trustees were to pay all Carew's debts and legacies out of the revenues of the barony, and to protect the residual interest in Idrone of Lady Margaret, who was named executor of the will. After that, the barony was to pass first to Carew's cousin Peter Carew, the eldest son of his uncle George, and, if Peter died without heirs, to his younger brother George. Carew added a codicil on 26 November 1575, the day before his death, providing for several additional legacies and giving instructions for the payment of debts. Two of Carew's creditors, Henry Davells and Mr. Rogers the elder, were given first call on the Idrone revenues. Roger Hooker was one of seven men to have a bequest of £40 out of Idrone, and various smaller bequests from the barony revenues went to other servants, including "my man Hamyllian £20, my man Warberton £20, my man Smolkin £4, Denys of the buttery 20s, Watt of the kitchen 20s, Bess my laundress £3, and my man Parker 20 nobles sterling." Carew confirmed Lady Margaret as executor of the will and beseeched her to forego any profits from the barony until all debts and legacies had been settled.[48]

Carew's second term of service with Essex ended about August or September 1575. On 6 August the queen wrote to Essex to inform him of the reappointment of Sir Henry Sidney as lord deputy and to thank him and his captains for all their efforts in Ulster.[49] Enclosed with the letter to Essex was a separate letter to Carew, Captain Malbie, and others thanking them personally for their service to Essex, "especially considering that in all services and hard accidents you have continued still with our cousin when others have left him."[50] Sidney landed in Ireland in September, and Essex returned to England before the end of the year.[51] The financial accounts kept for the Essex expedition by the Irish treasurer at war close on 30 September, and include an overpayment of £17 20d made to Carew and still unreimbursed at the time of his death.[52] Carew's attention was back on Idrone by 12 August, when Deputy Fitzwilliam responded to an earlier petition from Sir Peter by ordering Robert Harepool, the constable of Carlow Castle, to restore cattle and other cess exactions wrongfully levied on Carew's Idrone tenants.[53] Carew had to complain of Harepool again on 9 September. The dispute over cess exactions in Idrone had evidently grown considerably, for Carew agreed to enter into bonds of £100 to pay any lawful exactions Harepool could prove before the deputy. In light of this, Harepool was ordered to restore the undefined pledges Carew had given earlier for payment. Carew's complaint concerned Harepool's disregard for a previous order from the lord deputy to restore the pledges.[54]

The dispute with Harepool indicates the likelihood of Carew's presence at Leighlin by August 1575. It was perhaps about this time that Carew wrote from Leighlin to Hooker, who had returned to Devon, asking him to come again to Ireland to take charge of concluding the Munster suits. Hooker was hesitant to return to Ireland a third time, for Sir Peter had to write to Lady Margaret and to friends in Devon and ask them to persuade Hooker to agree. Hooker yielded to these persuasions, and perhaps to the satisfaction of knowing that Carew needed him, and took ship from Exmouth, intending to go directly to Munster and land at Cork. But the crossing was stormy and difficult and the ship was driven instead into Wexford, which was only about 15 miles from Leighlin. After conferring with Hooker at Leighlin, Sir Peter decided to put his cousin and heir Peter in charge of Leighlin and Idrone and to take himself to Ross to await the outcome of Hooker's negotiations with the landholders in Munster.[55] Just when or even if Carew had obtained permission from the queen to proceed with his Munster suits is not known. Perhaps when the queen allowed Carew to take part in the Essex expedition she also gave him permission to carefully re-open the Munster claims. There was, however, clearly still concern of what might happen in Munster if he did so; the promises not to meddle in Munster that Essex extracted from Carew at the end of 1573 prove that. At any event, by 1575 Carew obviously felt himself free to try to regain his family's ancient holdings in the region.

Hooker arrived in Munster just as the chief gentlemen of the county were gathered in quarter sessions, which likely dates Hooker's arrival to September 1575. The bold decision to give over Leighlin to his heir apparently convinced the gentlemen that Carew was serious about coming to live among them in Munster. Lord Courcy, the Lord Barry Oge, the O'Mahones, the O'Dricolls, and various other Anglo-Irish gentlemen and Irish chieftains, many of whom had approached Carew at the end of 1569 about coming to some settlement, all accepted Carew's claim and discussed terms with Hooker. All agreed to hold their lands from Carew at whatever "reasonable rents" Carew wished to assess. In the matter of past rent due, the gentlemen as a group agreed to give one year's rent for their combined holdings, which they estimated at 3,000 cattle valued at a mark a head, or more than £2000. Carew was to receive this rent within three months of his coming to live amongst them in Munster. They were also to furnish him from time to time with supplies for the household he would set up, a provision the practical Hooker insisted upon.[56]

When news of these agreements made its way around Cork, the chronically rebellious earl of Desmond, the chief landholder in the area, the Lords Barrymore and Roche, and several other important Munster gentlemen came to Hooker "and pretended great joy, and much gladness," that Carew was coming to live among them. They promised to meet him when he came to Munster and honourably conduct him into the county. Desmond, "extolling him very much," wrote letters to Carew "requesting that they might join in friendship and live together as good friends, whereof he would be very glad." Hooker dispatched messengers to Carew informing him of his success and urging him to come to Munster. Carew immediately hired a bark and prepared to ship his household goods, sending the messenger back overland to Hooker with the details of his plans. Hooker, meanwhile, set about doing what he did best—arranging all the practical details of Carew's transfer of residence. Advised by Davells, Hooker found a suitable house for Carew in Cork, and then travelled 10 miles to Kinsale to rent for Carew another residence, "builded after the English manner," from the town's chief magistrate. In the harbor of Cork, Hooker obtained sugar and spices from a merchant of Bristol and sack from a merchant of Exeter. The gentlemen of the region kept their promise and began to provide beef, mutton, wheat, wood, and other necessary items for the house in Cork. And so Hooker spent his days gathering these necessities and awaiting Carew's arrival in Cork.[57]

Carew never came to Cork because, in Hooker's words, God was pleased "to appoint him to another journey." Just as he was about to set out for Cork from Ross, Carew fell ill with what Hooker called "an impostumation of the bladder, which was supposed to have grown upon him for want of that ordinary purgation which nature desires." The abscess interfered with Sir Peter's ability to urinate and so debilitated him that "he lay for dead." A surgeon was called to make an incision and open the abscess, which gave Sir Peter some relief and strength enough to make the codicil to his will. A messenger was dispatched to Cork to fetch Hooker, with whom Carew especially wanted to speak. Carew lingered for another day after amending his will; he was in great pain, but endured it calmly, spending most of his time in prayer. The end came on 27 November 1575. Sir Peter's last words were a prayer. Hooker arrived two days later, too late to discover what Sir Peter had wanted to say to him.[58]

Sidney wrote to the Council in England on 15 December, the day of Carew's funeral, to inform them that "Sir Peter Carew is lately departed this world,"[59] but news of Sir Peter's death had already reached England by the first week of December. On 9 December an anonymous correspondent from Windsor informed Lord Deputy Sidney of "the great grief of many, of the death of good Sir Peter Carew." It was the opinion of all men, continued the writer, that Sir Peter was a man "of such rare virtue and singular good parts as is seldom to be found in these our days." Then the practical concerns of the living intruded, and the letter writer got to his main point; Carew had left Idrone to his cousin Peter, a young man who could hardly hope to hold the barony if he did not also have the keeping of Leighlin as Sir Peter had. The writer made suit to Sidney to continue the friendship he showed to Sir Peter by allowing his heir to hold Leighlin, and by favoring the young man with advice and counsel as to the ways and practices of Ireland, with which the younger Peter Carew was as yet unfamiliar.[60]

In Ross, the only service left for Hooker to perform for the man he called his "dear friend" was to see him "honourably interred and buried." After being disembowelled and "chested," the body remained in the house at Ross until 15 December, when it was carried by water to Waterford. The funeral was solemn and grand, attended by Lord Deputy Sidney and the entire Irish Council, as well as by the mayor and alderman of Waterford and "an infinite number of people." Hooker, in characteristic fashion, noted every detail of the funeral. The funeral procession to the church was led by soldiers and pikemen, marching two by two and pointing their guns and pikes downwards. A black-clad trumpeter, "sounding the dead sound," preceded Carew's black-clad servants, who marched also by twos and carried Sir Peter's standard, helm, crest, sword, and coat of arms. The coffin, bearing "escutcheons of his arms," came next, carried by four Carew servants. Last came the mourners, including the lord deputy and his retinue. After the sermon, the corpse was carried to the south side of the chancel, next to the altar, and there buried, the trumpeter sounding the whole time the earth was being cast into the grave, which was almost a quarter of an hour.[61]

As the coffin was lowered into the grave, the Lord deputy pronounced the following valediction:

> Here lies now, in his last rest, a most worthy, and noble, gentle knight, whose faith to his prince was never yet stained, his truth to his country never spotted, and his valientness in service never doubted—a better subject the prince never had.[62]

Queen Mary, had she been alive, might have quibbled with those sentiments, but certainly none of the mourners objected to the deputy's words. When the grave was filled, the drummers struck up and all the soldiers discharged their guns several times, filling the church with smoke and hiding the mourners from one another. Outside, the great guns of the town joined those aboard ships in the haven and those specially set up in the church-yard in firing a last salute. Next day, Carew's yellow pennons with black lions, and all his standards and accoutrements, were set up over the grave as a memorial to a man who, in Hooker's words, "left behind him many testimonies of his sincerity in religion, of his truth to his prince, faith to his country, uprightness in conversation, and just dealings with each man."[63] Hooker then left the gloomy church and stepped into the cold December darkness, ready to return once and for all to Devon.

---

[1] Hooker, "Life," p. 97.

[2] Queen Elizabeth to Sir Henry Sidney, 17 May 1570, *Sidney State Papers*, p. 127. For the Butlers' formal document of submission, see Lambeth, Carew MS 611, f. 162.

[3] Hooker, "Life," p. 97.

[4] Sir Henry Sidney to Sir Peter Carew, 28 May 1570, PRO, SP63/30/106.

5   Sir Peter Carew's Suits Concerning His Irish Lands, Undated, Lambeth, Carew MS
    605, f. 45. For the queen's response to these suits, see Queen Elizabeth to Sir Henry
    Sidney, 30 June 1570, *Sidney State Papers*, pp. 134-35.

6   Petitions and Offers of Sir Peter Carew Concerning His Irish Lands, 1571, Lambeth,
    Carew MS 606, f. 97. For particulars of Carew's claim to the Dullogh, see John
    Hooker's Notes on Sir Peter Carew's Title to the Dullogh, Lambeth, Carew MS 606,
    f. 80.

7   Queen Elizabeth to Sir William Fitzwilliam, 21 February 1572, Lambeth, Carew MS
    605, f. 30.

8   Order of Lord Deputy and Irish Council Concerning the Cess on Idrone, 16 February
    1573, Lambeth, Carew MS 605, ff. 30a-31; John Hooker's Notes on Sir Peter
    Carew's Suit for Freedom from Cess for Idrone, 1571, Lambeth, Carew MS 606, ff.
    75-77.

9   John Hooker's Notes and Transcriptions of Documents Relating to the Tallon Suit,
    1572-73, Lambeth, Carew MS 606, ff. 66-68.

10 John Hooker to Sir Peter Carew, 20 January 1573, Lambeth, Carew MS 605, f. 24.

11 John Hooker's Notes and Transcriptions of Documents Relating to the Tallon Suit,
    1572-73, Lambeth, Carew MS 606, ff. 69-73.

12 John Hooker to Sir Peter Carew, 23 October 1572, Lambeth, Carew MS 605, f. 38.

13 John Hooker to Sir Peter Carew, 20 January 1573, Lambeth, Carew MS 605, f. 24.

14 APC, VIII, p. 18.

15 Queen's Commission for Meering and Bounding Idrone, 14 September 1572,
    Lambeth, Carew MS 606, ff. 77-78; Report of the Boundary Commission, 6 October
    1572, Lambeth, Carew MS 606, ff. 78-79.

16 Report of the Boundary Commission, 6 October 1572, Lambeth, Carew MS 606, ff.
    78-79; *Calendar of Patent and Close Rolls of Chancery in Ireland*, pp. 549-50.

17 John Hooker to Sir Peter Carew, 20 January 1573, Lambeth, Carew MS 605, f. 24.

18 Hooker, "Life," pp. 97-98.

19 John Hooker to Sir Peter Carew, 23 October 1572, Lambeth, Carew MS 605, f. 38.

20 Lord Deputy Fitzwilliam and Chancellor Weston to Lord President Perrot, 26
    February 1573, Lambeth, Carew MS 605, f. 34.

21 John Hooker to Sir Peter Carew, 20 January 1573, Lambeth, Carew MS 605, f. 24.

22 After her liaison with the king, Mary Berkeley, Perrot's mother, married Thomas Perrot, who held lands in Pembrokeshire that eventually passed to the son his wife bore in 1527. Sir John Perrot also became the owner of the castle and lordship of Carew in Pembrokeshire, one of the most ancient Carew family holdings. Carew Castle had passed out of the family's hands when Sir Peter's grandfather, Sir Edmund, pledged it to Sir Rhys ap Thomas for money borrowed to support Sir Edmund's participation in Henry VIII's French campaign of 1513. When Sir Edmund failed to return from that campaign, Sir Rhys took up the pledge. The castle eventually came to the Crown through attainder; Perrot's claim to Carew Castle, which was first put forward in 1554, was based on Thomas Perrot's descent from Sir Rhys ap Thomas. Because of the differences Perrot, who was a Protestant, had with the Marian regime, his control of the castle was not secured until about 1562. Perrot extensively rebuilt the ancient Carew property and made it his seat. For more information on Perrot, see Hasler, *House of Commons*, III, p. 206 and *DNB*, pp. 906-07.

23 Lord President Perrot to Lord Deputy Fitzwilliam, 19 March 1573, PRO, SP63/41/40.

24 Ibid.

25 Lord Deputy Fitzwilliam and the Irish Council to Queen Elizabeth, 10 June 1573, PRO, SP63/41/37.

26 Lord Deputy Fitzwilliam and the Irish Council to the English Council, 10 June 1573, PRO, SP63/41/41.

27 Hooker, "Life," p. 99.

28 John Hooker to Sir Peter Carew, 20 January 1573, Lambeth, Carew MS 605, f. 24.

29 Ibid.

30 In their letter to the queen on 10 June, the deputy and Irish Council announced that they had taken order "for reformation of the cess of Odrone." See Lord Deputy Fitzwilliam and the Irish Council to Queen Elizabeth, 10 June 1573, PRO, SP63/41/37.

31 John Hooker to Sir Peter Carew, 8 March 1573, Lambeth, Carew MS 605, f. 208.

32 Queen Elizabeth to Lord Deputy Fitzwilliam, 14 March 1573, PRO, SP63/39/129.

33 Sir Peter Carew to the Lord Deputy, Undated, Lambeth, Carew MS 605, f. 42. In the closing to the letter, Carew wrote that he had up to that point followed his Irish suits three years in England and two years in Ireland, which would date the letter to about August 1573 if, as is likely, Carew placed the start of his Irish suits at the time

of his arrival in Ireland in August 1568. In a petition to the Council dated 1573, Carew asks again for relief of cess and puts the cost to him of defending Leighlin from the Butlers in 1569 at £3000. See *Calendar of the Carew Manuscripts*, vol. I (Nendeln, Liechtenstein: Kraus Reprint, 1974), p. 451.

34 Petitions and Offers of Sir Peter Carew, Undated, Lambeth, Carew MS 605, ff. 42-43. These petitions probably also date from 1573.

35 Walter Bourchier Devereux, ed., *Lives and Letters of the Devereux Earls of Essex, in the Reigns of Elizabeth, James I, and Charles I 1540-1646*, vol. I (London: John Murray, 1853), pp. 26-29, 33.

36 Hooker, "Life," pp. 99-100.

37 Sir Peter Carew to Lord Burghley, 16 September 1573, PRO, SP63/42/50.

38 Sir Peter Carew to Lord Burghley, 29 September 1573, PRO, SP63/42/66.

39 Hooker, "Life," p. 100.

40 Earl of Essex to the English Council, 2 November 1573, PRO, SP63/42/144.

41 For Tremayne's life, see Hasler, *House of Commons*, III, p. 526. Tremayne's brother Andrew had been one of Carew's fellow passengers on the bark that took him into exile in France in 1554.

42 Sir Peter Carew to Edmund Tremayne, 6 February 1574, PRO, SP63/45/9. Sir Thomas Smith's ill will stemmed from his belief that Carew had persuaded Essex to encroach upon his grant of the Ards peninsula in northern Ireland. Smith and his son obtained the Council's approval and the queen's grant of the Ards on which to plant an English colony. This private venture went sour when the government refused to support it with troops for fear of stirring rebellion. Smith's son suffered a horrible death at the hands of the Irish in the autumn of 1573, and Sir Thomas was left angry and bitter at many people. For more details, see Edmund Tremayne to Lord Burghley, 6 March 1574, PRO, SP63/45/7 and Ellis, *Tudor Ireland*, pp. 266-67.

43 Edmund Tremayne to Lord Burghley, 6 March 1574, PRO, SP63/45/7.

44 Hooker, "Life," p. 100.

45 Devereux, *Lives and Letters*, I, p. 54.

46 Instructions to Nicholas Malbie, 8 April 1575, Lambeth, Carew MS 628, f. 217a.

47 Queen Elizabeth to Sir Peter Carew, 12 April 1575, Lambeth, Carew MS 628, f. 290a.

48 Will of Sir Peter Carew, PRO, PCC 1 Carew, PROB 11/58.

49 Queen Elizabeth to the Earl of Essex, 6 August 1575, Lambeth, Carew MS 628, f. 231a.

50 Queen Elizabeth to Sir Peter Carew, 6 August 1575, Lambeth, Carew MS 628, f. 291.

51 Devereux, *Lives and Letters*, I, p. 120.

52 Accounts of Sir Edward Fyton, Treasurer at War for Ireland, 30 September 1575, Lambeth, Carew MS 628, f. 244.

53 Warrant from Lord Deputy Fitzwilliam to Robert Harepool, 12 August 1575, Lambeth, Carew MS 605, f. 49

54 Sir Peter Carew to Lord Deputy Fitzwilliam, 9 September 1575, Lambeth, Carew MS 605, f. 50.

55 Hooker, "Life," pp. 100-01. After relating all Sir Peter's close brushes with death, Hooker could not refrain from recording that the vessel which brought him to Ireland was shortly thereafter lost at sea with all hands in a terrible storm.

56 Ibid., pp. 101-04.

57 Ibid., pp. 104-05.

58 Ibid., pp. 105-06.

59 Sir Henry Sidney to the English Council, 15 December 1575, Lambeth, Carew MS 601, f. 43.

60 Unknown to Sir Henry Sidney, 9 December 1575, PRO, SP63/54/31.

61 Hooker, "Life," pp. 107-09.

62 Ibid., p.109.

63 Ibid., pp.108-09.

EPILOGUE

Sir Gawen Carew had shared deeply in the lives of his nephews Sir George and Sir Peter. He was often treated more like an older brother than an uncle. This close association has even misled some modern historians into calling Sir Gawen and Sir Peter brothers.[1] Sir Gawen outlived his nephew Sir Peter by almost a decade, dying sometime between the making of his will in October 1583 and the proving of the will in June 1585. He was about 80 years old at the time of his death. Despite three marriages, Sir Gawen, like both his nephews, had no children.

Although rarely at court after 1560, Sir Gawen continued to serve the queen in various capacities in Devon almost up to the time of his death. Even as late as March 1582, Sir Gawen served with the earl of Bedford and others on a commission to reform abuses in the postal service to the West Country. Sir Gawen was closely associated with the Protestant earl of Bedford during the years after 1560, and Carew signaled his close relationship with Bedford by naming the earl overseer of his will, "in token of the great love and good will that I have borne and do bear unto his lordship." Carew also bequeathed to the earl a covered cup of silver gilt, upon the cover of which were graven Carew's arms.[2]

Sir Gawen's will of 11 October 1583 begins by commending its maker "to the almighty and everlasting God. . . with assured hope of salvation in Christ's blood by the merits of his passion and death." After this Protestant opening, Carew directs that he be buried in St. Peter's Cathedral in Exeter should he die within 20 miles of the city. The tomb to be raised over his body was not to cost more than £40 and was to bear Sir Gawen's arms, and the arms of all three of his wives. Sir Gawen left his leased lands in Devon and Cornwall and all his "goods, chattels, jewels, plate, and household stuff" to his wife Elizabeth. At her death, all moveable property and the unexpired portions of all leases were to pass to his remaining nephew George Carew, who was described in the will as "of Leighlin in Catherlough," having come into possession of Idrone at the death of his elder brother in 1580.[3]

Sir Gawen's most important holdings were leases of former monastic properties in Cornwall and Devon obtained in the 1540s. The will refers to Henry VIII, from whom most of these properties were acquired, as "my late sovereign lord and master," phrasing that betrays an affection for the late king that probably neither Sir Gawen nor Sir Peter felt for any of his children.[4] Neither a sickly boy nor two women could match the dazzling king of their youths who had begun and made their careers and fortunes. By serving that monarch and his children, Sir Gawen Carew, although born only a fourth son, had done well in life.

Although named executor of her husband's estate by his will, Lady Margaret declined the office, and administration of the will was granted to Sir Peter's kinsman and servant John Wood of Luppitt in Devon.[5] But Wood's appointment on 20 February 1576 did not prevent Lady Margaret from being embroiled in the ongoing disputes and litigation concerning her late husband's extensive debts. A 1578 petition to Secretary Walsingham from Martin Constable, one of Carew's creditors, rehearsed the history of Sir Peter's debts since his demise. Constable claimed to have been a suitor to the Council for the past three years, asking continuously that the provisions of Carew's will calling for the payment of debts out of the revenues of Idrone be performed. Constable was himself owed £800 by the late Sir Peter, and stood bound for an additional £2000 of Carew's debts to other creditors. Constable complained that he had followed his suit at his own charge without help from the other creditors who were now attempting to have themselves paid before him. The petition asks that Constable be paid first, either by the other creditors or otherwise, that Constable be relieved of the bonds for Carew's other debts, and that the creditors to whom he is bound be paid before all others.[6] Despite Constable's petition and the intervention of the Council in the matter, the problem of Carew's debts remained unresolved.

Lady Margaret remarried in 1579, taking Sir John Clifton of Barrington in Somerset as her third husband.[7] In April 1580, both Lady Margaret and Clifton were named in a petition to the Council that called upon the feoffees of Idrone to fulfill the terms of Carew's will and settle the debts owed to the petitioners. The petition was shown to the queen herself, and the Council ordered Lady Margaret, Clifton, and the feoffees (among whom was John Hooker) to see that the petitioners were satisfied or show cause why they should not do so.[8] A year later, the Council ordered Clifton to call together the feoffees and cause them to make a lease of Idrone out of which the creditors demands could be met. But the Council's order contained no provisions for safeguarding the rights of George Carew, Sir Peter's heir to Idrone. Therefore, in September 1581, the Council agreed that George might himself collect the revenues of the barony and take order for applying the funds to his late cousin's debts. The feoffees were ordered to take bonds of George for the proper collecting and paying of the revenues, and were to demand of him a yearly accounting under oath of all the revenues collected.[9] Most of Sir Peter's debts were still outstanding when Lady Margaret died on 6 May 1583, eight years after her second husband.[10]

When Sir Peter Carew returned to Ireland in 1573, he brought with him his two young cousins, Peter and George Carew, sons of his uncle George, who died in 1583 at age 85. Both sons of George Carew stayed in Ireland after their cousin's death. Peter, the elder brother, inherited Idrone and his cousin's position at Leighlin. George, who had attended Oxford in 1572, was only about 17 when he witnessed Sir Peter's death in November 1575.[11] Both young men entered the queen's service in

Ireland; Peter obtaining knighthood from the lord deputy in September 1579, and George, also from the lord deputy, in February 1586.[12] The younger Sir Peter Carew died on 25 August 1580, in an ambush unleashed by Irish rebels on the deputy's army as it entered a narrow, wooded defile.

Idrone passed to the younger brother, George Carew, who got into serious trouble in 1583 for stabbing to death a man who was implicated in the death of his brother. George won his way back to favor in 1586, when Lord Deputy Sir John Perrot, the former president of Munster who had discouraged the queen from allowing Sir Peter to proceed with his Munster land claims in 1573, sent him to England to report the current state of Ireland. In performing this duty, he favorably impressed both the queen and Burghley. From 1586 until the end of the reign, Sir George Carew was to distinguish himself in the queen's service, especially in Ireland,[13] where he was appointed master of ordnance in 1588 and lord president of Munster in 1600. He was one of Lord Deputy Mountjoy's chief lieutenants in the crushing of the Irish rebellion and especially distinguished himself against the attempted landings by Spanish troops at Kinsale. He dealt ruthlessly with the Irish of Munster, and by 1603 could report the region largely pacified.[14]

Carew received immediate favor from James I. He became the queen's vice chamberlain and receiver of her revenues in October 1603. In 1605, the king created him Baron Carew of Clopton House, a property belonging to his wife, Joyce Clopton. He held various other appointments throughout the reign, including councilor for the colony of Virginia, governor of Guernsey, and privy councilor. Charles I created him earl of Totnes in February 1626. He died at his house in London in March 1629. Like his cousins, Sir George had no children; his heir was his niece Anne Carew, only daughter of his brother Sir Peter.[15]

Sir George Carew, unlike his cousin Sir Peter, had antiquarian interests. He was a close friend at the Jacobean court of the antiquaries Robert Cotton and William Camden. They perhaps helped him to order and annotate his own letters and papers, and encouraged him to purchase and collect other historical documents, especially those relating to Ireland and to his family. Many of the letters and documents generated by Sir Peter Carew and John Hooker during the Irish enterprise of 1568-75 survived as part of Sir George's carefully preserved collection. Hooker's biography of Sir Peter Carew also remained safe among Sir George's papers. On Carew's death, his papers passed to Sir Thomas Stafford, who had served with Sir George in Ireland and was reputed to be his illegitimate son. From Stafford, most of the Carew papers passed into the possession of Archbishop Laud, who deposited them in the Lambeth Library where they are still found today.[16]

---

[1] See, for instance, Murial St. Clare Byrne's misidentification of Sir Gawen in her commentary to volume VI of the *Lisle Letters*, p. 268. Ms. St. Clare Byrne also has Sir Gawen escaping to France with Sir Peter in 1554.

[2] Will of Sir Gawen Carew, PRO, PCC 34 Brudenell, PROB 11/68.

[3] Ibid. Sir Gawen was buried in Exeter Cathedral, in a small chapel near the Lady Chapel on the north side of the cathedral. A monument was raised in 1589 to the memory of Sir Gawen, his second wife Mary, and his second nephew named Peter, the eldest son of his brother George. The inscription is later than 1589, for it calls the younger Peter's brother George Carew baron of Clopton and earl of Totnes, which titles George did not acquire until the reigns of James I and Charles I, respectively. The inscription may have been added or extended when the tomb was refurbished by descendants of the Carew family in 1857. Although buried in Ireland, Sir Peter Carew also has a monument in Exeter Cathedral—a plaque on the south wall depicting Sir Peter kneeling in prayer.

4   Ibid.

5   Hasler, *House of Commons*, I, p. 542.

6   *Cal.SP Dom.*, Elizabeth, III, pp. 553-54.

7   *The Complete Peerage,* vol. XII (London: St. Catherine Press, 1953), p. 604.

8   APC, XI, pp. 438-39.

9   Ibid., XII, p. 363; XIII, p. 195.

10 *Complete Peerage*, XII, p. 604.

11 *Cal. Carew*, I, p. x.

12 Shaw, *Knights of England*, II, pp. 80, 84.

13 Hasler, *House of Commons*, I, p. 540.

14 "George Carew, Baron Carew of Clopton and Earl of Totnes," *DNB*, pp. 960-62; Hasler, *House of Commons*, I, pp. 540-410.

15 Ibid.

16 Ibid.

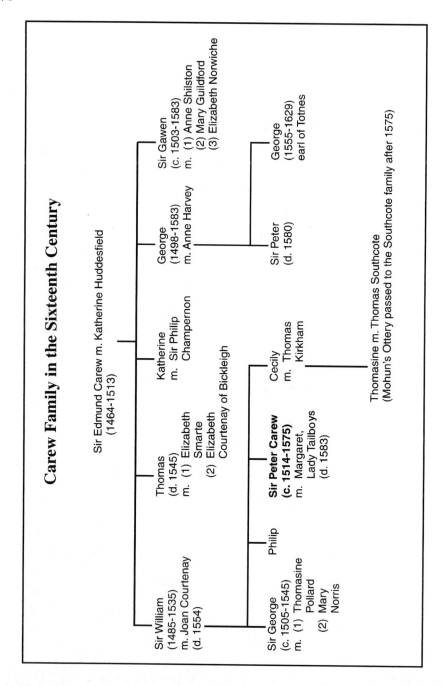

Carew Family in the Sixteenth Century

Sir Edmund Carew m. Katherine Huddesfield
(1464-1513)

Sir William
(1485-1535)
m. Joan Courtenay
(d. 1554)

Thomas
(d. 1545)
m. (1) Elizabeth
Smarte
(2) Elizabeth
Courtenay of Bickleigh

Katherine
m. Sir Philip
Champernon

George
(1498-1583)
m. Anne Harvey

Sir Gawen
(c. 1503-1583)
m. (1) Anne Shilston
(2) Mary Guildford
(3) Elizabeth Norwiche

Sir George
(c. 1505-1545)
m. (1) Thomasine
Pollard
(2) Mary
Norris

Philip

**Sir Peter Carew
(c. 1514-1575)**
m. Margaret,
Lady Tailboys
(d. 1583)

Cecily
m. Thomas
Kirkham

Sir Peter
(d. 1580)

George
(1555-1629)
earl of Totnes

Thomasine m. Thomas Southcote
(Mohun's Ottery passed to the Southcote family after 1575)

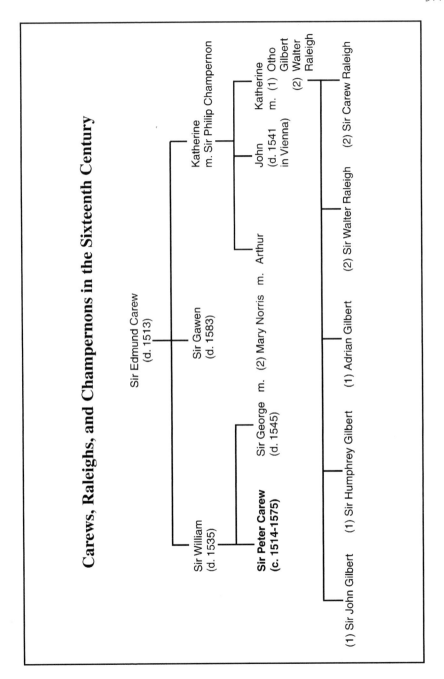

Carews, Raleighs, and Champernons in the Sixteenth Century

BIBLIOGRAPHY

Manuscript Sources

Archiepiscopal Library, Lambeth Palace, London:
Carew MSS 601, 605, 606, 611, 618, 628, 635

British Library, London:
Additional MSS 4797, 48017
Cotton MSS Calig. E IV, Titus B XII, Titus F VI, Vitellius B II
Egerton MS 2986
Harleian MSS 523, 5827
Lansdowne MS 155
Stowe MSS 141, 571

Cambridge University Library:
MS Mm. 1.32 (Memorandum book of John Hooker 1568-69)

Westcountry Studies Library, Exeter:
Abstracts of Inquisitions Post Mortem
       Thomas Carew, File 12(18)
       Joan Carew, File 26(55)
       Nicholas Carew, File 32(27)
       Nicholas Carew File 37(38)
       Nicholas Carew, File 129(35)
"Copies of Transcripts and Extracts from Wills and Other Records Collected by
       Miss Olive Moger," Vol. III
       Will of Sir William Carew

Devon County Record Office, Exeter:
MS 123M, Feoffment in Trust, Sir Edmund Carew
MS 484M, Manor of Mamhead Records
Calendar of the Archives of the City of Exeter
Calendar of the Archives of the Borough of Dartmouth
Exeter City Library. *Calendar of Deeds and Documents.* Nos. 68332-68522
Exeter City Library. *Precis of Deeds and Documents.* Nos. 30000-30250

Public Record Office, London:
Chancery, Inquisitions Post Mortem (C142)
Court of Requests, Bills of Complaint (REQ2)

Exchequer, Inquisitions Post Mortem (E150)
King's Bench, *Baga de secretis* (KB8)
King's Bench, *Placita coram rege* (KB27)
Prerogative Court of Canterbury, Wills (PROB11)
Star Chamber Proceedings, Henry VIII (STAC2)
Star Chamber Proceedings, Edward VI (STAC3)
State Papers Domestic, Henry VIII (SP1)
State Papers Domestic, Edward VI (SP10)
State Papers Domestic, Mary and Philip and Mary (SP11)
State Papers Domestic, Elizabeth (SP12)
State Papers, Ireland, Elizabeth (SP63)
State Papers Foreign, Mary and Philip and Mary (SP69)

Royal Irish Academy, Dublin:
MS 24.K.20 (Copies of Sir Henry Sidney's letters)

Contemporary Works, Calendars, and Other Printed Sources

Acts of the Privy Council of England. Edited by J.R. Dasent. Vols. I, III-VIII, X-XIII. London, 1890-1949.

The Antient History and Description of the City of Exeter. Exeter, 1765.

Bindoff, S.T., ed. *The House of Commons 1509-1558.* 3 vols. London: History of Parliament Trust, 1982.

Burke, John. *A Genealogical and Heraldic History of the Commoners of Great Britain and Ireland.* Vol. 1. London, 1836.

Calendar of Inquisitions Post Mortem for Cornwall and Devon. Edited by Edward Alexander Fry. Exeter: Devon and Cornwall Record Society, 1906.

Calendar of Letters, Despatches, and State Papers Relating to the Negotiations Between England and Spain. Edited by Royall Tyler et al. Vols. II-VIII, XII-XIII. London, 1969.

Calendar of Letters, Despatches, and State Papers Relating to the Negotiations Between England and Spain, Elizabeth. Vols. I, II. London, 1892-99.

Calendar of Patent and Close Rolls of Chancery in Ireland, 5 Henry VIII to 18 Elizabeth. Vol. I. Edited by James Morrin. Dublin, 1861.

Calendar of Patent Rolls, Edward VI. 5 vols. London: HMSO, 1924-29.

Calendar of Patent Rolls, Elizabeth. Vols. I-VIII. Nendeln, Liechtenstein: Kraus Reprint, 1976.

Calendar of Patent Rolls, Mary and Philip and Mary. 6 vols. London: HMSO, 1936-39.

Calendar of State Papers, Domestic, 1547-1580. London: HMSO, 1856.

Calendar of State Papers, Domestic, Edward VI. London: HMSO, 1992.

Calendar of State Papers, Foreign, Edward VI. Edited by W.B. Turnbull. London, 1861.

Calendar of State Papers, Foreign, Elizabeth. Vols. I-VII. Nendeln, Liechtenstein: Kraus Reprint, 1966-69.

Calendar of State Papers, Foreign, Mary. Edited by W.B. Turnbull. London, 1861.

Calendar of State Papers and Manuscripts, Relating to English Affairs, Existing in the Archives and Collections of Venice. Edited by R. Brown et al. Vols. VI, VII. London: HMSO, 1864-98.

Calendar of State Papers Relating to Ireland. Edited by H.C. Hamilton, E.G. Atkinson, and R.P. Mahaffy. 11 vols. London, 1860-1912.

Calendar of State Papers Relating to Scotland. Edited by J. Bain et al. Vols. I, IV. Edinburgh, 1898-1952.

Calendar of the Carew Manuscripts. Edited by J.S. Brewer and William Bullen. 6 vols. Nendeln, Liechtenstein: Kraus Reprint, 1974.

Calendar of the Close Rolls, Henry VII. 2 vols. London: HMSO, 1954, 1963.

Carew, Richard. "The Survey of Cornwall." In *Richard Carew of Antony: The Survey of Cornwall etc.* Edited by F.E. Halliday. London: Andrew Melrose, 1953.

Chambers, D.S., ed. *Faculty Office Registers 1534-1549.* Oxford: Clarendon Press, 1966.

Chronicle of Calais. Camden Series #35. London: Camden Society, 1846.

The Complete Peerage. Vol. XII. London: St. Catherine Press, 1953.

Cotton, W. and Henry Woollcombe, eds. *Gleanings from the Municipal and Cathedral Records Relative to the History of Exeter.* Exeter: James Townsend, 1877.

"Count de Feria's Dispatch to Philip II, 14 November 1558." Edited and translated by M.J. Rodriguez-Salgado and Simon Adams. *Camden Miscellany XXVIII.* 4th Series. London: Royal Historical Society, 1984, pp. 328-37.

Devereux, Walter Bourchier, ed. *Lives and Letters of the Devereux Earls of Essex in the Reigns of Elizabeth, James I and Charles I 1540-1646.* Vol. I. London: John Murray, 1853.

Devon and Cornwall Notes and Queries. [Carew Family Records.] Vol. 20 (1938/39).

"A Diary of the Expedition of 1544." *English Historical Review* 16 (1901): 503-07.

Ellis, Henry, ed. *Original Letters Illustrative of English History.* Series I. Vol. I. London: Harding, Triphook, and Lepard, 1825.

Entick, John. *A New Naval History: or, the Compleat View of the British Marine.* London, 1757.

Harte, Walter J., ed. *Gleanings from the Common Place Book of John Hooker, Relating to the City of Exeter (1485-1590).* Exeter, 1926.

Hartley, T.E., ed. *Proceedings in the Parliaments of Elizabeth I.* Vol. I: *1558-1581.* Leicester: Leicester University Press, 1981.

Hasler, P.W., ed. *The House of Commons 1558-1603.* 3 vols. London: History of Parliament Trust, 1981.

Historical Manuscripts Commission. "Acts of the Privy Council in Ireland, 1556-71." *Manuscripts of Charles Haliday of Dublin, Fifteenth Report,* Appendix 3. Edited by J.T. Gilbert. London, 1897.

——. *Earl of Egmont's Manuscripts, Seventh Report.* London, 1879.

——. *Report on the Records of the City of Exeter.* London, 1916.

——. *Salisbury Manuscripts, Ninth Report,* Appendixes 4 and 5. London, 1883, 1889.

Hooker, John. *The Description of the Citie of Excester.* Edited by W.J. Harte, J.W. Schopp, and H. Tapley-Soper. Exeter: Devon and Cornwall Record Society, 1919.

——. "The Discourse and Discovery of the Life of Sir Peter Carew." In *The Life and Times of Sir Peter Carew, Kt.* Edited by John Maclean. London: Bell and Daldy, 1857.

——. "John Hooker's Diary, or Journal, January 17 to February 23, 1568-9." In C. Litton Falkiner, "The Parliament of Ireland under the Tudor Sovereigns: With Some Notices of the Speeches of the Irish House of Commons." *Proceedings of the Royal Irish Academy* 25 (1904-05): 563-66.

——. "Hooker's Journal" [for the Parliament of 1571]. In *Proceedings in the Parliaments of Elizabeth I.* Edited by T.E. Hartley. Vol. I. Leicester: Leicester University Press, 1981, pp. 243-58.

——. "Life of Sir Peter Carew." In the *Calendar of the Carew Manuscripts.* Vol. 1.Nendeln, Liechtenstein: Kraus Reprint, 1974, pp. lxvii-cxviii.

——. "Life of Sir Peter Carew, of Mohun Ottery, co. Devon." *Archaeologia* 28 (1840): 96-151.

——. "The Order and Usage of the Keeping of a Parlement in England." In *Parliament in Elizabethan England: John Hooker's Order and Usage.* Edited by Vernon F. Snow. New Haven, Conn.: Yale University Press, 1977, pp. 115-94.

——. *An Original Manuscript of John Hooker, Chamberlain of the City of Exeter, 1555.* Edited by Herbert Edward Reynolds. (Now in the possession of the Dean and Chapter of Exeter Cathedral [no. 3520]). Belfast, 1787.

Howells, T.B., comp. *A Complete Collection of State Trials.* Vol. I. London: Hansard, 1816.

Hughes, Paul and James Larkin, eds. *Tudor Royal Proclamations.* 3 vols. New Haven, Conn.: Yale University Press, 1964-69.

Izacke, Richard. *Remarkable Antiquities of the City of Exeter.* London, 1681.

Jordan, W.K., ed. *The Chronicle and Political Papers of King Edward VI.* Ithaca, N.Y.: Cornell University Press, 1966.

Journal of the House of Commons, 1547-1628. London, 1803.

Kaulek, Jean, ed. *Correspondance Politique de MM. De Castillon et de Marillac: Ambassadeurs de France en Angleterre.* Geneva: Slatkine Reprints, 1971.

Leland, John. *The Itinerary.* Edited by Lucy Toulmin Smith. 5 vols. Carbondale: Southern Illinois University Press, 1964.

Letters and Papers (Foreign and Domestic) of the Reign of Henry VIII. Edited by James Gairdner et al. 21 vols. London, 1862-1932.

Letters and Papers Illustrative of the Reigns of Richard III and Henry VII. Edited by James Gairdner. 2 vols. London, 1861, 1863.

Maclean, John, ed. *The Life and Times of Sir Peter Carew, Kt.* London: Bell and Daldy, 1857.

Metcalfe, W. *A Book of Knights.* 2 vols. London, 1885.

Myers, James P., Jr., ed. *Elizabethan Ireland: A Selection of Writings by Elizabethan Writers on Ireland.* Hamden, Conn.: Archon Books, 1983.

Nichols, John Gough, ed. *The Chronicle of Queen Jane and of the First Two Years of Mary.* London: Camden Society, 1850.

—, ed. *The Diary of Henry Machyn.* London: Camden Society, 1848.

—, ed. *Literary Remains of King Edward the Sixth.* 2 vols. London, 1857.

O'Laidhin, Tomas, ed. *Sidney State Papers, 1565-70.* Dublin: Irish Manuscripts Commission, 1962.

Pocock, Nicholas, ed. *Troubles Connected with the Prayer Book Rebellion of 1549.* London: Camden Society, 1884.

Pole, Sir William. *Collections Towards a Description of the County of Devon.* London, 1791.

Ponet, John. *A Short Treatise of Politike Power.* 1556. Facsimile Edition. Menston, England: Scolar Press, 1970.

Quinn, D.B., ed. "Additional Sidney State Papers." *Analecta Hibernica,* no. 26 Irish Manuscript Commission (1970): 91-102.

Robinson, Hastings, ed. *Original Letters Relative to the English Reformation.* Cambridge: Cambridge University Press, 1846.

Rowe, Margery M. and Andrew M. Jackson, eds. *Exeter Freemen 1266-1967.* Exeter: Devon and Cornwall Record Society, 1973.

St. Care Byrne, Muriel, ed., *The Lisle Letters.* 6 vols. Chicago: University of Chicago Press, 1981.

Selve, Odet de. *Correspondence Politique.* Edited by G. Lefevre Pontalis, Paris: F. Alcan, 1888.

Shaw, William A. *The Knights of England.* Vol. II, *Knights Bachelors.* London, 1906.

Snell, Lawrence S., ed. *The Chantry Certificates for Devon and the City of Exeter.*
    Exeter: James Townsend and Sons, Ltd., 1963.
——. *The Suppression of the Religious Foundations of Devon and Cornwall.* Marazion,
    Cornwall: Wordens of Cornwall Ltd., 1967.
Snow, Vernon F., ed. *Holinshed's Chronicles of England, Scotland and Ireland.*
    (Hooker's 1587 edition). Vols. III, VI. London, 1808. Reprint, New
    York: AMS Press, Inc., 1976.
——, ed. *Parliament in Elizabethan England: John Hooker's* Order and Usage. New
    Haven, Conn.: Yale University Press, 1977.
State Papers of King Henry VIII. 11 vols. London: G. Eyre and A. Strahan, 1830-
    52.
Stoate, T.L., ed. *Devon Lay Subsidy Rolls 1524-7.* Bristol, 1979.
Strype, John. *The Historical and Biographical Works of John Strype.* Vol. 9, *Life of the
    Learned John Cheke.* Oxford: Clarendon Press, 1821.
Tomlins, T.E., ed. *The Statutes of the Realm.* Vol. IV London: The Record
    Commission, 1810-22.
Transactions of the Devonshire Association. [Carew Family and Exeter City Records.]
    Vols. 33 (1901), 67 (1935), 69 (1937). Plymouth and Exeter.
Vertot, René Aubert de, ed. *Ambassades des Messieurs de Noailles en Angleterre.* Vols.
    II-IV. Leyden, 1763.
Vivian, J.L., ed. *The Visitations of the Country of Devon.* Exeter, 1895.
Wriothesley, Charles. *A Chronicle of England During the Reigns of the Tudors.* Edited
    by W.D. Hamilton. Camden Society, New Series, #11, #20. London,
    1875, 1877.
Youings, Joyce, ed. *Devon Monastic Lands: Calendar of Particulars for Grants 1536-
    1558.* Torquay, Devon: Devon and Cornwall Record Society, 1955.

Secondary Works: Books

Andrews, K.R., Canny, N.P., and Hair, P.E.H., eds. *The Westward Enterprise:
    English Activities in Ireland, the Atlantic and America 1480-1650.*
    Detroit: Wayne State University Press, 1979.
Beer, Barrett L. *Northumberland: The Political Career of John Dudley, Earl of
    Warwick and Duke of Northumberland.* Kent, Ohio: Kent State
    University Press, 1973.
——. *Rebellion and Riot: Popular Disorder in England during the Reign of Edward VI.*
    Kent, OH: Kent State University Press, 1982.
Berleth, Richard. *The Twilight Lords: An Irish Chronicle.* New York: Barnes and
    Noble Books, 1994.
Bettey, J.H. *The Suppression of the Monasteries in the West Country.* Gloucester, Alan

Sutton, 1989.

Boggis, R.J.E. *A History of the Diocese of Exeter*. Exeter, 1922.

Bush, Michael L. *The Government Policy of Protector Somerset*. Montreal: McGill-Queens University Press, 1975.

Canny, Nicholas P. *The Elizabethan Conquest of Ireland: A Pattern Established 1565-76*. New York: Barnes and Noble Books, 1976.

Caraman, Philip. *The Western Rising 1549: The Prayer Book Rebellion*. Exeter: Westcountry Books, 1994.

Cornwall, Julian. *Revolt of the Peasantry 1549*. London: Routledge and Kegan Paul, 1977.

Curtis, Edmund. *A History of Ireland*. 6th ed. London: Routledge, 1988.

——. *Ireland in the Age of the Tudors: The Destruction of Hiberno-Norman Civilization*. London: Croom Helm, 1977.

Ellis, Steven G. *Tudor Ireland: Crown, Community and the Conflict of Cultures, 1470-1603*. London, Longman, 1985.

Elton, G.R. *The Parliament of England, 1559-1581*. Cambridge: Cambridge University Press, 1989.

Emmison, F.G. *Tudor Secretary: Sir William Petre at Court and Home*. London: Phillimore, 1961.

Falls, Cyril. *Elizabeth's Irish Wars*. London: Methuen, 1950.

Fletcher, Anthony. *Tudor Rebellions*. 2nd ed. London: Longman, 1979.

Froude, J.A. *History of England from the Fall of Wolsey to the Death of Elizabeth*. New York: Charles Scribner's Sons, 1881.

Gammon, Samuel Rhea. *Statesman and Schemer: William, First Lord Paget, Tudor Minister*. Hamden, Conn.: Archon Books, 1973.

Garrett, Christina Hallowell. *The Marian Exiles: A Study in the Origins of Elizabethan Puritanism*. Cambridge: Cambridge University Press, 1938.

Graves, MichaelA.R. *The Tudor Parliaments: Crown, Lords and Commons, 1485-1603*. London: Longman, 1992.

Gray, Todd, Margery Rowe, and Audrey Erskine, eds. *Tudor and Stuart Devon: The Common Estate and Government*. Exeter: University of Exeter Press, 1992.

Guy, John. *Tudor England*. Oxford: Oxford University Press, 1988.

Haigh, Christopher, ed. *The Reign of Elizabeth I*. Athens: The University of Georgia Press, 1987.

Halliday, F.E., ed. *Richard Carew of Antony: The Survey of Cornwall etc*. London: Andrew Melrose, 1953.

Harbison, E. Harris. *Rival Ambassadors at the Court of Queen Mary*. Princeton, N.J.: Princeton University Press, 1940.

Hoak, D.E. *The King's Council in the Reign of Edward VI*. Cambridge: Cambridge

University Press, 1976

Hoskins, W.G. *The Age of Plunder: The England of Henry VIII 1500-1547*. London: Longman, 1976.

—. *Devon*. Newton Abbot, Devon: David & Charles, 1972.

—. *Old Devon*. Newton Abbot, Devon: David and Charles, 1966.

—. *Two Thousand Years in Exeter*. Chichester: Phillimore, 1974.

Hosley, Richard, ed. *Shakespeare's Holinshed*. New York: G.P. Putnam's Sons, 1968.

Izon, John. *Sir Thomas Stucley, c. 1525-1578, Traitor Extraordinary*. London: Andrew Melrose, 1956.

Johnson, Paul. *Elizabeth I*. New York: Holt, Rinehart and Winston, 1974.

—. *Ireland: A Concise History from the Twelfth Century to the Present Day*. Chicago: Academy Chicago Publishers, 1980.

Jones, Norman. *The Birth of the Elizabethan Age: England in the 1560s*. Oxford: Blackwell, 1993.

Jordan, W.K. *Edward VI: The Young King The Protectorship of the Duke of Somerset*. Cambridge, Mass.: Harvard University Press, 1968.

—. *Edward VI: The Threshold of Power: The Dominance of the Duke of Northumberland*. Cambridge, Mass.: Harvard University Press, 1970.

Lehmberg, Stanford E. *The Later Parliaments of Henry VIII*. Cambridge: Cambridge University Press, 1977.

—. *The Reformation Parliament, 1529-1536*. Cambridge: Cambridge University Press, 1970.

Loach, Jennifer. *Parliament and the Crown in the Reign of Mary Tudor*. Oxford: Clarendon Press, 1986.

Loades, David. *Mary Tudor: A Life*. London: Basil Blackwell, 1989.

—. *The Reign of Mary Tudor: Politics, Government and Religion in England, 1553-58*. 2nd ed. New York: Longman, 1991.

—. *Two Tudor Conspiracies*. Cambridge: Cambridge University Press, 1965.

—. *The Tudor Court*. Totowa, N.J.: Barnes and Noble Books, 1987.

MacCaffrey, Wallace T. *Elizabeth I*. London: Edward Arnold, 1993.

—. *Elizabeth I: War and Politics 1588-1603*. Princeton, N.J.: Princeton University Press, 1992.

—. *Exeter, 1540-1640: The Growth of an English County Town*. Cambridge, Mass.: Harvard University Press, 1958.

—. *Queen Elizabeth and the Making of Policy, 1572-1588*. Princeton, N.J.: Princeton University Press, 1981.

—. *The Shaping of the Elizabethan Regime: Elizabethan Politics, 1558-1572*. Princeton, N.J.: Princeton University Press, 1968.

Mattingly, Garrett. *Catherine of Aragon*. Boston: Little, Brown and Company, 1941.

McKee, Alexander. *King Henry VIII's Mary Rose*. New York: Stein and Day, 1974.

Miller, Amos C. *Sir Henry Killigrew: Elizabethan Soldier and Diplomat.* Leicester: Leicester University Press, 1963.

Morton, Grenfell. *Elizabethan Ireland.* London: Longman, 1971.

Neale, J.E. *Elizabeth I and Her Parliaments 1559-1581.* New York: St. Martin's Press, 1958.

——. *Queen Elizabeth I: A Biography.* Chicago: Academy Chicago Publishers, 1992.

Parker, K.T. *The Drawings of Hans Holbein in the Collection of Her Majesty the Queen at Windsor Castle.* New York: Harcourt, Brace Jovanovish, Publishers, 1983.

Patterson, Annabel. *Reading Holinshed's* Chronicles. Chicago: University of Chicago Press, 1994.

Polwhele, Richard. *The History of Devonshire.* Exeter, 1793-1806.

Prince, John. *Damnonii orientalis illustres: Or the Worthies of Devon.* London, 1810.

Quinn, David Beers. *The Elizabethans and the Irish.* Ithaca, NY: Cornell University Press, 1966.

Rose-Troup, Frances. *The Western Rebellion of 1549.* London: Smith, Elder & Co., 1913.

Rowse, A.L. *Court and Country: Studies in Tudor Social History.* Athens: University of Georgia Press, 1987.

——. *The England of Elizabeth: The Structure of Society.* Madison: University of Wisconsin Press, 1978.

——. *The Expansion of Elizabethan England.* New York: Harper and Row, 1955.

——. *The Little Land of Cornwall.* Gloucester: Alan Sutton, 1986.

——. *Tudor Cornwall: Portrait of a Society.* 2nd ed. New York: Charles Scribner's Sons, 1969.

St. Leger-Gordon, Douglas F. *Portrait of Devon.* 2nd ed. London: Hale, 1968.

Scarisbrick, J.J. *Henry VIII.* Berkeley: University of California Press, 1968.

Slavin, A.J. *Politics and Profit: A Study of Sir Ralph Sadler 1507-1547.* Cambridge: Cambridge University Press, 1966.

Starkey, David. *The Reign of Henry VIII: Personalities and Politics.* London: George Philip, 1985.

Stone, Lawrence. *Family and Fortune: Studies in Aristocratic Finance in the Sixteenth and Seventeenth Centuries.* Oxford: Clarendon Press, 1973.

Sturt, John. *Revolt in the West: The Western Rebellion of 1549.* Exeter: Devon Books, 1987.

Westcote, Thomas. *A View of Devonshire in MDCXXX.* Exeter, 1845.

Willen, Diane. *John Russell, First Earl of Bedford: One of the King's Men.* London: Royal Historical Society, 1981.

Williams, Neville. *Henry VIII and His Court.* New York: Macmillan, 1971.

Williams, Norman Lloyd. *Sir Walter Raleigh.* Baltimore: Penguin Books, 1965.

Worth, R.N. *A History of Devonshire.* London, 1886.

Youings, J.A., ed. *Raleigh in Exeter 1985: Privateering and Colonisation in the Reign*

of Elizabeth I. Exeter: University of Exeter, 1985.
—. *Sixteenth-Century England*. New York: Penguin Books, 1984.

Secondary Works: Articles and Book Chapters

Adams, Simon. "Eliza Enthroned? The Court and Its Politics." In *The Reign of Elizabeth I*. Edited by Christopher Haigh. Athens: University of Georgia Press, 1987, pp. 55-77.

Bartlett, Kenneth R. "The English Exile Community in Italy and the Political Opposition to Queen Mary I." *Albion* 13, no. 3 (Fall 1981): 223-41.

—. "The Misfortune That Is Wished for Him: The Exile and Death of Edward Courtenay, Earl of Devon." *Canadian Journal of History* 14 (April 1979): 1-28.

Beer, B.L. London and the Rebellions of 1548-49. *The Journal of British Studies* 12, no. 1 (November 1972): 14-38.

Benson, J. "The Monument of Sir Peter Carew." *Devon and Cornwall Notes and Queries* 26, no. 2 (1954): 47-52; no. 3 (1954): 90-91.

Brigden, S.E. "Popular Disturbance and the Fall of Thomas Cromwell and the Reformers, 1539-40." *Historical Journal* 24 (1981): 257-78.

Canny, Nicholas P. "The Ideology of English Colonization: From Ireland to America." *William and Mary Quarterly* 30 (1973): 575-98.

—. "Rowland White's 'The Dysorders of the Irisshery' 1571." *Studia Hibernica* no. 19 (1979): 147-60.

Dunlop, Robert. "Plantation of Leix and Offaly." *English Historical Review* 6 (1891): 61-96.

Edwards, R. Dudley. "Ireland, Elizabeth I and the Counter-Reformation." In *Elizabethan Government and Society*, edited by S.T. Bindoff et al., 1966, pp. 315-39.

Falkiner, C. Litton. "The Parliament of Ireland under the Tudor Sovereigns: With Some Notices of the Speeches of the Irish House of Commons." *Proceedings of the Royal Irish Academy* 25 (1904-05): 508-66.

Harbison, E. Harris. "French Intrigue at the Court of Queen Mary." *American Historical Review* 45 (April 1940): pp. 533-51.

Hughes, James. "Sir Edmund Butler of the Dullogh, Knight." *Journal of the Royal Society of Antiquaries of Ireland* 11 (1870-71): 153-92, 211-31.

Loach, Jennifer. "Pamphlets and Politics, 1553-8." *Bulletin of the Institute of Historical Research* 48 (1975): 31-45.

Manning, R.B. "Violence and Social Conflict in Mid-Tudor Rebellions." *Journal of British Studies* 16 (1977): 18-40.

Mathew, David. "The Cornish and Welsh Pirates in the Reign of Elizabeth.

English Historical Review 39 (July 1924): 337-48.

Moody, T.W. "The Irish Parliament under Elizabeth and James I: A General Survey." *Proceedings of the Royal Irish Academy* 45, sect. C (1939): 41-81.

O'Laidhin, T. "Sir Henry Sidney's First Lord Deputyship." *Bulletin of Irish Commission of Historical Sciences* no. 80 (1957).

Quinn, David B. "Government Printing and the Publication of the Irish Statutes in the Sixteenth Century." *Proceedings of the Royal Irish Academy* 49, sect. C (1943-44): 45-129.

—. "Ireland and Sixteenth Century European Expansion." *Historical Studies* 1 (1958):20-32.

—. "The Munster Plantation: Problems and Opportunities." *Cork Historical and Archaeological Society Journal* 71 (1966).

—. "Parliaments and Great Councils in Ireland 1461-1586." *Irish Historical Studies* 3 (1942-43): 60-77.

Rowse, A.L. "Edward Courtenay, Last Earl of Devon in the Elder Line." In *Court and Country: Studies in Tudor Social History*. Athens: University of Georgia Press, 1987, pp. 61-101.

—. "Richard Carew, Antiquary." In *Court and Country: Studies in Tudor Social History*. Athens: University of Georgia Press, 1987, pp. 242-77.

—. "Sir Peter Carew, Soldier of Fortune." In *Court and Country: Studies in Tudor Social History*. Athens: University of Georgia Press, 1987, pp. 102-35.

Searley, A.W. "Haccombe. Part VII. Early Carew Period." *Transactions of the Devonshire Association for the Advancement of Science, Literature, and Art* 56 (1924): 309-26.

Slavin, Arthur J. "Cromwell, Cranmer and Lord Lisle: A Study in the Politics of Reform." *Albion* 9, no. 4 (Winter 1977): 316-36.

Thorpe, Malcolm R. "Religion and the Wyatt Rebellion of 1554." *Church History* 47, no. 4 (December 1978): 363-80.

Treadwell, Victor. "The Irish Parliament of 1569-71." *Proceedings of the Royal Irish Academy* 65, sect. C (1966-67): 55-89.

Usherwood, Stephen. "Sir Peter Carew, 1514-1575: 'Valientness in Service.'" *History Today.* 28, no. 4 (April 1978): 249-55.

Walker, Ronald Francis. "Carew Castle." *Archaeologia Cambrensis* 105 (1957): 81-95.

Youings, J.A. "The South-Western Rebellion of 1549." *Southern History* 1 (1979): 99-122.

—. "The Terms of Disposal of the Devon Monastic Lands, 1536-58." *English Historical Review* 69 (January 1954): 18-38.

Secondary Works: Unpublished Dissertations

Bartlett, K.R. "The English Exile Community in Italy Under Queen Mary I."
    Ph.D. thesis, University of Toronto, 1978.

Bradshaw, Brendan. "The Government of Ireland, c. 1540-1583." Ph.D. thesis,
    University of Dublin, 1980.

Harwood, William R. "The Courtenay Family in the Politics of Region and
    Nation in the Late Fifteenth and Early Sixteenth Centuries." Ph.D. dis-
    sertation, Cambridge University, 1978.

Whiting, R. "The Reformation in the South-West of England." Ph.D. disserta-
    tion, University of Exeter, 1977.

INDEX